Patrick Pinnell

W9-BRL-048

Place
Making

Developing Town Centers, Main Streets, and Urban Villages

Charles C. Bohl

Urban Land Institute

About ULI–the Urban Land Institute

ULI–the Urban Land Institute is a nonprofit education and research institute that is supported by its members. Its mission is to provide responsible leadership in the use of land in order to enhance the total environment.

ULI sponsors education programs and forums to encourage an open international exchange of ideas and sharing of experiences; initiates research that anticipates emerging land use trends and issues and proposes creative solutions based on that research; provides advisory services; and publishes a wide variety of materials to disseminate information on land use and development. Established in 1936, the Institute today has more than 17,000 members and associates from some 60 countries representing the entire spectrum of the land use and development disciplines.

Richard M. Rosan

President

Recommended bibliographic listing:

Bohl, Charles C. *Place Making: Developing Town Centers, Main Streets, and Urban Villages.* Washington, D.C.: ULI–the Urban Land Institute, 2002.

ULI Catalog Number: P45
International Standard Book Number: 0-87420-886-6
Library of Congress Control Number: 2002112463

Copyright 2002 by ULI–the Urban Land Institute
1025 Thomas Jefferson Street, N.W.
Suite 500 West
Washington, D.C. 20007-5201

Third Printing, 2006

Printed in the United States of America. All rights reserved. No part of this book may be reproduced in any form or by any means, electronic or mechanical, including photocopying and recording, or by any information storage and retrieval system, without written permission of the publisher.

Cover image credits—first image: Elkus/Manfredi Architects Ltd.; third image: Steve Hall/Hedrich-Blessing.

Sources, credits, and copyrights for photographs and graphic material in this book are as noted. Every effort has been made to accurately identify the sources and credits for all photographs and graphics. All other photographs appearing in this book (those without credits listed) are from the author's personal collection and cannot be reproduced or reused in any form without the written consent of the author.

This publication is made possible by financial support from the ULI Foundation.

Project Staff

Senior Vice President, Policy and Practice
Publisher
Rachelle L. Levitt

Vice President, Development Trends and Analysis
Project Director
Dean Schwanke

Vice President, Real Estate Development Practice
Gayle Berens

Director, Book Program
Managing Editor
Nancy Stewart

Manuscript Editor
Sandra F. Chizinsky

Art Director
Betsy VanBuskirk

Cover and Layout Design
Dever Designs

Director, Publishing Operations
Diann Stanley-Austin

Principal Author

Charles C. Bohl Charles C. Bohl is a research associate professor and director of the Knight Program in Community Building at the University of Miami's School of Architecture. Since 2000, he has been responsible for developing all aspects of the Knight Program into an innovative interdisciplinary curriculum that brings together outstanding scholars, architects, designers, community leaders, policy makers, theorists, and practitioners with an active interest in the process of community building and its relationship to the built environment of American villages, towns, cities, and suburbs. As director, Bohl oversees all of the Knight Program's activities including fellowship seminars and study tours held in cities throughout the United States, an annual symposium, an annual charrette, the work of graduate scholars in the Suburb and Town Design Program, and publications sponsored by the program.

Before joining the University of Miami, Bohl taught in the fields of planning and architecture at the University of North Carolina at Chapel Hill (UNC) and at North Carolina State University's School of Design. He was also a senior research associate at UNC's Center for Urban and Regional Studies where he established an interdisciplinary research program on smart growth and the new economy, and served as the senior fellow for the Weiss Urban Livability Program at UNC.

Bohl has published across disciplines with funding from the Fannie Mae Foundation, the Z. Smith Reynolds Foundation, the Urban Land Institute, and the North Carolina Department of Social Services and Department of Community Affairs. He also consults in the fields of planning and urban design. Bohl holds a bachelor's degree from New York University, a master's degree in urban and regional planning from the University at Albany, and has done his doctoral work in planning at UNC.

Contributing Author

Dean Schwanke is vice president, Development Trends and Analysis, in the Policy and Practice department at the Urban Land Institute in Washington, D.C. Over the past 20 years, Schwanke has authored or coauthored numerous books and reports for ULI and is the principal author of the *Resort Development Handbook* (1997), *Remaking the Shopping Center* (1994), and *Mixed-Use Development Handbook* (1987). He has served as the principal author of the annual *ULI Real Estate Forecast* since it began in 1996. He is currently researching and writing a new revised edition of the *Mixed-Use Development Handbook,* scheduled for publication in 2003. In 1999, he created ULI's conference program on place making and town center development, which he has continued to develop annually. Schwanke holds a BA degree from the University of Wisconsin–Madison and a master of planning degree from the University of Virginia.

Acknowledgments

Through the process of researching and writing this book I have had the honor and privilege of working with many innovative and talented individuals—real estate developers, architects, planners, traffic engineers, public works officials, retailers, builders—committed to the creation of town centers that can serve as the social, cultural, economic, and civic hubs of activity for American communities. As codes, regulations, standards, and business and finance practices all remain largely stacked against these projects, it goes almost without saying that behind every town center that is built stands a group of dedicated individuals—part visionaries, part pragmatists—who are wholly committed to the creation of great places.

First and foremost, my thanks to the developers and designers of these projects, who shared the experiences and hard-won insights gained through many years of putting together the vision, financing, planning, design, construction, and management of today's new town centers and main streets. My admiration and regard for these trailblazers only increased in the course of writing this book: without their vision and perseverance, there would be no new town centers, and very little in the way of an alternative vision for how to reassemble some of the residential, office, civic, and retail fragments of our metropolitan landscapes into central gathering places for our communities.

Among the many people who shared their thoughts, expertise, and time with me, I offer special thanks to R. John Anderson, Ray Bromley, Jaime Correa, George de Guardiola, Robert Davis, Bill Dennis, Diane Dorney, Victor Dover, Andrés Duany, Reid Ewing, Bob Gibbs, Rick Hall, Richard Heapes, Jennifer Hurley, Kevin Klinkenberg, Joe Kohl, Bob Kramer, Jean-François Lejeune, Bill Lennertz, Charlie Lockwood, Dick Loffelmacher, Art Lomenick, Richard Longstreth, Mike Mehaffy, Neal Payton, Elizabeth Plater-Zyberk, Doug Porter, Tim Rollins, Eileen Schlichting, Terry Shook, Lee S. Sobel, Yaromir Steiner, Rob Steuteville, Doug Storrs, Marilyn Waters, Mike Watkins, and Todd Zimmerman. Collective thanks to the staffs of Duany Plater-Zyberk; Dover, Kohl & Partners; and the Center for Urban and Regional Studies at the University of North Carolina at Chapel Hill.

Extra special thanks to David Salvesen, for pestering me to write all those book reviews for *Urban Land* and for introducing me to ULI; to my dissertation adviser, Professor David Godschalk, for having the patience and confidence that allowed me to "follow my bliss"; to my dissertation committee and mentors, Ed Kaiser, Phil Berke, Emil Malizia, and Paul Tesar, for their patience and support as I completely reversed the traditional progression from dissertation, to faculty position, to book publishing; to Mary Beth Powell, Bill Rohe, and the staff of the Center for Urban and Regional Studies, who provided a home, in Chapel Hill, North Carolina, for the first phase of the town centers laboratory; and to Elizabeth Plater-Zyberk, who provided a new home for the effort in Coral Gables, Florida, at the University of Miami's School of Architecture.

Thanks also to the Knight Fellows and Knight Scholars in Community Building, in particular: Lee S. Sobel, who shared my passionate interest in these places and provided a real estate finance perspective, some photos, some encouragement, and some humor along the way; Phil Langdon, my *consigliere* in the world of book publishing; Christopher Podstawski, who helped with the final preparation of graphics for the book; and Andrea Gollin, for always being there to answer those questions and accomplish those tasks that no one else could.

A heartfelt thanks to Dean Schwanke and the ULI staff for entrusting me with this assignment and for their patience and generosity throughout the research and writing phases. As the guiding force behind this project, Dean developed the initial concept for the book at ULI, reviewed and edited the entire manuscript, and wrote the bulk of chapter 5. Thanks also to the ULI manuscript review group—Thomas Brink, of RTKL Associates, in Dallas; Thomas D'Alesandro IV, of Terrabrook, in Reston, Virginia; George de Guardiola, of de Guardiola Development, Inc., in West Palm Beach, Florida; Richard Heapes, of Street-Works, in Alexandria, Virginia; and Charles Terry Shook, of Shook, in Charlotte, North Carolina—who provided valuable observations and comments. Designers, developers, and management staff also reviewed each of the case studies for their respective projects and provided factual checks and insights. And special (somewhat blurry-eyed) thanks to Sandy Chizinsky, whose words speak louder than most people's actions, and who read every word of the book (chapter, verse, and some in between the lines), and did a superb job on the copyediting phase of the book. Thanks also to Dever Designs, who did an exemplary job in the graphic design and layout for the book.

To these and to the many others who helped make this work possible, especially my parents, Norma and Dan; my father- and mother-in-law, Joe and Betty; and my family—my wife, Lisa Marie, and my children, Zachary, Sawyer, and Madison: May all your worlds be graced by beautiful, wondrous, enduring places that possess the magic that can make you forget where you were going and be happy to be right where you are.

Charles C. Bohl
Research Associate Professor and Director
Knight Program in Community Building
School of Architecture
University of Miami
Coral Gables, Florida

Contents

Foreword

In his 1999 bestseller, *A Man in Full,* Tom Wolfe wrote of the placelessness of so many of our suburban landscapes, including the easternmost reaches of the San Francisco Bay area.

> *He had driven through that whole area, from Vine Hill, where he lived, on east to Pittsburg [California] and beyond, and it was now one vast goulash of condominiums and other new, cheap housing. The only way you could tell you were leaving one community and entering another was when the franchises started repeating and you spotted another 7-Eleven, another Wendy's, another Costco, another Home Depot. The new landmarks were not office towers or monuments or city halls or libraries or museums but 7-Eleven stores.*

Generations of suburbanites have now come to realize that a 7-Eleven, as useful as it is, does not a place make.

This book talks about the creation of *suburban places,* which many would consider an oxymoron. But that wasn't always the case. Contrary to popular belief, suburbs are not a modern phenomenon. Prior to the 19th century, wherever you had a major city like London or Paris, Cairo, or Beijing, you had outlying development—a few homes, a shop or two—that eventually grew into a recognizable and separate village: a suburb.

Suburbs—as we understand them in the United States—really saw their genesis in the early 1800s. These were places that were deliberately designed to be physically and symbolically separate from the increasingly large, immigrant-filled, polluted, and noisy U.S. cities. The creation of these first suburbs was also driven by transportation: it had to be easy for a businessman, for example, to travel from his suburban home to the city.

By the early 20th century, when railroads and trolleys were widespread and reliable, virtually every major U.S. city had its suburbs. It was during this period that several classic new communities emerged, such as Chestnut Hill and the Main Line, outside Philadelphia; Scarsdale, outside New York; Chevy Chase, outside Washington, D.C.; the great North Shore suburbs, like Lake Forest, outside Chicago; and even Beverly Hills, a master-planned community whose first lots went on the market in 1906. These early prototypical suburbs were not entirely bedroom communities. They were more like villages, clustered around train stations and boasting little main streets with neighborhood-serving shops, a few apartments, a church, a post office, and a library: real places.

With the rise of the automobile in the 1920s and 1930s, these early suburbs—and dozens of newer ones—really reached their heyday. In most instances, they continued to cluster around train or trolley stations and village centers. But they started to get bigger, because people could now drive their cars to the train station.

The post–World War II suburban boom was also transportation-driven, but now it was strictly automobiles and freeways, not rail, that pushed suburban development. These new communities, like Long Island's Levittown or Los Angeles's San Fernando Valley, were different from the suburbs of the 1920s and 1930s in one other key factor: they didn't have a main street or a village center unless they happened to engulf an older community. They weren't *places*. They were simply street after street of single-family homes, with an occasional school thrown in. But there were no true public realms, no civic centers, no main streets.

Some people claim that the regional shopping malls that grew up on the outskirts of these suburbs were simply the new version of a public realm. I disagree. A public realm is about community, not simply about consumerism. A public realm is an outdoor space in the heart of a community with a variety of uses. It is infused with civic pride and the lofty dreams of the community. A regional mall, by itself, is not.

Most post–World War II suburbs were bedroom communities. They were great places to raise families, offering good housing at a reasonable cost. But they weren't true places. This, of course, is the crux of our suburban dilemma today. How do you define "a place"?

A combination of many things—from architecture, to cultural institutions, to topography, history, economy, and physical appearance—create place. But there is one more key factor: you must have social interaction to have a true place. Many suburbs stymied social interaction by physically fragmenting our lives. Our homes, jobs, shopping, entertainment, houses of worship, and civic institutions were all separated from each other. In effect, most suburbs became the antithesis of true places.

The New Town Movement of the 1960s rose up in direct response to these placeless suburbs. Following European examples, these new towns were conceived as balanced and virtually self-contained communities—with housing of all kinds and price ranges; office and industrial jobs; and retail, entertainment, schools, houses of worship, and parks, all within close distance by foot, bicycle, or automobile. These new towns were all about creating place.

Unfortunately, the new towns that were built also adopted many elements from modernist urban design that worked against place making, including large zones of separate uses and high-speed roadways designed exclusively for automobiles. They did, however, represent a genuine, community-scale planning effort to create distinctive, coherent places.

Most of the original new towns fell into financial trouble. Of the two dozen or so true new towns that were planned in the 1960s, only a handful went into full-scale development, including Reston, Virginia; Columbia, Maryland; Irvine, California; and our company's Valencia, California.

The vast majority of suburban development in the 1960s, 1970s, and 1980s continued to take the form of placeless communities. The last few generations of Americans have rarely had the experience of coming together on a tree-lined street to shop, to walk after dinner, or to talk with friends, because typical suburbia reduced the street to a single-purpose, pedestrian-intimidating traffic arterial.

Fortunately, in recent years, the pendulum has begun to swing away from this development pattern. More and more people want to return to the traditional main street or town center, particularly as our lives become more mobile, more global, more computerized, and more hectic. Despite all the talk about "going virtual," people still want a sense of belonging, a sense of community: a place.

A new development trend is helping to put the place back into our communities. In a deliberate attempt to create a sense of place and identity, and to gain an edge when competing with other areas for future development and increased tax revenues, post–World War II suburbs across the country are building main streets from scratch or reinvigorating old town centers.

At Newhall Land, we believe that these multidimensional main streets are a key to suburban place making. That's why we are building one, named Town Center Drive. And that's why hundreds of other new suburban town centers, main streets, and urban villages are planned, under construction, or already completed across the United States. These new main streets are sprouting up in virtually every kind of post–World War II community—from a sprawling suburb like Schaumburg, near Chicago, to Disney's new town of Celebration, Florida. They also take many forms—from streets that are several blocks long to tree-shaded town squares and village greens.

These new suburban main streets are *not* outdoor shopping malls masquerading as main streets. Like the small-town main streets of the pre–World War II years, they have a full range of everyday uses and activities—including office, retail, entertainment, hotels, housing, and civic institutions like public libraries—all integrated within a pedestrian-friendly environment. They are places in every sense of the word, and they are creating a sense of place for their suburban communities.

Most important, town centers are enjoyed by people. As Fred Kent, president of Project for Public Spaces, once commented, "People like to gather in settings that attract other people. They like streets with stores. They like to move chairs before sitting in them, even if they move them right back to the position they found them in. And there are few things that people enjoy watching more than a passing parade."

Main streets and town centers are passing parades, motherhood and apple pie. They are old-fashioned and very contemporary. They are quaint and urban. Most important, they create a sense of place . . . without a 7-Eleven.

In the near future, we may look back on the post–World War II decades as an anomaly—as the only time when communities lacked a true main street or "place."

Gary Cusumano
Chief Executive Officer and President
Newhall Land
Valencia, California

Place
Making

Developing Town Centers,
Main Streets, and Urban Villages

Introduction

> *"A town in which men have worked hard all day at their great engines ought to be glittering and gay at night, if only for an hour or two. Think of the energy, the organisation, the drive of purpose required [in their daily work] ... why, a minute fraction of these could fill this dark street with light, music, and gaeity.*
>
> —J. B. PRIESTLY, *English Journey*

Over the past 30 years, American suburbs have gradually become more fully developed—with a complete range of houses, apartments, hotels, shopping centers, office and industrial parks, and public buildings in a pattern frequently referred to as suburban sprawl. When measured in raw statistical terms (acreage, square footage, and employment), suburbs are no longer simply bedroom communities and have become more economically and socially diverse. Thanks to an expanding network of roads and highways, residents can find a wide variety of goods and services, and employment and recreational opportunities, all within short commutes of their homes. Increasingly, however, suburban areas are becoming victims of their own success.

With the development of new shopping malls, strip shopping centers, office parks, and roadside restaurants and hotels, suburbanites who once wished for wider selections of merchandise and better restaurants closer to home have found new meaning in the time-honored warning: "Be careful what you wish for. You may get it." In many regions, as more and more people are compelled to take to the highways for each and every activity, that "short commute" to everything has become longer, more congested, and more stressful. It's as if the prophecy of Judge Doom (the cartoon villain of *Who Framed Roger Rabbit?*) for 1947 Los Angeles had come true:

> *Eight lanes of shimmering cement running from here to Pasadena! I see a place where people get on and off the freeway, off and on, off and on, all day and all night. . . . I see a street of gas stations, inexpensive motels, restaurants that serve rapidly prepared food, tire salons, automobile dealerships, and wonderful, wonderful billboards as far as the eye can see. My God, it'll be beautiful!*

Suburban sprawl has been characterized as development that is relatively low density, spread over large areas, and segregated into single-use zones of single-family homes, apartment complexes, office parks, shopping malls, and commercial strips.[1] According to a survey conducted in 2000 by the Pew Charitable Trust for Civic Journalism, sprawl has become a major policy issue nationwide, equaling or surpassing perennial concerns like crime, education, and taxes. "Sprawl is now a bread-and-butter community issue," explains Jan Schaffer, executive director of the Pew Center, "with dramatic frustrations over sprawl and growth now edging out more traditional issues."[2]

But while concern about growth has typically revolved around traffic congestion and environmental impacts, community livability and quality of life issues have recently become central to the debate. Moreover, concern about livability extends beyond residents to business and community leaders, who regard the negative effects of sprawl as a threat to their ability to compete with other regions.[3] Maturing suburban and "edge city" landscapes typically lack a center, a place that establishes an identity for the community and offers residents and visitors an opportunity to come together, and to meet and mingle face-to-face.[4] "It's a character issue and an identity issue," says Robin Traubenik, planning chief for New Lenox, an edge city near Chicago, Illinois. "Here there's nowhere to take your kids on a Saturday and walk around. There's a feeling something's missing."[5]

An Emerging Response to Sprawl

In recent years, new town centers, main streets, and urban villages have attracted intense interest from the development community. Whether modest village centers on the suburban fringe or bustling urban districts created on infill sites, main street and town center developments are making waves as promising new forms of real estate development. Urban "place making"—via the effective programming and design of a mix of uses, within a pedestrian environment—is not simply a dream of urban designers and city planners but a marketable development concept that is increasingly being embraced by both the public and the private sectors.[6] There is also a growing appreciation among community leaders, planners, and developers of how town centers, main streets, and urban villages can put communities "on the map," and establish a strong identity for residential developments. The public apparently agrees: in a recent survey, an astounding 86 percent of suburban homebuyers expressed support for the concept of a mixed-use town center clustered around a village green.[7]

But while suburbanites are attracted by main streets and town centers, they also demand convenient automobile access. Similarly, the offices, retail businesses, and service establishments that might occupy main street and town center developments often have "suburban expectations" that are inconsistent with the format of a traditional town center. Thus, developers, planners, and urban designers are faced with the challenge of reinventing traditional town centers in ways that can serve suburban populations.

Place Making: Developing Town Centers, Main Streets, and Urban Villages is the result of extensive site visits, research, and interviews with the professionals who are involved in the planning, design, and development of the projects that are literally reshaping the American urban and suburban landscape. The projects presented in this book—the first generation of new main streets and town centers created in nearly 50 years—are pioneering efforts that, taken collectively, have broken most, if not all, of the conventional rules of development. As a result, new town centers and main streets have involved compromises, and a good deal of pragmatic, trial-and-error experimentation. But what is most striking about these projects is not their flaws but their success—despite the challenges and roadblocks that have confronted them.

This book responds to the need for timely information on best practices, and on lessons learned by those who have been involved in developing leading-edge main street and town center projects.

Chapter Outline

Chapter 1, "The Place-Making Trend," identifies and discusses the key factors driving the development of town center and main street projects.[8] These include the desire for a stronger sense of place and community identity in suburbs; changing demographics and lifestyles that favor mixed-use centers; market forces that are driving innovation in retail, office, entertainment, and apartment properties; and the emergence of public policies that promote smart growth and the new urbanism.[9]

Chapter 2, "Learning from the Past: Town Centers and Main Streets Revisited," takes a look back at the history and evolution of American town centers and main streets, from colonial towns to mid-19th-century company towns, turn-of-the-century streetcar suburbs, and the garden cities of the early 20th century. The chapter also covers the more recent part of this history and evolution, including the disintegration of town centers into more specialized development products, like shopping centers, and the experiments involving the creation of modernist-influenced town centers for mid-20th-century new towns. The chapter shows how early-20th-century examples, like Kansas City's Country Club Plaza and Princeton's Palmer Square, have continued to provide valuable models for mixing uses; balancing the needs of pedestrians and automobiles; and creating distinctive, enduring places.

New town centers and main streets represent a dramatic break from the conventional design of shopping centers, office parks, and apartment complexes. To find good models for the types of streets, outdoor spaces, buildings, and mix of uses and activities required for a town center, designers and developers have had to look back at the great streets, plazas, and centers of historic cities and towns. Chapter 3, "Timeless Design Principles for Town Centers," identifies some of the lessons that can be learned from traditional towns and cities and intro-duces some basic urban design considerations for streets, public spaces, and buildings in town centers.

Chapter 4, "Emerging Formats for Town Centers, Main Streets, and Urban Villages," provides an overview of the wide variety of projects being planned and built, including

- New village and town centers created for maturing master-planned communities;
- Town centers and main streets planned or under development for new urbanist communities;
- Existing main streets that have been reinvented;
- Urban villages;
- Mall-to-main-street conversions, which retrofit or replace failed shopping centers with town centers or main streets;
- Transit villages;
- Mixed-use office parks;
- Publicly initiated suburban town centers.

Chapter 5, "Launching a New Town Center: Feasibility and Financing," reviews the major issues to be tackled, including development objectives, market analysis, feasibility and financial analysis, financing, and the role of the public sector. The chapter also highlights a number of obstacles and potential pitfalls for town center developers. Chapter 6, "Breakthrough Projects Revisited," considers a number of breakthrough projects and highlights their significance and development history. The breakthrough projects profiled in the chapter are

- Miami Lakes Town Center, Miami Lakes, Florida;
- Princeton Forrestal Village, Princeton, New Jersey;

- Mashpee Commons, Mashpee, Massachusetts;
- Reston Town Center, Reston, Virginia;
- Mizner Park, Boca Raton, Florida.

Chapter 7 presents detailed case studies of different types of exemplary projects, including village centers, town centers, main streets, transit villages, and urban villages. The description of each project includes information on the site, the mix of uses, the market, the regulatory framework, and the level of public partnership involved. The chapter takes an in-depth look at the urban design of each project, and provides insights from the key players who were directly involved in project design, planning, development, marketing, and management. The following projects are profiled in the case studies:

- CityPlace, West Palm Beach, Florida;
- Easton Town Center, Columbus, Ohio;
- Haile Village Center, Gainesville, Florida;
- Market Square in Kentlands/Lakelands, Gaithersburg, Maryland;
- Market Street at Celebration, Celebration, Florida;
- Orenco Station Town Center, Portland, Oregon;
- Southlake Town Square, Southlake, Texas;
- Town Center Drive, Valencia, California.

Chapter 8, "A Compendium of Planning and Design Ideas for Town Centers," brings together all the lessons of the previous chapters in a concise summary of the key planning and design principles that distinguish town center projects from other types of developments. The chapter describes what works—and what doesn't—for different types of projects in different types of settings, and details the qualities that contribute to long-term success.

Learning from Experience

By whatever name the projects are called—village center, urban village, town center, transit village, or main street—the developers of these projects all shared an ambition to create unique places with lasting value, rather than standardized developments to be quickly built and sold. This goal has yielded daunting challenges—as lenders, developers, planners, designers, builders, public works departments, and tenants struggle and experiment in an effort to create settings that are more compact, mixed-use, pedestrian- and transit-oriented and that have a stronger civic character than anything produced in recent decades. These are projects that have challenged long-held assumptions about consumers, retailing practices, street standards, building design, parking arrangements, housing types, office space, marketing, and a host of related issues. Town center projects require a skillful effort to balance the needs of residents and visitors, automobiles and pedestrians, living spaces and working spaces, and public spaces and private spaces. Town centers may also involve satisfying the requirements of small retail stores

and big boxes; casual and fine-dining restaurants; small professional offices and large corporate ones; civic facilities; and commercial entertainment. Such efforts require careful planning—but even more important, they require the flexibility to adapt to situations and circumstances that could not be anticipated.

This book brings together the collective wisdom and experience that have been gained from the first generation of town center and main street projects to be built in over five decades. Some experienced overnight success, while others were years in the making. Together they represent some of the most exciting developments in recent years, providing real-world examples of how developers, designers, and communities can create sustainable, livable, and profitable alternatives to sprawl, and places with lasting value to the community.

Notes

1. The term *sprawl* has been used by observers of urban phenomena as far back as 1958, when William Whyte published an essay on sprawl in *Exploding Metropolis;* it has been used in policy studies since at least 1974, when the Real Estate Research Corporation published *The Costs of Sprawl.* In the academic and policy arenas, the definition of the term—and the question of whether it exists at all—continue to arouse considerable debate. The explosion of magazine and newspaper articles on sprawl in recent years, however, suggests that the many implications of the term have become part of our common language. For a sampling of the literature on sprawl, including the controversy surrounding its definition and impacts, see Ivonne Audirac and Maria Zifou, *Urban Development Issues: What Is Controversial in Urban Sprawl? An Annotated Bibliography of Often-Overlooked Sources* (Chicago: Council of Planning Librarians, 1989); Andrés Duany, Elizabeth Plater-Zyberk, and Jeff Speck, *Suburban Nation: The Rise of Sprawl and the Decline of the American Dream* (New York: North Point Press, 2000); Reid Ewing, "Characteristics, Causes, and Effects of

Sprawl: A Literature Review," *Environmental and Urban Issues* (winter 1994); Reid Ewing, "Counterpoint: Is Los Angeles-Style Sprawl Desirable?" *Journal of the American Planning Association* 63, no. 1 (1997); Peter Gordon and Harry W. Richardson, "Point: Are Compact Cities a Desirable Planning Goal?" *Journal of the American Planning Association* 63, no. 1 (1997); Doug Kelbaugh, "The Costs of Sprawl," *Cascadia Forum* 1, no. 1 (October 1993); Real Estate Research Corporation, *The Costs of Sprawl: Environmental and Economic Costs of Alternative Residential Development Patterns at the Urban Fringe* (Washington, D.C.: U.S. Government Printing Office, 1974); Dwight Young, "Alternatives to Sprawl" (paper presented at the Alternatives to Sprawl conference, Washington, D.C., 1995).

2. Brad Knickerbocker, "Forget Crime—But Please Fix the Traffic," *Christian Science Monitor,* February 16, 2000.

3. See, for example, Neal R. Peirce, "Bank of America Chief Champions Smart Growth," *Nation's Cities Weekly* 22, no. 18 (1999); and Bank of America, *Beyond Sprawl: New Patterns of Growth to Fit the New California* (San Francisco: Bank of America, California Resources Agency, Greenbelt Alliance, and Low Income Housing Fund, 1995); Lisa Wormer and Gil Shamess, eds., *Profiles of Business Leadership on Smart Growth: New Partnerships Demonstrate the Economic Benefits of Reducing Sprawl* (National Association of Local Government Environmental Professionals, 1999).

4. The term *edge city* was coined by journalist Joel Garreau in his 1991 book, *Edge City: Life on the New Frontier,* to describe the high concentrations of office and retail space in suburban areas outside of cities and traditional downtowns.

5. Quoted in Craig Savoye, "Vanilla Suburbs Seek an Identity," *Christian Science Monitor,* December 30, 1999, 1.

6. Throughout Raymond Unwin's classic 1909 text, *Town Planning In Practice,* he italicizes the word *place,* giving it a special emphasis and meaning. In the chapter entitled "Of Centres and Enclosed Places," he explains: "The *place* is the more modern form of the Greek agora and the Roman forum. We have no English word exactly equivalent. The English market-place was often a true *place,* but not always. The English word 'square,' besides limiting the shape to a regular form, denotes something often quite different. We must, therefore, be content with the simple French word *place;* it has the advantage of being essentially the same word as the Italian *piazza* and the German *platz;* and if at present it does not convey a sufficiently definite idea, perhaps it may be possible for us to pack more meaning into it."

7. Brooke Warrick and Toni Alexander, "Looking for Hometown America," *Urban Land,* February 1997.

8. The phrases *town center* and *main street* will be used as generic terms to refer to the wide variety of places and projects discussed throughout the book. Distinctions between different types of projects will be discussed in detail in chapter 4.

9. For those who are unfamiliar with the new urbanism, it represents a major movement in planning and architecture that is based on the urban design principles of traditional towns, cities, and main streets—as preserved and experienced in places like Nantucket, Savannah, Charleston, and Old Town Alexandria. The role of the new urbanism in the growing number of main street and town center projects is discussed in greater detail at the end of chapter 1.

The Place-Making Trend

There's no there, there. —GERTRUDE STEIN, *Everybody's Autobiography*

Too much of anything is too much for me.

—PETE TOWNSEND, *"Too Much of Anything"*

Morning in Haile Village Center, Gainesville, Florida.

In sharp contrast to the suburban character of the surrounding neighborhoods and to the sprawling strip development that ripples along the fringes of Gainesville, Florida, Haile Village Center offers narrow streets and alleys, apartments and townhouses above shops and offices, a meetinghouse, and a village green. Why would the developer, Robert Kramer, have undertaken the challenging, long-term process of planning, designing, and building a mixed-use village center with a traditional layout and design? When several possible reasons for undertaking such a project were posed to him—such as the growing desire to provide suburban towns with an identity and a sense of place; to create more walkable neighborhoods; and to develop "smarter," more sustainable communities, he smiled and replied, "I thought the reason was to make money."

And so it must be, if town centers are to flourish. But Kramer was also driven by a desire to create a unique new place—and he has pursued a vision of that place steadfastly for many years.

Kramer and his partner, Matthew Kaskel, spent the early years of Haile Plantation's development thinking carefully about just what kind of place the village center should be. From the very beginning, they envisioned it as a traditional village center, and visited dozens of small towns and villages to collect ideas, writing out lists of social, community, and civic qualities and activities that the center should foster. But without their confidence in the center's ability to turn a profit, it would never have been built.

Today there are nearly 100 new town center projects of various types planned or under construction, and older main streets and downtowns are being renovated in an estimated 6,000 communities of all sizes.[1] After a break of nearly 50 years, why are so many plans and projects for new, mixed-use town centers, main streets, and urban villages now emerging?[2]

Until recently, the perception was that there was no money to be made in main street and town center projects. While developers and local redevelopment agencies worked hard to create successful mixed-use projects in downtown areas, fine-grained and pedestrian-friendly mixed-use developments in the suburbs continued to be viewed as inherently risky. Proposals for urban-scale, mixed-used developments in suburban settings were associated with the lunatic fringe, and were met with severe skepticism by financiers, potential tenants, local neighborhood groups, and public officials. Only edge-city locations were acceptable grounds for experimentation, and then only on a scale designed for the automobile, not for pedestrians. Why are main street and town center projects suddenly the focus of attention? What forces have come together to transform these projects from risky trips down memory lane into attractive investments and trend-setting developments? The forces are many, and include changing market demands, shifting public policy, new urban design ideas, and the cultural changes that are occurring as the tastes and attitudes of the Depression-era generation yield to those of the baby boomers, Generation X-ers, and beyond.

Marketing "community" at Lakelands, the home of Market Square, in Gaithersburg, Maryland.
Courtesy Natelli Communities.

The "Quest for Community"

According to *Real Estate Development: Principles and Process*, "the excitement of identifying an unfulfilled human need and creating a product to fill it at a profit is the stimulus that drives development."[3] Without sufficient demand for main street and town center settings, developers would not be going to such great lengths to build these complex and challenging projects, and municipalities would be extremely reluctant to approve and invest public funds in them. But with virtually no track record, what are the indications that there is a demand for such projects? What human needs are they designed to fulfill?

While surveys indicate that Americans continue to embrace the single-family home, they also reveal an extraordinary discontent with what Reid Ewing refers to as "the rest of the suburban package." In "Counterpoint: Is Los Angeles–Style Sprawl Desirable?", Ewing summarizes a wide variety of research supporting this view, including 11 studies indicating that "given the choice between compact centers and commercial strips, consumers favor the centers by a wide margin."[4] Lending further support are the 1995 American LIVES survey, which found that nearly 70 percent of those surveyed were unhappy with suburbs as they currently exist, and the Pew Center's February 2000 survey, in which "sprawl" was cited as the number one concern across the nation.[5] Much of the torrent of media attention focused on sprawl targets the patchwork of strips, centers, and "pods" of separate retail, office, and multifamily developments—an agglomeration that many people consider unattractive, congestion-inducing, and mind-numbingly monotonous.

According to real estate analyst Christopher Leinberger, "the real estate development industry now has 19 standardized product types—a cookie-cutter array of office, industrial, retail, hotel, apartment, residential, and miscellaneous building types."[6] Leinberger notes that the formulas for these product types have been refined over many decades, making them relatively "easy and cheap to finance, build, trade, and manage." These development products are clearly successful at meeting the needs of businesses and consumers and form the very fabric of our metropolitan regions. However, while the real estate industry has become very good at building these projects, the projects themselves are not very good at building communities.

One alternative touted by smart growth advocates and new urbanists is to reconfigure portions of suburban office, retail, and higher-density residential development on infill sites to create traditional town centers or urban villages. These town centers would be designed as compact, mixed-use, pedestrian-oriented places—of the sort that could provide communities with a focal point and civic identity.

"Third places" as an endangered species: a parking lot "café" in Durham, North Carolina.

Outdoor dining at Mizner Park, in Boca Raton, Florida.

Americans' genuine dissatisfaction with sprawl and their interest in alternatives appear to be two sides of the same coin. The American LIVES survey, in which a remarkable 86 percent of suburban home-buyers stated a preference for town centers, also found that 29 percent favored the *status quo,* with "shopping and civic buildings distributed along commercial strips and in malls."[7]

These sentiments, often described as a "quest for community," are apparent in the titles of recent books, such as Philip Langdon's *A Better Place to Live,* Terry Pindell's *A Good Place to Live: America's Last Migration,* and James Howard Kunstler's *Home From Nowhere.*[8] For the authors of these and other books and articles, the elements most commonly identified as missing are what sociologist Ray Oldenburg has referred to as "third places." Third places are the traditional community gathering places found outside the home (our "first place") and the workplace (our "second place") and include cafés, taverns, town squares, and village greens.[9] Where development is completely organized around the requirements of automobile travel, third places either become islands in a sea of parking, cut off from nearby neighborhoods—or, in the case of town squares and village greens, they become extinct. Many observers are convinced that these community gathering places are the missing ingredients that people in suburban areas and edge cities are looking for today. As Pindell writes, "Towns and cities whose social life coalesces around such places rather than the country club and the private home meet the first criteria for people looking for a good place to live today."[10]

Newly created settings, like Mizner Park's Plaza Real and Reston Town Center's Fountain Square and

The space between buildings—the public realm—such as at Reston Town Center's Fountain Square, Reston, Virginia, enables a town center or a main street to act as the "third place" for nearby neighborhoods.

ice-skating pavilion, are proving that these types of community gathering places are not simply nostalgic archetypes advanced by urban-history buffs, but real magnets for residents and visitors. Like colonial New England villages, today's town center projects typically revolve around a central plaza or park that establishes a public atmosphere and provides an ideal setting for the cafés, taverns, and bistros celebrated by Oldenburg. In fact, it is the space *between* buildings— the public realm of plazas, greens, squares, and walkable streets—that enables a town center or a main street to act as the third place for nearby neighborhoods and communities.

Smyrna Town Center, the emerging town center of Smyrna, Georgia.
Courtesy Sizemore Floyd Architects.

Place Identity

Closely related to the quest for community is the growing appreciation of how town centers, main streets, and urban villages can "put communities on the map," and establish a strong identity for new residential communities and existing towns and suburbs. Maturing edge cities, like Schaumburg, Illinois, and Owings Mills, Maryland—still touted by Joel Garreau, author of *Edge Cities,* as the wave of the future—are particularly likely to experience an identity crisis as the sum of their parts fails to add up to a community. When asked to explain the reasoning behind Baltimore County's proposal to create a

town center for Owings Mills, the county executive explained, "It will give this community a heart, an identity, and a focal point."[11] Even Tysons Corner, Virginia, the epitome of Garreau's edge city, is moving forward with a town center project. Commenting on the proposal, Fairfax county supervisor Gerald E. Connolly explained, "The idea is to try to put some personality into Tysons." As architect Rod Henderer, vice president of RTKL Associates, Inc., added, "There's a huge amount of office space, but there's never been a civic heart to Tysons. This is a measure to give that to Tysons. Most cities have a sense of place about them. Tysons does not, and it needs one."[12]

For MPCs developed in the 1960s and 1970s, which consisted of hundreds or thousands of acres of low-density suburban neighborhoods, a town center can provide both a literal and symbolic center for the community in a way that a golf course and clubhouse cannot. Early village centers, like those in Columbia, Maryland, and Reston, Virginia, used a combination of innovative and conventional retail forms but fell short of expectations as both commercial and community centers. Reston's Lake Anne Village, for example, placed housing over retail along a lakefront, an innovative approach that performed poorly, in part, because it offered limited visibility from nearby roads that were not high-traffic to begin with. But whereas Lake Anne Village Center has continued on, with a core of longtime residents who feel quite connected to the center, other small village centers within Reston and Columbia that were oriented toward neighborhood shopping were outright failures and have been closed.

In recent years, MPCs approaching buildout, like Valencia, in California, and Miami Lakes and Haile Plantation, in Florida, have chosen traditional urban designs for their main streets and town centers. In contrast to the shopping centers of Columbia, Maryland, which are ringed by parking lots, Haile Village Center's Main Street can be quickly transformed into a pedestrian setting for farmers' markets and community festivals. And unlike Columbia, Haile Village Center has a main street, a central green and fountain area, and a meetinghouse, which provide gathering places for homeowners' association meetings, retirement parties, weddings, receptions, and other public and private events and celebrations.

For new communities, such as the traditional neighborhood developments (TNDs) of Celebration, in central Florida, and Kentlands and Lakelands, in Gaithersburg, Maryland, town centers provide an instant identity and a "downtown" that is capable of distinguishing these communities from residential subdivisions and planned unit developments that lack a pedestrian-oriented core. With their sales offices and information centers strategically located in the downtown, the town centers in these communities act as ports of entry. Visitors and potential homebuyers often discover the town center first, with its

Mizner Park's Plaza Real, a popular outdoor gathering place in Boca Raton.

refreshing, pedestrian-scale shopping and its public gathering spaces, then explore the residential neighborhoods.

The value of establishing a strong identity is also apparent in the mixed-use, urban village–style projects being developed by apartment builders like Post Properties, Inc.; Trammell, Crow Residential; and AvalonBay Communities. The mix of uses, the urban ambience, and the pedestrian-oriented public realm immediately distinguish places like Post's Riverside, near Atlanta; Addison Circle, in Addison, Texas; and Phillips Place, in Charlotte, North Carolina, from

Haile Village Center, the heart of Haile Plantation, a 1960s master-planned community in Gainesville, Florida. *Courtesy Haile Plantation Corporation.*

other apartment, condominium, and townhouse complexes in those markets. Builders of MPCs and TNDs, and residential developers like Post, are discovering that people are willing to pay a premium to live in settings that include more traditional, pedestrian-oriented centers of the sort that can give the community a stronger identity. Early homebuyer surveys in Orenco Station, a new urbanist community near Portland, Oregon, showed that potential residents were so excited about the town center concept that the developer decided to spur home sales by putting the first phase of the town center on a fast track—a strategy that has paid off, both by quickening the pace of residential sales and by leading to more rapid appreciation in prices.

Riverside, one of Post Properties's mixed-use, urban village–style projects near Atlanta, Georgia, embodies an urban ambience that distinguishes it from other apartment communities in Atlanta. © *Steve Hinds.*

Changing Preferences and Tastes

As Dolores Hayden shows in *Redesigning the American Dream,* the residential, commercial, and office settings of post–World War II suburbs were planned and designed largely to meet the needs of families that consisted of a working husband, a stay-at-home mom, and children.[13] More recently, Dowell Myers has observed that the "traditional family of breadwinner father and stay-at-home mom now accounts for barely one-tenth of all households," and working mothers have become the norm.[14] Married couples with children represented only 26.7 percent of all households in the 1990 census and had slipped to 23.5 percent by 2000; the other three-quarters of American households were made up of singles, families with no children, and single parents with children. According to the 2000 census, "nonfamily households" will soon account for one-third of all American households, and one-quarter of households currently consist of persons living alone.

American households are also growing older and more ethnically diverse. These demographic changes have important implications for real estate markets: for example, as compared to families with children, singles, couples with no children, and retirees are more likely to be attracted to smaller, lower-maintenance housing clustered within walking distance of employment, services, amenities, people, and activities. These demographic trends, together with the general lack of such diverse, mixed-use environments in America's suburbs, are bolstering the development of new town centers and urban villages.

New Housing Concepts: Selling Lifestyle, Not Density

Recent years have witnessed a resurgence in downtown housing markets that is being driven by young professionals, empty nesters, and others looking to escape traffic congestion, gain better access to urban amenities, and find lower-maintenance housing options. While suburban residential markets continue to dominate, housing permits in large cities more than doubled between 1991 and 1998, "growing at a faster rate than that of suburbs and metropolitan areas

Creating Places for a Changing America

On the basis of survey research conducted by their marketing and communications firms, American LIVES, Inc., and InterCommunicationsInc, Brooke Warrick and Toni Alexander summarized, for developers, some of the broader implications of America's changing demographics:

- The change from mass-market standards to niche market differentiation, both by life stage and by lifestyle.
- The change from unplanned suburbs to master-planned communities.
- The change from suburban anonymity and individualism to a yearning for community.
- The change from contemporary to neotraditional styling.
- The change from strip-commercial suburban sprawl to compact, highly defined town centers.[1]

These trends translate into a growing dissatisfaction, among significant segments of homebuyers, consumers, and businesses, with the conventional real estate product types described by Christopher Leinberger, and indicate the need for more diverse residential, retail, hotel, and office formats.[2]

Resident surveys conducted by Post Properties, Inc., a major developer of suburban apartment complexes in the South and West, showed that "the apartment dwellers who had sought out the security and space of the suburbs were starting to get sick of the commute."[3] As John Williams, chief executive officer of Post Properties,[4] observed, "By the early 90s, it was evident there was a rebellion, or sea change, in people's attitude about where they wanted to live."[5]

1. Brooke Warrick and Toni Alexander, "Looking for Hometown America," *Urban Land*, February 1997.
2. Christopher Leinberger, "The Market and Metropolitanism," *Brookings Review* 16, no. 3 (fall 1998).
3. Lisa Davis, "A Different Vision: Post Properties CEO John Williams Stops to Plant the Roses," *Delta Sky Magazine,* May 2000.
4. Since resigned.
5. Andrés Duany, Elizabeth Plater-Zyberk, and Jeff Speck, *Suburban Nation: The Rise of Sprawl and the Decline of the American Dream* (New York: North Point Press, 2000), 255.

in general."[15] As one observer notes, "These new homes all share . . . one feature that, except on rare occasions, the suburbs do not offer: refreshing views of older, often refurbished, historical settings—the rediscovered charm of the inner city."[16]

While urban living is gaining wider appeal, rustic loft conversions and renovated historic townhouses can satisfy only a portion of the demand for intown residences. At the same time, renters and purchasers looking for urban ambience expect all the conveniences they have become accustomed to in more suburban locations, including up-to-date layouts; modern plumbing, telecommunications, and electrical systems; convenient parking; and a sense of safety and security. These twin demands—for an urban lifestyle with suburban amenities—have created opportunities for savvy developers and innovative public sector agencies to integrate higher-density housing into town center and main street projects.

Despite the scarcity of market data on the potential demand for housing in town center projects, and the strong skepticism of real estate professionals, demand for residential properties in town centers continues to exceed expectations in a wide variety of markets. Most surprising of all is the strong demand for housing above retail shops and offices. For example, Orenco Station's lofts and live/work units—residential types that were completely untested in the market—have garnered prices that are unprecedented in Portland's outlying suburbs.[17] Despite being located just minutes away from competing properties with beachfront views, the apartments above the shops and cafés of Mizner

Park, on an inland site in Boca Raton, have proven extremely popular—particularly those facing the bustling Plaza Real. And in suburban Gaithersburg, Maryland, three-story live/work units in Kentlands's town center are being snapped up at prices that far exceed those of much larger single-family homes in the area. Projects like Post Properties's Uptown Place, in Charlotte's Fourth Ward, are succeeding where no new apartments have been built in more than a decade, and other Post residential properties offering urban settings and amenities command premiums in markets—such as Atlanta, Dallas, and Denver—that have a large supply of multifamily housing options.

Thomas D'Alesandro, of Terrabrook, which is developing the second phase of Reston Town Center, points out that the center

> *currently has over 1,500 homes, ranging from rental to high-rise condos and also townhouses. Prices are substantially higher than those for similar housing units a few miles away. Over 700 apartments are now under construction, by Trammell, Crow Residential, right inside the urban core of Reston Town Center, and about 70 additional condo units are planned to start construction in 2002 in another high-rise tower.*

While the compact forms of town centers and urban villages are touted for their potential to reduce automobile trips, support transit, and help preserve open space, town center projects are not marketed on the basis of their higher density, a term that conjures up negative images in the minds of many potential renters and homebuyers. Instead, marketers focus on the attractiveness of town centers to those who are looking for the benefits of intown lifestyles and for the urban amenities they provide. Town center and main street projects are promoted as "live, work, play" settings that offer some relief from the totally automobile-dependent lifestyles of "soccer moms," business commuters, and others who feel trapped by suburban sprawl. While some are lured to town center and main street projects by the promise of a more bohemian lifestyle of bistros and art galleries, many others wish only to simplify their lives and experience a stronger sense of community. As John Williams, chairman and chief executive officer (until recently) of Post Properties, has said, Post Properties's urban villages are "a blend of old-fashioned neighborhood living and 21st-century technology and convenience."[18]

The same urban lifestyle qualities that draw people to live in town centers are also proving attractive to the guests of hotel chains and inns. Travelers who are already harried by busy schedules and frequent travel to unfamiliar places welcome the opportunity to walk from their hotel room to offices and lunch meetings during the day, and to restaurants, entertainment, gymnasiums, and public gathering spots in the evening, without having to climb into a car. A town center residence or hotel room also offers something rarely found in suburbia: a "room with a view," overlooking the public space and street life of the community.

Evolving Retail Realms

Just as housing above retail has been met with raised eyebrows and smirks, main street retail has faced skepticism from all sides. Critics continue to point to the struggles of historic main streets, and to the presumed incompatibility of big-box formats and main street shop spaces and locations. Most of all, skeptics focus on the time-tested rules of retailing, which dictate specific requirements for highway visibility, traffic counts, parking, building orientation, signage, and tenant mix.

While these conventional rules are no less relevant today, a number of retailing trends are fueling the need for continued innovation in retail formats. These trends include steady declines in the number and length of mall visits; overbuilding in retail markets; the increasing importance of e-commerce; and, in particular, the uproar over sprawl and the dull sameness of many retail settings. Since the 1980s, retail space has been growing five to six times faster than retail sales: the United States is currently flooded with almost 5 billion square feet (465 million square meters) of retail space, of which 500 million square feet (46 million square meters) is vacant.[19] Continued overbuilding in the retail sector has created a zero-sum situation—an intense, accelerated form of "retail Darwinism," in which retail properties either compete successfully and grow stronger or die off.[20]

The challenges facing retail developers have become a recurring theme of *Emerging Trends in Real Estate*, a publication issued by Pricewaterhouse-Coopers. The 2000 report described the situation quite simply: "There's too much retail. That's the problem." One analyst quoted in the report estimates that "from 20 percent to 30 percent of retail is redundant," adding that "we're really underdemolished."[21] The 2002 report found much the same: "America is overstored—too many formats cannibalize each other . . . and, so far, the Internet only nibbles away at market share. . . . Dead and dying malls litter the nation's suburbs. . . . Most power centers are risky propositions, as category killers and discounters battle amongst themselves in submarket-by-submarket survival 'contests'."[22] The one bright spot identified are the new shopping centers—commonly known as "lifestyle centers"—that are adopting a main street and town center format. "Lifestyle centers . . . continue to be promoted as the new-wave format. . . . They'll end up stealing business from the other

Mainstream retailers on main streets: Banana Republic, the Bombay Company, Talbots Kids, and Talbots Petites line up in Reston Town Center, Reston, Virginia.

categories, particularly malls."[23] Other factors cited by PricewaterhouseCoopers as affecting malls and shopping centers include traffic, changing consumer tastes, boredom with redundant formats, time-constrained lifestyles, and "questionable entertainment strategies."[24] Such turmoil is bringing the pressure for innovation in retail properties to unprecedented levels.

On the demand side, surveys report approval ratings of 70 to 80 percent, and higher, for town centers and main street projects.[25] The revived interest in town centers and main streets has not gone unnoticed by retailers and developers, who have been rediscovering older main streets in places like

A main street store for Barnes & Noble at Bethesda Row in Bethesda, Maryland.
Courtesy Federal Realty Investment Trust.

Westport, Connecticut; Winter Park, Florida; and Santa Monica, California. Mainstream retailers like Ann Taylor, Banana Republic, the Body Shop, the Gap, J. Crew, Pottery Barn, Restoration Hardware, Talbots, Victoria's Secret, and Starbucks are actively seeking out main streets, both old and new. Federal Realty Investment Trust, a leader in the revitalization of entire blocks of older downtowns over the past two decades, has applied the same principles used in its successful revitalization efforts to create new projects, such as Pentagon Row, in Arlington, Virginia. The trust describes these new projects as "a new vision for main street."[26] Shopping center owners and developers are also keenly aware of trends and are rapidly introducing

lifestyle centers and what have been called "main street malls." After attending a national shopping center conference, retail expert Bob Gibbs estimated that nearly one-third of all proposed shopping centers fell into one of these two categories and incorporated elements of new urbanist planning and design.[27]

A common misconception holds that town center projects are limited to upscale boutiques and espresso bars. Projects like Mashpee Commons, in Cape Cod, Massachusetts; McKenzie Towne Centre, in Calgary, Alberta; and the Uptown District, in San Diego, California, are dispelling this myth and proving that big boxes and standard shopping center tenants like pharmacies, supermarkets, and video stores can be designed for main street settings. In fact, Market Square, in Gaithersburg, Maryland, has been designed to incorporate four big-box stores within a main street setting. To blend various combinations of Leinberger's 19 development types within a town center format, developers, retailers, planners, and designers have literally had to think outside the box. The challenge is twofold: first, to find urban designers who are capable of reconfiguring the standardized site and building formats used for shops, restaurants, cinemas, hotels, and offices that have been developed in strips and centers; and second, to persuade planners, retailers, financiers, developers, and local government to implement designs that break all the rules.

By far the clearest sign of retail evolution, however, can be seen in the conversion of former shopping malls and strip centers into town centers and main streets. In the case of Mizner Park, the transformation required the complete demolition of the original mall and the construction of a new urban boulevard. In

Top: Turning malls into main streets: Eastgate Mall, a failing shopping center in Chattanooga, Tennessee. *Courtesy Dover, Kohl & Partners.*

Bottom: The development plan for Eastgate Mall's transformation into Brainerd Town Center. *Courtesy Dover, Kohl & Partners.*

other cases, such as Mashpee Commons, conversion has involved a combination of demolition and rehabilitation. Still other malls and strip centers, such as Eastgate Mall, in Chattanooga, Tennessee (now Brainerd Town Center), and the Winter Park Mall, in Winter Park, Florida, are undergoing gradual transformations. Most of these projects are located on infill sites that offer both challenges and opportunities, and strong public/private partnerships are typically required to make the projects happen. As one Williams-Sonoma executive sees it, "We're going through a time I refer to as the de-malling of America."[28]

The challenge for the planners, designers, and developers of main streets and town centers is to create places that are more than simple reconfigurations of conventional retail projects. Richard Heapes, the principal designer for Mizner Park and other main street projects, has cautioned against the "malling of main street," an approach that is typified by simplistic changes (for example, removing the rooftop of a shopping mall and renaming it a town center). As Gary Bowden, formerly with RTKL Associates and now a professor at the University of Maryland, states, "Main street is not two strip centers face-to-face; the developers of these kinds of centers require a city-builder mentality, and they require patience."

New Workplace Environments

In addition to creating more lively and interesting places to live and shop, main street and town center projects are beginning to attract a variety of employers, ranging from small, independent offices providing professional services (e.g., the law, real estate, insurance, and health care offices in Haile Village Center and Gaithersburg's Market Square) to the world headquarters of major corporations (e.g., the AT&T headquarters, located in Redmond Town Center, Washington; the headquarters of Princess Cruises, located in Valencia Town Center Drive, Valencia, California; and several corporate headquarters located in Reston Town Center, Virginia).

As many high-technology manufacturing operations become less noxious as land uses, they are also beginning to consider town center locations, which are viewed as offering a higher quality of life than typical industrial parks. Apple Computer and JVC have located manufacturing facilities in Laguna West's town center, near Sacramento, California, and some office and technology parks—such as Legacy Town Center, in Plano, Texas, the headquarters of EDS—are beginning to transform themselves from single-use work zones into mixed-use, pedestrian-oriented town centers.

Small, owner-occupied professional offices on Main Street in Haile Village Center.

AT & T Wireless Headquarters, in Redmond Town Center, Redmond, Washington.

Both for companies that would otherwise be isolated in office and technology parks, and for "new economy" workers who are tired of the "virtual world" of computers, e-mail, and telecommuting—and eager for face-to-face contact—town centers and mixed-use environments offer an appealing alternative. Charles Lockwood, who has written on the suburban town center and main street phenomenon, has observed that "more and more people want to return to the traditional main street, particularly as their lives become more mobile, more global, and more computerized. Despite all the talk about 'going virtual,' people still need to feel they belong to a community."[29]

The home-based workforce, in particular, is drawing a great deal of attention from homebuilders and from the developers of town centers and main streets. Although estimates vary, the number of home-based businesses and workers is already substantial and is expected to grow rapidly in the coming years. According to an article on the live/work homes featured at the 2001 International Builders' Show,

In America today, nearly 20 million businesses call an office home. Home-based businesses are one of the fastest-growing segments of commerce, and every week 8,000 people make the decision to combine their work and living space. Add to these figures the millions of people who work out of their homes for employers based elsewhere, and the number of people who work from their residences exceeds 55 million.[30]

These numbers are fueling the growing interest in live/work buildings; in addition, communities are under pressure to revise their zoning and building codes to allow a broader mix of uses—in particular, the inclusion of small businesses—in residential areas. In response to this demand, *Builder* magazine, Beazer Homes, and Duany Plater-Zyberk & Company worked together to create Live/Work 2001, three permanent models of comfortable, contemporary urban homes that accommodate very different businesses and adaptable living spaces. The project was constructed in Atlanta's historic warehouse district, Castleberry Hill, and was the focal point of the 2001 International Builders' Show.[31]

Advancing Leisure and Entertainment Concepts

In recent years, shopping centers of all types have been incorporating more entertainment elements—including cinema complexes, restaurants, and entertainment-oriented retailers—to lure and retain shoppers. Urban entertainment centers (UECs) have also evolved as a new and separate category of development. And, according to industry expert Michael Beyard, UEC formats are branching out, moving from freestanding entertainment centers toward "mixed-use

Office park to town center: A conceptual plan for transforming a portion of the Legacy Office Park, in Plano, Texas, into Legacy Town Center. *Courtesy Legacy.*

projects that are infused with entertainment and entertaining retailers in an entertaining environment." Town centers and main streets create ideal settings for leisure and entertainment-oriented activities.

Retail entertainment uses are increasingly migrating to urban, mixed-use, and town center settings—in part because these settings are in themselves more entertaining, as well as more authentic—and this combination has the potential to create a stronger destination and a better experience for the visitor. CityPlace and Easton Town Center, which are among the case studies in this book, offer prime examples of town centers that incorporate retail entertainment uses. In many town centers, retail entertainment uses are now primary uses, and the growth of the retail entertainment concept over the past decade has helped to fuel the town center movement.

Town center and main street settings offer a range of benefits for retail entertainment uses. The mix of uses offered in town centers—including residential, office, and civic elements—strengthens the sense of place and can thus enhance the retail entertainment component. For example, the town hall on the green of Southlake Town Square, in Southlake, Texas, provides a strong sense of place for that development and offers something that is atypical of festival marketplaces and freestanding UECs. Moreover, town center and main street settings are frequently connected to an existing network of streets and blocks, which creates connections to surrounding areas and enhances the integrity of the development as a true urban experience.

The design and tenant mix of town centers enable them to provide a lively combination of both commercial and nonprofit leisure and entertainment activities. Town center bistros, cafés, and shops are clustered around public skating rinks and amphitheaters, and movie theaters spill out onto public plazas rather than onto parking lots. And the farmers' markets, outdoor community concerts, and Fourth of July celebrations once held, for the sake of convenience, in the courtyards of shopping malls and in the parking lots of strip commercial centers are now being drawn to the more traditional, open-air streetscapes and public greens and plazas of town centers, which provide a more authentic community atmosphere and seem uniquely tailored for these events.

Nothing can substitute for good site location, a sound market analysis, and a carefully designed tenant mix and leasing strategies, but town centers have

an additional dimension that boils down to "Walt Disney World 101." After decades of painstaking surveys and analysis, Disney's management team discovered that it was not the "attractions" that were fueling the repeat business that is absolutely essential to Disney's economic success—it was the quality of the built environment itself! The same is true for town centers and main streets.

What keeps people coming back to town centers and main streets is not simply the commercial activity—there are comparable stores in competing locations, and visitors often arrive with no specific plan of activity—but the casual public setting that town centers provide for meeting, mingling, strolling, and people watching. As Daniel Brents, vice president of Gensler, in Houston, has observed, "[it's] as much about congregating as it is merchandising." The attractiveness of town center formats as places for congregating yields the essential ingredients that fuel the commercial success of town center tenants: customers and foot traffic.

Smart Growth, Sustainable Development, and Livable Communities

In response to both media attention and the public outcry against sprawl, government agencies and nonprofit organizations have taken actions to encourage the development of town centers, main streets, and urban villages. One of the earliest initiatives designed specifically to revitalize historic main streets and town centers was the National Main Street Program of the National Trust for Historic Preservation. First piloted in 1977, the program has grown and evolved over the years and now includes more than 1,200 local Main Street programs in 43 states. More recently, large foundations such as the Heinz Endowment, the MacArthur Foundation, and the Turner Foundation have begun funding research and initiatives related to smart growth.

ULI has long sought to promote best practices in land use and development, and has for many years actively promoted smart growth and mixed-use development. ULI began conducting research and promoting mixed-use development as early as the mid-1970s, and published *Mixed-Use Developments: New Ways of Land Use* in 1976. Six years later, ULI published the recommendations of the Council on Development Choices for the 80s, which stated: "The mingling of work and commerce with residences makes for healthy and vibrant neighborhoods. Instead of separating houses from everything else, the Council recommends efforts to create a mix of land uses in our neighborhoods and communities." More recently, ULI has joined with the Environmental Protection Agency (EPA) and numerous nongovernmental organizations to promote smart growth. In 1999, ULI began sponsoring an annual conference called "Place Making: Developing Town Centers, Transit Villages, and Main Streets."

Examples of just how widely the concepts of smart growth, sustainable development, and livable communities have spread include the EPA's national Sustainable Development Challenge Grants and its regional Smart Growth/Livable Communities initiatives; the Transportation and Community and System Preservation (TCSP) pilot program of the U.S. Department of Transportation; a variety of initiatives undertaken by the Center for Livable Communities, an arm of California's Local Government Commission; and the 1990s Eastward Ho! movement, in southeastern Florida. The growing number of initiatives and programs reveals an emerging coalition of interest groups—focused on environmental protection, historic preservation, real estate development,

Top: The smart growth movement is having a large impact on local, regional, and state land use and transportation planning.

Bottom: Abacoa Town Center, the heart of the Abacoa new urbanist community in Jupiter, Florida, includes a main street with residential over retail.

Among the strong and dramatic steps that West Palm Beach has taken to redevelop its downtown is the successful revitalization of Clematis Street.

conservation, transit, housing, and community development—that see how their own agendas dovetail with the development of town centers. Compact, mixed-use, pedestrian- and transit-oriented centers are regarded as the key to realizing common goals: reducing air pollution, traffic congestion, and infrastructure costs; preserving open space, farmland, and natural habitat; and creating more livable neighborhoods and communities. The Sierra Club's current antisprawl campaign, which actively promotes infill development and compact growth, is one of the most high-profile examples of these shared agendas.[32]

The public sector is also providing direct support for the creation of town centers, main streets, and urban villages through a variety of smart growth initiatives. Smart growth, which originated in the growth management movements of states like Florida, Maryland, Oregon, and Vermont, has evolved into a much wider, more diverse effort to address the shortcomings of current development policies and practices. Compact, mixed-use, pedestrian-oriented centers are a key component of the smart growth agenda and of all smart growth legislation. Public initiatives to cluster development in community-oriented activity centers are spreading rapidly among all levels of government: municipal (the city of Seattle's Urban Villages comprehensive plan); regional (the Portland 2040 plan); state (New Jersey's Communities of Place plan); and even federal (the HOPE VI Program, and the community design guidelines set by the Department of Housing and Urban Development for its Homeownership and Enterprise Zone programs). Key research institutions and trade organizations for real estate developers and builders, including ULI and the National Association of Home Builders, are also actively engaged in the public policy dialogue on smart growth.[33]

Internationally, there are very active town center initiatives in France, Germany, the United Kingdom (U.K.), and other European countries. The U.K. Department of the Environment has maintained an active research agenda on the design of, market for, and performance of different types of town centers, and the Urban Villages Group, based in the U.K., has brought together a consortium of architects, planners, developers, and public officials from throughout Europe to promote the development of mixed-use urban villages.

Harbor Plaza, a revitalized section of Suisun City, California. *Courtesy City of Suisun City.*

At the local level, the American Planning Association's Growing Smart initiative, the sustainable development movement, transit-oriented development strategies, and the new urbanism have led a large and growing number of villages, towns, and cities across the United States to adopt ordinances that promote the creation of mixed-use centers. Communities have also come to recognize the importance of urban design in creating successful centers. In Illinois alone, three suburban communities have commissioned design competitions to develop town centers and have drawn hundreds of submissions and inquiries from around the globe. Public investments in transit lines, land acquisition, parking garages, and infrastructure improvements have also been vital in moving many town center and main street projects forward.

The unique combination of community and commercial elements in town center projects makes them natural situations for the creation of public/private partnerships. Communities like Silver Spring, Maryland; Smyrna, Georgia; Suisun City, California; Washington, New Jersey; and West Palm Beach and Kendall, Florida, have all taken dramatic steps to initiate main streets and town centers. Others, such as Boca Raton, Florida, and Tualatin, Oregon, have partnered with developers to carry out specific projects. Still others, such as Portland's Orenco Station, have used the location of transit stations to focus development.

The New Urbanism

Recent trends in architecture and urban design have also proved instrumental in the creation of town centers, main streets, and urban villages. The new urbanism has been described by Herbert Muschamp, architecture critic for the *New York Times,* as the "most important phenomenon to emerge in American architecture in the post–Cold War era."[34] The movement, which now has its own official organization—the Congress for the New Urbanism, complete with its own charter, annual conferences, and a growing membership—attracts comparisons to the International Congress of Modern Architecture, the equivalent organization for modernism, even while defining itself in direct opposition to modernist architecture and planning.

New urbanists strongly support revitalizing old town centers and main streets, and reconfiguring portions of newer retail, office, and higher-density residential growth to transform them into village centers, town centers, and urban districts. New urbanist planning and design firms such as Calthorpe Associates, in San Francisco; Correa Valle Valle, Dover, Kohl & Partners, and Duany Plater-Zyberk & Company, in Miami; Gibbs Planning Group, in Birmingham, Michigan; Lennertz Coyle & Associates, in Portland, Oregon; and Moule & Polyzoides, in Los Angeles, have all worked on significant numbers of town center and main street projects on both greenfield and infill sites.

Many large and diversified planning and design firms have also created specialized units that focus on town center and main street design. These include large international firms, like RTKL Associates and EDAW, as well as small and medium-sized firms like

Cooper Carry; Cooper, Robertson & Partners; Elkus/ Manfredi Architects Ltd.; Shook; and Street-Works, to name just a few.

The new urbanism has adopted what Andres Duany has described as a pragmatic neotraditional philosophy. In *Suburban Nation,* Duany and his coauthors, Elizabeth Plater-Zyberk and Jeff Speck, note that "the term *neotraditional* was coined by the Stanford Research Institute to describe the ethos of the baby-boom generation, the generation that is expected to be culturally dominant until the year 2030." Among the examples used to illustrate the concept of neotraditionalism, the authors cite the "Mazda Miata, a car that looks, sounds, and handles like a British roadster but maintains the rate-of-repair record of a Honda Civic."[35]

In similar fashion, town center and main street developers and designers learn from and apply the best urban design practices from the "traditional urbanism" found in historic town centers and main streets, while pragmatically adapting them to modern lifestyles, business practices, and technologies. The next two chapters follow a similar course, taking a look back at how town centers and main streets have evolved over time, and reconsidering the qualities and characteristics of enduring places that might still provide a basis for successful town centers today.

Notes

1. Craig Savoye, "Vanilla Suburbs Seek an Identity," *Christian Science Monitor,* December 30, 1999, 1.
2. The phrases *town center* and *main street* will be used as generic terms to refer to the wide variety of places and projects discussed throughout the book. Distinctions between different types of projects will be discussed in detail in chapter 4.
3. Mike E. Miles, Emil E. Malizia, Marc A. Weiss, Gayle L. Berens, and Ginger Travis, *Real Estate Development: Principles and Process* (Washington, D.C.: ULI, 1991), 15.
4. Reid Ewing, "Counterpoint: Is Los Angeles–Style Sprawl Desirable?" *Journal of the American Planning Association* 63, no. 1 (1997): 107–126.
5. See Brooke Warrick and Toni Alexander, "Looking for Hometown America," *Urban Land,* February 1997, 27–29, 51, 53; and *Sprawl Now Joins Crime as Top Concern* (Washington, D.C.: Pew Center for Civic Journalism, February 15, 2000), www.pewcenter.org/about/pr/pr_ST2000.html. For additional survey results, see Ivonne Audirac and Anne H. Shermyen, "An Evaluation of Neotraditional Design's Social Prescription: Postmodern Placebo or Remedy for Suburban Malaise?" *Journal of Planning Education and Research* 13 (1994): 161–173; Ivonne Audirac, Anne H. Shermyen, and Marc T. Smith, "Ideal Urban Form and Visions of the Good Life," *Journal of the American Planning Association* 1, no. 3 (Autumn 1990): 470–483; Sidney N. Brower, *Good Neighborhoods: A Study of In-Town and Suburban Residential Environments* (Westport, Conn.: Praeger Publishers, 1996); Ewing, "Los Angeles–Style Sprawl"; and Rob Steuteville, "Section 16—Sales and Consumer Response to the New Urbanism," in *New Urbanism and Traditional Neighborhood Development: Comprehensive Report and Best Practices Guide* (Ithaca, N.Y.: New Urban News, 2000): 16-1–16-10.
6. Christopher Leinberger, "The Market and Metropolitanism," *Brookings Review* 16, no. 3 (fall 1998).
7. Warrick and Alexander, "Looking for Hometown America."
8. As early as 1958, Robert A. Nisbett published a book entitled *The Quest for Community* (it was reissued in 1969). See also Lloyd W. Bookout, "Building Community in America's

Suburbs," in *ULI on the Future: Building More Livable Metropolitan Areas* (Washington, D.C.: ULI, 1997); James Howard Kunstler, *Home from Nowhere* (New York: Simon & Schuster, 1996); Philip Langdon, *A Better Place to Live* (Amherst, Mass.: University of Massachusetts Press, 1994); Terry Pindell, *A Good Place to Live: America's Last Migration* (New York: Henry Holt & Company, 1995); Warrick and Alexander, "Hometown America."

9. Ray Oldenburg, *The Great Good Place* (New York: Paragon House, 1989).

10. Pindell, *Good Place,* 4.

11. David Nitkin, "Vision of Owings Mills Builds on Main Street: Proposed Town Center Would Curtail Sprawl, Give Area 'a Heart'," *Baltimore Sun,* January 4, 2000.

12. Michael D. Shear, "New Town Center Planned to Put a 'Heart' in Tysons Design Aims to Appeal to Pedestrians," *Washington Post,* February 24, 1999.

13. Dolores Hayden, *Redesigning the American Dream: The Future of Housing, Work, and Family Life* (New York: W. W. Norton), 1984.

14. Dowell Myers, "Demographics and Sociology," in *ULI on the Future: Land Use in Transition,* ed. Dean Schwanke (Washington, D.C.: ULI, 1993).

15. Alexander von Hoffman, *Housing Heats Up: Home Building Patterns in Metropolitan Areas* (Washington, D.C.: Brookings Institution, 1999).

16. David C. Dozier, "Room with a View," *Urban Land,* November/December 1999.

17. Live/work housing is also referred to as "flex housing" because of its ability to adapt space for retail, service, and residential use (that is, to be "flexible" concerning use).

18. PR Newswire, "New Urbanism Validated in Atlanta with Lease-up of Post Riverside" (http://www.prnewswire.com/ [January 12, 2000]). Williams has since resigned.

19. Richard Moe and Carter Wilkie, *Changing Places: Rebuilding Community in the Age of Sprawl* (New York: Henry Holt & Company, 1997), 147.

20. Numerous articles have reported on the overbuilding of retail properties and on the decline in visits to shopping malls. Hacknett cites an industry survey that revealed a nearly 50 percent decline in the number of trips, stores visited, and hours spent in shopping malls during the 1980s. See "Malls Losing Their Allure: Spurned Shopping Centers Add Services to Attract Harried Consumers," *Sunday Times Union* (Albany, N.Y.), September 4, 1994, E-1, E-3. See also Moe and Wilkie, *Changing Places,* and Timothy Egan, "Retail Darwinism Puts Old Malls in Jeopardy," *New York Times,* January 1, 2000.

21. PricewaterhouseCoopers and Lend Lease Real Estate Investments, *Emerging Trends in Real Estate 2000* (New York: PricewaterhouseCoopers and Lend Lease Real Estate Investments, 1999).

22. PricewaterhouseCoopers and Lend Lease Real Estate Investments, *Emerging Trends in Real Estate 2002* (New York: PricewaterhouseCoopers and Lend Lease Real Estate Investments, 2001).

23. Ibid.

24. PricewaterhouseCoopers and Lend Lease Real Estate Investments, *Emerging Trends 2000.*

25. Rob Steuteville, *New Urbanism and Traditional Neighborhood Development: Comprehensive Report and Best Practices Guide* (Ithaca, N.Y.: New Urban News, 2000).

26. Ann O'Hanlon, "Pentagon City Project Starts; Development to Include Shops, Apartments, Skating Rink," *Washington Post,* July 22, 1999.

27. Steuteville, *New Urbanism and Traditional Neighborhood Development,* 4-3.

28. Mitchell Pacelle, "Chain Stores Discover Main Street," *Raleigh News & Observer,* February 18, 1996. (Reprinted from the *Wall Street Journal.*)

29. Charles Lockwood, "Retrofitting Suburbia," *Urban Land,* July 1998.

30. "Live/Work 2001 Homes Planned for International Builders' Show" (http://www.prnewswire.com/ [June 8, 2000]).

31. Ibid.

32. See the Sierra Club's Web page on sprawl for additional information: http://www.sierraclub.org/sprawl/.

33. NAHB position statements on smart growth can be found at http://www.nahb.org/smartgrowth/default.htm.

34. Herbert Muschamp, "Can New Urbanism Find Room for the Old?" *New York Times,* June 2, 1996.

35. Andrés Duany, Elizabeth Plater-Zyberk, and Jeff Speck, *Suburban Nation: The Rise of Sprawl and the Decline of the American Dream* (New York: North Point Press, 2000), 255.

CHAPTER 2

Learning from the Past:

Town Centers and Main Streets Revisited

> *For five millennia, our human settlements were built to human scale, to the five- or ten-minute walk, which defined neighborhoods, within which all of life's necessities and many of its frivolities could be found.*
>
> —ROBERT DAVIS, *Developer and Town Founder, Seaside, Florida*

Town center, main street, and urban village projects represent a dramatic break from the single-use, automobile-oriented formats that have dominated planning and real estate development since the 1950s. Recent efforts to create town centers reflect, in part, a reconsideration of the form and function of central places in historic settlements. The size and proportions of Rome's Piazza Navona, for example, inspired Boca Raton's Mizner Park.[1] But the Italian piazza served as a point of reference, not as a model to be literally reproduced. And while the ancient Roman city of Bath, England, is cited by John Williams, chief executive officer (until recently) of Post Properties, Inc., as an inspiration for Post Riverside, it clearly did not serve as a blueprint for this or other new urbanist projects undertaken by Post. The distant and recent past, however, provide both inspiration and some important lessons for developing 21st-century town centers and main streets.

As the master planner and architect Raymond Unwin noted nearly 100 years ago, in order to create great places we cannot simply copy the best historic places. Nor, today, can we expect one successful town center to serve as a literal model for another project at a different site, in a different city, serving a different market: variations in site characteristics; in local and regional climate, technology, culture, lifestyle, and architecture; and in the scale and requirements of shops, restaurants, and civic institutions all have to be taken into account.

Although Unwin warns against literally copying the design of historic settings, he also maintains that it is *essential* to study "old towns and their buildings." While critics are quick to label interest in historic precedents as nostalgia, the piazzas, market squares, and town centers created before the advent of the automobile embody thousands of years of collective wisdom about urban place making. Despite vast technological and societal changes, our physical dimensions and the way we perceive our environment have changed little over the millennia. When we step out of our automobiles and begin walking through places, we experience them much as our ancestors did. We *see* the buildings, streets, walkways, and trees; we *hear* the sounds of people and activities; we *feel* the sun and wind on our skin; we sense the openness or enclosure of the outdoor spaces; and we pick up subtle cues about the ambience and relative safety of places.

> *Physically, emotionally, intellectually, any change in man's nature is so gradual as to be inconsequential in respect to the design of a specific place. . . . the [Campidoglio's] perfection of spatial balance and scale—as correct today as in the sixteenth century because man's perception of space and scale have not changed. Proportion, scale, form, rhythm, value—these are timeless qualities of design, not to be confused with "style" and "taste" which vary in the utmost.*[2]

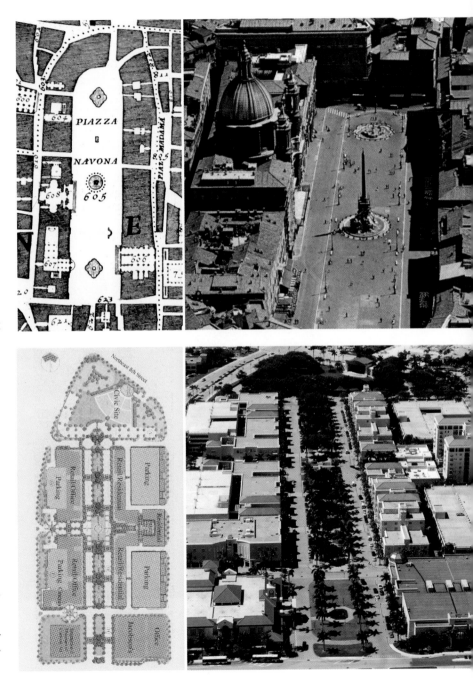

Learning from the past: The size and proportions of Rome's Piazza Navona served as an inspiration for the design of Boca Raton's Mizner Park.
Top left: Camillo Sitte, Der Städtebau nach seinen künstlerischen Grundsätzen, 5th ed. (Vienna: Karl Graber, 1922). Bottom left: City of Boca Raton Community Redevelopment Agency. Top right: Photo Alinari; courtesy Ministero Aeronautico U.S.P. Bottom right: Crocker & Company.

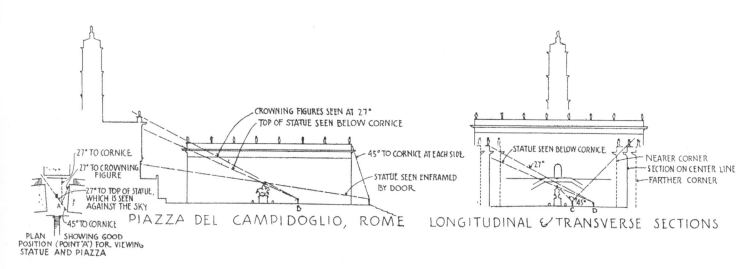

CROWNING FIGURES SEEN AT 27°
TOP OF STATUE SEEN BELOW CORNICE

27° TO CORNICE
27° TO CROWNING FIGURE
27° TO TOP OF STATUE, WHICH IS SEEN AGAINST THE SKY
45° TO CORNICE

PLAN SHOWING GOOD POSITION (POINT "A") FOR VIEWING STATUE AND PIAZZA

45° TO CORNICE AT EACH SIDE
STATUE SEEN ENFRAMED BY DOOR

PIAZZA DEL CAMPIDOGLIO, ROME

STATUE SEEN BELOW CORNICE
27°
45°

NEARER CORNER
SECTION ON CENTER LINE
FARTHER CORNER

LONGITUDINAL & TRANSVERSE SECTIONS

The study of human scale and the perception of urban space remain as relevant today as they were during the Renaissance. Pictured: Werner Hegemann and Elbert Peets's study of the Piazza del Campidoglio in Rome.
Werner Hegemann and Elbert Peets, American Vitruvius: An Architect's Handbook of Civic Art *(New York: The Architectural Book Publishing Co., 1922).*

Old main streets in places like Georgetown, in Washington, D.C., provide lessons on how mixed uses, pedestrians, and sport utility vehicles can happily coexist.

While recent history provides endless examples of places designed to accommodate a single activity served by automobiles, it provides very few examples of places that are designed to skillfully mix activities in a pedestrian setting. Because town centers currently represent something new to developers and designers, many projects touted as such are little more than shopping centers and commercial strips with a few cosmetic changes. Creating places with staying power will require much more than plentiful parking, decorative streetscaping, and chain stores selling the latest fashions. To find examples of places that have been built to a human scale, and that offer a mix of uses, a strong civic character, and an enduring sense of place, we need to look to the past, then decide how best to apply these lessons to a world populated by virtual offices, Starbucks, and sport utility vehicles.

This process of rediscovery and adaptation is exactly what an earlier generation of architects and planners carried out, between 1900 and 1930, under the banner of "civic art"; the thought and work of those years continue to inspire today's place makers, particularly new urbanist designers.[3]

Both the recent and the distant past offer inspiration and important lessons for the development of 21st-century town centers. This chapter takes a brief look back at the history and evolution of town centers and main streets in the United States, beginning in the colonial era and highlighting a few more recent examples from the late 19th and early 20th centuries that are still considered important precedents today. The next chapter will then consider some of the timeless qualities and characteristics of enduring places that might inform current efforts to create successful town centers. Taken together, however, these two chapters can only hint at the complexity of the art of place making. Readers who wish to obtain a deeper understanding need to study the original sources, including both texts and the places themselves, and consult practitioners who are steeped in the knowledge of both.

Town centers and main streets have experienced dramatic changes over the course of U.S. history in response to a wide variety of factors, including major shifts in the patterns of employment, housing, and construction; in transportation technologies; and in retailing practices. Periods of industrialization, urbanization, and rising affluence have been followed by periods of sociodemographic change, suburbanization, and deindustrialization. The town centers created during each successive era reflect an ongoing reconsideration of the scale, composition, and pertinence of neighborhood, village, and town centers for a rapidly changing world.

Colonial Centers and Courthouse Squares

Located at militarily defensible sites along key trade routes, at crossroads, and at ports, early colonial examples of village and town centers reveal the cultural values and economic enterprise behind their planning and design. Spanish settlements were clearly guided by *The Laws of the Indies*. Signed by the King of Spain in 1573, *The Laws of the Indies* are considered to be the first planning code of the

Americas, and set forth detailed planning and design guidelines for colonial towns and cities where life revolved around a central plaza.

The design of cities and towns established under *The Laws of the Indies* is often used as a precedent for contemporary new urbanist and town center projects, but Jean-François Lejeune, of the University of Miami School of Architecture, has noted some important differences. Compared with new urbanist communities, Spanish colonial towns and cities typically had larger blocks; larger, much more open public plazas; no alleyways; and streets terminating in views of the surrounding landscape rather than in views of buildings. The large blocks accommodated a variety of courtyard building types and allowed, in addition to the larger public spaces of the main plazas, the creation of more intimate, semipublic spaces within housing blocks. Similar combinations of private courtyard housing and public plazas can be found in ancient Greek and Roman cities, and throughout the early Muslim world, including Moorish Spain.

In colonial New England, houses were grouped around a village green, or commons, that was communally owned and dominated by a meetinghouse (later, a town hall) and a church. Like the Spanish plazas, the commons were often larger than those now advocated by urban designers, since their primary purpose was for grazing livestock: farmers often lived in the village center and "commuted" to their fields.

Excerpts from *The Laws of the Indies* (1573)

If the boundaries are populated, ... try to learn about the place, the contents and quality of the land, the nation(s) to which the people there belong, who governs them, and carefully take note of all you can learn and understand.

On arriving at the place where the new settlement is to be founded ... a plan for the site is to be made, dividing it into squares, streets, and building lots, using cord and ruler, beginning with the main square from which streets are to run to the gates and principal roads and leaving sufficient open space so that even if the town grows, it can always spread in the same manner. Having thus agreed upon the site and place selected to be populated, a layout should be made in the following way....

The main plaza is to be the starting point for the town; if the town is situated on the seacoast, it should be placed at the landing place of the port, but inland it should be at the center of the town. The plaza should be square or rectangular, in which case it should have at least one and a half its width for length inasmuch as this shape is best for fiestas....

The size of the plaza shall be proportioned to the number of inhabitants ... taking into consideration the growth the town may experience. [The plaza] shall be not less that 200 feet wide and 300 feet long, nor larger than 800 feet long and 530 wide. A good proportion is 600 long and 400 wide.

From the plaza shall begin four principal streets: One [shall be] from the middle of each side, and two streets from each corner of the plaza; the four corners of the plaza shall face the four principal winds, because in this manner, the streets running from the plaza will not be exposed to the four principal winds....

Around the plaza as well as along the four principal streets which begin there, there shall be portals, for these are of considerable convenience to the merchants who generally gather there; the eight streets running from the plaza at the four corners shall open on the plaza without encountering these porticoes, which shall be kept back in order that there may be sidewalks even with the streets and plaza.

In cold places the streets shall be wide and in hot places narrow....

The streets shall run from the main plaza in such manner that even if the town increases considerably in size, it will not result in some inconvenience that will make ugly what needed to be rebuilt, or endanger its defense or comfort.

Here and there in the town, smaller plazas of good proportion shall be laid out....

The temple ... shall be separated from any other nearby building, or from adjoining buildings, and ought to be seen from all sides so that it can be decorated better, thus acquiring more authority.... [All adjacent buildings] shall be built in a manner that would not embarrass the temple but add to its prestige.

They shall try as far as possible to have the buildings all of one type for the sake of the beauty of the town.

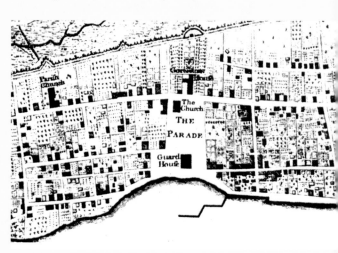

The Laws of the Indies, signed by the King of Spain in 1573, established the primacy of the central plaza in Spanish colonial cities. Pictured: a plan detail for the city of St. Augustine, Florida, which was established in the 16th century. *University of Miami Slide Library Collection.*

Source: Excerpted from a translation by Axel Mundigo and Dora Crouch included in "The City Planning Ordinances of The Laws Of The Indies Revisited, I," *Town Planning Review* 48 (July 1977): 247–268; and from "The Law of the Indies," a translation by Ramon Trías included in Jean-François Lejeune, ed., *The New City*, vol. 1 (University of Miami School of Architecture, 1991), 18–33.

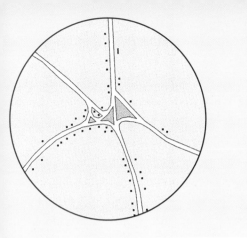

Shirley Center, Massachusetts (founded 1753).
Reprinted, by permission of the author and publisher, from Keller Easterling, American Town Plans *(New York: Princeton Architectural Press, 1993).*

The early settlers did, however, have a clear sense of the town center's role in the life of the community. The founding of Shirley Center, Massachusetts, in 1753, reflects what residents felt was important about their town center, and the balance they were seeking to achieve:

> *The committee made its report and recommendations (their "town plan"). The cornerstone would be the Meetinghouse (the "sacred tree" that went with the moot-hill). On one side would be the Churchyard, dedicated to eternity. On the other side the Common, devoted to posterity. Around this would be "clustered," besides the homesteads and the Town Hall, the Meetinghouse, Schoolhouse and Country Store. They would make the "five senses" that constitute a complete rural community: home, government, religion, education, and commerce.*[4]

The town center as democratic common was a departure from the European town centers that the colonists had left behind, which were dominated by the church and by the buildings of the monarchy and merchant guilds. It would take centuries for royal hunting grounds and estates to be transformed into the parks and public spaces of modern European cities. American colonial town centers, in contrast, recalled the agoras of ancient Greece, and established a strong tradition of public space that continues to this day. This tradition manifests itself in contemporary court cases concerning the right to

The Green, of New Haven, Connecticut, was the central square of the original nine squares of the 17th-century town.

assemble and protest in shopping malls—which have served, for several decades, as the *de facto* central gathering places of the American suburbs.

Early Railroad Towns

The new variations that the industrial revolution brought to town centers and main streets stemmed primarily from changes in transportation technologies. The introduction of railroads and streetcar systems brought about the first generation of "transit-oriented development," making possible the creation of company towns like Lowell, Massachusetts

sold. The Pullman Arcade Building, a large, mixed-use building, incorporated a two-level arcade containing a theater, a library, a bank, offices, and shops. In the late 19th century, these streets and squares became the scene of enormous labor unrest when workers organized to protest the all-encompassing control that George M. Pullman exerted over the lives of workers in his company town. Thus, historic main streets and town centers were not simply places to live, work, and gather socially, but also places to organize militias, launch protests, make speeches, and carry out the public life of the community.

(1822), and Pullman, Illinois (1880), and of early suburbs like Llewellyn Park, in Orange, New Jersey (1853), Lake Forest, Illinois (1856), and Garden City, New York (1869).[5]

Pullman, Illinois, built by the manufacturer of Pullman railroad cars, was a small town with a sophisticated urbanism. The town plan consisted of a grid relieved by a central public square. The Market Square was enclosed by four colonnaded two-story apartment buildings that faced the Central Market Hall building, where fresh produce and other goods were

Early railroad suburbs like Llewellyn Park and Lake Forest, conceived as retreats from increasingly industrial and overcrowded cities, initially dispensed with formal town centers; instead, they were centered on the railroad station and on an open, natural meadow, or "ramble."[6] One early exception was

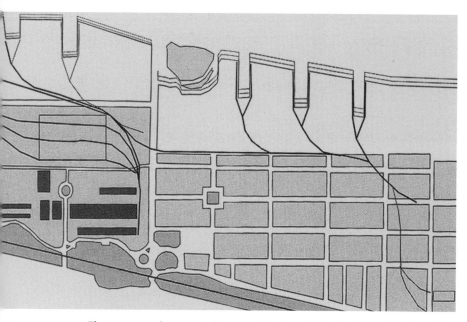

The streets and squares of town centers have historically provided a public realm for all manner of social, cultural, and economic activities, including—in the case of Pullman, Illinois, pictured here—labor uprisings. *Reprinted, by permission of the author and publisher, from Keller Easterling,* American Town Plans *(New York: Princeton Architectural Press, 1993).*

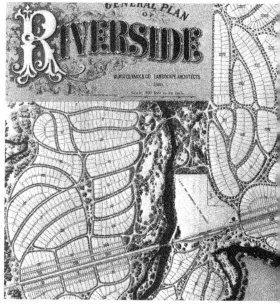

Frederick Law Olmsted and Calvert Vaux's plan for Riverside, Illinois (founded 1869), where a landscaped "ramble" forms the central spine of the community. The community also included a town center focused on the rail station, which was originally the primary mode of commuting to and from Chicago. *University of Miami Slide Library Collection.*

Riverside, Illinois (1869), designed by Frederick Law Olmsted and Calvert Vaux, which contained a distinct town center—a railroad station, commercial and civic buildings, and a water tower that became a symbol of the community.[7] Thus, even with a settlement pattern that emphasized low density and open space—and despite marketing that introduced the concepts of the business commute and the separation of workplace and dwelling—Riverside found reasons to maintain a town center that responded to the needs and expectations of potential homebuyers, residents, and visitors. It offered convenience, access to shopping, a civic character, aesthetic appeal, and a sense of place—of having arrived somewhere.

The streetcar suburbs of the late 19th century came even closer than the railroad suburbs to contemporary notions of transit-oriented development. In contrast to the railroad suburbs, where estate homes lined meandering, curvilinear roads set in bucolic landscapes, streetcar suburbs represented dense, incremental extensions of older urban cores. Many of these neighborhoods—including Roland Park, in Baltimore; Myers Park, in Charlotte, North Carolina; and the inner-ring suburbs of Boston—remain highly desirable today.[8] As these neighborhoods have been repopulated and revitalized, interest in restoring transit service has also grown. In 1994, as a part of a broader revitalization, trolley service was reintroduced to Dilworth, Charlotte's first streetcar suburb.

The Garden City Movement and Civic Art

Increasing automobile ownership early in the 20th century introduced the most serious challenge for the design and function of town centers and main streets, a challenge that continues to this day. The advent of the automobile also coincided with two other important developments: the emergence of the Garden City Movement, which produced neighborhoods, towns, and villages that continue to be influential today, and the birth of the town planning profession—which, in its first decades, was immersed in the principles and practice of civic art. Each of these early-20th-century developments had a lasting impact on the planning and design of town centers.

The Garden City Movement, advanced by Ebenezer Howard at the end of the 19th century, emerged as a town-scale response to "agricultural depression" and the conditions of "Victorian slum cities."[9] At about the same time, the work of leading figures like Werner Hegemann, John Nolen, Barry Parker, Elbert Peets, Raymond Unwin, and the Olmsted brothers—practitioners trained in architecture, physical planning, and design—led to the emergence of town planning as a profession. Heeding Howard's call to decentralize overcrowded cities, these early town planners generated what are now considered classic town plans, characterized by modified grid patterns in which radial avenues and boulevards converged on strong focal points and town centers.[10] The plans incorporated urban parks, village greens, promenades, and pocket parks, and reserved prominent sites for civic uses. Streets were designed to strike a balance between pedestrian and vehicular needs, accommodating shade trees, sidewalks, and street furnishings while also providing visibility and the convenience of drive-by access and on-street parking. Buildings fronted the right-of-way, and arcades, colonnades, galleries, balconies, stoops, and attached plazas all helped to establish the street as a viable public realm.

These early town planners designed places according to the principles of civic art advanced by Camillo Sitte, Hegemann, Peets, and Unwin.[11] As interpreted and promoted by Unwin, civic art was not about urban beautification but about "adopting an orderly framework of streets and public spaces within which the work of individual architects could take its place, and introducing such devices as axial views, expansive public squares, and formal groupings of buildings" that, in effect, set the stage for human activity.[12] As Witold Rybczynski writes, the aim of Unwin's work was to "explain what it is that makes towns and cities of the preindustrial period so pleasing, and to formulate specific principles of urban design that can be adapted to the modern period."[13] This is very similar to what the new urbanism seeks to do, drawing on both pre-20th-century precedents and on the classic town-planning work of the 1900–1930 era. To their credit, the early

The plan for Letchworth, England (founded 1904), by Raymond Unwin and Barry Parker, where 12 streets and boulevards converge on a large town square that is dominated by civic buildings. *Raymond Unwin,* Town Planning in Practice: An Introduction to the Art of Designing Cities and Suburbs, *2d ed. (London: T. F. Unwin, 1911).*

town planners applied the principles of civic art equally, no matter what they were working on —the implementation of L'Enfant's plan for Washington, D.C.; early federal experiments with low-income housing; wealthy speculative communities like Coral Gables, Florida; "company" towns like Kingsport, Tennessee; or working-class neighborhoods in industrial cities, like Seaside Village, in Bridgeport, Connecticut.

The team of Unwin and Parker planned numerous garden cities and suburbs in England. The village center they planned for the model industrial village of New Earswick (1902), just northeast of York, included a modest folk hall, a village green, and a row of shops with residences above, all of which provided the village with a central gathering place and an identity that were true to its medieval motif. In the much larger town center that the team designed for Letchworth (1904), 12 streets and boulevards converge on a large town square that is dominated by major municipal and religious structures.[14]

The town center of Hampstead Garden Suburb (1906), near London, is dominated by two imposing churches that face each other across a vast green: both the scale and the composition are more like that of an oversized medieval church square than of a mixed-use town center. Unlike Letchworth, however, Hampstead includes a subsidiary center—a small village green surrounded by a school, stores, various public buildings, tennis courts, and bowling greens. This center is within a short walk of the major shopping area—two blocks of Germanic medieval buildings positioned along the main highway, which serve as a monumental gateway to the town.

Unwin's perhaps most striking move was to *decrease* the width of most streets at a time when the

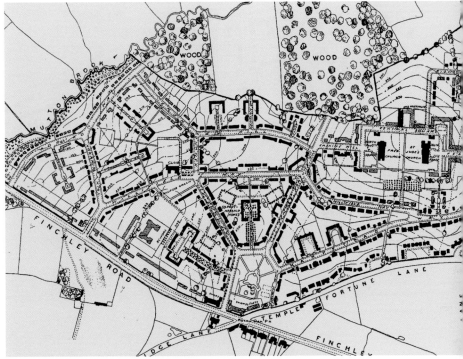

In contrast to the town square in Letchworth, the central square (upper-right-hand portion of the plan detail) for Hampstead Garden Suburb (founded 1906), near London, is rectangular and accessed by just a few principal streets. The commercial center is located at the intersection of streets (center of plan detail), where the buildings form a monumental entrance. *Raymond Unwin,* Town Planning in Practice: An Introduction to the Art of Designing Cities and Suburbs, *2d ed. (London: T. F. Unwin, 1911).*

The mixed-use center of Hampstead Garden Suburb, near London, pictured here in 2001. *Rick Hall.*

automobile was becoming increasingly common. He offered two reasons for this decision: to increase available open space without increasing the size of the entire community, and to slow traffic in neighborhood areas (a technique that has only recently made a comeback in the form of traffic calming). Both of these choices preserved the viability of central places by maintaining reasonable walking distances from homes to other activities, and balancing the needs of pedestrians and vehicles. In contrast to the chicanes, speed bumps, and rumble strips that make up the repertoire of today's traffic calming tech-

developments; and a fine-grained mix of dwellings, civic structures, shops, and workplaces.

Similar experiments with town planning were taking place at the same time on the other side of the Atlantic. The town center of Forest Hills Gardens, New York (1911–1912), is Station Square, "a brick-paved plaza dominated by the tower of the Forest Hills Inn, bordered on one side by the embankment of the railroad station and on the other three by a continuously arcaded building, containing apartments and shops, that spans the two principal streets leading from it into the residential neighborhoods of the village."[15] Additional parks, churches, and corner stores are spread throughout the plan, but Station Square clearly anchors the community and acts as a dramatic gateway. The two principal streets and a greenway connect the square with a mix of single-and multifamily housing, most of which is located little more than a five-minute walk from the station.

As with so many towns from this era, the town center in Yorkship Village, New Jersey (1916), is highlighted by the diagonal convergence of streets in the geographic center of the town. This thoroughly traditional center is composed of three-story civic and commercial buildings surrounding a village square, and is within a ten-minute walk of all the original residences. Created as part of the Emergency War Housing initiative of 1917–1918, the village was connected to the industries of Camden, New Jersey, by a streetcar line. Unlike so many of the urban neighborhoods in and around Camden's declining industrial base, Yorkship Village (now part of Fairview) has survived largely intact.[16]

What is striking about the places planned and built during the classic era of town planning, between 1900 and 1930, is that appealing and enduring urban places were still being created while the automobile was becoming more widespread. Along with the shopping villages discussed in the next section of this chapter, these places stand as reminders that automobiles and town centers are not

Grosvenor Atterbury's plan for Forest Hills Gardens, New York (founded 1911–1912), an early example of a transit-oriented, pedestrian-friendly, mixed-use suburb. *Peter Hall,* Cities of Tomorrow *(Oxford, U.K.: Blackwell, 1988).*

niques, Unwin and his contemporaries were more likely to employ decorative fountains, monuments, and statues, which slowed traffic at intersections and traffic circles while enriching the community with public art and a sense of place.

Unwin and Parker also made use of the *close,* a more urban version of today's suburban cul de sac. Other characteristics of Unwin and Parker's work include a diverse mix of housing types; the application of formal principles of civic art to town-scale

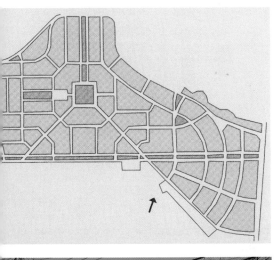

Top: Yorkship Village, in Camden, New Jersey (founded 1918). *Reprinted, by permission of the author and publisher, from Keller Easterling,* American Town Plans *(New York: Princeton Architectural Press, 1993).*

Bottom: Seaside Village, pictured here in 2001, was built in Bridgeport, Connecticut, during the First World War. A contemporary of Yorkship Village, Seaside Village remains a viable neighborhood in the midst of widespread decay. *Rick Hall.*

natural enemies: people have found creative ways to accommodate the needs of both for a long time—but until recently, we had simply forgotten many of the lessons.

Early Shopping Villages

Experiments in early town planning were paralleled by experiments in master-planned commercial centers. In the early 20th century, changes in the production, distribution, and sale of goods made it possible to quickly construct centers devoted primarily to shopping—hence the emergence of the term *shopping center,* which describes a more specialized entity than *town center.* Whereas the agora, the medieval market square, and the colonial town commons evolved gradually to support complex social, civic, and economic activities, the evolution of modern shopping centers has involved a steady shrinkage of civic and residential functions in favor of economic ones (a shift that some observers believe makes shopping centers more vulnerable to short-term changes in retailing). The increasing specialization and automobile orientation of shopping centers, however, took place slowly at first, and many pre–World War II shopping centers continue to be cited as good precedents for today's town centers.

In *Making a Middle Landscape,* Peter Rowe explores four types of retail realms that evolved during the 20th century: the strip commercial center,

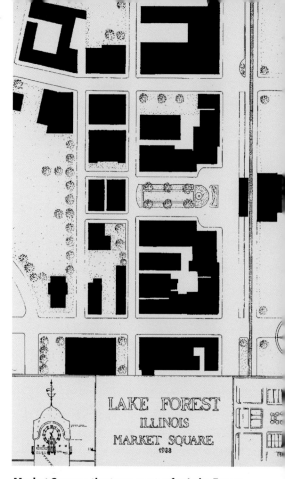

Market Square, the town center for Lake Forest, Illinois, was established in 1916; in 1979, it was added to the National Register of Historic Places as the first planned suburban shopping center. *Drawing by students at the University of Miami School of Architecture; courtesy Jean-François Lejeune.*

the roadside franchise, the shopping village, and pedestrian malls.[17] Rowe notes that early retail forms on the urban fringe mimicked many of the design elements of main streets and town centers. These retail centers typically contained a mix of uses and maintained better connections with surrounding residential areas than today's shopping centers. Shopping villages also often included clock towers, formal squares, and greens that explicitly recognized the social and civic dimensions of these places within the community. Examples of these early retail forms include "taxpayer blocks"—inexpensive, low-rise buildings that were constructed, and then rented out, to "temporarily" enable the owner of the block to pay his or her property taxes; Shaker Square, a modified strip center developed in 1929 for Shaker Heights, a suburb of Cleveland, Ohio; Country Club Plaza, developed beginning in the early 1920s for the Country Club District of Kansas City, Missouri; Highland Park Shopping Village, developed in Dallas in 1931; and Cameron Village, developed in 1948 for Cameron Park, in Raleigh, North Carolina.[18]

Lake Forest, Illinois, resisted the notion of a town center for 60 years, until the addition of Market Square, in 1916. On the one hand, Market Square illustrates the shift away from traditional town centers, anchored by religious and civic institutions, toward centers devoted primarily to shopping. Nevertheless, Market Square continues to be widely hailed as a classic plan for an American town center conceived during the early automobile era; in 1979, it was added to the National Register of Historic Places as the first planned suburban shopping center.

Market Square's reputation is derived from the simple elegance of its traditional urban design, which has been described by Robert A. M. Stern and John Massengale as "a charming, intimately scaled group of buildings arcaded along the street and surrounding a lovely square."[19] The formal common, complete with a memorial fountain honoring its architect; the open-air pedestrian arcades; and the prominent clock tower all contribute to a strong sense of place. The streetfront and the square are lined with two-story buildings containing ground-floor shops with offices and residences above. Angled, on-street parking spaces are provided in front of the shops; "shipping courts" located behind each block are reserved for deliveries, utilities, and trash collection.

The community has recently formed a non-profit revitalization organization, Market Square 2000, which is raising funds to restore the streets and public spaces of Market Square, all of which are owned and maintained by the City of Lake Forest. As the Market Square 2000 effort proclaims, "the original plan for Market Square by Howard Van Doren Shaw is not only still beautiful, it continues to serve our community well and works as a model throughout the country."[20] After 86 years in existence, Market Square continues to perform an important role as the town center for Lake Forest.

The planned community of Shaker Heights (1921) represents an interesting hybrid of an early suburb and a classic town plan. Covering nearly 4,000 acres (1,620 hectares), Shaker Heights combines higher-density areas, based on a modified grid pattern, with lower-density curvilinear areas. The town center consists of 12 one- and two-story neo-Georgian commercial buildings arranged in an octagonal layout. The center is bisected by a transit line, an arrangement that foreshadowed the contemporary transit-oriented development models advanced by Peter Calthorpe.

Top: Lake Forest's Market Square, pictured here in 2000. *Michael Morrissey.*

Bottom: Early-20th-century shopping village and transit-oriented development at Shaker Square (founded 1926), the commercial center for Shaker Heights, Ohio. *Reprinted, by permission of the author and publisher, from Keller Easterling, American Town Plans (New York: Princeton Architectural Press, 1993).*

Although the center is primarily commercial, Rowe has described its layout and appearance as creating a "formal square and symbolic community center" that is reinforced by the pedestrian connections to the adjacent neighborhoods.[21] The neo-Georgian facades and enclosure give the center "a picturesque quality . . . reminiscent of some of the qualities of the high street tradition of English towns."[22]

Today's town centers also have much in common with early shopping villages such as Cameron Village, Highland Park Village, and Country Club

Plaza—shopping villages that were developed to meet the daily needs of residents from the surrounding master-planned communities. Begun in 1931, Highland Park Village was created to provide a shopping area and town square for Highland Park, a planned community started in 1907 (and now part of the Dallas, Texas, metropolitan area). To gather ideas, the developers and architects traveled to sites in California and Mexico, and to Barcelona and Seville, in Spain. The resulting design included a central plaza and narrow streets lined with Spanish Mediterranean buildings—complete with terra-cotta tile roofs, stucco walls, arcades, arched doors, and intricate ironwork. The site has undergone substantial redevelopment since the mid-1970s and now includes an extensive network of brick paths and walkways, lush landscaping, benches, and trees. Highland Park Village has also been added to the National Register of Historic Places. More than 70 years after its creation, the 9.9-acre (four-hectare) site includes 200,000 square feet (18,580 square meters) of retail space and 46,200 square feet (4,290 square meters) of office space.

Kansas City's Country Club Plaza, begun in 1922, is a third precedent regularly cited by contemporary developers and designers for its quality and longevity. Country Club Plaza was developed as the commercial hub for the Country Club District, a planned community on the outskirts of Kansas City started by developer J. C. Nichols in 1907.

The distinctive layout and design of Highland Park Village have helped it to survive and prosper through seven decades of change in retailing, and to remain a highly popular destination for shopping and dining.
Michael Morrissey.

Unlike Lake Forest and Highland Park Village, Country Club Plaza lacks a large, formal public space; instead, the shopping village takes the form of an urban district—where public space is dispersed in small attached plazas and sidewalk cafés, and the street itself creates the continuous thread of the public realm.

Like Highland Park Village and Market Square, Country Club Plaza took many years to fully develop and continued to evolve as the years went by and fashions changed. What has remained constant for each of these settings is their distinctive architecture and urban design, which have allowed them to adapt to the changing demands of retail, dining, office, and entertainment establishments and to accommodate growing numbers of automobiles while maintaining an urban fabric. In Country Club Plaza, this evolution has involved the transition from parking lots to structured parking as density and land values increased—providing some validation for similar transformations, often viewed skeptically, that are planned for today's town centers.[23] The enduring charm of the buildings and public spaces that continues to attract visitors year after year has also convinced mainstream retail establishments to adapt to the traditional urban ways of doing business found in these older shopping villages.

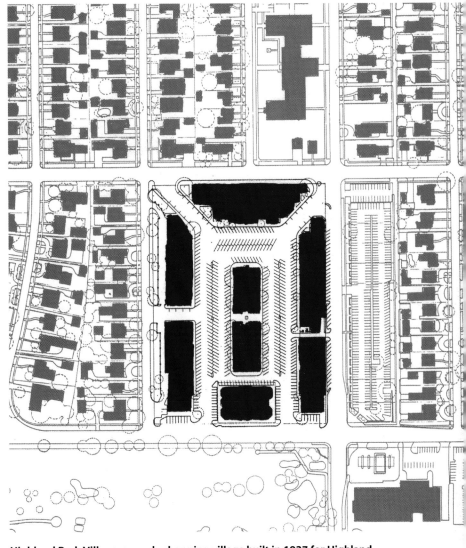

Highland Park Village, an early shopping village built in 1937 for Highland Park, in Dallas, Texas. *Drawing by students at the University of Miami School of Architecture; courtesy Jean-François Lejeune.*

Kansas City's Country Club Plaza: An Enduring Prototype

J. C. Nichols, one of the original organizers of ULI and the founder of the J. C. Nichols Company, developed Country Club Plaza beginning in 1922, as the commercial center for Kansas City's Country Club District. The Plaza has evolved gracefully over the course of eight decades, and continues to be cited as one of the best examples of a commercial district that was developed using traditional urban blocks, streets, and buildings, and that accommodated the automobile from the very outset.

An Urban Design Perspective

The Plaza is one of the unique urban places in America, and is a wonderful example of several important features of good urbanism.

An Easily Adaptable Urban Form

When J. C. Nichols began building the Plaza 80 years ago, it was a simple neighborhood shopping center consisting of small, locally owned shops and offices. Eventually, it grew into a regional shopping center—and, as is the case with all urban districts and developments, it continued to change (with some prodding). Now an entertainment destination as well, the Plaza offers both entertainment retail and niche restaurants. No doubt this change will continue. All the while, the Plaza's beauty and intimacy have enabled it to maintain its place as a community icon and a beacon of pride.

Detail and Playfulness

Each block has buildings that provide a wonderful level of design detail for passersby, and the urban environment offers many playful fountains, sculptures of human figures, and decorative streetscapes that "keep the eye moving" in a lively visual feast.

More Urban Equals More Success

As the Plaza and its immediate surroundings have become more urban, the area has become more successful. Each decade has brought increasing density and urbanization in and around the Plaza, as infill sites are developed and smaller buildings are replaced with larger ones. The hotels and offices adjacent to the Plaza are some of the most desirable in the region, and the housing is certainly the most expensive. Despite having been developed as a suburban shopping center, Country Club Plaza is now both highly urban and highly successful, although it is very different from the typical suburban shopping centers that feature big-box stores and acres of surface parking.

Turning a Mall Inside Out

As the store mix has evolved to include those establishments commonly found at upscale suburban malls, the Plaza has demonstrated that these stores can be successful in a mall "turned inside out"—that is, where there are through-streets, ample sidewalks, on-street parking, and sidewalk storefronts. Even with successful suburban malls in the region, the Plaza is still the location of choice for every national retailer or vendor, if space is available.

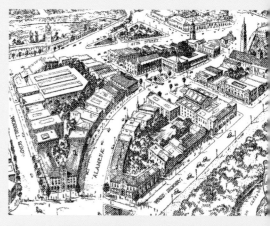

Edward Buehler Delk's rendering of the original plan for J. C. Nichols's Country Club Plaza, founded in 1922 in Kansas City. *The J. C. Nichols Company.*

Although there are no residential units within Country Club Plaza, the center is surrounded by high-density apartments and condominiums, many within walking distance of the Plaza. *Kevin Klinkenberg.*

From its founding, the Plaza has strived to balance the needs of pedestrians and automobiles. *Kevin Klinkenberg.*

Hiding Off-Street Parking

The Plaza actually has an abundance of off-street parking to complement the on-street parking, but it is hidden in midblock garages, in garages disguised as buildings, and in garages with street-level retail. Because of the historical pattern of the Plaza's development, the small to medium-sized garages are spaced throughout the district, enabling them to blend seamlessly into the urban form. Moreover, the necessity of fitting into an increasingly dense and urbanized area forced the garages to take on unique characteristics, including unusual angles, varying parking arrangements, and shared ramps. The Plaza also provides proof that, if planned properly, the surface lots of today's town center projects can evolve into structured parking, as dictated by density and the project's continued growth and success.

Diverse Activities at the Sidewalk Level

While much of the Plaza consists of two-story structures, the second floor is often given over to office uses. The shopping center has long had a mix of department stores, small retailers, restaurants, and entertainment vendors, and a range of uses of varying densities—residential areas; office space; and civic, institutional, and hotel facilities—are directly adjacent to the Plaza.

Shortcomings

While the Plaza has many exceptional qualities, it does have a few shortcomings that are worthy of mention. The edges of the shopping center are clearly defined, but the district lacks a true "center" that could serve as a public gathering space. Although it can be argued that there are many smaller "centers," such as the fountain areas, small courtyards, and plazas, it is a principle of traditional urban design that neighborhoods and districts should have clearly delineated centers.

Moreover, the Plaza is clearly a "shopping" center: civic uses are relegated to the edges of the development, and are sometimes not at all well connected to the Plaza itself. This arrangement is not the fault of the developer, as the design of adjacent streets and structures was beyond the developer's control. Nevertheless, the relegation of civic uses to the outskirts of the Plaza does not always serve nearby residents well.

In addition, although the recent renovation of Brush Creek has significantly improved the civic spaces, Mill Creek Park and the Nichols Fountain—the best civic spaces—are at the edge of the Plaza. And, although Mill Creek is one of the finest and most heavily used parks in the city, it is not well integrated with the shopping center.

Finally, the Plaza would be even more wonderful if the branch library were located within the shopping area instead of across the creek.

The Plaza has adapted well over time: for example, parking lots have been transformed into parking garages that are skillfully concealed by liner buildings. *Kevin Klinkenberg.*

Recent Infusion of Additional Parking

More aggressive development of the Plaza's remaining parcels, as well as redevelopment of some underperforming parcels, has recently begun. The design of the newer development has generally been successful (though a new office tower is out of scale), but there is some concern about the infusion of parking—3,000 spaces, to accommodate some new structures and anticipated demand. The Plaza—following the "cars moving slowly" theory—has always maintained a delicate balance between automobile and pedestrian needs. The additional parking and the intensity of office development have the potential to tip this balance against pedestrians, causing much more automobile congestion and degrading the center's overall atmosphere.

The Evolution of a Town Center

Like most good places, the Plaza is, to an extent, a victim of its own success. For example, because it has not been emulated in the Kansas City area, it has little competition as an urban entertainment district and has become an entertainment destination for suburbanites and tourists. Thus, with each passing month, it serves the surrounding neighborhood less and less and visitors more and more. National chains have increasingly forced out local merchants, and the tenant mix has become less balanced and more upscale, driving out many moderately priced operations. Moreover, because basic services—drugstores, barbershops, a grocery store—have disappeared, nearby residents must now drive elsewhere for these services rather than walk. Although such an outcome may be natural when a given metropolitan region offers only one attractive urban area, it is unfortunate for locals.

Country Club Plaza is important as a model not only of shopping village design but as an example of the evolution of a shopping center and urban district over time. In pursuing the goal of more and better town center and urban village development, planners and redevelopment officials too often embrace development plans that promise (given enough incentives and control) to transform an entire area in just a few years, through a single "white knight" entity. While the Plaza was developed under the guiding light of architect Edward W. Tanner from 1925 to 1974, and under the oversight of the Nichols Company throughout most of its lifetime, it is important to remember that the Plaza developed continuously, in the course of many decades, and that many hands have been involved—including those of new owners Highwoods Properties, who recently purchased the property and have implemented numerous changes. New town centers should be planned with this long-term evolution in mind as well.

Source: Kevin Klinkenberg, principal, 180 Degrees Design Studio, Kansas City, Missouri.

Numerous cafés and small plazas establish a continuous flow of indoor and outdoor space, where visitors can sit, talk, drink, dine, and people watch.
Kevin Klinkenberg.

Traditional architectural styling, public art, fountains, and walkways provide the Plaza with much of its charm.
Kevin Klinkenberg.

Top: The colonial village theme is carried out through a variety of distinctive buildings, ranging in height from three to five stories, that use traditional materials (including brick, stone, wood, and stucco), and exhibit careful attention to architectural detail. *Michael Morrissey.*

Bottom: A newer addition to Palmer Square, maintaining the scale, vertical mix of uses, and pedestrian orientation of the original 1937 plan. *Palmer Square Management, LLC.*

One final example that is often cited as an enduring model for town centers and main streets is Palmer Square, the 7.7-acre (three-hectare) town center across from the main entrance of Princeton University. Originally the site of a busy stagecoach stop between New York and Philadelphia, Palmer Square was built in 1937 by Edgar Palmer, who envisioned it as a town center for the university—a place where people would work, live, dine, and socialize. Thomas Stapleton designed the square and the original buildings to resemble those found in colonial villages near Philadelphia. Palmer bequeathed the site to Princeton University in his will, but at the time of his death, in 1943, only two sides of the square had been completed.

The site was sold in 1981, and additional construction carried out from 1985 through 1990 completed the enclosure of the square. The design for the expansion was sensitive to the original Stapleton plan: the newer buildings and parking garages blend into the context of the historic fabric of the square. Although it maintains the appearance of a town center that has evolved over time, Palmer Square is in fact owned by a single company that employs contemporary retailing practices for leasing, tenant mix, marketing, programming, hours of operation, and parking management. A fully mixed-use town center, the square now offers more than 105,000 square feet (9,750 square meters) of retail in 55 stores; 140,000 square feet (13,000 square meters) of office space; a 216-room hotel (an expansion of the original Nassau Inn); apartments; and condominiums.

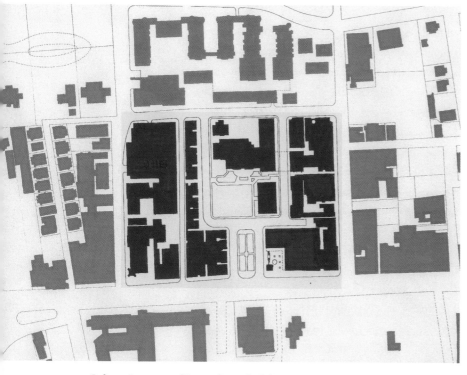

Palmer Square and its environs, in Princeton, New Jersey. *Drawing by students at the University of Miami School of Architecture; courtesy Jean-François Lejeune.*

Town Centers in Transition

Throughout the 20th century, town centers and main streets continued to be redefined by trends in real estate development, transportation, and planning. In Radburn, New Jersey (1928), dubbed a "town for the motor age," the central places of the community were defined in terms of schools: one elementary school for each neighborhood, and one high school for every three neighborhoods, all linked by a loosely defined commons composed of greenways and parks. Radburn's commercial core—its stores, offices, and apartment buildings—was placed at the periphery, along a major avenue near a rail station. Using schools as the key elements of town, village, and neighborhood centers became increasingly difficult, however: the large amount of land required for single-story buildings, athletic fields, and parking lots made the centers too diffuse to support pedestrian-oriented activities, in-town housing, and a vibrant street life.

The town center for Greenbelt, Maryland, constructed by the Resettlement Administration in the 1930s, captures the continued evolution of the type of shopping center that made its first appearance in Lake Forest, Illinois. Located along a roadway near the geographic center of the town, Greenbelt's center positioned parking lots at the rear of the buildings on two sides of the complex. Multiple pedestrian connections linked the center's courtyard to a nearby pool, a recreation area, a school, and the surrounding neighborhoods. The center included a grocery store, retail shops, a theater, a gas station, and a bank, as well as a post office, a government office, police and fire stations, and a youth center. However, the center avoided the creation of pedestrian-oriented urban streets in favor of separate roadways and paths for vehicles and pedestrians, and lacked the formal public spaces found in early shopping villages. Housing, clustered in superblocks, was also separated from the center. Despite the inclusion of diverse shops and facilities in the center's original design, it was symbolically weak as a town center, and the amount of open space between the center and surrounding land uses gave the impression that the buildings were set in a field.

Changes in town centers, such as those in Greenbelt, reflected the growing influence of the automobile on the planning and design of town centers. Frank Lloyd Wright's plans for Broadacre City (1928) expressed his vision of the ways in which the automobile would radically transform American settlement patterns. Wright's city of the future included all the elements of a large town center—government buildings, hotels, retail centers, churches, schools, and dwellings—but these were dispersed over many miles of open countryside, in isolated pockets of development linked by highways and rail lines. Wright based his vision on the ideals of Thomas Jefferson, who believed that land ownership and agricultural life were central elements of American democracy. Under Wright's plan, each household would own a home and enough acreage to carry out subsistence farming; household members would commute—primarily via automobile—to workplaces, commercial activities, and cultural facilities. Broadacre City was also conceived as an alternative to Le Corbusier's (circa 1920) Ville Radieuse, a high-density, urban vision of superhighways and high-rise "towers in a park." In these visions and in others, such as Norman Bel Geddes's Magic Motorways pavilion at the 1939 World's Fair, there was no place for a pedestrian-oriented town center or main street, only for specialized "pieces" of them that

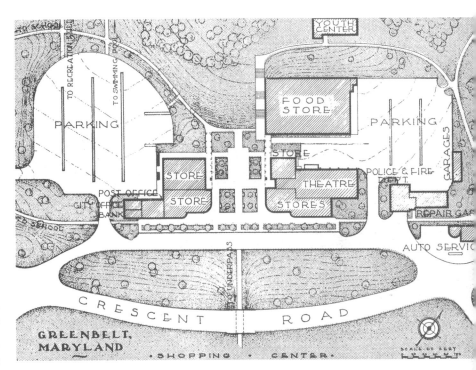

Clarence Stein considered the shopping center and community center combination "the most important forward step" made by Greenbelt, Maryland (founded 1935), in the New Town movement. Greenbelt's town center exhibits the continued evolution from traditional town center to commercial shopping center that occurred in the mid-1930s. The core shopping area remained a pedestrian plaza, with pathways connecting the center to the neighborhoods. Parking was located behind the commercial buildings.
Reprinted, by permission of the publisher, from Clarence S. Stein, Toward New Towns for America, *7th ed. (Cambridge, Mass.: MIT Press, 1989).*

would be linked together by the new, wide-open highways that were the central features of these plans.

Following World War II, the increasing scale and specialization of development—office and industrial parks, retail strips and centers, and resi-

In its attempt to reinvent town centers and main streets, the New Town movement, beginning in the 1950s, adopted a blend of modernist architecture and planning and conventional shopping-center formats. Pictured: the entry to the Milton Keynes Town Centre, in England. *James Moore.*

dential subdivisions and apartment complexes—appeared to herald the end of traditional town centers and main streets. The "town centers" produced between 1950 and 1980 for MPCs and new towns dwarfed their predecessors and adopted modernist, automobile-oriented planning and design. These were efforts to invent a completely new type of town center that emphasized mobility and specialized land uses, provided separate routes for vehicles and pedestrians, and replaced formal squares and village greens with vast open spaces.

In place of the pedestrian-oriented neighborhood unit of the 1930s, the master plan for the 6,750-acre (2,730-hectare) new town of Reston, Virginia, included five separate villages, each with its own center, as well as a town center to serve an anticipated population of 75,000 residents. Las Colinas, a 12,000-acre (4,860-hectare) MPC begun in 1973 in Irving, Texas, in the Dallas–Fort Worth Metroplex, included a 960-acre (390-hectare) "urban center" consisting of office and retail space organized around a canal.

Woodbridge, developed between 1976 and 1992 in Irvine, California, provides an example of the scale and the specialization of land uses in more moderately sized MPCs: the 1,700-acre (690-hectare) site has 200 acres (80 hectares) of open space, 150 acres (60 hectares) of retail and office uses, 100 acres (40 hectares) for eleven school sites, 30 acres (12 hectares) for eight churches, and a 25-acre (10-hectare) town center. The population of 26,000 is dispersed in low-density pockets separated into multifamily units, apartments, apartments for seniors, and single-family housing serving various market segments. Government and civic uses, some of the definitive elements of traditional town centers, are absent from the site.

The town centers created for postwar new towns and MPCs typically adhered to a principle of strict separation of pedestrians and vehicles—effectively killing the street, depriving it of any opportunity to shape or to contribute to the town center. No longer would visitors follow a grand boulevard or a meandering side street to arrive in a great square or plaza. Instead, they would enter a building after a

Traditional town center civic uses, such as a post office and library, were included in the British new town of Cumbernauld's largely enclosed, climate-controlled town center. *Rick Hall.*

short walk across a parking lot. Gathering places would include conventional shopping centers and malls, and grand, spacious plazas bordered—but not really enclosed—by austere, modernist structures rather than by the traditional hodgepodge of architecture and building types. In sum, modernist town centers failed to recreate the pedestrian character, human scale, and intimate public spaces of historic centers. Instead of achieving a kind of timelessness, by embodying both the identity and memory of a community as it ages and matures, many of the town centers created in the 1960s now appear hopelessly trapped in time.

Lake Anne Village Center, the original modernist town center of Reston, Virginia, is one of the most innovative efforts from this era. The center incorporates many ideas shunned by other new towns and MPCs of the era, including vertically mixed uses (residences over shops), and a piazza that is partially enclosed by a crescent-shaped, multistory building that opens onto Lake Anne. Although there are no streets, and the modernist architecture is austere, Lake Anne Village Center has attracted and

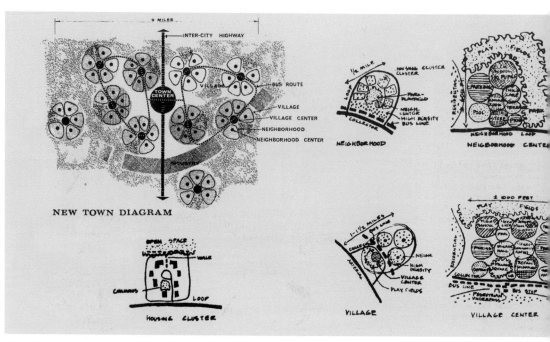

The planning diagrams for Columbia, Maryland, illustrate how the concepts of neighborhoods, neighborhood centers, villages, village centers, and town centers evolved beginning in the 1950s—becoming larger, more automobile-oriented, and more specialized in new towns and in large, master-planned communities.
Morton Hoppenfeld, "A Sketch of the Planning Building Process for Columbia, Maryland," American Institute of Planners Journal, *November 1967.*

maintained a loyal base of residents, including Robert E. Simon, Reston's founder, who returned to live in the community after a 30-year hiatus. As a retail center, however, the village center has never performed well, in part because it did not incorporate a main street and in part because it lacked visibility from nearby roadways. Fairfax County recently designated Lake Anne Village Center a historic preservation district—which is ironic, given that the modernist inspiration for its architecture and urban design reflected an effort to break with all sense of tradition and historic influence.

In contrast to the approach used at Lake Anne Village Center, many early new towns and MPCs attempted to create village centers simply by including convenience stores and shopping centers in the overall plan; examples include Reston's lesser-known village centers and the town center of Columbia, Maryland. As Reid Ewing has noted, many of these were "buried within residential areas."[24] The lack of visibility from arterials contributed to their dismal performance, and most of these centers have been moved to locations better oriented to capture both internal and external consumers.

For every town center created for a new town or MPC, hundreds of shopping centers were being built, forming the commercial nuclei of suburban communities. Peter Rowe has noted that early planning reformers, including Clarence Perry and Clarence Stein, "equated the roles of shopping centers with schools and playgrounds in an attempt to create a sense of suburban community."[25] Victor Gruen, an architect and designer considered by many to be the "grandfather" of the modern shopping mall, boasted, "We can restore the lost sense of commitment and belonging; we can counteract the phenomenon of alienation, isolation and loneliness and achieve a sense of identification and participation."[26]

Purely from the perspective of design, several authors have explored the parallels between shopping malls and historic urban forms such as town centers and main streets. Barry Maitland and Peter Rowe, for example, have identified elements of the interior layout of shopping malls that are consistent with traditional urban forms—in particular, the use of arcades (mall areas) and plazas (courts), and the general layout of main streets.[27] These similarities end at the mall parking lot, however.

In reality, shopping centers such as those in Shaker Heights and Lake Forest, which contained the vestiges of a compact, mixed-use, pedestrian-oriented civic space, were quickly superseded by forms designed strictly for retailing and the automobile. Shopping malls, shopping centers, and commercial strips gradually eliminated civic uses, replaced pedestrian linkages to the surrounding community with parking lots, and concentrated on marquees and interior design. Many shopping malls are now much larger than entire towns from the colonial era, and represent the opposite extreme from the traditional town center and main street.

The public's disillusionment with malls stems, to some degree, from the narrow range of land uses and activities they accommodate, and from the com-

Reston, Virginia, and other new communities developed after World War II, expanded the scale and composition of the traditional town and city across thousands of acres.

Lake Anne Village Center, in Reston, Virginia, mixes traditional town center elements—including a piazza, outdoor dining, and offices and apartments above shops—with the heavy modernist aesthetic of the 1960s.

plete privatization of all space—from the parking lot to the interior courtyards and walkways. The owners and developers of shopping centers have responded by pumping up the entertainment component of malls, and carrying out extensive redesigns of the facades, interior spaces, and storefronts. But while shopping centers have gone through many changes over the years, they have remained essentially single-use retail centers based purely on an economic rationale—and, in many ways, represent the antithesis of traditional town centers. The success of town centers reveals that reconnecting commercial spaces with communities can serve both economic and civic interests equally well.

Nevertheless, the hierarchy of neighborhood, community, and regional shopping centers that has evolved remains highly relevant to today's town centers and main streets. Retail issues such as scale, trading area, and tenant mix are still fundamental considerations in planning for town center and main street projects.

In the 1970s and 1980s, attitudes toward pedestrian-friendly multiuse and mixed-use formats began to change—in part because of the influence of Jane Jacobs's book *The Death and Life of Great American Cities,* which highlighted the importance of mixed uses in providing strength and vitality for urban neighborhoods and districts.[28] Although most of the new mixed-use projects that emerged during these years were dominated by office space and located in downtowns, and few included anything resembling a main street or a town center format, several pioneering examples reintroduced some of the

concepts of place making and city building. In San Francisco's Embarcadero Center, for example, which was begun in 1966 and completed in 1981, four large office buildings, a large hotel, and retail space are arranged around pedestrian plazas and walkways, creating a new, modernist urban district that remains an important destination and icon for the city.

The emergence of the festival marketplace was critical in establishing the viability of open-air shopping environments. Projects developed by the late James Rouse of the Rouse Company, and designed by the late Benjamin Thompson, beginning in the 1970s—including Boston's Faneuil Hall and Baltimore's Harborplace—were pioneering efforts that brought exciting new urban retail and entertainment environments to the city in the form of open-air, pedestrian-friendly settings. But even these projects were built around pedestrian plazas or waterfront promenades, and did not include a true main street. Ironically, the resurrection of the town center concept would require the reintroduction of streets that could accommodate both pedestrians *and* cars.

Because recent history provided so few examples of how to build a traditional town center, designers and developers of today's early town center and main street projects, such as Mashpee Commons, Mizner Park, Reston Town Center, and Seaside's town center, began to look further back in time for ideas and inspiration. The next chapter follows in their footsteps and considers some of the timeless ingredients of traditional town centers that are being adapted and reintroduced in contemporary projects.

Notes

1. Charlie Siemon, land use attorney and adviser on the development of Mizner Park, interviewed by author, January 12, 2000.
2. Jere Stuart French, *Urban Space: A Brief History of the City Square,* 2nd ed. (Dubuque, Iowa: Kendall/Hunt Publishing Co., 1983), 27.
3. Two essential volumes from this period that have been reissued in recent years and represent treasure troves for would-be town center designers: Raymond Unwin, *Town Planning in Practice* (1909; reprint, New York: Princeton Architectural Press, 1994); and Werner Hegemann and Elbert Peets, *American Vitruvius: An Architect's Handbook of Civic Art* (1922; reprint, New York: Princeton Architectural Press, 1999); both

A small portion of the Dolphin Mall, one of the latest generation of regional shopping malls, which opened in Miami, Florida, in 2001. The mall is spread across 120 acres (49 hectares) and includes 1.4 million square feet (130,060 square meters) of space. While the urban design of shopping malls has represented the antithesis of town centers, shopping malls' market logistics; tenanting strategies; and leasing, marketing, and management practices remain essential ingredients for the success of town center projects.

books were indebted to Camillo Sitte, *The Art of Building Cities: City Building According to Its Artistic Fundamentals,* trans. Charles T. Stewart (Westport, Conn.: Hyperion Press, 1979).

4. Benton Mackaye, *Expedition Nine: A Return to a Region* (Washington, D.C.: Wilderness Society, 1969), 4–6. A "moot-hill" was a hill where meetings or councils were held.

5. Dates in parentheses indicate the year in which the community was founded.

6. Robert A. M. Stern and John Montague Massengale, *The Anglo-American Suburb* (London: Rizzoli, 1981), 44–45.

7. Ibid., 24.

8. See Sam Bass Warner, *Streetcar Suburbs: The Process of Growth in Boston 1870–1900* (1962; reprint, New York: Atheneum, 1976).

9. Peter Hall, *Cities of Tomorrow* (Oxford, U.K.: Blackwell, 1988), 91–92.

10. See Witold Rybczynski, *City Life: Urban Expectations in a New World* (New York: Scribner, 1995), chap. 2, "The Measure of a Town," 35–50; chap. 6, "Civic Art," 131–148.

11. Hegemann and Peets, *American Vitruvius;* Sitte, *Art of Building Cities;* Unwin, *Town Planning in Practice.*

12. Rybczynski, *City Life,* 133.

13. Ibid., 194.

14. See Hall, *Cities of Tomorrow,* 94–100.

15. Stern and Massengale, *Anglo-American Suburb,* 34.

16. Rybczynski, *City Life,* 191–192.

17. Peter Rowe, *Making a Middle Landscape* (Cambridge,

Mass.: MIT Press, 1991), 110.

18. Ibid., 119–120.

19. Stern and Massengale, *Anglo-American Suburb.*

20. Market Square 2000 Web site (http://www.lfc.edu/marketsquare2000/faq.html [November 6, 2000]).

21. Rowe, *Middle Landscape,* 112.

22. Ibid.

23. The conversion of parking lots to parking structures has, in fact, occurred in Reston town center and is planned for Kentlands Square shopping center, where the parking lot is laid out in a manner that could accommodate urban streets and blocks in the future.

24. Reid Ewing, *Developing Successful New Communities* (Washington, D.C.: ULI, 1991), 142–143.

25. Rowe, *Middle Landscape,*139.

26. V. Gruen and Larry Smith, *Centers for the Urban Environment* (New York: Van Nostrand Reinhold, 1973), 11.

27. Barry Maitland, *Shopping Malls: Planning and Design* (New York: Nichols Publishing Co., 1985); Rowe, *Middle Landscape.*

28. Jane Jacobs, *The Death and Life of Great American Cities* (New York: Random House, 1961).

CHAPTER 3

Timeless
Design Principles for Town Centers

Though the study of old towns and their buildings is most useful, nay, is almost essential to any due appreciation of the subject, we must not forget that we cannot, even if we would, reproduce the conditions under which they were created; the fine and all-pervading tradition is gone, and it will take generations for any new tradition comparable to the old one to grow up. While, therefore, we study and admire, it does not follow that we can copy; for we must consider what is likely to lead to the best results under modern conditions, what is and what is not attainable with the means at our disposal. —RAYMOND UNWIN, *Town Planning in Practice*

own centers have their roots in the ceremonial, religious, military, trade, and administrative centers of preindustrial settlements stretching back over five millennia. The Greek city-states, Roman crossroads and military towns, European medieval villages, English towns and country villages, and American colonial settlements all revolved around flourishing central cores. What is sometimes overlooked today, however, when new town centers and main streets are often thought of as isolated "projects," is that these traditional cores did not stand alone, but were always woven into the fabric of a larger, essentially residential community—whether village,

The Plaza Mayor, in Madrid, Spain, begun in 1617, shows how completely historic town centers were integrated into cities. Offering a dramatic contrast to the surrounding pattern of irregular blocks and streets, the square plaza is lined with six-story houses with arcaded shops on the ground floor and second-floor balconies that face the plaza. The buildings also arch over the streets that lead into the plaza, making the experience of entering the plaza even more dramatic. *Kevin Klinkenberg.*

Detail of the Mashpee Commons master plan, showing the proposed residential neighborhoods (center and lower left) that will build on and connect with the original town center (upper right). *Imai/Keller, Inc., Architects and Planners.*

town, or city—and sized appropriately. Although transportation technology has made it possible for commercial centers to serve people throughout far-flung trade areas, the interweaving of town centers and residential neighborhoods remains key to the creation of places that have enduring value, a strong identity, and round-the-clock activity.

This is not to say that the centers cannot come first. Historically, towns and cities have grown outward from a core centered on economic activities (such as a mill) and transportation routes (such as a port or a railway station). While critics have questioned the timing and economic logic of building town centers early in the development of a large residential community—like Florida's Celebration, for example—retail expert Bob Gibbs has argued that town centers can and should be built wherever there is sufficient market demand.[1] Town centers can then gradually add residential neighborhoods and grow into full-fledged towns, rather than the other way around. This is the reverse situation for most master-planned communities, where the town center is planned as a future component after much of the residential phase has been completed and the population in and around the project has grown large enough to support commercial development. In most master-planned communities, however, the town center is planned as a future component, to be built only after the better part of the residential phase is complete and the population in and

around the project is large enough to support commercial development. But the resulting delay in the construction of the town center can generate anxiety among new homebuyers and disappointment among existing residents of the surrounding community, both of whom may have to wait many years for convenient access to shops and services.

A wise alternative is to choose a location where there is already sufficient demand to support commercial development and to build the town center first; the gradual addition of residential neighborhoods will allow the area to grow into a full-fledged town. This is exactly the strategy of the developers of Mashpee Commons, in Cape Cod, Massachusetts,

Preeminent public space in a simple plaza in Amsterdam. *World Idea Network.*

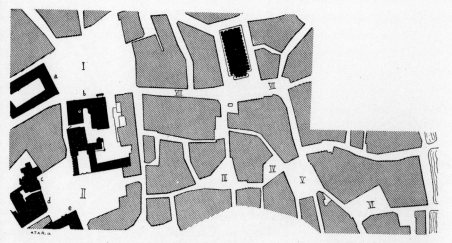

Fig. 47. Bruges. I. Grand'Place.—II. Place du Bourg.—III. Place Saint-Jean.—IV. Place des Biscayens.—V. Place Jean van Eyck.—VI. Marché du Mercredi.—VII. Place de la Vieille Bourse.—VIII. Rue Flamande.—a. Market halls.—b. Hôtel provincial.—c. Chapelle du Saint Sang.—d. Hôtel de Ville.—e. Palais de Justice

The medieval city of Bruges, Belgium, exemplifies the multicentered nature of historic town centers. Rather than being focused on a single large gathering space, Bruges offers a wide variety of plazas and squares, which are made possible by the city's irregular pattern of blocks and streets. *Camillo Sitte,* Der Städtebau nach seinen künstlerischen Grundsätzen, *5th ed. (Vienna: Karl Graber, 1922).*

who are adding four residential neighborhoods to surround a highly successful town center. A similar approach has been taken in Easton Town Center, near Columbus, which tapped pent-up demand for retail and entertainment uses. Regardless of which comes first, however, town centers have never existed apart from the town proper or from the residential populations that give town centers their life and purpose.

While the suburban realm suffers from too little concentration of activities—to the point where there *is* no center in a traditional sense, the haphazard concentration of too many conflicting activities in a single nucleus also goes against most historic prece-

dents. In all but the smallest of hamlets, traditional towns have almost always had not one, but *many* centers, of different types and scales, serving different purposes. There might be one or more market squares, a civic center, a parade ground, a church plaza, a *rambla,* and any number of open spaces—parks, village greens, waterfronts, promenades, and areas surrounding key landmarks and activities. A city might have a business district, an arts district, a waterfront district, a nighttime entertainment district, and other specialized areas distinguished by natural and built features and clusters of synergistic businesses and activities. Some of these centers have supported a vibrant public life for the entire community and its visitors, while others maintain a more subdued, residential, or contemplative character and a less public atmosphere. Some are "hardscapes" of brick and stone, while others are "softscapes"—green landscapes and gardens.

This chapter takes a closer look at the timeless characteristics of town centers, with a focus on the public gathering places, streets and pathways, and buildings that are typically found in town centers. In considering a combination of past and present examples, the chapter explores the rediscovery and adaptation of these timeless characteristics for today's town centers and main streets.

providing a public realm for everyday social life; housing bustling marketplaces and places to meet, mingle, and "people watch"; and providing a backdrop for more exceptional events such as fairs, festivals, coronations, protests, and even revolutions.[2] And although the marketplace role of the agora, the forum, and the market square was important, this was not "consumer space" in the sense that a shopping mall is, but was clearly recognized and experienced as public space, with a civic character that transcended the commercial activities that took place there. The way that the public space was used in historic town centers represents a good standard for today's town centers and main streets: if the *only*

The Plaza, in Santa Fe, New Mexico, has been in continuous use for nearly three centuries. The rustic, 330-foot by 360-foot (100-meter by 110-meter) plaza is surrounded by buildings on all four sides, which include arcaded walks reserved for Native Americans selling handmade items.

Gathering Places

One of the key features of successful town centers, past and present, is the variety of attractive public gathering spaces they contain. These urban open spaces differ significantly from the more fluid and spacious parks and open spaces commonly found in today's suburban areas. Throughout urban history, public plazas, village greens, and town squares have been the focal points of towns and town centers,

In Covent Gardens, in central England, the central square is surrounded by a variety of civic and retail uses. *World Idea Network.*

A traditional New England village green in Falmouth, Massachusetts.

reason people come there is to shop, then the project has fallen short of creating the type of magnetic destination where people go to become engaged in the community and to experience the place itself.

The agoras and forums of ancient Greek and Roman cities; the great cathedral squares, civic squares, and marketplaces of medieval and Renaissance cities; and the town squares, commons, and main streets of early American towns and villages all provided centers around which community life revolved. Designers in search of inspiration for new projects need look no further than the plazas of early Spanish-American

cities; the squares of colonial Savannah and Philadelphia; the greens of New England villages; or any number of European piazzas, squares, and urban parks. In fact, historians and designers have devoted lengthy studies to such settings in an effort to pinpoint the qualities that made them work in the past—and that allow so many of them to continue to work to the present day.[3] While many of these public spaces had very rustic beginnings—as garrisons, as fields for livestock, or as the setting for militia drills—they gradually took on a wider variety of roles and meanings as the communities surrounding them grew and matured. In effect, as a community became more urban, its gathering places did as well—a shift that was reflected in the construction of buildings that further enclosed and defined the space, and in the addition of walkways, statues, art, monuments, lighting, and more formal landscaping in the gathering place itself.

The agora of ancient Athens is often cited as embodying many of the ideal qualities that today's town centers aspire to recreate. In *City: Rediscovering the Center,* William Whyte refers to the need to "return to the agora," to reestablish public spaces within our towns and cities where people can "meet and talk," and that create a sense of place.[4] In its earliest form, the Athenian agora was little more than a farmers' market, consisting of roughly 15 acres (six hectares) of open space conveniently located near people's homes. Over time, the space became partially enclosed by various public buildings, shrines, and a stoa (an open colonnade) that "served as a general-purpose structure and eventually became the frame for rows of shops."[5] The agora was a thoroughly

Types of Urban Open Space

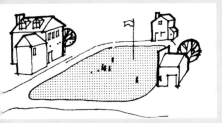

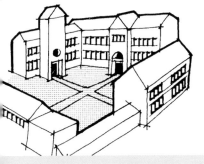

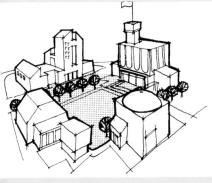

In *Urban Space,* Jere Stuart French identifies nine types of squares found in American cities: civic square, collegiate square, green, mall, market square, parade ground, parvis (church square), residential square, and rotary.[1] The accompanying drawings represent six of the types of squares identified by French.

In *Town and Square: From the Agora to the Village Green,* Paul Zucker makes additional distinctions between what he calls the closed square, the dominated square, the nuclear square, grouped squares, and the amorphous square.[2] Other, even more specific types of urban open spaces—such as courthouse squares, courts, and small urban parks—do not fit either within either French's or Zucker's typologies. There are, moreover, other types of urban open space—such as balconies, terraces, patios, and roof gardens—that are associated with individual buildings. Town centers are most often distinguished by the layers and complexity of their urban open space network, rather than simply by the presence of a single central plaza.

Drawings by Michael Doty. Reproduced, by permission of the author, from Jere Stuart French, *Urban Space* (Dubuque, Iowa: Kendall/Hunt Publishing Company, 1978).

1. Jere Stuart French, *Urban Space* (Dubuque, Iowa: Kendall/Hunt Publishing Company, 1978).
2. Paul Zucker, *Town and Square: From the Agora to the Village Green* (New York: Columbia University Press, 1959).

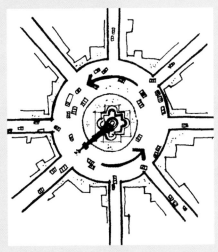

Left, top: A parade ground, which is similar to a New England village green.

Left, second down: A residential square.

Left, third down: A parvis, or church square.

Left, fourth down: A collegiate square, a closed square often found on college campuses.

Left, bottom: A civic square.

Left: A rotary. Smaller variations of rotaries are appearing in new town centers.

mixed-use setting, where the commercial, social, athletic, entertainment, and civic activities of the community all shared the same space. Whyte concludes that "the agora at its height would be a good guide to what is right. Its characteristics were *centrality, concentration,* and *mixture,* and these are the characteristics of the centers that work best today."[6]

One additional characteristic considered crucial to creating good public gathering places is *enclosure.* Camillo Sitte emphasized this particular aspect in *City Planning According to Artistic Principles,* which

was originally published in 1889 and would come to influence a generation of town planners in Europe and the United States. One of these was Raymond Unwin, who recommended that the creation of places should not involve "the complete enclosure of a continuous ring of buildings, like a quadrangle, for example; but a general sense of enclosure resulting from a fairly continuous frame of buildings, the breaks in which are small in relative extent and not too obvious."[7] Unwin discusses numerous examples, including the Piazza Erbe, in Verona, and the Piazza Navona, in Rome—which, despite being accessible by eight and nine different streets, respectively, still manage to provide a strong sense of enclosure. To maintain this spatial quality, streets are designed to meet at the corners of plazas and are angled and aligned in ways that prevent them from cutting straight across the centers of squares or plazas.

Both the urbanists of Unwin's era and the new urbanists of today stress that a sense of enclosure depends heavily on the proportional relationship between the size of the open space and the height of the surrounding buildings. As Robert Orr, an architect who was involved in the early days of Seaside, a new urbanist community in the Florida panhandle, explains, "People tend to congregate in tight spaces, like at cocktail parties. People huddle in the kitchen or in doorways, rarely in the middle of rooms."[8]

While emphasizing that the design of good plazas is not a science, Werner Hegemann and Elbert Peets, in their venerated tome on civic art, suggested that the ratio of height to width found in the best plazas ranges from 1:1 to 1:3.[9] Six decades later, Richard Hedman came to a similar conclusion in his primer, *Fundamentals of Urban Design,* which suggests that this is not an antiquarian standard but one based on the

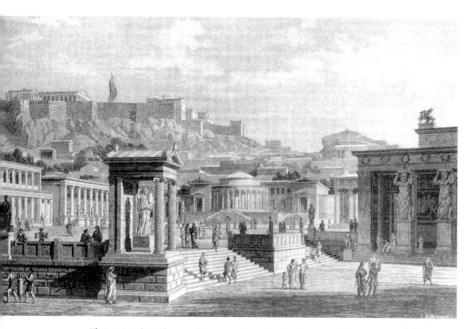

The agora in Athens—the archetypal mixed-use, multipurpose public gathering space. *Jakob von Falke,* Hellas und Rom *(Stuttgart: Spemann, 1878).*

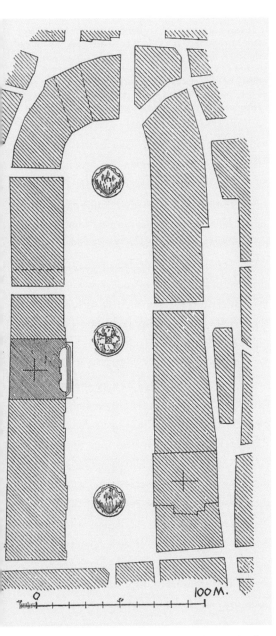

Rome's Piazza Navona, which dates back to antiquity, maintains a strong sense of enclosure while accommodating the entrances of nine streets. *A. E. Brinckmann, Platz und Monument als kunstlerisches Formproblem, 3d ed. (Berlin: E. Wasmuth, 1923).*

unchanging nature of human scale.[10] The authors of both books based their recommendations on the relationship between the proportions of urban spaces and the angles at which people standing within a plaza typically look at buildings. There are, however, many exceptions to this general rule, including some of the great urban spaces of Europe, and the central plazas of Spanish colonial towns and cities. In Spanish colonial town centers, the plazas tend to be much larger and more open, and public spaces are defined not only by buildings but by the sky and the surrounding landscape, which may terminate the views down the long streets that lead out of town.

The degree of openness that visitors experience in larger spaces can be influenced by the height of monuments within the plaza (for example, the obelisk at the center of St. Peter's Square, in Rome), and by the use of regularly spaced trees along the edge of a square. The great Renaissance architect Andrea Palladio recommended proportional standards here as well, stating that "all the edifices made round a piazza ought not to be higher than the third part of the breadth of the piazza, nor lower than the sixth."[11] Discussing a contemporary example, Andrés Duany has noted that Seaside's Central Square is actually oversized in relation to the surrounding buildings. To create a more

In towns such as York, England, historic squares are often turned into parking lots to address the lack of adequate parking. Although designing parking lots so that they can serve as plazas when they are empty of cars is desirable, such lots work best as interior courts and at the periphery of the town center, rather than in the core. *World Idea Network.*

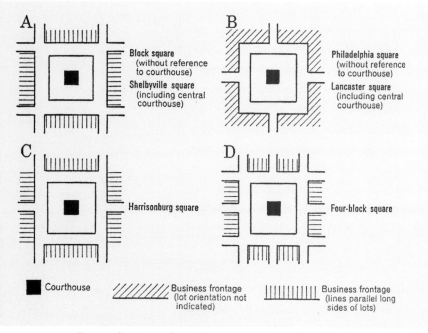

A. Block square (without reference to courthouse)
Shelbyville square (including central courthouse)

B. Philadelphia square (without reference to courthouse)
Lancaster square (including central courthouse)

C. Harrisonburg square

D. Four-block square

■ Courthouse

///// Business frontage (lot orientation not indicated)

|||||||| Business frontage (lines parallel long sides of lots)

Four major types of courthouse-square plans found in the eastern United States, as identified by E. T. Price. Note that in the orientation of streets, and the location of public buildings in the very center of the square, these plans break most of Camillo Sitte's artistic principles for designing enclosed places. © *American Geographical Society; reproduced, with permission, from Edward T. Price, "The Central Courthouse Square in the American County Seat,"* Geographical Review 58, no. 1 (January 1968).

human scale for the space, the design called for a canopy of regularly placed palm trees at the edge of the green.[12] The courthouse squares that became common in parts of the American South; in southwestern "frontier" towns (particularly in Texas); and in the Midwest, beginning in the 1820s, are another exception. In these towns the squares are dominated by the courthouses themselves, which are typically located in the center of the square.[13]

While suburban developments are typically characterized by too little enclosure, too much enclosure can also be a problem. In an interesting parallel with the evolution from main streets to shopping malls, R. E. Wycherley notes that agoras, which for hundreds of years were designed as integral parts of a city's street network, gradually became more enclosed and secluded from the city proper. Some eventually became completely enclosed, a transformation that Wycherley associates with the "disintegration of the city."[14] Similarly, many of today's town center and main street projects run the risk of becoming isolated enclaves within cities and suburbs, rather than integrated centers that can grow and evolve with the areas around them.

The point here is not to suggest absolute standards for plazas or greens but to remind town center planners, designers, and developers that centuries of thought and experimentation have gone into the creation of successful public gathering places—and that both this body of knowledge, and the places themselves, constitute resources that should not be ignored in the planning and design of today's town centers. Thoughtful use of such resources can help planners and designers resist the temptation to create, in their enthusiasm, haphazard combinations of open space of all shapes and sizes, filled with fountains, statues, trees, and shrubs of all varieties, surrounded by a potpourri of historicist buildings, each of a different height and style.

It is also important to realize that not all historic gathering places have aged gracefully over time. Simply drawing on a historic precedent without adapting it to automobiles, climatic differences, access requirements, and other factors that shape 21st-century life is asking for trouble. Many piazzas and squares have turned into parking lots, and hundreds of main streets in cities and towns across the United States have been bypassed—sometimes literally, by means of highways that circumvented the downtown business district—and forgotten.

The resort town of Seaside shows just how much urban variety can be packed into a mere 80 acres (32 hectares). Robert Davis, Seaside's founder and developer, has noted that the town center is much larger than it would have been if it had been designed solely for the number of homes in Seaside.[15] Since the entire vicinity lacked anything like a town center, Davis presumed that Seaside's town center would one day serve the population of a much larger area and would need to be sized accordingly. This assumption has proven to be prophetic, as Seaside has evolved into a magnet for tourists, and there has been considerable growth along the Route 30a corridor, which fronts Seaside's town center. This new development includes WaterColor, a 500-acre (200-hectare), 1,170-unit new urbanist community by Arvida/St. Joe that wraps around Seaside's northern perimeter and will ultimately put over 2,000 residents and seasonal visitors within walking and biking distance of Seaside's Central Square.

Seaside's town center consists, first, of Central Square, a large town green in the form of an outdoor amphitheater that is modeled, in part, on squares found in Charleston and Savannah. The green includes a stage for concerts and special events, and is surrounded by multistory buildings with shops, restaurants, offices, meeting rooms, and lofts. Directly across the street is Downtown Seaside, a beachfront bazaar that includes a bustling collection of stalls, kiosks, and restaurants inspired by Italian street markets. A third center of activity, Ruskin Place, lies just north of Central Square. Modeled after Jackson Square, in New Orleans, the center combines live/work buildings and an intimate, enclosed central space to create a more subdued, residential character. A fourth center, the Lyceum, provides a formal, dignified civic space with educational facilities. The layout is modeled after Thomas Jefferson's plan for the central green at the University of Virginia, and the early renderings are reminiscent of the agoras and forums of ancient Greece and Rome.[16] While the list of precedents that inspired Seaside's many squares is impressive, the inspirations were all liberally adapted to Seaside's site conditions and indigenous plant life, to

Arvida's WaterColor project wraps around Seaside (lower center), Florida, and will greatly expand the seasonal and year-round market for Seaside's town center. *Arvida, a St. Joe Company; master plan by Cooper, Robertson & Partners.*

local and regional architectural traditions, and to the needs of what Davis has described as a "holiday town" that functions much like a "horizontal hotel" (while many of Seaside's homes are rented out for much of the year, visitors stay in individual cottages and bungalows rather than in one of the high-rise hotels or condominiums that are ubiquitous on the beaches of Florida's panhandle). Each of Seaside's public gathering places is either contiguous to Central Square or linked to it by a major street, reinforcing the centrality and importance of the main square. With their diverse

Top: A bustling, open-air market along Seaside's beach just across the street from Central Square.

Bottom: The quiet repose of Ruskin Place, just a one-mi walk from Seaside's Central Square.

qualities and the broad range of activities that they support, these gathering places, viewed collectively, form a much richer town center than could possibly have been achieved by any one of them individually.[17]

Streets and Pathways

The scale and variety of pathways (often referred to as *paseos*), alleys, and streets found in historic towns and villages also provide important precedents for the planning and design of new town centers and main streets. Both Sitte and Frederick Law Olmsted emphasized that each street should be designed as an artistic unit.[18] Unwin restated this sentiment quite simply: "It was not deemed enough that a road should serve as a means of communication from one place to another, it was also desired that it should afford some dignity of approach to important buildings, and be a pleasant way for the passer-by."[19] The

Surrounded on three sides by mixed-use buildings, Seaside's Central Square serves as a multipurpose space for performances and social gatherings.

way that streets and pathways weave through the town center, connecting its buildings and public spaces, can provide pedestrians with a sense of discovery and delight that is seldom experienced in the suburban landscape, and that is essential to the town center experience.

As Allan Jacobs's *Great Streets* and *The Boulevard Book* illustrate, successful boulevards and main streets do not require lavish materials or fancy streetlights and furniture to make them comfortable, attractive, and functional places to live, work, shop, and stroll.[20] The appeal of great streets stems more from the provision of ample sidewalks and appropriate street trees, and from the presence of building frontages whose windows, doors, and awnings are oriented toward the sidewalk, forming a consistent street wall. As Robert Orr has noted, "You start by thinking of buildings as part of the street. The street hasn't been a civic space for a long time."[21]

Like great plazas and squares, great streets also offer a sense of enclosure, and are built on a human scale that is related to the proportion between the

The ratio of street width to building height defines streets as places within town centers, rather than as mere transportation corridors. Pictured: a retail street in Utrecht, the Netherlands.

height of the buildings and the amount of open space (in this case the space between the facades of the buildings that face one another). Streets in suburban areas are typically many times wider than the heights of the buildings that line them, often reaching ratios of 1:6 and higher. Such wide streets prevent any sense of spatial enclosure from being achieved and are more difficult for pedestrians to cross. The types of historic urban streets that are considered models for town centers typically achieve much tighter proportions, approaching a 1:1 relationship, and as a result they are much more success-

At a maximum width of 20 feet (six meters), the narrow streets of historic Charleston, South Carolina, provide an extraordinary network of well-defined urban space.

Wide streets with deep setbacks and low-rise build-ings make it virtually impossible to establish the type of enclosed space experienced on traditional main streets. Pictured: a typical suburban commer-cial street (Palm Beach County, Florida).

ful at creating a sense of enclosure. Higher ratios will produce greater spatial enclosure. Some of the most distinctive urban streets in medieval cities have ratios of 3:1 or higher, and streets in large cities like New York and San Francisco achieve much higher ratios.[22]

Where historic streets are relatively wide in rela-tion to buildings, the addition of an unbroken canopy of street trees has often been used to intro-duce a more human scale. Another way to define streets and boulevards is to bring the buildings up to and over the sidewalks—by adding arcades, colon-nades, awnings, stoops, balconies, and terraces. This must be done carefully, however, on commercial main streets, where an unobstructed view of store-front displays is essential. Two of the most important methods used historically to heighten the sense of enclosure are *deflected* and *terminated* vistas. Deflect-

ed and terminated vistas are particularly useful where a separate square or plaza is lacking and the street itself is the central gathering place. In the case of deflected vistas, both sides of the street offer a consistent street wall, but the street is gently curved, or "deflected," so that the view ahead remains closed and continu-ously changes as the viewer moves along the street. Gordon Cullen, a major figure in the English town-scape movement in the 1960s, advocated the addi-tion of such "kinks" to improve the character of "lin-ear villages" in England—which, like many Amer-ican towns, consist of a straight street running past a few blocks of downtown buildings. Cullen felt that deflected vistas enhanced the "serial vision" of the pedestrian—the experience of the town as a series of sequential images.[23]

As the name indicates, a terminal vista consists of a straight street that ends with a view of a building or landmark, often a building of special significance, such as a church or meeting hall. This does not mean that all vistas need to be terminated: one alternative can be seen in the design of Renaissance streets that offer an "infinite" perspective. An alternative to the use of buildings to deflect and terminate vistas can also be found in many Spanish colonial cities and in the frontier towns of the western United States. Stefanos Polyzoides, an architect and urban designer

A building can terminate a vista without terminating the street itself. This street, in Charleston, South Carolina, continues around the tower at the top of the street and down the other side of the hill.

The spatial definition of relatively wide urban streets, such as this one in Georgetown, in Washington, D.C., can be enhanced through deflected vistas.

Since the success of town center projects depends heavily on their ability to create a pedestrian-friendly atmosphere, developers and designers should carefully consider examples of older traditional boulevards, promenades, streets, and alleyways designed primarily for pedestrian use. At the same time, however, as the pedestrian-only plazas built in the 1960s and 1970s proved, it rarely makes sense to completely exclude vehicular traffic, which helps support businesses and makes use of on-street parking. On-street parking, in turn, provides convenient access to shops, helps slow traffic, and creates a buffer that shields pedestrians on the sidewalk from street traffic. Some of the best

active in California and the Southwest, has observed the "daylighting" of streets in these towns, meaning that the street grid opens out in such a way that vistas terminate in the natural landscape of mountains, fields, and bodies of water.

Almost as important as the main street itself are the alleyways, side streets, and walkways that usher pedestrians to and from the main street and other destinations. Frequent side streets and other through-block passageways (paseos) enable pedestrians to access the main street without having to walk around large blocks or across major thoroughfares. The small, irregular blocks and intricate, organic web of streets, paths, and alleys in medieval villages represent some of the most porous networks for pedestrian movement.

King Street, Charleston's main street.

precedents are older streets that have achieved a balance between vehicular and pedestrian needs, either through careful adaptation over time—or, in the case of some town centers and shopping villages planned and designed early in the automobile age, between 1910 and 1930—by design. It may also be desirable to create somewhat larger blocks, without alleyways, to accommodate interior courtyards and gardens that can enhance residential development in the town center.

Top right: While older alleyways are often converted to pleasant pedestrian passageways, town centers also need service areas, which can be provided by "working alleys." This one, in historic downtown Fort Myers, Florida, is used for parking, utilities, trash bins, and deliveries.

Right: A narrow, pedestrian-only shopping street in Amsterdam.

Bottom right: Attractive, inviting alleyways provide pedestrian passageways through many blocks in historic Charleston.

Bottom left: Philadelphia Alley, in Charleston.

Left: The first main-street–oriented Saks Fifth Avenue store in the country was developed on King Street, in Charleston. The experimental format—two stories and 55,000 square feet (5,110 square meters), about one-third to one-half the size of a typical Saks—has been very successful, and other chains have now introduced main-street formats, sometimes referred to as "resort stores."

Above: A suburban version of Saks attached to Miami's new Dolphin Mall: the same retailer as on Charleston's King Street, in a drastically different building and setting.

Town Center Buildings

Perhaps the most difficult aspect of creating new town centers involves the design and construction of appropriate building types, on which so much of a town center's success depends. Buildings not only need to effectively mix land uses and activities but must (1) define the public realm of streets and urban open spaces; (2) create a human-scale, immersive environment that maintains the atmosphere of a traditional town center throughout; and (3) balance the needs of businesses and civic facilities (which require delivery areas and public access) and the

needs of residents (who need privacy and quiet). Buildings at the edges of the town center must also provide a smooth transition between the commercial character of the core and the residential character of adjacent neighborhoods. Here again, historic main streets and town centers provide rich material for consideration.

Given the importance of building design, it is not surprising that the urban design codes and guidelines created by new urbanists place far more emphasis on the types of buildings that are appropriate to various sections of town centers than on the particular land uses and activities permitted. For example, the same retail operation that is housed in a one-story warehouse building surrounded by parking lots along a suburban roadway can be housed in a multistory building facing an urban street in a town center. The building type, the way it is positioned on its lot, and the relationship between the building and the street change dramatically, but the land use does not.[24]

fish merchants, booksellers, and all manner of activities.[25] While a stoa may or may not be a desirable element in a town center today, the principle of providing relatively cheap, flexible space in either temporary or permanent structures deserves more attention than it receives.

One of the best examples of a new town center that has made good use of flexible, temporary space is Seaside. Developer Robert Davis realized early on

The buildings on and around Seaside's Central Square are designed to accommodate a wide variety of potential uses. Many of the buildings are also designed so that they can eventually be moved to other sites in the town when the market supports construction of larger, more permanent buildings on the square.

There is certainly nothing new about mixed-use buildings. As Wycherley notes, "the stoa or open colonnade . . . was found to be a useful general-purpose building and became especially characteristic of the agora," providing flexible space for bankers,

that it would be many years before the market would support the construction of the five-story buildings around Central Square that were envisioned in Seaside's code. To activate the public space and realize some economic benefits in the meantime, Davis began building movable, temporary buildings along the streetfront, placing small kiosks on the edge of the

Above: Small, inexpensive kiosks allowed Seaside to introduce a variety of unique retail shops early in the town center's development.

Right: Seaside's kiosks have a minimal amount of interior space, with at least as much covered outdoor space for open-air merchandising.

where it will serve as the home for a new charter school. According to Davis, these buildings are inexpensive to build, and the cost of constructing them can be amortized over a few years, after which they can be moved or donated for civic uses, and replaced with more substantial buildings. In new urbanist or master-planned projects that cannot support the immediate construction of a full-blown town center, this approach offers maximum flexibility at minimal

town green and in the beachfront bazaar of Downtown Seaside. Downtown Seaside itself was initiated in 1981, with the construction of two eight-foot (2.5-meter) -square shacks where Davis established a gathering place for Saturday flea markets. These were eventually joined by buildings modeled after sharecroppers' cabins (a building type reflecting the local architectural heritage) and by a Florida panhandle version of the Parthenon temple, which was built on the beach.

The temporary buildings at Seaside have housed a mind-boggling assortment of shops, services, and offices over the years; for a time, one kiosk on the town green provided a lilliputian home for the Seaside Institute. Another structure, a two-story building that housed a bookstore on Central Square for several years, is being relocated to the Lyceum,

cost, while providing an opportunity to establish the character of the town center early on in a project.

Some of the first permanent buildings to house a vertical mix of uses emerged in early Roman times; Dimitri Procos identifies the Roman *tabernae* as the predecessors of all vertical shop/dwelling combinations found in traditional towns.[26] Some of the most extensive and best-preserved examples can be found in Trajan's Market, in Rome. In his classic book on preindustrial cities, Gideon Sjoberg notes that virtually *all* land uses and buildings in the preindustrial era were mixed, and that a person would commonly "reside, produce, store, and sell his wares within the confines of the same structure."[27] Medieval towns and villages, in particular, grew into extraordinarily dense, mixed-use communities composed primarily of live/work structures.

The reintroduction of live/work (or "flex") units in a number of contemporary projects recalls these historic precedents; examples include Haile Village Center (Gainesville, Florida), Kentlands/Lakelands town center (Gaithersburg, Maryland), Orenco Station (Portland, Oregon), Rosemary Beach (Walton County, Florida), and Seaside. Live/work variations include lofts that incorporate both living and work space, units in which living space is located *above* work space, and units that are located *near* work spaces (such as an accessory building).[28] Similarly, projects like Post Properties's Riverside, in Atlanta, and Addison Circle, in Addison, Texas, with their dense concentration of housing and their urban-village character, are attempts to recapture some of the qualities of the European villages and towns celebrated by Lewis Mumford for their human scale, pedestrian-friendly qualities, seamless mix of land uses and activities, central public spaces, and distinctive sense of place and community.[29]

With an estimated 55 million Americans now performing at least some work out of their homes, however, live/work units are far from being merely nostalgic housing forms.[30] Increasingly, people are looking for arrangements in which their workplaces are closer to where they live—whether they live above the workplace, live near it, or literally work and live in the same space. Some observers of economic trends view the members of the new economy workforce, with their predilection for working at or near their homes, as a high-technology version of the home-based craftsmen of the early industrial revolution, an era in which home life and the workplace blended together. As management guru Charles Handy has observed, "For the first time in human experience, we have a chance to shape work to suit the way we live instead of shaping our lives to fit our work. We would be mad to miss the chance."[31]

The most essential typological element of mixed-use buildings for town centers, however, is the shopfront. Whether a town center is composed of one-story buildings or 20-story buildings, the articulation of the ground-floor facade has a major impact on the town center's allure and viability as a retail address, and on the establishment of the street as a public realm. Ample first-floor ceiling heights, generous storefront windows, clearly defined entrances, pedestrian-oriented signage, ambient lighting, and canopies have all contributed to the composition of the prototypical shopfronts found in traditional town centers and main streets.

Nothing new under the sun: mixed-use buildings and live/work structures were the norm for medieval towns and villages. Pictured: a detail from "Le Gouvernement des Princes." *Bibliothèque de l'Arsenal, Paris.*

Today, emphasis on the design of shopfronts sometimes leads to the neglect of buildings' lower stories—those that are just above the ground floor, and clearly visible from the street, but that are increasingly occupied by parking garages. The vitality of traditional main streets and town centers is reinforced by the habitable space (offices, apartments, restaurants, lofts) that overlooks—and maintains a connection with—the street. Although it is true that contemporary buildings must respond to more stringent codes and tenant requirements than their predecessors, many of these regulations concern only the internal design of the buildings: by studying the structures found in historic main streets and town centers, architects and designers of town centers can still learn a great deal about how to accommodate a wide range of shops, offices, and living space; how to maintain a connection between the upper floors and the street life below; and how to effectively frame the street as a public space.

Buildings also do much more than house people and shops: they establish the design vocabulary of places and the visual rhythm of streetscapes. Architectural elements that contribute to the overall sense of place include:

- Height (of both buildings and individual floors);
- Scale and massing;
- The extent to which buildings are attached or detached from one another;
- The spacing between buildings and the street;
- The proportions of windows, bays, doorways, porches, and other features;

Town centers should take advantage of the views of lively streets and public spaces by locating offices, restaurants, and living space on upper floors, with windows and balconies opening onto the street.

- Architectural style;
- Materials, finishes, and textures;
- A number of other elements, including shadow patterns, landscaping, the location and treatment of entryways, and the response of buildings to climate and topography.[32]

One of the challenges facing the designers and developers of town center buildings is to balance the need for both harmony and diversity. In traditional

A Typology of Main Street Buildings

In *The Buildings of Main Street: A Guide To American Commercial Architecture,* Richard Longstreth identifies 11 building types common to American main streets, categorizing them on the basis of the composition of their facades and their number of stories.[1] While commercial buildings have generally increased in overall size and depth to accommodate larger enterprises, historic shopfront facades embody visual and functional elements that can serve as models for main streets of any era. Relatively narrow shopfronts, for example, allow pedestrians to take in a large number of shops within a short walking distance (just as they can within shopping malls). A major goal of new town centers is to emulate the variety of building types, styles, materials, and colors found in traditional, main street buildings that were constructed over many decades by many different builders. The diagrams in this feature box offer a sampling of the categories in Longstreth's typology of main street buildings; the photos, all from Charleston, South Carolina, illustrate some of the categories.

All diagrams: Richard W. Longstreth, The Buildings of Main Street: A Guide to American Commercial Architecture *(Walnut Creek, Calif.: AltaMira Press, 2000). Reproduced by permission of the author.*

1. Richard W. Longstreth, *The Buildings of Main Street: A Guide to American Commercial Architecture* (Walnut Creek, Calif.: AltaMira Press, 2000).

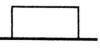

Above: A one-part commercial block.

Right: A one-part commercial building.

Above: A two-part commercial block.

Right: The most common type of main street building is what Longstreth refers to as the two-part commercial, which is composed of two distinct zones: a ground-floor retail element, and upper stories reserved for more private residential and office uses.

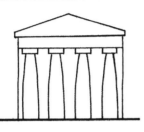

Above: A temple front.

Right: A temple front building next to two-part commercial variations.

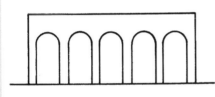

Above: An arcaded block.

Right: A variety of Longstreth's types, including a vault, an arcaded front, and two-part commercial variations.

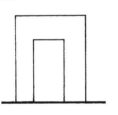

Above: A vault.

Right: "None of the above." One of the many five-and-ten-cent stores of S. H. Kress & Company, which were once found on main streets throughout the United States; this one now houses a Williams-Sonoma. The Kress building's unique combination of elements places it outside the 11 types of main street buildings Longstreth identifies.

town centers, this balance evolved naturally: the buildings that were added incrementally, over many decades and centuries, were constructed of different materials and reflected changing architectural styles and norms—but shared notions, for example, of the appropriate distance between buildings and the street and sidewalk; about how windows and doors address the street; and even about the general proportions of doorways, windows, and ceiling heights. In short, buildings responded to the *context* of adjacent buildings, streets, and public spaces. Major exceptions were typically limited to important civic buildings, such as cathedrals, palaces, and guildhalls,

The newer buildings of Charleston Place, an infill project on Meeting Street, are similar to the historic buildings in their scale and setbacks, but appear flat and lack the visual variety that distinguishes most main streets.

which were intentionally distinguished from neighboring structures to symbolize their special significance to the community.[33]

Contemporary development occurs much more rapidly: the design and construction of town centers and main streets is usually condensed into just a few short phases. Too often, in an effort to create a strong overall identity for a project, or because too few architects and builders are involved in design and construction, the balance is tipped to emphasize harmony at the expense of diversity. One of the key challenges for today's town center and main street projects is to emulate the balance between harmony and diversity that occurred naturally in the past.

Harmonious building types with a diversity of styles create a visually interesting streetscape along Meeting Street, in Charleston.

Notes

1. Robert Steuteville, "Retail Expert Sees a Shift Back to Main Street," *New Urban News* 4, no. 6 (1999).

2. There is considerable literature on squares, piazzas, and other forms of "urban space." See, for example, Jere Stuart French, *Urban Space: A Brief History of the City Square,* 2nd ed. (Dubuque, Iowa: Kendall/Hunt Publishing Co., 1983); Rob Krier, *Urban Space,* trans. Christine Czechowski and George Black (New York: Rizzoli, 1979); and Paul Zucker, *Town and Square: From the Agora to the Village Green* (New York: Columbia University Press, 1959). See also Duany Plater-Zyberk & Company, *The Lexicon of the New Urbanism,* June 3, 1999 ed. (Miami: Duany Plater-Zyberk & Company, 1999), sec. E.

3. See, for example, Zucker, *Town and Square*; French, *Urban Space*; and Peter Swift, "Dr. Josef Stubben's History of Public Squares," *Council Report II* (Miami: Knight Program in Community Building, 2002), 16.

4. William H. Whyte, *City: Rediscovering the Center* (New York: Doubleday, 1988), 337.

5. Ibid., 339.

6. Ibid., 340 (emphasis added).

7. Raymond Unwin, *Town Planning in Practice* (1909; reprint, New York: Princeton Architectural Press, 1994), 197.

8. Craig Savoye, "Vanilla Suburbs Seek an Identity," *Christian Science Monitor* 92, no. 26 (1999): 1.

9. Werner Hegemann and Elbert Peets, *American Vitruvius: An Architect's Handbook of Civic Art* (1922; reprint, New York: Princeton Architectural Press, 1999), 42ff.

10. For more detailed discussions of the psychophysical aspects of design on a human scale, see Richard Hedman and Andrew Jaszewski, *Fundamentals of Urban Design* (Washington, D.C.: Planners Press, 1984), 58–60; and the discussion of "spatial definition" in Duany Plater-Zyberk & Company, *The Lexicon of the New Urbanism* (Miami: Duany Plater-Zyberk & Company, June 12, 2000), sec. H2.1.

11. Andrea Palladio, *Four Books of Architecture* (New York: Dover Publications, 1965), bk. 3, ch. 2, p. 59, as cited in French, *Urban Space,* 78.

12. Remarks made by Andrés Duany during a walking tour of Seaside, November 1999.

13. See the discussion in R. V. Francaviglia, *Main Street Revisited: Time, Space, and Image Building in Small-Town America* (Iowa City: University of Iowa Press, 1996), 94.

14. R. E. Wycherley, *How the Greeks Built Cities,* 2nd ed. (London: Macmillan, 1967), 83. Also discussed in Whyte, *City,* 340ff.

15. Remarks made by Robert Davis during a walking tour of Seaside, January 2000.

16. Background on the precedents considered in the design of Seaside's central public spaces can be found in Steven Brooke, *Seaside* (Gretna, La.: Pelican Publishing Company, 1995), 93–97, 107–117.

17. Zucker, in *Town and Square,* refers to this arrangement as "grouped squares."

18. Camillo Sitte, *City Planning According to Artistic Principles* (1889; reprint; New York: Random House, 1965).

19. Quoted in Witold Rybczynski, *City Life: Urban Expectations in a New World* (New York: Scribner, 1995), 185.

20. Allan B. Jacobs, *Great Streets* (Cambridge, Mass.: MIT Press, 1993); Allan B. Jacobs, Elizabeth Macdonald, and Yodan Rofé, *The Boulevard Book: History, Evolution, Design of Multi-Way Boulevards* (Cambridge, Mass.: MIT Press, 2002).

21. Savoye, "Vanilla Suburbs Seek an Identity,"1.

22. Duany Plater-Zyberk & Company, *Lexicon* (2000), sec. H2.1.

23. Gordon Cullen, *Townscape* (London: Architectural Press, 1961), 221. See also Duany Plater-Zyberk & Company, *Lexicon* (2000), sec. H2.1, the discussion of deflected and terminated vistas.

24. See James Krohe, "'Types' Replace 'Uses,'" *Planning* 62, no. 11 (November 1996): 11.

25. Wycherley, *How the Greeks Built Cities,* 52.

26. Dimitri Procos, *Mixed Land Use: From Revival to Innovation* (Stroudsburg, Penn.: Dowden, Hutchinson, and Ross Inc., 1976).

27. Gideon Sjoberg, *The Preindustrial City: Past and Present* (New York: The Free Press, 1965), 103.

28. One of the best sources of information on the topic of live/work is the Live/Work Institute, http://www.live-work.com.

29. See Lewis Mumford, "The Contribution of the Village" and "Principles of Medieval Town Planning," in *The City in History: Its Origins, Its Transformations, and Its Prospects* (New York: Harcourt Brace Jovanovich, Publishers, 1961).

30. PR Newswire, "Live/Work 2001 Homes Planned for International Builders' Show" (http://www.prnewswire.com [June 8, 2000]).

31. As quoted in Richard Florida, *Competing in the Age of Talent* (Pittsburgh, Penn.: R. K. Mellon Foundation, Heinz Endowments, and Sustainable Pittsburgh, 2000).

32. Adapted from Hedman and Jaszewski, *Fundamentals of Urban Design,* 14.

33. And even these structures were adapted over time, to suit new rulers or regimes: witness the reuse of religious buildings as churches, mosques, or synagogues, depending on the religion of the ruling power.

CHAPTER 4

Emerging Formats for

Town Centers, Main Streets, and Urban Villages

> *"We are seeing a national rebirth of traditional town centers."*
>
> —JIM CONSTANTINE, *Director of Planning and Research, Looney Ricks Kiss*
>
> *"These projects are literally transforming the urban landscape in America."*
>
> —DEAN SCHWANKE, *Vice President, Development Trends and Analysis, ULI*

Recent years have witnessed an explosion of interest in, and extensive experimentation with, the creation of new town centers, main streets, and urban villages. While these projects differ in scale, location, mix of land uses, and degree of transit orientation, all have been conceived and advanced in the spirit of creating lively, diverse, pedestrian-friendly places to live, work, shop, or simply enjoy the company of others. This chapter provides a broad overview of the many types of projects emerging in the United States and Canada.

A confusing assortment of terms is often used to describe the new projects being built: town centers, village centers, urban villages, transit villages, lifestyle centers, urban entertainment centers, and main streets. One reason for the profusion of terms is the desire, on the part of planners and developers, to indicate that projects are based on new concepts—while at the same time associating them with the traditional types of places that have wide appeal.

To begin to sort out the range of projects that are being built, two sets of characteristics must be taken into account: first, the project's position and performance as a commercial center, and second, the characteristics of the urban design. When considered in terms of their size, trade area, and retail tenant mix, new town center formats can be categorized according to the standard criteria that ULI, the National Association of Convenience Stores (NACS), and the International Council of Shopping Centers (ICSC) use to categorize shopping centers. As defined by the NACS, for example, a convenience store corresponds, in terms of size and trade area, to a neighborhood store in a traditional neighborhood development (TND). When it comes to site location, overall square footage, and retail tenant mix, town center projects are typically planned much like their retail counterparts, depending on whether they are expected to perform as neighborhood, community, or regional shopping centers.

In practice, however, projects can be difficult to categorize. A project like Florida's Haile Village Center, for example, with 30,000 square feet (2,790 square meters) of retail and another 130,000 square feet (12,080 square meters) of office space is comparable in size to a neighborhood shopping center, but is not comparable in terms of site location or tenant mix. Projects like Easton Town Center, outside Columbus, and CityPlace, in West Palm Beach, approximate the scale, retail mix, and market of regional shopping centers—yet projects less than half their size, like Market Street at Celebration, in Florida, are also called town centers.

While the commercial elements of new town center formats operate much like shopping centers, what most clearly sets town centers apart is their urban

CORRELATION OF RETAIL DEFINITIONS CSD ←————————→ TND

The following definitions are taken from the Shopping Center Development Handbook published by the Urban Land Institute (ULI), and from the National Association of Convenience Store (NACS).

CONVENTIONAL
SUBURBAN
DEVELOPMENT

TRADITIONAL
NEIGHBORHOOD
DEVELOPMENT

The ULI Convenience Store ←————————→ **The TND Neighborhood Store**

A convenience store is a retail business that provides a convenient location for quick purchases from a wide array of products (predominantly food). Convenience stores are typically less than 5,000 sq ft with convenient pedestrian access and parking, and extended hours of operation.

The ULI Convenience Center ←————————→ **The TND Main Street Shops**

A convenience center, similar to a convenience store, provides for the sale of personal services (dry cleaning, barber shop, shoe repair) and convenience goods (food, drugs, and sundries). The convenience center is anchored by some type of personal/convenience retail such as a minimarket. It has a typical gross leasable area of about 20,000 sq ft.

The ULI Neighborhood Center ←————————→ **The TND Town Center Shops**

A neighborhood center provides for the sale of convenience goods and personal services for the day-to-day needs of the immediate neighborhood. The supermarket is the principal tenant. In theory, the neighborhood center has a typical gross leasable area of 50,000 sq ft. In practice, it may range in size from 30,000 to 100,000 sq ft.

The ULI Regional Center ←————————→ **The TND Shopping District**

A regional center provides for the sale of general merchandise (apparel, furniture, and home furnishings) in depth and variety, as well as a range of services and recreational facilities. It is anchored by one or two full-line department stores of generally not less than 75,000 sq ft. In theory, its typical size is 450,000 sq ft of gross leasable area; in practice, it may range from 300,000 to 850,000 sq ft. The regional center is the second largest type of shopping center, providing services typical of a business district yet not as extensive as those of the super regional mall.

RETAIL TYPE BY SIZE & SERVICE AREA

ULI	TND	Size (sq ft)		Service Area (radius)	
		Min	Max	Min	Max
Convenience Store	Neighborhood Store	800	5,000	1/4 mile	1 mile
Convenience Center	Main Street Shops	15,000	25,000	1 mile	2 miles
Neighborhood Center	Town Center Shops	30,000	100,000	2 miles	5 miles
Regional Center	Shopping District	300,000	850,000	5 miles	15 miles

Although town center formats represent a dramatic break from the design of shopping centers, the size, trade areas, tenant mixtures, leasing, and management practices of shopping centers remain applicable to town centers. Duany Plater-Zyberk & Company, *The Lexicon of the New Urbanism, June 3, 1999 ed.* (Miami: Duany Plater-Zyberk & Company, 1999).

design. The "rural-urban transect" presented in *The Lexicon of the New Urbanism* offers a useful conceptual framework for sorting out town center formats.[1] The transect categorizes settlement patterns into six general types of environments ("zones"), which range from places with a very rural quality, to places with a suburban quality, to places that are increasingly urban.

What establishes the distinctive character of each of these settings is the way in which everything—the height, setback, and types of buildings; the landscaping and the types of urban open space; the character of the streets, alleys, and passageways; the design of streetlights and street furniture; the types and placement of street trees—acts to reinforce the essential character that makes each of these zones a distinctive place. Commercial settings found in traditional towns and cities can also be placed along this rural-urban continuum—progressing from the corner store, to neighborhood and village centers, to main streets and town centers, to the dense urban core areas within cities.

For example, a village center could be characterized by a single block of large, single-family building types adapted for mixed uses; gently curving streets and uncurbed lanes; and a village green with an informal, garden-style arrangement of trees and foliage. A town center is more likely to contain multiple blocks; taller, mixed-use buildings built more closely together and set closer to the sidewalk; more urban streets and alleys; and formal squares with a combination of paved walkways and small grassy areas. An urban center would have still taller buildings, which would be attached to one another and form a consistent street wall; the streets would be recognizably urban; and the plazas, courts, and squares would be more formal, with more hardscape surfaces, and with more formal landscaping.[2]

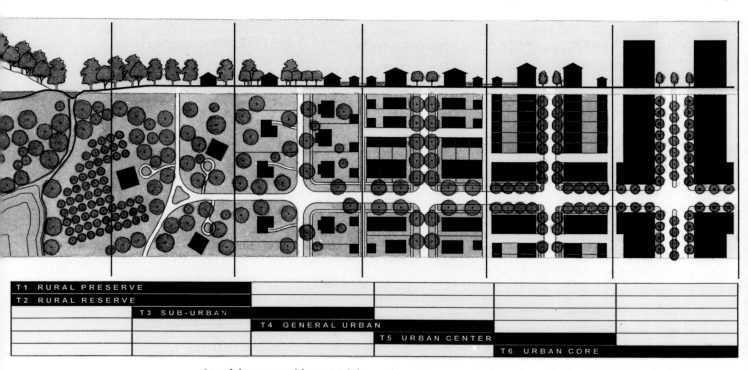

T1	RURAL PRESERVE				
T2	RURAL RESERVE				
		T3 SUB-URBAN			
			T4 GENERAL URBAN		
				T5 URBAN CENTER	
					T6 URBAN CORE

A useful conceptual framework for sorting out town center formats can be found in the "rural-urban transect" presented in Duany Plater-Zyberk & Company's *The Lexicon of the New Urbanism*.

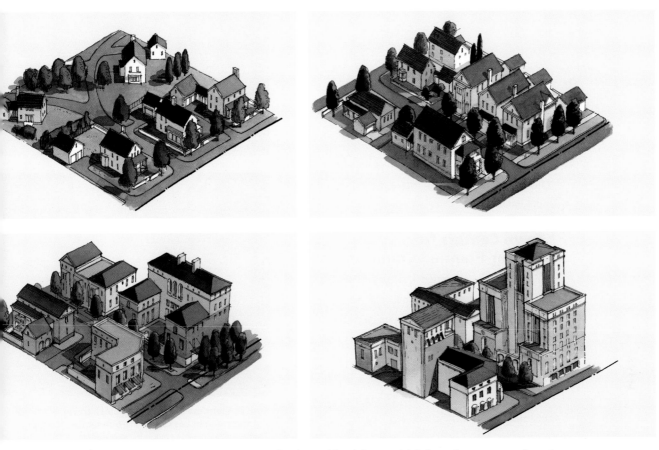

Top left: The "sub-urban" zone of the transect is a low-density residential area with informal green space, large homes on generous lots, and houses set back from curving streets. *James Wassell/Duany Plater-Zyberk & Company.*

Top right: The "general urban" zone is primarily residential but more urban and compact than the sub-urban zone, and is located closer to the town center. A mix of various housing types often share a common setback and garden wall. A regular row of street trees create a canopy for the residential streets. Corner stores and live/work units might be found here. *James Wassell/Duany Plater-Zyberk & Company.*

Bottom left: The mixed-use "urban center" is composed of two- to five-story buildings with retail at street level and commercial and residential uses above. The alignment of storefronts forms a continuous street wall, and open space takes the form of regularly shaped streets, squares, greens, and plazas. *James Wassell/Duany Plater-Zyberk & Company.*

Bottom right: The "urban core," which contains the most dense construction within the tallest buildings, often occurs along major thoroughfares but may also be located along waterfronts or in other areas where property values are highest. The urban core is either thoroughly mixed use or within walking distance of a mixed-use urban center. *James Wassell/Duany Plater-Zyberk & Company.*

All manner of town center projects are now popping up all over the United States and Canada as part of traditional neighborhood developments; as extensions of existing downtowns in older towns and cities; as entirely new districts within suburban communities and edge cities; as retrofitted shopping malls, office campuses, and apartment complexes; as urban and suburban infill developments; and as town centers for maturing master-planned communities (MPCs).[3] Defying one of the fundamental assumptions of shopping malls—that only a climate-controlled environment can draw visitors—these open-air projects are also being built in all types of climates, from Cape Cod to the Pacific Northwest, and from temperate climates in Florida, California, and the Southwest to regions with harsh winters in the Midwest and Northeast. Projects are as small as village centers and as large as multiblock town centers, and incorporate everything from small "mom-and-pop" shops and live/work

buildings to large corporate office buildings, apartment blocks, big-box retailers, entertainment centers, and hotels.

Town Centers for Master-Planned Communities

In contrast to conventional, single-use developments, MPCs incorporate a greater mix of land uses and activities, and link homes with shopping, recreational activities, and employment. As the residential portions of these projects become built out, they are beginning to face what is often their final challenge—creating a downtown for the community. Throughout the 1980s, the majority of MPCs followed a typically suburban approach: clustering shopping centers, enclosed malls, offices, and hotels in nodes along key roadways, where there was little or no residential development and all residents and visitors arrived by automobile.

Even MPCs that took bold steps to create unique settings—such as Las Colinas Urban Center, in Irving, Texas—have struggled to create truly urban environments with an active street life that extends beyond the nine-to-five workday. The center, which houses 25,000 workers in 8 million square feet (743,220 square meters) of office space, consists primarily of high-density office buildings; these are interspersed with shops—organized in a half-dozen Mediterranean-style blocks—which surround a canal and Williams Square, home to the world's largest equestrian sculpture. However, because an arterial separates the high-density office core from a large cluster of stores, and multifamily residential housing is concentrated in separate areas,

Top: The landmark bridge and clock tower overlooking the canal in Las Colinas Urban Center, Irving, Texas. *Las Colinas Association, Irving, Texas.*

Bottom: The traditional architecture of the bridge and clock tower yields to the conventional appearance of the office buildings and parking garages of Las Colinas. The lack of residential and civic uses— and of a more fine-grained mix of retail, entertainment, and dining—has hampered ambitions to make this a diverse, active town center for Las Colinas. *Las Colinas Association, Irving, Texas.*

the overall effect is more single use than mixed use.[4] Despite a 97 percent office occupancy rate, retailers and restaurants have struggled in the 960-acre (388-hectare) urban center, in part because of the limited amount of housing nearby. Las Colinas also lacks the types of civic uses that can strengthen the connection between town center projects and the surrounding community. Thus, while office space at the center has achieved an enviable density, and while the center itself possesses the accoutrements of an urban place, the activity and diversity that characterize a successful town center continue to elude it.

With over 400 acres (162 hectares) of land remaining in the center, Las Colinas is now looking to residential growth as the key to its future vitality.[5] RTKL Associates was recently employed to create a new master plan that incorporates a light-rail transit village and a large residential component within the center. The light rail will connect to the Dallas–Fort Worth Airport, and will help reposition Las Colinas as a corporate office center in a more traditional town center setting.

One of the earliest MPCs to break out of the typical suburban approach to commercial development was Miami Lakes Town Center, which lies in the heart of the 3,000-acre (1,210-hectare) Miami Lakes MPC developed by the Graham Companies.

The fountain square at the entrance to Miami Lakes's narrow Main Street is surrounded by ground-floor retail, with offices and apartments on the upper floors—an extraordinary urban design for an early 1980s project.

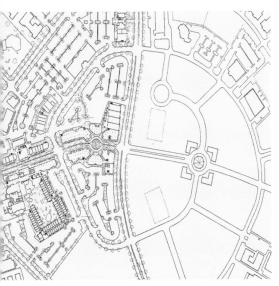

Miami Lakes Town Center in Florida. The existing town center is to the west (left), and the expansion is taking place to the east (right). Ludlam Road runs through the center of the site from north to south, forming a central axis with Main Street. As it moves west from Ludlam, Main Street enters into a circular plaza with a fountain and a majestic tree, gently curves to the southwest, then runs alongside two blocks of two- to four-story mixed-use development and a third block of three-story urban townhouses. *Drawing by University of Miami students. Courtesy Jean-François Lejeune.*

The original core of the town center—a 27-acre (11-hectare), two-block main street completed in 1985—was an early forerunner of the current wave of town center projects. The plan broke many of the conventional rules of retail centers: it lacked large anchor stores, placed apartments and offices above retail shops, and incorporated an unusual street layout—including a narrow, tree-lined main street—and an overall plan that Lester Collins, the original planner and architect, likened to the chambers of a nautilus shell. The town center is currently beginning an expansion under an amended plan crafted by Dover, Kohl & Partners, a leading new urbanist firm based in South Miami.

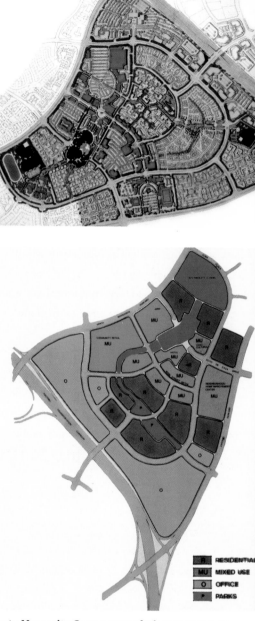

This aerial view of the early phases of Santa Margarita Center in Orange County, California, shows the two shopping centers that are being linked by a main street that curves through the center of the site. Extensive parking lots are concentrated in the center of the shopping centers, and are therefore masked from nearby residential development—although in most places, the residential and commercial areas are separated by walls. *EDAW, Inc.*

Santa Margarita Center, part of a larger, 250-acre (101-hectare) mixed-use urban core for the master-planned community of Rancho Santa Margarita, incorporates 310,000 square feet (28,800 square meters) of retail space, including multiple big-box stores. *EDAW, Inc.*

The underlay zoning for Santa Margarita's urban center works against a more fine-grained mix of uses, but the Main Street section of the plan introduces greater flexibility. *EDAW, Inc.*

Although Miami Lakes was an anomaly in the early 1980s, it anticipated trends in today's MPCs, many of which are seeking to create town centers characterized by pedestrian-oriented streets, human-scale buildings, and open-air public settings. Mirroring trends in retail formats, some MPCs are creating hybrids that combine pedestrian-friendly main streets with more typical suburban commercial developments. Some examples of hybrid combinations in MPCs include Valencia Town Center Drive

and Santa Margarita Center, both in California; the Streets at Southpoint, in Durham, North Carolina; and the Marketplace at Cascades Town Center, in Loudoun County, Virginia.

The first phase of the $100 million Valencia Town Center Drive project, developed by the Newhall Land and Farming Company, consists of a main street with major retail, office, and hotel uses.

The town center is directly adjacent to, and integrated with, the Valencia Town Center regional mall, which was developed in an earlier phase. At Santa Margarita Center, Altoon + Porter Architects and EDAW have created a downtown civic plaza in the midst of a 350,000-square-foot (32,520-square-meter) commercial mixed-use core. Although the center includes big-box formats; curvilinear streets; and large, surface-parking lots, it also includes open-air piazzas, promenades, and colonnades along a central spine.

The Marketplace at Cascades Town Center, planned by Sasaki Associates and Development Design Group (DDG) for the Cascades MPC, includes three separate retail components in nine buildings on a 21-acre (eight-hectare) site. The 213,660 square feet (19,850 square meters) of retail in the town center are divided up into a neighborhood shopping center, a community shopping center, and a main street area that acts as an urban retail and entertainment district. DDG describes the town center as a "hybrid development," in which the main street–style Southbank Commons section acts as a village hub and connects the two conventional shopping centers, one of which is anchored by a major supermarket and pharmacy. The project employs several traditional design elements, including a grid layout, with portions of the streets

Top: One of the many plazas interspersed within the Santa Margarita Center; framed by buildings with office over retail, the plaza offers views of nearby residential neighborhoods. *EDAW, Inc.*

Bottom: Like Santa Margarita's Center, the Marketplace at Cascades Town Center, in Loudoun County, Virginia, incorporates three commercial sections, including a main street that connects two open shopping areas. Pictured here is the main street section, known as Southbank Commons. The three sections of the town center incorporate over 200,000 square feet (18,580 square meters) of retail space for the 105-acre (42-hectare) Cascades master-planned community. *Development Design Group.*

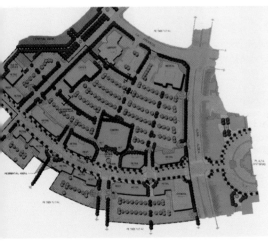

The Main Street section of Santa Margarita Center brings buildings up to the street and includes some office and residential over retail (adjacent to a paseo that connects to a nearby residential neighborhood). *EDAW, Inc.*

Becoming "Real" Town Centers

Rancho Santa Margarita residents voted in 1999 to become an incorporated city, and Miami Lakes easily passed a similar ballot in November 2000. As master-planned communities evolve into incorporated cities and towns, the need for city halls, police departments, libraries, and other civic buildings and institutions will grow—and the town centers of these communities will be the natural location for these uses. Public spaces will also be needed for farmers' markets, performances, bandstands, and other uses and activities that the community wants to nurture and that may extend beyond what the developer initially envisioned.

The possibility of eventual incorporation means that sites must be reserved for civic institutions far in advance of their becoming a reality. If town center and main street projects hope to avoid the fate of many festival marketplaces, they will need to distinguish themselves through the provision of civic institutions and high-quality public spaces. Even in cases where large, planned communities and suburban areas are not incorporated, however, the presence of civic institutions and a mix of housing within a town center can help to transform town center projects into inhabited places with a sense of permanence and community character.

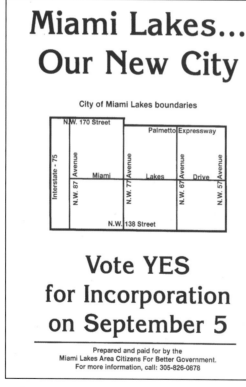

As large master-planned communities and traditional neighborhood developments evolve into incorporated municipalities, their need for town centers with sites for town halls, libraries, and other civic institutions will grow.

At Haile Village Center, part of the unincorporated community of Haile Plantation, in Gainesville, Florida, the Meeting Hall is used year-round for hundreds of community meetings, weddings, receptions, and other special events.

lined with buildings characterized by traditional architectural styles and materials.

Town centers within MPCs vary greatly in size and in the degree of urbanism they incorporate. At one end of the spectrum is Haile Village Center, with its gently curving main street, Craftsman-style

Haile Village Center's traditional one- to two-story buildings, narrow streets and lanes, and mature landscaping provide a small-town ambience.

Reston Town Center represents a more urban place, with high-rise buildings, dense development, and brick plazas. *Sasaki Associates, Inc.*

meeting hall, and village green; at the other end are large, mixed-use urban districts and commercial centers like Reston Town Center, with its wider, straighter main street; high-rise, stone-and-glass buildings; and brick plaza.

In Haile Village Center, developers Bob Kramer and Matthew Kaskel worked diligently over the past decade, making incremental additions to the center and paying careful attention to the kinds of urban design details that would evoke the main streets of historic Florida communities. The center now includes 32 one- and two-story buildings housing over 45 shops, service businesses, and restaurants that are designed to meet the everyday needs of both

Haile Plantation's 8,000 residents and those who live in the vicinity of this growing suburb of Gainesville. The center's human scale; traditional brick and stick-frame detached buildings; narrow streets, lanes, and passageways; and sensitive incorporation of a mature landscape create a village atmosphere

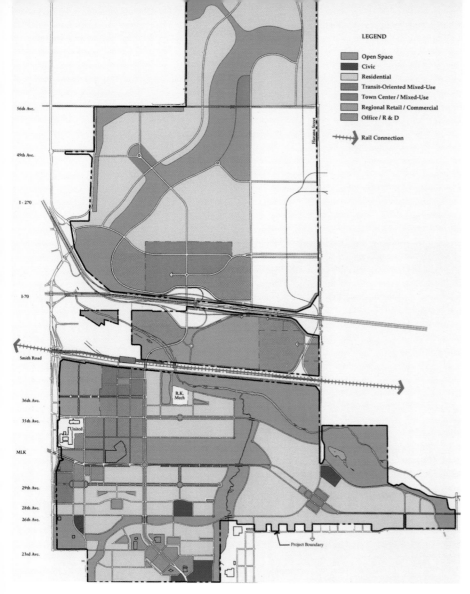

LEGEND

- Open Space
- Civic
- Residential
- Transit-Oriented Mixed-Use
- Town Center / Mixed-Use
- Regional Retail / Commercial
- Office / R & D
- ‐‐‐‐‐ Rail Connection

Touted as the largest infill project in the United States, the 4,700-acre (1,900-hectare) redevelopment plan for Stapleton Airport, in Denver, Colorado, includes five areas designated for a variety of pedestrian-oriented commercial centers and two large areas designated for regional retail and commercial uses, such as regional malls. *Calthorpe Associates.*

that distinguishes Haile Village Center from virtually all other projects in its class.

At the opposite end of the spectrum, Reston Town Center incorporates high-rise office towers housing major corporations; a 500-room hotel; a rapidly developing residential component; multiple parking structures; and a mix of retail, dining, and entertainment tenants—all of which have combined to make it a regional destination. Compared with Haile Village Center, Reston's architecture, streetscape, and public spaces create a much more formal, urban character.

While some town centers in MPCs have had difficulty attracting visitors from outside their borders, one recently completed project has been an extraordinary success. Easton Town Center, described by its developers as a "leisure-time destination center," is the heart of a new, 1,200-acre (485-hectare), mixed-use suburban district in the northeast quadrant of Columbus, Ohio. Phase I of Easton Town Center opened in July of 1999 and attracted over 11 million visitors, generating more than $150 million in sales in

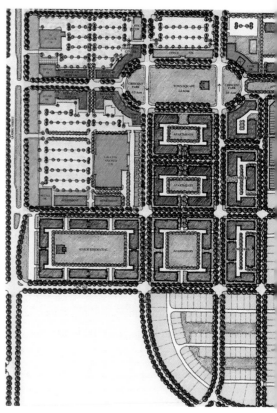

A detailed plan for a major town center in the Stapleton redevelopment plan. *Calthorpe Associates.*

Easton Town Center, in the suburbs of Columbus, Ohio, attracted 11 million visitors in its first year. *Development Design Group.*

Village and Town Centers in New Urbanist Communities

Town centers and main streets can also be found across a wide spectrum of new urbanist projects. And, where sufficient market demand exists, town centers are being constructed as part of the early phases of large TNDs, such as the 640-acre (258-hectare) San Elijo Ranch project, in San Diego, which will include 224,000 square feet (20,810 square meters) of retail and 767 residential units.[8] In Civano (Tucson, Arizona), the first neighborhood center houses a café, a gallery, shops, a meeting hall, and offices in southwestern-style buildings that incorporate 14 different types of sustainable systems and materials.

its first year in operation and far exceeding the developer's expectations.

Encouraged by the success of projects like Easton Town Center, the rapidly growing city of Miramar—home of several MPCs just northwest of Miami—has unveiled plans for a $130 million, 54-acre (22-hectare) town center. In addition to a new city hall, a cultural arts center, and a library, the town center will include 290,000 square feet (26,940 square meters) of office space, 115,000 square feet (10,680 square meters) of retail space, and 225 residential units. The design for the town center, by Torti Gallas and Partners•CHK, Inc., has been described as "the cutting edge of a new urbanism, with its mixed municipal, office, retail, and residential uses set among gardens, plazas, and walkways."[6] According to Bob Payton, Miramar's assistant city manager, "It creates a close neighborhood 'feel' and will become the civic and commercial heart of our rapidly developing community."[7]

Kentlands, in Gaithersburg, Maryland, had to wait nearly ten years for its town center, until exceptional circumstances and strong community support led to the development of Kentlands Market Square. The Town Paper.

Like earlier MPCs, however, most TNDs have had to wait until substantial portions of their residential neighborhoods were completed before a town center or main street project could be initiated. Early TNDs, like Laguna West (Sacramento, California), Kentlands (Gaithersburg, Maryland), and Harbor Town (on Mud Island, directly adjacent to downtown Memphis), have struggled to make the ambitious plans for their town centers a reality. Others, such as Lakelands (Gaithersburg, Maryland), Avalon Park (Orlando, Florida), and Middleton Hills (Madison, Wiscon-

At the King Farm traditional neighborhood development, in Montgomery County, Maryland, a high-density employment center is located in the northwestern portion of the site, and a village center is located in the heart of the community's residential portion. *Torti Gallas and Partners·CHK, Inc.*

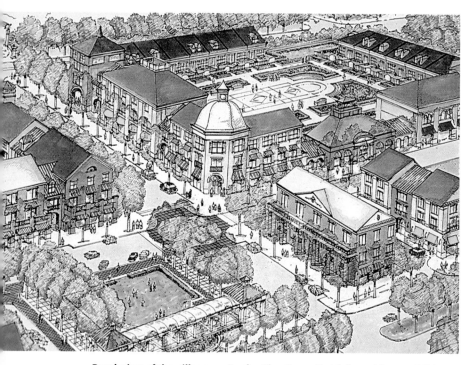

Rendering of the village center for King Farm. *Torti Gallas and Partners·CHK, Inc.*

sin), have justified subsidies for corner stores and modest neighborhood centers, which the developers regarded as key amenities and marketing tools in the early stages of the projects. Finding workable formats and stable proprietors is also a challenge, and TNDs like Southern Village (Chapel Hill, North Carolina) and Belmont Green (formerly Belmont Forest, in

Loudoun County, Virginia), have seen store operations come and go as new formats and proprietors are tested.

Village centers are also emerging in TNDs such as Southern Village (see feature box), and King Farm (Montgomery County, Maryland).[9] Billed as a convenience center, King Farm's village center, located 15 miles (24 kilometers) northwest of Washington, D.C., offers 130,000 square feet (12,080 square meters) of commercial space, including a Safeway food and drugstore, a dry cleaner, a hair salon, a video store, two restaurants, and a deli, all geared for residents of the TND and other nearby neighborhoods. With its three-story buildings and 12- to 18-foot (3.6- to 5.4-meter) sidewalks, however, the King Farm village center resembles anything but a conventional shopping center. Parking is available on the street and in rear lots behind buildings, which pedestrians can access via midblock archways and passages. The two floors above the retail shops include 1,200–1,600-square-foot (110–150-square-meter) townhouses served by elevators; additional multifamily housing being added on adjacent streets will provide a transition from the mixed-use core to the residential edge of the village center.

Other examples of TNDs with village centers planned or under construction can now be found throughout the United States, including Amelia Park (Amelia Island, Florida); Coffee Creek Center (Chesterton, Indiana); Daniel Island (Charleston, South Carolina); Fairview Village (Portland, Oregon); Northwest Landing (Dupont, Washington); Rosemary Beach (Fort Walton Beach, Florida); Tannin (Orange Beach, Alabama); and Trillium, Vermillion, the Village of Woodsong, and the Green at Scott's Mill (all in North Carolina), to name but a few. Each of these projects is attempting to respond to market conditions and current local opportunities, while providing a community gathering place for residents of the TND.

By emphasizing housing and services that support aging in place, Joel Embry's Amelia Park, for example, located on 106 acres (43 hectares) in the middle of Amelia Island, is being positioned to serve not only the residents of the TND, but also the large and growing retirement population of Fernandina Beach. The village centers in Rosemary Beach and Tannin are positioned on key roadways along the Florida panhandle and Alabama's Gulf Coast, in areas where seasonal populations and tourism play a large role. The 38-acre (15-hectare) Village of Woodsong, which is located near an existing library, church, middle school, shopping center, and other amenities, is positioning its village center to accommodate small workplaces, neighborhood shops, services, cafés, and a number of public gathering spaces for local residents.

The Green at Scott's Mill also incorporates an existing school and church, and connects to the street network of Apex, a small town in central North Carolina. The Scott's Mill project centers on a village green that will provide a new focal point for both the TND and the existing town. The green will

Southern Village Corner Store and Village Center

Southern Village, in Chapel Hill, North Carolina, exhibits many of the challenges facing the development of commercial areas within traditional neighborhood developments (TNDs) in smaller communities. To demonstrate commitment to new urbanist principles early on, the developer constructed a mixed-use building—housing a corner store and café, with offices on the second floor—in the center of the first residential neighborhood. The 2,000-square-foot (190-square-meter) corner store has been subsidized since it opened in 1995 and has gone through three operators, although the level of subsidy decreased as the community grew to include over 700 homes (as of 2001). The most recent proprietor developed a close connection with the community and offered a winning combination of café fare, prepared meals, and everyday sundries, but he has since moved on, and the market has been reinvented once again.

In Southern Village, a traditional neighborhood development in Chapel Hill, North Carolina, a mixed-use building houses a corner store and café. *D. R. Bryan.*

When the developers were asked if they would do it again, Jim Earnhardt, the project manager, responded, "It showed the residents we were doing something different. I visited Kentlands and spoke to the developers. In hindsight they would have liked to have a corner store from the beginning."[1] Although the Southern Village market and café struggled financially, topping out at $87 per square foot ($936 per square meter) under its previous owner, it did succeed in providing a focal point and social center for the community's early years.

While homeowners in the surrounding Arlen Park neighborhood remain big supporters of the café, the TND's overall center of gravity has shifted toward the 70,000-square-foot (6,500-square-meter) village center now being built in another part of the TND. The location of the village center traded some roadway visibility for a somewhat more central site that is surrounded by the project's highest-density housing, including apartments, condominiums, and townhouses. The village center also benefits from the presence of an adjacent park-and-ride lot, and incorporates a new elementary school, a new church, and a daycare center. The first two structures within the core area were office buildings, with space designed to accommodate retail and service businesses on the ground floors; with the exception of the space occupied by a dry cleaner, however, these ground-floor spaces are otherwise occupied by offices.

Anchoring the village center is a four-screen cinema with stadium seating, which plans to show outdoor movies on the village green during the summer months. Future plans call for restaurants; a 50-room inn and conference center; a satellite facility for an academic department of the University of North Carolina at Chapel Hill, which is nearby; and a block of retail stores, including a small grocery store and pharmacy. Attempts to attract a grocery store, however, have been thwarted by zoning for the site's small-area plan, which limits the maximum store size to 15,000 square feet (1,390 square meters).

Surveys, interviews, and focus groups conducted by the developers and the author clearly indicate that the plan to build a village center was a key factor in many residents' decisions to locate in Southern Village. Early residents have been eagerly awaiting the development of the village center since first moving in, and some have approached the developers about starting small businesses in the center or relocating their offices there. One homeowner plans to move his small business to the village center as soon as the lease runs out on his current location in a suburban office park.

Residents recognize the challenges involved in creating a village center that is both community oriented and economically viable. As one resident put it, "We need a balance between attracting outside investment and meeting the needs of residents. Preserving a 'community feel' is the key." Residents also want the architecture of the village center to be consistent with the neotraditional design of the housing, and are interested in having a mix of unique and interesting shops and restaurants, as well as a fountain or some other focal point that would act as a central gathering place.

1. Rob Steuteville, *New Urbanism and Traditional Neighborhood Development: Comprehensive Report and Best Practices Guide* (Ithaca, N.Y.: *New Urban News,* 2000) 4-4.

be surrounded by approximately 60,000 square feet (5,570 square meters) of retail, service, and community uses and a mix of live/work units, housing for seniors, and attached and detached homes.

Corner stores and village centers have typically been developed as integral features of, and amenities for, the larger TND community, rather than as aggressively competitive shopping centers. Corner stores, in particular, frequently require subsidies and do not generate high rates of return in and of themselves. What they can do, however, is offer the community a focal point and a sense of place that can greatly enhance its appeal—as well as its property

The entrance to WaterColor, in South Walton County, Florida, is framed by two complementary mixed-use buildings, a hotel with a corner store and café on the ground floor, and the building pictured here, which contains offices with condominiums above. *Cooper, Robertson & Partners.*

values and home sales. Because this sense of place is increasingly important in community design, many developers are willing to undertake corner stores and village centers despite their potential for modest returns, in order to add authenticity and a competitive edge to the larger TND. Increasingly, however, the town centers of TNDs are being positioned to tap existing market demand and stand on their own as competitive commercial enterprises even while the population of the TND is still growing.

New urbanist projects also include some exceptional cases, such as Celebration's town center, which was virtually complete in the first phase of development, and Mashpee Commons, which is being developed "in reverse": a town center was developed for an existing market, and neotraditional neighborhoods will be added in later phases. As highlighted in chapters 6

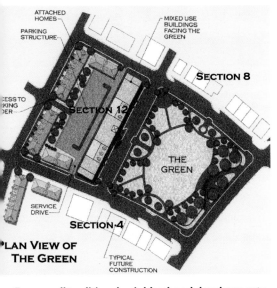

Even small traditional neighborhood developments, such as the Green at Scott's Mill, in the small town of Apex, North Carolina, are incorporating two- to four-story mixed-use buildings, clustered around a village green, to serve as the village centers for both the development and the residents of the town. *Carter Crawford, P.A.*

and 7 of this volume, these projects differ radically in their scale, design, and tenant mix: Celebration, for example, incorporates just 67,500 square feet (6,270 square meters) of retail space (including 11,150 square feet—1,040 square meters—for the cinema), while Mashpee Commons boasts over 280,000 square feet (26,010 square meters) of retail space. Another case study presented in chapter 7 focuses on the Market Square and "Midtown area," which straddles the Kentlands and Lakelands TNDs. Yet another variation on the town center concept, Market Square offers one potential model for mainstream developers who are looking to meld conventional big-box and main street retail, and to include secondary streets that are lined with live/work buildings.[10]

One of the most complex and ambitious TND town centers currently under development is Abacoa Town Center, located in the heart of the 2,055-acre (830-hectare) Abacoa TND, in Jupiter, Florida. The 35-acre (14-hectare) town center was developed by de Guardiola Development, of West Palm Beach, and

A view of Kentlands Market Square, looking toward Kentlands Square Shopping Center, which is just across Kentlands Boulevard. To the rear of the small shops along Market Street are four big-box stores.

features 100,000 square feet (9,290 square meters) of retail; 55,000 square feet (5,110 square meters) of office space; a 17-screen, 80,000-square-foot (7,430-square-meter) cinema; 412 apartments (including units above shops); and a one-acre (0.4-hectare) theater green with an open-air stage—all in a town center setting. Adjacent to the main street are two university facilities (Florida Atlantic University's Jupiter Campus and the Honors College); Roger Dean Stadium (home to a minor-league team and to the spring training camps of the St. Louis Cardinals and the Montreal Expos); a hotel and conference center; and a public golf course. Parking is provided in three parking structures, in on-street spaces, in parking courts, and in sur-

At Market Street at Celebration, the architecture and urban design create the ambience of a small town center, with a modest amount of retail square footage and a fine-grained mix of retail, office, residential, and civic uses.

face lots to the rear of buildings. Phase I of Abacoa Town Center was completed in late 2000, and the $65 million project has moved ahead rapidly while the early phases of the community's residential areas are still being built. Neither the public sector nor the TND developer provided any subsidies, and the project has proceeded strictly on its own merits. In addition to residents in the town center's multifamily units and nearby single-family neighborhoods, the market for the shops and restaurants in the town center includes college students, baseball fans, and golfers—all of whom are within walking distance of the main street.

In a more common pattern for TNDs located in suburban areas, portions of town centers come online at different phases in the overall development of TNDs. In Harbor Town and other projects, for example, multifamily housing was created at an early stage, which helps to build up the necessary density and market for the retail uses to be developed later. In other cases, civic uses might be established first; in Fairview Village, for example, a public elementary school, a private school, the Fairview City Hall, the Fairview Columbia Library, a new post office, and a

One of several civic uses built in Fairview Village, Oregon, in advance of the town center's commercial uses. *Holt & Haugh, Inc.*

Fairview City Hall also houses the planning and engineering department and the police department. *Holt & Haugh, Inc.*

Town Center Drive, the main street of Abacoa, a traditional neighborhood development located in the northern suburbs of Palm Beach County, Florida, is lined with four- to five-story buildings containing a mix of ground-floor retail, office, and multifamily residential.

community church provide an enviable civic infrastructure for the town center and TND.

On the international front, the Urban Villages Group and the Prince of Wales have sponsored efforts to promote traditional urbanism in the United Kingdom; one example—the Poundbury project, designed by Léon Krier—is a mixed-use extension of an existing town that is based on a classic Western European model. In Australia and New Zealand, which are becoming world leaders in pub-

million, represents one of the most advanced projects. Although lacking dwelling units and a vertical mix of uses, the center incorporates the mainstream tenant mix found in community shopping centers, proving that town centers need not be limited to boutique retailers and high-priced bistros.

One of the most ambitious projects moving forward in Canada is Cornell, a 2,400-acre (970-hectare) TND with an expansive town center encompassing both a village center and a main street live/work area; an "entertainment village"; a town park and lakefront promenade; both a conference hotel *and* a convention hotel; two office campuses; and a rich mixture of housing types, civic spaces, and parks. The market has embraced the first phase of the town center: second-story apartments over retail space sold quickly, and street-level commercial space—which includes a coffeehouse, a bank, a health food store, and a self-service laundry—also

McKenzie Towne Centre, in Calgary, Alberta, incorporates standard community shopping-center tenants such as an IGA grocery store, a bank, a drugstore, a hair salon, and a video store. *Carma Developers.*

lic sector efforts to encourage the use of traditional urbanism to manage the growth and redevelopment of cities and regions, the movement is referred to as *reurbanization.*

But, outside of the United States, Canada—where TNDs are proliferating—has by far the largest number of town center and main street plans and projects. Canadian projects include Cornell (Markham, Ontario), McKenzie Towne (Calgary, Alberta), Montgomery Village (Orangeville, Ontario), Oak Park (Ontario), Terwillegar Towne (Edmonton, Alberta), the Village at Niagara-on-the-Lake (Ontario), and at least 18 other TNDs.[11]

With over 100,000 square feet (9,290 square meters) of retail space, McKenzie Towne Centre, which opened in 1999 at a cost of approximately $23

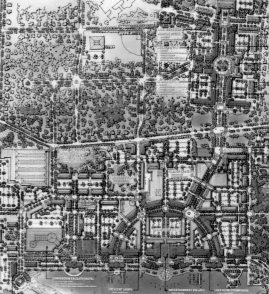

A portion of the expansive Cornell Towne Centre, a 250-acre (101-hectare), 6.6 million-square-foot (613,160-square-meter) development at the heart of Cornell, a traditional neighborhood development in Markham, Ontario. In addition to a village center, the town center includes Main Street Cornell, which is located to the north, and offers townhouses, residential towers, and retail shops oriented around a central plaza and fountain. A hotel anchors the north end of Main Street, and many offices and live/work accommodations serve an adjacent medical center. *Development Design Group.*

Nurturing Village Centers with "Corner Stores"

Because market conditions rarely support the early development of full-blown town centers, the majority of traditional neighborhood developments (TNDs) under development incorporate smaller-scale commercial centers—often a corner store at the outset, and eventually a neighborhood or village center. However, TNDs that begin with a simple corner-store format, often with offices or apartments located on the second floor, have encountered many obstacles. Some view Seaside's Modica Market, in business since 1989 and never subsidized, as a successful prototype, but it still took three years—while the resort town was built out and began attracting increasing numbers of regional visitors and tourists—for the store to turn a profit.

Seaside, Florida's Modica Market, the prototype corner grocery store for a traditional neighborhood development.

The interior of a market in WaterColor, Florida.

Other fledgling TNDs have eschewed the use of isolated corner stores in the interiors of neighborhoods in favor of more centrally located mixed-use buildings. The first mixed-use buildings at I'On, a 243-acre (98-hectare), 760-home TND in Mount Pleasant, South Carolina, currently house a salon, an interior design store, a day spa, a sales office, and the offices of the I'On Company. The construction of these two buildings initiated the development of I'On Square, a village center that will eventually house 30,000 square feet (2,790 square meters) of local shops and offices. To take advantage of local drive-by traffic, the village center is located at the entrance to the TND.

I'On Square, in Charleston, South Carolina, was initiated with two two-story mixed-use buildings at the entrance to the I'On traditional neighborhood development.

In Canada, the developers of Inverness Square, in the McKenzie Towne TND, have worked hard to attract and retain appropriate tenants for the main building in the neighborhood center. The Inverness General Store has struggled, but has benefited from the fact that rental mailboxes are located inside it. The mailboxes, which generate steady foot traffic, are paid for through mandatory association fees

Inverness Square, in McKenzie Towne, a traditional neighborhood development in Calgary, Alberta, typifies the struggle to find the right mix of tenants for small neighborhood centers, and the need to support businesses with outside customers without disrupting the residential character of the neighborhood. *Carma Developers.*

that are also used to maintain the building's clock tower. While residents enjoy having the store within Inverness Village, some office tenants are less satisfied with the location, and some have moved to a larger village center that was completed in a later phase of the TND's development. The developer then pursued a rezoning that would have permitted a private school to occupy a portion of the town center's main building, but local residents resisted, fearing the introduction of school-related traffic into the village.

To improve the viability of small-scale commercial uses, developers have been experimenting with hybrid retail operations that combine elements of grocery stores, general stores, and pharmacies; offer prepared foods; and incorporate cafés, video rental operations, and other businesses. One innovative example is Miss Cordelia's, the 6,000-square-foot (560-square-meter) mixed-retail operation opened by developer Henry Turley for his Harbor Town TND. Unable to identify a small-scale grocer to locate in the TND, Turley started Miss Cordelia's in the

town center's first commercial building. The store zeroed in on the types of goods people were looking for by directly contacting Harbor Town residents, logging more than 200 product requests in its first three weeks of operation. Profitable from the outset, Miss Cordelia's now tops $300 per square foot ($3,230 per square meter) in sales, which Turley credits to the fact that "people recognize there is something different here ... that shopping at Miss Cordelia's is the best way to meet neighbors."[1]

The grocery store is a single-story building that shoppers enter from a rear entrance; two other sides of the 10,400-square-foot (970-square-meter)

Harbor Town, a traditional neighborhood development (TND) on Mud Island, near Memphis, offers an innovative cluster of shops that are cradled between multistory apartment and mixed-use buildings. The shops are adjacent to the town square and a Montessori school, and are within walking distance of many of the TND's single-family homes. *John Van Fossen.*

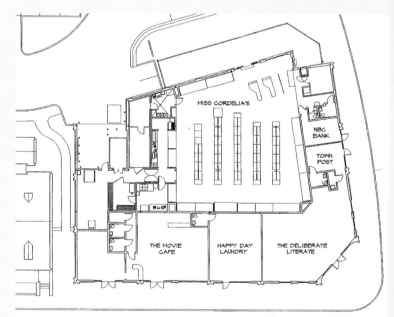

Miss Cordelia's grocery store, in Harbor Town, is lined with small shops that face the town square and streets; parking is to the side and rear of the building. *The Henry Turley Company.*

A dry cleaner and a hybrid "video and pizza" store create an active streetfront lining one wall of Miss Cordelia's grocery store; the street wall is continued in the adjacent multifamily residential buildings. *John Van Fossen.*

meters) of retail, 8,000 square feet (740 square meters) of office and service space, and apartments and condominiums—all in two- and three-story buildings—has introduced a vertical mix of uses and helped enclose the main square. In addition to the grocery store, the tenant mix now includes a deli, a barbershop, a video center, a card and gift shop, a day spa, a beauty salon, a dry cleaner, and the offices of lawyers and other professionals. The town center also includes

building, which face the street and Harbor Town Square, are lined with a mix of small shops, including the 2,000-square-foot (190-square-meter) Movie Café, which includes a pizzeria, bar, and video rental shop. To create retailing that is consistent with the needs of a TND, Turley believes in packing in as many small-scale, multifaceted operations as possible. "A typical suburban shopping center is renting square footage," he says, "We are renting merchant count [i.e., maximizing the number of stores per square foot, rather than the amount of square feet per store]. We are always trying to get them to take less [space]—like everyone else, merchants have been 'encultured' with the wrong ideas. Everyone thinks that bigger is better."[2]

The small town center of Harbor Town has continued to grow: the addition of another 6,000 square feet (560 square

The parking lot, shopping carts, and store entrance are at the rear of Miss Cordelia's grocery store, providing the convenience of a conventional market without disrupting the main street with parking or blank walls along the square. *John Van Fossen.*

a 10,000-square-foot (929-square-meter) Montessori school (K–8), 210 apartments, and 21 condominiums. The final building will add another restaurant and ground-floor retail, with lofts on the upper floors, and will complete the enclosure of Harbor Town Square.

1. Rob Steuteville, "First Commercial Building Opens in Harbor Town," *New Urban News* 3, no. 2 (1998): 1, 3–4.
2. Ibid.

The main street entrance to the cluster of shops facing Harbor Town Square. *John Van Fossen.*

leased at a solid pace.[12] Much of the 1.8 million square feet (167,230 square meters) of office space and 300,000 square feet (27,870 square meters) of retail space approved for the TND will be located in the town center.

Suburban Infill Town Centers

A growing number of town center projects are also being planned and built by private developers to serve existing suburban markets, rather than as the centerpieces of growing MPCs and TNDs. Some of these are infill projects or extensions of existing town centers and edge cities: examples include Redmond

Top: Redmond Town Center and vicinity. *LMN Architects.*

Bottom: Locating parking in garages and to the rear of buildings helps maintain Redmond Town Center's main street urban design. *LMN Architects.*

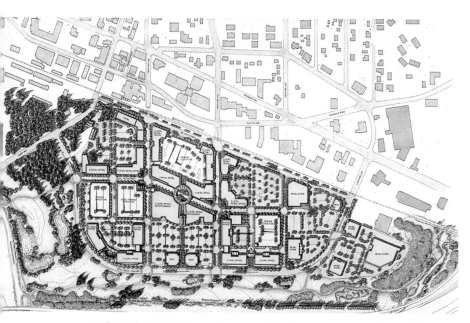

Redmond Town Center, in Redmond, Washington, is a suburban infill town center with a mix of retail, entertainment, office, and hotel uses, and a strong connection to the street grid of an existing town. *LMN Architects.*

Town Center, in Redmond, Washington, the home of Microsoft; Owings Mills Town Center, which is taking shape in an edge city in Baltimore County, Maryland; and Phillips Place, located in the South Park area, an edge city near Charlotte, North Carolina. Other projects involve new town center districts within largely residential suburban areas: examples of this type include Southlake Town Square (Southlake, Texas); Prescott Valley Town Center (Prescott Valley, Arizona); Westglen Town Center (West Des Moines, Iowa); and Addison Circle (Addison, Texas).

The 1.65-million-square-foot (153,290-square-meter) Redmond Town Center combines land uses normally developed independently, including a lifestyle shopping center, an office campus, two hotels, a cinema, and multifamily housing. The project extends the street grid of downtown Redmond across a rail line, and provides a new focal point for an existing town that is located in the center of a much larger suburban region. At Westglen Town Center, in contrast—a new, 95-acre (38-hectare) district in a suburban setting—developer Tim Urban and the design firm of Shook have planned to incorporate mainstream grocery and community shopping-center tenants in a lower-density format that blends conventional suburban commercial uses and main street designs.

In Arizona, the Fain Signature Group has initiated development of a large, multifaceted town center district that will serve as the heart of Prescott Valley, a rapidly growing suburban community that is north of Phoenix and situated on some of the 72,000 acres (29,140 hectares) that the Fain family has assembled since the 1870s. The plans for the 500-acre (200-hectare) master-planned district, which is surrounded by residential neighborhoods and strip commercial development, are reminiscent of the modular composition found in Reston's town center district. Prescott Valley Town Center will weave together a mix of elements, including a new, mixed-use main street designed by Calthorpe Associates, a 39-acre (16-hectare) entertainment center, a town hall and civic center, a neighborhood shopping center, a large medical complex, a college, and a variety of housing; a technology park has also been proposed for inclusion in the district.

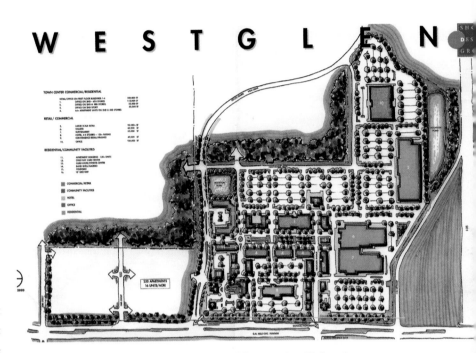

The plan for Westglen, a town center planned for West Des Moines, Iowa.
Tim Urban.

In Denver, Colorado, 11 acres (4.5 hectares) of what was once Lowry Air Force base is being transformed into the Lowry Town Center. The project will include 118,000 square feet (10,960 square meters) of retail space and 14,000 square feet (1,300 square meters) of second-story office space, laid out along a new main street with a public plaza. The town center is anchored by a 56,400-square-foot (5,240-square-meter) Albertson's grocery store and

Lifestyle Centers and Town Centers

In recent years, the shopping center industry has witnessed the rapid rise of a new format known as *lifestyle centers,* in which open-air shopping is organized along main streets. According to a recent report by the International Council of Shopping Centers (ICSC), of the 30 lifestyle centers constructed since 1985, 18 have been constructed since 1997, and plans for new lifestyle centers are proliferating at the annual ICSC conferences.[1]

The term *lifestyle center* was coined (and trademarked) in 1987, by developers Dan Poag and Terry McEwen, when they built the Shops at Saddle Creek, in the Germantown area of Memphis. Attempts by the ICSC to define lifestyle centers, however, have shown how elusive the concept can be: in

Some urban entertainment centers, like the Shops at Sunset Place, in Miami, are now being referred to as lifestyle centers.

Washingtonian Center, in Gaithersburg, Maryland, is a compact lifestyle center that includes structured parking. Small retail shops, organized along a main street, are anchored by larger stores such as Target, Barnes & Noble, and Galyan's; the development also includes a cluster of restaurants around a small fountain plaza.

terms of gross leasable retail space, for example, centers range widely, from as little as 90,000 square feet (8,360 square meters), at One Pacific Place, in Omaha, Nebraska, to as much as 760,000 square feet (70,610 square meters), at the Summit Shopping Center, in Birmingham, Alabama. The 30 projects identified as lifestyle centers by the ICSC included well-known urban entertainment centers like Cocowalk and the Shops at Sunset Place (both in Miami), retail-only centers like Mount Pleasant Towne Centre (Mount Pleasant, South Carolina), and full-blown mixed-use town centers like Reston Town Center and Southlake Town Square. About half of the centers did not have a cinema, and while the number of restaurants averaged 5.5 per center, the count ranged from as few as one to as many as 15 dining establishments. Some projects that are generally regarded as lifestyle centers, such as the Avenue at White Marsh (White Marsh, Maryland) and Washingtonian Center (Gaithersburg, Maryland), did not even appear on the list.

Generally, lifestyle centers are characterized more by their upscale retail, dining, and entertainment tenants and less by their mix of uses and urban design, whereas town centers and main streets put more emphasis on the latter. In fact, the original idea behind lifestyle centers was to place high-quality shopping mall tenants in a spruced-up, strip mall format. By offering a smaller shopping center layout and placing parking closer to individual stores, developers of lifestyle centers hoped to draw customers who had been put off by the typical shopping mall experience. In keeping with Poag & McEwen's original vision, lifestyle centers often have no anchors, provide less gross leasable area and lower overhead than shopping malls, and are filled with tenants identified as "lifestyle retailers"—specialty stores such as Restoration Hardware, Pottery Barn, Ann Taylor, and others that carry merchandise catering to the affluent target market.

While some regard as superficial the extra attention paid to the architecture and streetscape in early lifestyle centers, the format's growing popularity has led to continuous refinements, and more and more elements of traditional urban design are appearing in new lifestyle centers. Lifestyle centers typically do not, however, attempt to achieve the more fine-grained mix of retail, office, civic, and residential uses; the variety of urban open spaces; and the community orientation of town center projects.[2]

1. "Lifestyle Centers—A Defining Moment," *ICSC Research Quarterly* (winter 2001–2002).
2. See K. Dube, "Lifestyle Center Pioneers Open Aspen Grove," *Shopping Center Today* (http://www.icsc.org [May 25, 2002]); M. Barker, "What's a Lifestyle Center?" *Shopping Center Today* (http://www.icsc.org [May 25, 2002]).

includes many tenants typically found in neighbor-hood shopping centers. To strengthen the center's aesthetic appeal and better serve the neighborhood being built around it, the grocery store is located in the heart of the project, rather than on the busy arte-rial that is adjacent to the center.

Southlake Town Square, one of several urban cen-ters being created in automobile-oriented suburban communities and edge cities in Texas that have grown rapidly in recent decades, is one of the most well rounded of these projects, incorporating an even mix of retail and office space, a post office, a town hall, a courthouse, a library, and residential units above retail. The project also includes Grand Avenue, a promenade that terminates in a traditional town square dominated by a courthouse. (See case study in chapter 7.)

Urban Redevelopment Town Centers

Urban villages and town centers are also appearing on urban infill sites and in redevelopment areas, including brownfield sites. Among the high-density projects cur-rently underway on brownfield sites is Atlantic Station, an Atlantic Steel industrial site in midtown Atlanta that is now being redeveloped as a major mixed-use urban center with a variety of housing, office, retail, hotel, and other uses. Similarly, Victory, located on a brownfield site adjacent to downtown Dallas, is pro-ceeding with a high-density urban development plan that includes office space and a variety of other uses, including a major arena that is already complete.

In Southlake Town Square, a new town center for an existing suburban com-munity in Texas, the town hall will provide a civic anchor for 2 million square feet (185,810 square meters) of retail and office uses. *Cooper & Stebbins, L.P.*

Federal Realty's $78 million Pentagon Row proj-ect, recently completed on an 18.5-acre (7.5-hectare) infill site directly across Interstate 395 from the Pentagon, is contiguous with the Pentagon City mixed-use development, which features a mall, a hotel, a Metro station, high-rise office buildings, and high-density residential uses. Pentagon Row serves the large nearby workforce as well as residents of the more than 2,500 high-rise residential units that surround the site, and offers over 300,000 square feet (27,870 square meters) of specialty and service retail, a 45,000-

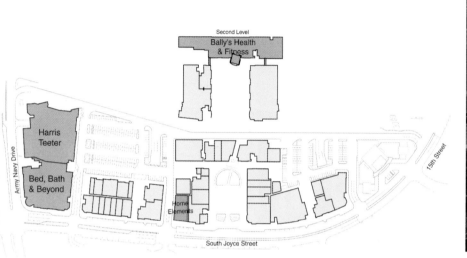

The site plan for Pentagon Row, in Arlington, Virginia, which mixes big-box retailers, a major grocery store, a health club, 500 apartment units, and a variety of small shops clustered around an urban plaza. *Federal Realty Investment Trust.*

square-foot (4,180-square-meter) grocery store, ten restaurants, and 500 residential apartments. Restaurants with café-style outdoor seating are clustered around the project's centerpiece, an urban square with a full-sized skating rink.

Other examples of infill and redevelopment projects include Salt Lake City Gateway, Uptown Dallas, and the Uptown District, in San Diego.

Inner-city and public housing redevelopment efforts, including those being undertaken by the Department of Housing and Urban Development's HOPE VI program, are also incorporating main street formats. New urbanist town centers and main streets in inner-city neighborhoods include Lexington Terrace, in Baltimore, Maryland; Chestnut Court, in Oakland, California; and Salishan, in Tacoma, Washington. One of the most ambitious HOPE VI

Top: A street corner at Pentagon Row, with a view of the Pentagon and the Washington Monument in the background. *Steve Hinds.*

Bottom: Parking lots are located at the interior of Pentagon Row (and underground as well), and many shops have entrances from both the parking lot and the street (on the opposite side of the building). *Steve Hinds.*

efforts, Park DuValle, in Louisville, Kentucky, includes a 25,000-square-foot (2,320-square-meter) town center and an expansion plan incorporating both big-box formats and smaller-scale retail, with office uses and apartments above.[13]

NEIGHBORHOOD CENTER

Town centers are being planned for redeveloped public housing projects such as Salishan, in Tacoma, Washington. *Torti Gallas and Partners•CHK, Inc.*

Existing Main Streets Reinvented

Throughout the United States, the past decade has witnessed the rediscovery and revitalization of both the older main streets of cities and towns, and the relatively newer main streets of suburban downtowns. The now-vibrant Park Avenue, in Winter Park, Florida, and Clematis Street, in West Palm Beach, Florida, are examples of older main streets. One of the most dramatic reinventions of an older main street is the Third Street Promenade, in Santa Monica, California. By the 1970s, Third Street had devolved into a moribund pedestrian mall, and the construction of Santa Monica Place, an enclosed shopping mall, had left the surrounding Bayside District virtually lifeless. After five years of planning and a year of construction, Third Street Promenade opened in 1989 and became a run-away success story. Much more than a main street revitalization program, the project involved a complete redesign and redevelopment of the three-block pedestrian mall, an undertaking that was facilitated by a strong public/private partnership.

As project master planners, the Roma Design Group, reintroduced automobile traffic for portions of the day; developed a coordinated program of signage, landscaping, and street furniture; and created expansive sidewalks (up to 30 feet—10 meters—wide) to accommodate outdoor dining, kiosks, and pedestrian amenities. To boost the concentration of nighttime activities, new city codes required that movie theaters and other entertainment uses be located within the district; excluded service uses, such as banks; and banned offices from the ground floor. Density bonuses have also strengthened the urban ambience of the district: buildings now range from three to six stories in height, and floor/area ratios are as high as 3.5. The success of the Third Street Promenade has now spilled over into the surrounding Bayside District, a 53-acre (21-hectare) area that incorporates nearly 1 million square feet (92,300 square meters) of office space, 1 million square feet (92,300 square meters) of retail and entertainment uses, over

170,000 square feet (15,790 square meters) of civic uses, 178 residential units, and 86 hotel rooms.[14]

In Highland Park, Illinois, Renaissance Place, located on a five-acre (two-hectare) parcel bordering the existing downtown, is adding 200,000 square feet (18,580 square meters) of retail, office, and residential development. The project includes 72,000 square feet (6,690 square meters) of specialty retail and restaurants, 40,000 square feet (3,720 square meters) of office space, and 32 apartments in a vertical mixed-use, main street arrangement. The tenant mix includes both national upscale retailers and unique local merchants, and is anchored by a relatively small—48,000-square-foot (4,460-square-meter)—urban-style Saks Fifth Avenue and a five-screen art house movie theater. Residents of this established, upscale suburb of Chicago feel strongly about preserving Highland Park's distinctive identity; the mayor, who views the project as consistent with the history and character of the town, describes Renaissance Place as a combination of "thoughtfully designed, landscaped open spaces and low-rise brick buildings in keeping with downtown Highland Park's refined atmosphere."[15]

The major player in the redevelopment of main streets in the United States in recent years has been Federal Realty Investment Trust, based in Rockville, Maryland. Founded in 1962, Federal Realty currently holds over 120 prime retail properties, including conventional shopping centers, in major markets throughout the United States. Over the past decade, however, Federal Realty has carved out a niche in the redevelopment of urban main streets—and, in 1994, officially launched its Main Street Retail program,

A newly created street corner at Renaissance Place, in Highland Park, Illinois. *Davis Street Land Company.*

Bethesda Row, in Bethesda, Maryland, is Federal Realty Investment Trust's "laboratory" for creating mixed-use main streets. *Federal Realty Investment Trust.*

which targeted the acquisition of select retail properties in established downtown shopping areas. The program now encompasses 91 main street retail properties in approximately 20 cities, including Bethesda, Maryland; Evanston, Illinois; Forest Hills, New York; Greenwich, West Hartford, and Westport, Connecticut; San Antonio, Texas; Pasadena, San Diego, and Santa Monica, California; and Winter Park, Florida.

Federal Realty's formula has involved the acquisition of one or more contiguous blocks of property; the creation of pedestrian-friendly main streets (through the rehabilitation of old buildings, the construction of new buildings, and the improvement of streetscapes); and a winning combination of "street-smart" retail tenants such as Banana Republic, Barnes & Noble, the Disney Store, Eddie Bauer, the Gap, the

Limited, Pottery Barn, and Saks Fifth Avenue. The ground-floor retail mix includes entertainment and dining; office space and, increasingly, multifamily housing are located on the upper floors. Bethesda Row, billed as Federal Realty's "laboratory," incorporates five city blocks (8.1 acres—3.2 hectares) in Bethesda's central business district, and involved the creation of 330,000 square feet (30,660 square meters) of retail, office, and entertainment uses, as well as multifamily residential units.

Although Federal Realty is now refocusing its mission as an investment trust and will no longer develop large, capital-intensive development projects like Pentagon Row and Santana Row, Steven Guttman, Federal Realty's chief executive officer, remains bullish on the long-term value of the company's main street retail assets, which it will continue to hold and manage.

Urban Villages

While retail is obviously a key element in town centers, apartment buildings and residential uses can also play a definitive role, and several apartment developers are incorporating a mix of uses and new urbanist design into their new projects. When high-density multifamily properties are mixed with retail and other uses, such efforts frequently yield what is characterized as an urban village. The principal distinction

Top: Addison Circle, the new town center for Addison, Texas. *Steve Hinds.*

Bottom: Post Legacy, the mixed-use residential component of Legacy Town Center, has brought places to live, shop, and dine into the heart of the enormous Legacy office park in Plano, Texas. *Steve Hinds.*

between an urban village and a town center is a higher intensity of residential development and a lower emphasis on commercial uses.

In recent years, Post Properties has been a leader in this field, but other firms, such as Trammell Crow Residential and AvalonBay Communities, among others, have also been pursuing this market. A $3 billion corporation headquartered in Atlanta, Post Properties specializes in the development and management of apartments; most of the firm's 35,000 units are located in over 100 communities in sprawling suburban areas in the South and Southwest. In a move that paralleled the transformation at Federal Realty, chief executive officer John Williams redirected the development of nearly 7,000 new apartment units in a completely different direction: the units would be integrated into high-density, pedestrian-oriented, mixed-use projects. Part of this strategy involved the acquisition of the Dallas-based Columbus Realty Trust, which was already experimenting along the same lines. Commenting on the company's change in direction, Williams said, "We have no interest at all in building suburban garden apartments."[16] The company's vision statement now reads "To Build Better Neighborhoods."

Under this new mission, Post's new projects remained heavily focused on apartments, but began to incorporate some condominiums and townhouses, as well as a mix of neighborhood retail, service businesses, and restaurants. This mix of uses is arranged in high-density pockets of development characterized by small urban public spaces and traditional urban streetscapes, with retail on the ground floor and offices and residences above. The majority of Post's projects are located on urban infill sites. Some—like Uptown Square, in Denver, and Roosevelt Square, in Phoenix—involve the adaptive use of existing structures; others—like Parkside, in Atlanta—blend into and connect with 100-year-old neighborhoods. High-profile projects include Riverside, in Atlanta; Harbour Place, in Tampa Bay; and Addison Circle, in Addison, Texas. Riverside was designed by DPZ, and both

Post Harbour Place, in Tampa, Florida. *Steve Hinds.*

only offer a mix of uses and activities and a pedestrian atmosphere, but achieve a subjective sense of place that can be difficult to describe, but that people recognize when they experience it.[17]

As apartment specialists, Post Properties has found it beneficial to partner with other development groups, like Federal Realty, in arrangements that allow each partner to focus on its area of expertise—and that yield a mixed-use whole that is greater than the sum of its parts. Projects that Post and Federal Realty have

Harbour Place and Addison Circle were planned by RTKL Associates. In a reflection of the change in the corporate culture, Post's headquarters were also relocated to urban village settings: its corporate headquarters are in Riverside, and its Dallas headquarters in Addison Circle.

The Dallas–Fort Worth area is currently a hotbed for urban village development; in addition to the Post projects, other developments include United Commercial Realty's Knox Street project, in Knox-Henderson; the Henry S. Miller Company's West Village project, north of the central business district; and Mockingbird Station, a large, transit-oriented project being developed by UC Urban. Billed as "live, work, play" settings, these projects and others like them have worked to achieve the density, residential emphasis, and resident-oriented mix of uses that characterize urban villages. Developers agree that to succeed, an urban village format must not

Post Riverside has introduced suburban Atlantans to European-style living.
Steve Hinds.

cooperated on include Pentagon Row, in Arlington, Virginia, and Lindbergh City Center, in Atlanta. Post also partnered with TrizecHahn on Paseo Colorado, a project in the heart of downtown Pasadena, California, that involved retrofitting the Plaza Pasadena shopping mall.

Like Federal Realty, Post Properties has more recently refocused on managing properties, and has cut back on new development—including the sort of large-scale, mixed-use development that is viewed as unusually capital-intensive and risky for real estate investment trusts that grew largely by acquiring and managing existing properties. Thomas Brink, of RTKL Associates, which has designed numerous projects for both Post Properties and Federal Realty, notes that developers and designers should focus on one initial question when approaching these residential/retail combinations: "Is this a retail project with residential, or is it a residential project with support retail? The entire approach to planning and designing the project hinges on this initial understanding."

Reinvented Retail Centers

Edward Bennett's plan for downtown Pasadena, developed in the 1920s, created a dramatic view—punctuated by plazas and by civic buildings—down the length of Garfield Avenue. Fifty years later, with the construction of the Plaza Pasadena shopping mall, which enclosed a portion of the street and incorporated it within the mall, Bennett's "city beautiful" vision was literally closed off. At the behest of the city, Moule & Polyzoides completed a Civic

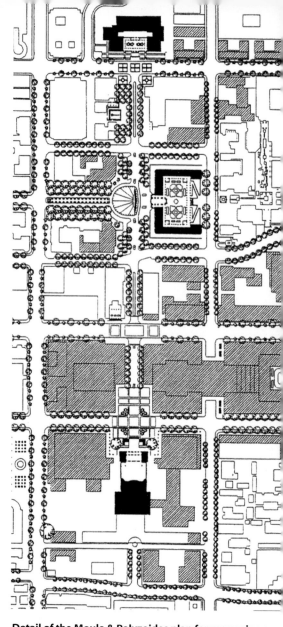

Detail of the Moule & Polyzoides plan for reopening a key axis through the Plaza Pasadena shopping mall, and thereby restoring the urban fabric of the original 1920s Bennett Plan. *Moule & Polyzoides.*

Center Master Plan in 1998 that called for the north-south axis of the 1925 Bennett plan to be restored, and for Plaza Pasadena to be transformed from a monolithic, inward-facing, enclosed retail mall into three separate blocks of mixed-use buildings that would front the street.

To the surprise of many, TrizecHahn, the original developer and owner of the mall, embraced the plan for Paseo Colorado. The redevelopment plans, designed by Ehrenkrantz Eckstut & Kuhn and RTKL Associates, called for the interior portion of the mall to be torn down, for Garfield Avenue to be reopened, and for an urban village to be created in the civic center area. The shopping mall has been reconfigured as 560,000 square feet (52,030 square meters) of ground-floor commercial uses topped by four stories of residential units, including about 400 apartments constructed by Post Properties. The tenant mix includes shops, restaurants, a health club, a gourmet market, a day spa, cinemas, and other retail and entertainment establishments. The project, which cost more than $200 million, opened in late 2001 and has been embraced by both the city and the local market: 60 percent of the planned 75 shops and restaurants were preleased before ground breaking.

The redevelopment of shopping centers and strip commercial areas into main streets, town centers, and urban villages has become increasingly common in recent years. A recent study on "greyfield" shopping malls identified 140 dying malls and another 249 maturing, "troubled" malls that were at the end of their life cycle and had the potential to become greyfields within five years.[18] According to Lee S. Sobel, the author of *Greyfields No More,* a greyfield property is an abandoned or struggling single-use commercial property located in an older suburban or urban setting that contains an abundance of excess parking. (The term refers to the faded asphalt that dominates these properties; greenfields, in contrast, are characterized by agricultural land or grassy fields, and brownfields are contaminated, industrial infill sites.)

Malls that meet the criteria for greyfields (age, location, average acreage, and square footage) are further classified as dying or troubled, depending on how poorly they compare to other malls. Industry rankings range from A to D: "A+" malls have sales per square foot of $400 and up (per square meter of $4,300 and up) and "D" malls have sales of less than

$100 per square foot ($1,075 per square meter). Greyfield malls operate at the C+, C, and D levels. Malls with sales of less than $200 per square foot ($2,150 per square meter) are considered vulnerable to becoming greyfields within five years, and those with sales of less than $150 per square foot ($1,615 per square meter) are classified as dying greyfield

The demolition of this portion of the Plaza Pasadena shopping mall was the first step in the process of restoring the north-south axis of the 1925 Bennett Plan and transforming the mall into a multiblock, mixed-use main street. *Moule & Polyzoides.*

malls.[19] Sobel's study highlighted the considerable market potential of these properties—which average 500,000 square feet (46,450 square meters) and 45 acres (18 hectares), and many of which are located in inner-ring suburbs. These sites can be attractive locations for redevelopment as higher-density, mixed-use,

Top: One of many inner-ring suburban shopping malls facing extinction throughout the United States, Kingsdale Shopping Center is now slated to be transformed into a town center for Upper Arlington, Ohio. *ACP Visioning & Planning, Ltd.*

Middle: Phase I of the Kingsdale redevelopment is focused around a new square that will form the focal point for the new town center. *ACP Visioning & Planning, Ltd.*

Bottom: Phase II will add moderate- to high-density housing on short blocks throughout the former mall site. *ACP Visioning & Planning, Ltd.*

pedestrian-oriented neighborhoods, main streets, and town centers.

Some mall retrofits have involved total demolition; Boca Raton Mall, for example, was demolished for the construction of Mizner Park, and a Sears was demolished for the Uptown District, in San Diego. Others have consisted of incremental adaptations of older shopping centers; the transformation of the New Seabury Shopping Center into Mashpee Commons and the redevelopment of Chattanooga's Eastgate Shopping Mall, which became Brainerd Town Center, are examples. As Mashpee demonstrates, plans to convert shopping centers and enclosed malls into open-air main streets and town centers are not limited to the Sunbelt. Mall conversion efforts have been proposed in places like Syracuse, New York (Lafayette Mall), Upper Arlington, Ohio (Kingsdale Shopping Center), and the epitome of postwar suburban America, Levittown, New York.

An inner-ring suburb of Columbus, Upper Arlington was developed early in the 20th century and modeled after the Country Club District, in Kansas City, but never developed a town center area like that of Country Club Plaza. The residents of this suburban community, which eventually incorporated as a separate city, now view the fading Kingsdale Shopping Center property as a golden opportunity to establish a downtown for the community and provide property tax relief by adding office and retail uses to the city's predominantly residential base. The redevelopment plan, prepared by ACP Visioning & Planning and adopted by the city, calls for the 38-acre (15-hectare) superblock site to be broken up into more than a

The Winter Park Mall, in Winter Park, Florida, is being gradually transformed into a mixed-use town center—Winter Park Village—with a street grid, on-street parking, and urban public spaces. *Lee S. Sobel.*

dozen blocks; streets that are currently cut off at the perimeter of the mall property will be extended throughout the site and connect with the city's existing street network. The mix of retail, office, residential, and civic uses called for in the plan would replace parking lots with structures and significantly increase the density of development, raising the floor/area ratio from 0.19 to 0.76.

Opportunities for mall retrofits are becoming so widespread that firms like Dover, Kohl & Partners have carved out a niche developing plans for them. Dover, Kohl worked with the Gibbs Planning Group on the creation of redevelopment plans for the ongoing transformation of Eastgate Mall into Brainerd Town Center, and on the conversion of Winter Park Mall into a main street–oriented development known as Winter Park Village. In recent decades, Winter Park Mall had declined precipitously while the town's historic main street, Park Avenue, grew steadily stronger and more vibrant. In a major role reversal, Park Avenue became a model for how to redevelop the mall property. Dover, Kohl also teamed with DPZ to develop a plan for the gradual transformation of the classic sprawl surrounding the massive Dadeland Mall into a town center for Kendall, Florida.

Other projects that involve the replacement of a shopping mall with a mixed-use neighborhood include City Center Englewood, in Englewood, Colorado, and the Crossings at Mountain View, a completed project in Mountain View, California. Both projects were planned and designed by Calthorpe Associates, a leader in transit-oriented development (TOD). At the Crossings at Mountain View, a walkable neighborhood adjacent to a new Caltrain commuter station incorporates a variety of single-family and multifamily housing

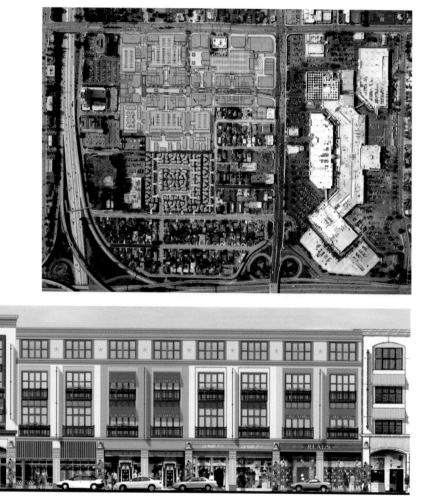

Top: The Santana Row project, in San Jose, California, replaced the Town and Country Mall with a main street and an intense mix of retail, office, and housing. *Federal Realty Investment Trust.*

Bottom: Santana Row's main street will be lined with four-story mixed-use buildings with on-street parking. *Federal Realty Investment Trust.*

types and a small amount of commercial uses. City Center Englewood also includes plans for a light-rail line at the heart of the project.

Federal Realty, which has focused much of its attention on the redevelopment of existing main streets, is now applying many of the same principles employed in its redevelopment projects to the creation of entirely new main streets and to the redevelopment of shopping centers and malls. In San Jose, Federal Realty's ambitious Santana Row development, located on the former site of the Town and Country Mall, offers 680,000 square feet (63,170 square meters) of retail space, 1,200 residential units, 200 hotel rooms, a variety of public gathering spaces, and over 5,200 parking spaces on a 40-acre (16-hectare) site. According to the project's designer, Richard Heapes, of Street-Works, Santana Row is one of the very few town center and main street projects that does not involve any public sector subsidies or incentives, a fact that he attributes to the extraordinarily strong real estate market in the region.

Smaller retail centers have also been redeveloped as main street projects. In Shirlington Village (Arlington, Virginia), a main street setting with buildings dating back to the 1940s, redevelopment will involve 125,000 square feet (11,610 square meters) of existing retail and the addition of 150,000 square feet (13,940 square meters) of new retail, 400 residential units, 250,000 square feet (23,230 square meters) of office space, and a 125-room hotel.

Transit Villages

Even in suburban cities in the South and West (like Charlotte, North Carolina, and Sacramento, California) ever-increasing traffic congestion has led to a renewed interest in transit development. Along with pedestrian-friendly village environments, transit-

Top: Rendering of the vision for the Crossings in Mountain View, California. *Calthorpe Associates.*

Bottom: At the Crossings, mixed-use buildings on the corner closest to the transit station lead to the townhouses. *Calthorpe Associates.*

oriented projects are striking a responsive chord with homebuyers, many of whom are making home purchases based on little more than the promise of future transit service. Mixed-use formats based on traditional towns and villages have been embraced, in part, for their potential to create desirable, high-density residential neighborhoods clustered around transit stations—an arrangement that can, in turn, reinforce transit ridership. Transit villages represent an exciting alternative to the "transit station in a parking lot" designs of past decades, in which stations were surrounded by park-

and-ride lots and provided few opportunities for joint real estate development.

Transit agencies, municipalities, and developers are now collaborating to create special area plans, design guidelines, and partnership arrangements that support transit initiatives. The Pacific Northwest and California have been particularly active in planning for transit villages, and design firms like Calthorpe Associates, based in San Francisco, and Lennertz Coyle & Associates, based in Portland, Oregon, have specialized in the planning and design of TODs.

In Richmond, California, for example, Richmond Transit Village is being developed on an infill site directly adjacent to a multimodal transit station offering bus service and connections to both the regional and national rail systems (BART and Amtrak,

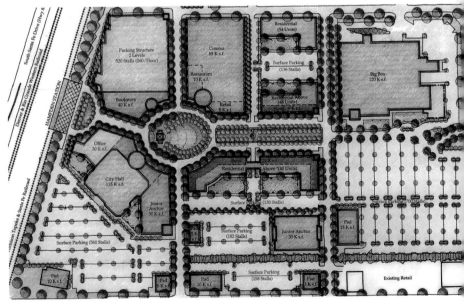

Malls to main streets: City Center Englewood, in Englewood, Colorado (above), and the Crossings, in Mountain View, California (above left), both involve the transformation of old shopping center sites into transit-oriented neighborhoods. *Calthorpe Associates.*

respectively). BART and the Richmond Redevelopment Agency sponsored a competition to develop the plan and selected the Olson Company to develop the site. The plan, crafted by Calthorpe Associates, will replace surface parking lots and vacant land with high-density multifamily housing; small-lot, single-

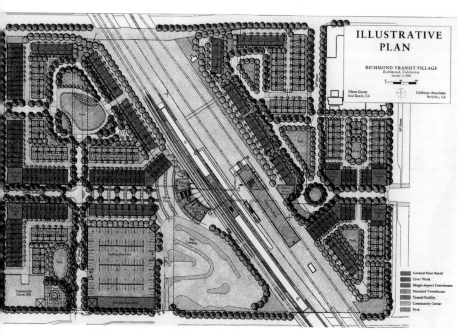

ILLUSTRATIVE PLAN

RICHMOND TRANSIT VILLAGE
Richmond, California
October 11, 2001

Olson Group   Calthorpe Associates
Seal Beach, CA   Berkeley, CA

Ground Floor Retail
Live / Work
Single-Aspect Townhouse
Standard Townhouse
Transit Facility
Community Center
Park

Richmond Transit Village, in Richmond, California, has replaced parking lots with a dense, mixed-use urban village. *Calthorpe Associates.*

Top: The plan for a transit village in the small town of Cornelius, North Carolina, which lies in the path of the rapid metropolitan expansion of Charlotte. The town center is focused around a new town hall, which will be encircled by a crescent-shaped main street. *Shook.*

Bottom: The construction of the new town hall signals the beginning of a new town center in Cornelius. *Shook.*

family housing; a performing arts center; a plaza that will include retail; and a new parking garage that will include storefronts at ground level.

One of the most talked about transit-oriented projects is Orenco Station, a 210-acre (85-hectare) TND located in the western suburbs of Portland, Oregon, and connected to downtown via the new MAX light-rail line. Because of the strength of the existing market, as well as additional demand generated by a major arterial that runs through the site, Pacific Reality Associates developed a town center for the TND in the early stages of the project. One of the few nearly completed examples of a transit village located in a suburban area, Orenco Station provides some important lessons about the relationship between transit stations, highways, and town centers, which will be explored in the case study of this project included in chapter 7.

In Charlotte, North Carolina, voter approval of a sales tax to help fund a $1 billion regional rail initiative, and the adoption, by many communities, of new urbanist planning and design principles, have combined to trigger plans for transit villages and town centers in many towns and small cities in the metropolitan region. The 100-year-old town of Cornelius, for example, retained the Charlotte-based firm of Shook to plan and design a new downtown centered

Early streetcar suburbs and in-town neighborhoods—like those within Charlotte, North Carolina's Trolley District depicted here—have witnessed the reintroduction of trolley service in recent years, while newer suburbs are experiencing trolley service for the very first time. *Shook.*

on the light-rail line. A new town hall, retail stores, and live/work units have been built to date. Cornelius has been aggressive in committing $5.2 million to acquire 120 acres (49 hectares) east of the light-rail track, and has hired DPZ to draft development standards calling for a mix of apartments, condos, offices, and commercial uses clustered around a rail station. The project will add 950 residential units to this small southern town.

Encouraged by the development of the nearby 350-acre (140-hectare) Vermillion TND, by Nate Bowman, Huntersville acquired 30 acres (12 hectares) adjacent to Vermillion and hired DPZ's Charlotte office to come up with a specific development plan. Bowman is now working with the town to develop a transit village, focused on the old Anchor Mill property and a proposed light-rail station, that will provide Huntersville with a new town center. Similar preparations for transit villages are taking place in the towns of Davidson and Pineville.

In addition to undertaking a light-rail initiative, Charlotte is redeveloping the area known as the Charlotte Trolley District. A grass-roots effort 20 years in the making, the redeveloped district was mas-

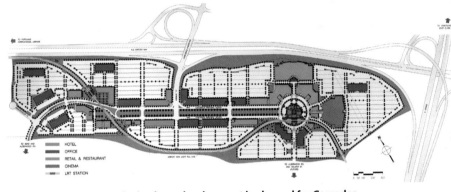

Intensive workplace and mixed-use development is planned for Cascades Station, a transit-oriented development near Portland, Oregon's airport. *LMN Architects.*

ter planned in a community design workshop led by Shook. The Trolley District project will include the revival of the historic trolley line and the development of as many as 11 neighborhood-based stops along the trolley's route. The two-mile (3.2-kilometer) trolley line will reestablish the link between the downtown and a number of intown neighborhoods, including the trendy warehouse district.

Transit-oriented projects are also being planned on a large urban scale; Lindbergh City Center, for example, a major project being developed by Carter & Associates, will involve 47 acres (19 hectares) surrounding a proposed MARTA station located on the outskirts of Buckhead, a suburb of Atlanta. Billed as "the country's first true transit-oriented development," the project will include 1.2 million square feet (111,480 square meters) of office space, much of it earmarked for 3,500 workers from Bell South—which, as part of its commitment to smart growth initiatives, is a key partner in the project. Other elements of Phase I include 330,000 square feet (30,660 square meters) of retail and dining (490,000 square feet—45,520 square meters—at buildout), 220 apartments (400 at buildout), and 288 condominiums (600 at buildout). Unlike many transit villages, which are focused on residential uses, Lindbergh City Center will be a major employment center.

New Urbanist Workplaces

Many of the projects described so far incorporate moderate amounts of office space, much of it located above ground-floor retail. Some also include live/work buildings that blend townhouses with ground-floor offices and retail. Several recent and proposed projects, however, are attempting to incorporate large-scale office and manufacturing uses within town centers and mixed-use districts. In *The Fractured Metropolis,* Jonathan Barnett notes that in many ways, Reston Town Center represents "an office park themed as a downtown."[20] While business and technology parks are far from becoming obsolete, there are signs that not

all companies and workers are enamored of 100,000-square-foot (9,290-square-meter) "work boxes" with 1,000-foot (305-meter) setbacks, surrounded by nothing of more interest than passive, "campuslike" green space; other large office buildings; and acres of parking.

New Urban News has identified 35 mixed-use, new urbanist projects that will incorporate from 400,000 to over 6 million square feet (37,160 to 557,420 square meters) of commercial space, includ-

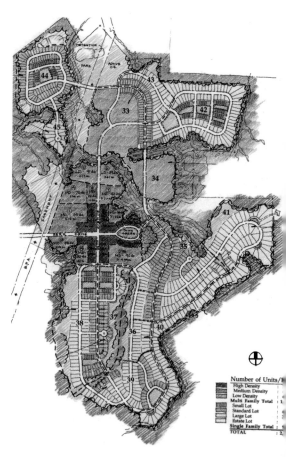

Issaquah Highlands is a 2,000-acre (809-hectare) new urbanist project located 17 miles (27 kilometers) east of Seattle, Washington, in the hills above the town of Issaquah. The plan includes 3,250 dwelling units and a high-density town center.
Calthorpe Associates.

ing offices, light industrial uses, and research and development facilities.[21] Examples include Abacoa (Jupiter, Florida); Celebration (Orlando, Florida); Coffee Creek (Chesterton, Indiana); Northwest Landing (Dupont, Washington); Post Properties's Riverside (Atlanta); and Addison Circle (Addison, Texas); the Victory project, in Dallas (4 million square feet— 371,610 square meters—of office space planned); and the Atlantic Station project, which includes plans for 6 million square feet (557,420 square meters) of office space on a 135-acre (55-hectare) brownfield site in midtown Atlanta.

One of the largest projects is Issaquah Highlands, a 2,000-acre (809-hectare) new town located 17 miles (27 kilometers) east of Seattle, Washington, that will be Microsoft's second major campus. Issaquah Highlands will offer a high-density town center with 400,000 square feet (37,160 square meters) of commercial space distributed along a street grid and around public spaces. The same street grid will connect to a 3 million-square-foot (278,710-square-meter) office district. The town center will also provide a mixed-use transition between the project's intense concentration of employment uses and its residential neighborhoods.

Town center projects vary widely in their approach to incorporating large-scale office uses. Celebration, for example, includes loft office space in the town center and campus-type, single-use districts along the major highways at the edge of the site. The layout of Redmond Town Center revolves around a 350,000-square-foot (32,520-square-meter) lifestyle shopping center and main street; multistory buildings within the town center house all 1.5 million square feet (139,350 square meters) of office space. In San Mateo, California, the Bay Meadows Specific Plan incorporates a 500,000-square-foot (46,450-square-meter) campus-style office district within a mixed-use neighborhood. Multistory office buildings in Bay Meadows enclose one end of a linear park that connects with mixed-use districts, residential neighborhoods, and a Caltrain commuter rail station.

The town center for Issaquah Highlands will offer 400,000 square feet (37,160 square meters) of commercial uses and high-density residential housing along a major north-south arterial. *Calthorpe Associates.*

The King Farm TND has taken a different approach, creating two separate mixed-use districts: a village center, which is centrally located within the TND and incorporates community-oriented uses such as a grocery store, a dry cleaner, and a variety of coffee shops and restaurants; and Irvington Centre, an employment district with nearly 3 million square feet (278,710 square meters) of planned office space. King Farm Boulevard provides a direct link between the two centers. The composition of the site plan reveals some of the underlying zoning that remained in place, challenging the designer's and developer's creativity in pursuing a mixed-use TND.

Irvington Centre adds a major employment center to the King Farm traditional neighborhood development. *Torti Gallas and Partners•CHK, Inc.*

Irvington Centre—described as "a first-class business center that offers an urban atmosphere in a suburban setting"—is located in the southern portion of the site, near the Interstate 270 interchange and the proposed light-rail line. Although it is primarily an employment center, Irvington Centre also includes shops, services, and fine dining oriented toward business users. The buildings of Irvington Centre line the streets, enclosing formal public spaces, and parking is clustered behind buildings, in courtyards and in structures.

Pedestrian-friendly mixed-use office projects are also being incorporated into major suburban commercial centers, including maturing edge cities in search of stronger civic identities. Tysons Corner, Virginia, is a burgeoning edge city with over 80,000 workers and 20 million square feet (1,858,060 square meters) of office space. As the county executive notes, however, "We have almost nothing . . . that is pedestrian-friendly."[22] As part of an effort to address that problem, the Towers Crescent project will introduce an 18-acre (seven-hectare) pedestrian-oriented town center—made up predominantly of office, retail, and restaurant uses—into the space between the Tysons Corner Center shopping mall and a Marriott Hotel. Designed by RTKL and Sasaki Associates, the firms that worked on Reston Town Center, the Towers Crescent project will offer pedestrian-oriented streets

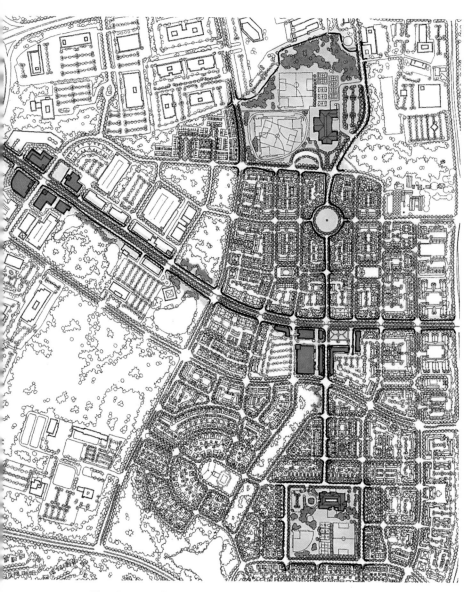

King Farm Boulevard, in Gaithersburg, Maryland, provides a direct connection between the village center (center of the plan) and Irvington Centre (at the western edge of the site). *Torti Gallas and Partners•CHK, Inc.*

and ground-floor retail, restaurants, and office buildings—all grouped around a central plaza punctuated by a large fountain. The project faces extraordinary challenges in connecting with adjacent land uses—and, while it remains to be seen how well an island designed for pedestrians will perform within a sea of automobiles and highways, the project has the potential to create a unique, walkable, human-scale place within a setting often criticized as placeless.

Projects are also grappling with ways to incorporate light industry within mixed-use, pedestrian-friendly settings. In Civano, an environmentally sensitive 65-acre (26-hectare) business park—which

New, mixed-use buildings in Legacy Town Center, in Plano, Texas. *Steve Hinds.*

currently includes a 31,000-square-foot (2,880-square-meter) photovoltaics manufacturing plant—is being developed directly adjacent to the retail and residential center of the community. In Laguna West, which is still struggling to develop its mixed-use retail core, there are Apple Computer and JVC manufacturing plants totaling 750,000 square feet (69,680 square meters), plus another 180,000 square feet (16,720 square meters) of warehouse space, located directly across from the town center district.

The project that truly captures the essence of "reinventing the office park," however, is Legacy Town Center, a $500 million mixed-use town center on a 150-acre (60-hectare) infill site within the vast, 2,665-acre (1,078-hectare) Legacy Office Park, in Plano, Texas, 15 miles (24 kilometers) north of Dallas. The town center will provide shops, restaurants, and nearby housing options for some of the 36,000 people who work in the park, including the 15,000 who work for Electronic Data Systems, which owns the park. According to Legacy director Marilyn Kasko, "The corporations in Legacy recognize this opportunity to enhance the quality of life for many of their employees while increasing their productivity. The nine-to-five workday isn't the standard anymore—workers can't spend hours in their cars each day. This town center is the ultimate amenity for the 36,000 employees in Legacy."[23]

The components that make up the town center include a mixed-use main street area, dubbed the Shops at Legacy; a community entertainment district;

an urban village with lofts, townhouses, and apartments developed by Post Properties; a 404-room Doubletree Hotel; and a three-acre (1.2-hectare) landscaped park, as well as smaller parks and civic spaces. The project is planned to incorporate some 450,000 square feet (41,810 square meters) of retail, 60,000 square feet (5,580 square meters) of loft office space on upper floors, another 250,000 square feet (23,230 square meters) of office space in a separate building, and a mix of 2,700 residential units (including 384 units in Post Legacy Phase I). According to Kasko, "Our goal is to create a good environment where people can be creative."[24]

Publicly Initiated Suburban Town Centers

While private sector interests initiated the majority of the projects described in this chapter, the public sector is also playing an increasingly active role in planning for, promoting, and facilitating the construction of town centers and main streets, especially in the suburbs. These projects are viewed as serving a number of public purposes connected with smart growth, transit development, and economic development; perhaps most important, they are viewed as a means of creating more livable communities with a strong sense of place.

Dozens of town center plans and projects are being initiated by communities throughout the United States. In Illinois alone, town center initiatives have been undertaken in Channahon, New

The Schoolhouse Square section of Olde Schaumburg Centre District, the town center initiated by the Village of Schaumburg. The town center has replaced disconnected commercial parcels with more compact, mixed-use, interconnected development, but is still struggling with details, such as the relationship of buildings to the street. *Village of Schaumburg.*

Lenox, Plainfield, Schaumburg, and Vernon Hills. Leadership is coming from many sources, including local governments and the nonprofit sector. In Channahon, for example, the Catholic Diocese of Joliet has spearheaded efforts to create a village center for the community. After identifying the need for a community gathering place, the diocese donated a 100-acre (40-hectare) parcel of land as the site of the village center and sponsored a design competition that drew 337 registrants and 133 submissions from across the country.

The community-initiated effort in Illinois that has made the most progress, however, is the Olde Schaumburg Centre District in the Village of Schaumburg, an edge city of Chicago. In its effort to create a town center for a community characterized by shopping malls and strip development, the village government implemented a variety of initiatives—including the creation of a town center overlay district and a tax increment financing district, and public investments in parks, civic buildings, and a 65-foot (20-meter) clock tower on the town square. Although most of the community has embraced Olde Schaumburg, the project also has its critics, including one who described the center as a "pedestrian-oriented parking lot." While the majority of public sector difficulties involve financial and regulatory issues, Olde Schaumburg illustrates how challenging it can be for suburban communities to rediscover the essence of good urbanism.

In California, communities like the City of Brea, Glendale, Pasadena, Santa Monica, and Suisun City are all pursuing different types of main street and town center projects. Suisun City, located about halfway between Sacramento and San Francisco, is one of the most interesting efforts, as it involves the complete redevelopment of a small, older town center that had become surrounded by automobile-oriented suburbs.[25] In the late 1980s, after a *San Francisco Chronicle* survey of the Bay Area's 98 municipalities ranked Suisun City last in quality of life, a new mayor and an active citizens' group pushed forward a redevelopment plan, adopted in 1990, that focused on creating a new town center. Over the past decade, the city has worked steadily to clean up its polluted harbor and improve its main street and historic buildings. Suisun City has also initiated infill development throughout the Old Town Harbor area, resulting in the construction of new downtown housing, a new town plaza and performance setting, a marina, and civic institutions (including a new city hall).

In most suburban communities, where regulations and codes were written for automobile-oriented, single-use development, the challenges of creating town centers can be daunting. In Tualatin, Oregon, a suburban community about ten miles (16 kilometers)

south of Portland, 20 years elapsed between the time the city created a new redevelopment district, in 1975, and the 1995 ground breaking for the 19-acre (8-hectare) Tualatin Commons town center. Tualatin Commons is a mixed-use suburban redevelopment made up of offices, rowhouses, a hotel, restaurants, and live/work units dubbed "hoffices" by their designer. The centerpiece of the town center consists of a public plaza and promenade that surround a manmade lake. These amenities are credited with boosting the performance of the hotel and office buildings. According to David Leland, a real estate consultant involved in

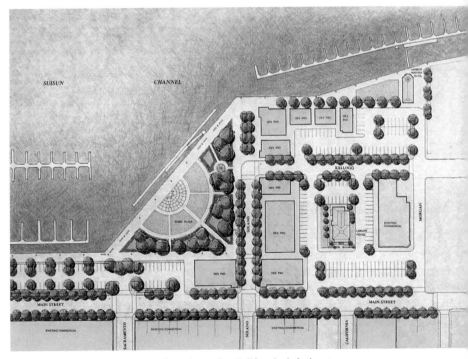

This industrialized harbor area in Suisun City, California, is being transformed from a brownfield into the city's town center. *Suisun City.*

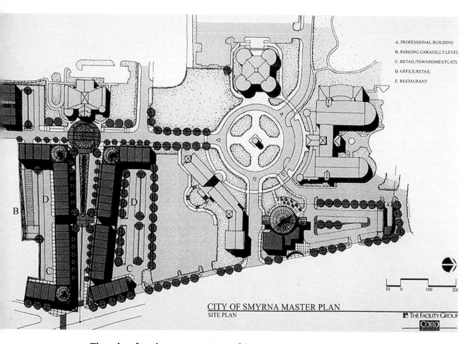

A. PROFESSIONAL BUILDING
B. PARKING GARAGE(2.5 LEVEL)
C. RETAIL/TOWNHOMES/FLATS
D. OFFICE/RETAIL
E. RESTAURANT

CITY OF SMYRNA MASTER PLAN
SITE PLAN

The plan for the town center of Smyrna, Georgia, where several civic buildings will be clustered around a large traffic circle. *Sizemore Floyd.*

the project, office space is leasing at rates 25 percent above market rents. The Tualatin Commons project shows how strong the desire is to create central gathering places in the suburbs, and how even small communities like Tualatin, with a population of about 20,000, can create such places through proactive planning, public investment, partnerships with capable developers, and perseverance.[26]

Community-initiated town center projects can also be found up and down the east coast of the United States, especially in the suburbs of major metropolitan areas of Florida, Georgia, Maryland, New Jersey, North Carolina, South Carolina, and Virginia. In states such as Florida, Maryland, and New Jersey, which have enacted strong growth management and smart growth legislation in recent years, there is statewide support for planning efforts aimed at encouraging more compact development patterns. In other states there are significant regional pockets of activity, including communities near Atlanta, Georgia; Charleston, South Carolina; and Charlotte, North Carolina.

Small communities, like Washington Township, New Jersey (population 48,000), and Mint Hill, North Carolina (population 11,567), are proactively planning and developing small village and town centers to help preserve their identity. They are also looking to village and town centers as ideal settings for higher-density housing, civic buildings, parks, transit stations, and community facilities. Washington Township, a rapidly growing community located 20 minutes from downtown Philadelphia, hired Anton Nelessen and Associates to develop a plan for a 350-acre (142-hectare) TND district that includes a new town center for the community. The plan for Mint Hill, developed by Shook for the town and the McAdams Company, will create a 50-acre (20-hectare) town center with shops, restaurants, and offices. The focal point for Mint Hill's town center is a green promenade, terminating in a plaza in front of a new, 20,000-square-foot (1,860-square-meter) town hall. The plan also includes a theater, a YMCA, and a supermarket, and calls for the use of building types and architectural styles based on the vernacular traditions of the antebellum South.

Two of several town center and transit-oriented plans developed for communities in Maryland as part of the state's smart growth initiatives. *Torti Gallas and Partners•CHK, Inc.*

As would be expected in the case of many community-initiated projects, civic institutions, village greens, and plazas represent key components of the plans for main streets and town centers. In Holly Springs, North Carolina, where the downtown has never been much more than a crossroads, a plan involving a private developer calls for a new town center to meet the needs of the town's growing population. The plan focuses on a village green that is dominated by a town hall in the center; on one side of the green is an amphitheater, and on the other a library and a chamber of commerce building; rows of shops and offices line the other two sides of the green.

Just as small towns are responding to the spread of development in the Charlotte metro area, at least two suburban satellites of Atlanta have taken strong

steps to preserve their small-town character. Decatur, about 10 miles (16 kilometers) east of downtown Atlanta, developed a town center plan aimed at creating an inviting, walkable shopping district. The City of Smyrna (population 30,000), about 10 miles (16 kilometers) northwest of downtown Atlanta, has pursued a similar route. Both jurisdictions have attempted to realize their visions for town centers incrementally, nudging and cajoling commercial interests and enlisting the help of developers in efforts to bring buildings up to the street, locate parking in back, and bring about alternatives to strip commercial formats. Smyrna has been the more proactive, investing heavily in a village green and several civic buildings that have helped to attract private sector investment in office space, retail, and housing. The efforts of the town, the downtown development authority, and Sizemore Floyd Architects, of Atlanta, resulted in a ULI Award for Excellence in 1997.

The largest number of public sector initiatives, including transit villages and town centers planned for unincorporated areas and small towns, are in Maryland, where there is a strong commitment to smart growth. Higher-density efforts are moving forward in suburban cities like Bethesda, Owings Mills, Rockville, and Silver Spring. In Anne Arundel County alone, Torti Gallas and Partners•CHK, Inc., has developed sophisticated transit village and town center plans for Annapolis Center, Hanover Junction, Jessup Center, and North Linthicum Center.

In Silver Spring, a suburban business district in Montgomery County where there was widespread popular opposition to an earlier plan involving a massive office complex and megamall, officials and developers have now signed an agreement to redevelop the center of the district as a town center for the community. The $321 million project will include 1 million square feet (92,900 square meters) of retail, office, residential, and civic space and will emphasize community-oriented commercial shops rather than department stores or entertainment attractions. The project involves heavy public subsidies, amounting to $132 million in state and county funds, to support the construction of a multimodal transit center, parking garages, a public square, townhouses, and a civic building. Public funds are also being provided for the restoration of the 400-seat Silver Theatre, which will be run by the American Film Institute.[27]

In Owings Mills, Baltimore County is backing a $26 million effort to create a pedestrian-oriented main street with shops, offices, 300 homes, a county library, and a college campus, all clustered around a town green.[28] In downtown Bethesda, Federal Realty is now in the fourth phase of its five-block Bethesda Row project. Finally, in Rockville, the city and a group of developers have worked together to clear away yet another dead mall to make way for a new town center incorporating 1.5 million square feet (139,360 square meters) of office, retail, and urban housing on a 7.75-acre (three-hectare) site.

In Florida, increasingly widespread efforts to create main streets and town centers involve older communities such as Stuart, Ft. Myers, Winter Park, and Winter Springs; newer communities such as Kendall; and emerging areas such as the 1,100-acre (445-hectare) redevelopment plan for the Orlando Naval Training Center. By far the most ambitious and rapidly moving effort to date, however, is the 55-acre (22-hectare) CityPlace project, located in the heart of West Palm Beach. The result of a bold redevelopment process initiated under Mayor Nancy Graham over a decade ago, the $550 million project is redefining the downtown.

The number of community-initiated projects touched on here show that, far from being just a passing fad in real estate development, the town center movement is widespread and deep-rooted. The case studies presented in chapters 6 and 7 will take a more in-depth look at projects that provide a rich source of information for the planning, design, and development of town centers and main streets.

Notes
1. Duany Plater-Zyberk & Company, *The Lexicon of the New Urbanism,* June 3, 1999 ed. (Miami: Duany Plater-Zyberk & Company, 1999).
2. For a European perspective on how to categorize and plan for town centers, see Urban and Economic Development Group, *Vital and Viable Town Centres: Meeting the Challenge* (London: HMSO, 1994).
3. Hundreds of small towns and cities throughout the United States are currently working to revitalize historic main streets and town centers through the National Main Street Program. The focus of this book, however, is on projects that involve the substantial creation of new main streets and town centers rather than the revitalization of existing buildings.
4. Site visit report by architect John Montague Massengale,

received as an Internet communication, Monday, September 13, 1999.

5. Peggie Evans, "Population Key for Las Colinas' Urban Center Development," *Dallas Business Journal* 19, no. 51 (1996): 1–2.

6. Ed Duggan, "Miramar Plans $130 Million Project to Create City Center," *Business Journal Serving South Florida,* August 11, 2000.

7. Ibid.

8. The term *new urbanism* was coined to describe a broad movement in architecture, planning, and urban design that adopts urban design practices from traditional urbanism and applies them to new development and redevelopment. New urbanism includes greenfield, infill, and redevelopment work and is being applied at local, regional, state, and federal levels. Although the term *new urbanism* superceded the earlier terms, *neotraditional planning* and *traditional neighborhood development* (TND), the term *TND* continues to be applied, especially to large, master-planned communities—such as Kentlands and Celebration—that adopt a new urbanist approach to planning and design.

9. Southern Village has both a corner store, located within one of its residential neighborhoods, and a village center, located near the center of the property and adjacent to an arterial roadway.

10. Robert Steuteville, "Market Square Is a Retail Prototype," *New Urban News* 4, no. 6 (1999): 7.

11. Robert Steuteville, "New Urbanism in Canada," *New Urban News* 3, no. 2 (1998): 7–11.

12. Robert Steuteville, "New Urbanism Makes Progress in Canada," *New Urban News* 4, no. 2 (1999): 6–8.

13. Terry Poulton, "Park Duvalle Town Center Work Ready to Start," *Business First: The Weekly Business Newspaper of Greater Louisville,* June 2, 2000.

14. See the case study of the Third Street Promenade in Michael D. Beyard et al., *Developing Urban Entertainment Centers* (Washington, D.C.: ULI, 1998), 214–223.

15. Press release, Davis Street Land Company, September 1, 1999.

16. Katheryn Hayes Tucker, "Saying Goodbye to the 'Burbs," *New York Times,* March 5, 2000, pp. 1ff.

17. Trey Garrison, "Urban Villages Offer Residents Intimate Feel," *Dallas Business Journal,* February 2, 1998.

18. "Greyfields Regional Mall Study" (2001), downloaded on February 15, 2002 from http://www.cnu.org/cnu_reports/ Greyfield_Feb_01.pdf. The study was conducted by PricewaterhouseCoopers, the Harvard Graduate School of Design, and Continuum Partners, with funding from the Surdna Foundation, and was published by the Congress for the New Urbanism.

19. Lee S. Sobel, *Greyfields No More* (San Francisco: Congress for the New Urbanism, 2002).

20. Jonathan Barnett, *The Fractured Metropolis* (New York: HarperCollins, 1995).

21. Rob Steuteville, *New Urbanism and Traditional Neighborhood Development; Comprehensive Report and Best Practices Guide* (Ithaca, NY.: New Urban News, 2000), 5-1–5-6.

22. Michael D. Shear, "New Town Center Planned to Put a 'Heart' in Tysons Design Aims to Appeal to Pedestrians," *Washington Post,* February 24, 1999.

23. Post Properties, press release (www.prnewswire.com [October 20, 1999]).

24. "In the Works . . . Legacy Town Center," *Planning* 64, no. 6 (1998).

25. See the online journal *Terrain* for a thorough case study of Suisun City's town center redevelopment efforts (http://www.terrain.org/Archives/Issue_3/Suisun/suisun.html [October 24, 2000]).

26. See the online journal *Terrain* for a thorough case study of the Tualatin Commons project (http://www.terrain.org/ Archives/Issue_4/tualatin/tualatin.html [October 25, 2000]).

27. "Scaled-Down Downtown Brightens Silver Spring," *Planning* 64, no. 6 (1998).

28. David Nitkin, "Vision of Owings Mills Builds on Main Street: Proposed Town Center Would Curtail Sprawl, Give Area a Heart,'" *Baltimore Sun,* January 4, 2000.

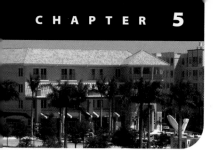

CHAPTER 5

Launching a New Town Center:
Feasibility and Financing

"Do not be afraid to dream ... and then set out to make it happen."

—J. C. NICHOLS, *a founding member of ULI*

The credo "It's a place, not a project," and the directive to create "immersive environments" both point toward fundamental differences between conventional, single-use real estate development and town center or mixed-use projects. More than most other types of real estate projects, successful mixed-use development requires a capable, experienced, and diverse development team; thorough planning; substantial and "patient" capital; and a great deal of creativity.

To be successful, a project needs:

- Sound objectives;
- A viable development entity;
- A thorough market analysis that takes account of market synergy;
- A creative development strategy that is targeted to market needs;
- A thorough financial analysis to determine the project's feasibility and assess financial alternatives;
- A sound financing plan;
- A plan and design that will yield functional and marketable buildings for each use, while achieving synergy between uses and creating a sense of place for the project as a whole.

Knowing what type of place is being created sounds like common sense, but is in reality a crucial step that is commonly ignored. Failing in this could result in a project with a built-in identity crisis—a place where the pieces conflict with one another (most often because of a mix of urban and suburban buildings, streets, and open spaces). The determination of what sort of place will be created will affect the scale and mix of land uses and the nature of the commercial tenants to be assembled.

For visitors, town centers and main streets provide a very different experience than what would be encountered in shopping centers, and their urban design and land use mix represent radical departures from the conventional shopping-center format; nevertheless, town center and main street projects need to emulate many of the tenanting, management, and marketing practices that have made shopping centers so successful. Thus, at the same time that town center projects are experimenting with combinations of local and regional retail, entertainment, dining, cultural, and civic uses, their retail strategies (including tenant mix, leasing, and management) should be largely consistent with those that have proven successful for various categories of shopping centers over the past several decades.[1]

Decisions about the development program and concept should flow naturally from market studies, site location, the overall character of the existing community and of adjacent land uses, the proposed density of the project, transit access, and other factors. First and foremost, however, town center developers need to determine how receptive the community is to ideas that run against typical land use regulations—such as the vertical mixing of uses; narrow streets, alleys, and lanes; shared parking; flex housing units; and the wide assortment of other changes required to create a pedestrian-oriented environment. Developing a town center is difficult enough even when the community is supportive, but it becomes a daunting, time-consuming task where there is inflexibility or outright opposition.

A key nonfinancial objective of the Cascade Station project, which is being developed by the Trammell Crow Company and Bechtel outside of Portland, Oregon, is to provide concentrated, transit-oriented development capable of spurring public and private investment in a 5.5-mile (8.9-kilometer) light-rail spur connecting downtown Portland to the Portland International Airport. *LMN Architects.*

Development Objectives and the Development Team

Both financial and nonfinancial development objectives must be well defined from the outset. The objectives may be quite different depending on who is involved: a private developer may be seeking to maximize return on investment, a public entity may be seeking to revitalize a commercial area or create a center for an area that has none, and the developer of a master-planned community may be seeking to create a sense of place for the community while also obtaining a reasonable return. The nature and relative importance of these objectives will shape the project; and, as planning and development continue, all decisions will be tied in one way or another to these initial objectives—either because each decision will be evaluated in terms of its conformance to the spirit of the objectives, or because some decisions may lead to a reassessment of the initial objectives.

Moreover, in a complex deal with numerous players from the public and private sectors—often the case with town center or mixed-use projects—differing objectives usually lead to conflicts. Thus, it is important that all parties understand the objectives of the other parties from the outset.

Whatever entity initiates the project and however many participants are involved in the venture, ultimately the project must be undertaken and controlled by a master developer. Master developers of mixed-use projects should have, at a minimum:

■ Enough organizational depth—including a multi-talented, resourceful real estate team—to respond to opportunities and problems. Entrepreneurial spirit is necessary, but it is no substitute for strong management.

■ The ability to endure potentially higher levels of risk and longer lead times until profits are realized.

■ Access to sizable financial resources (and "patient money"), especially at the early stages. During the project's most critical early stages, considerable equity capital will be needed to fund predevelopment costs; and, during the construction phase, debt capital sources must allow the developer to defer the amortization of debt until a stabilized income stream is achieved.

■ Substantial control over the subject property and all major aspects of the development process. When an unforeseen marketing, financial, engineering, or political problem arises, the master developer must be able to swiftly assess its impact on the entire development and rearrange financing or scheduling if necessary. Having to answer to numerous sources and levels of command is a definite liability for the developer of a mixed-use project.

Pentagon Row, in Washington, D.C., is an example of how developers can partner to create mixed-use projects, allowing each firm to focus on its area of expertise. Federal Realty Investment Trust developed and manages the retail component, while Post Properties developed and manages the residential units located on the upper floors. *Steve Hinds.*

Master developers of town centers are, by definition, involved in multiple product lines, not in a single type of real estate. Because these product lines vary significantly and require different approaches and skills, this factor in itself can create significant problems: many developers who are highly proficient in creating one type of product, for example, have run into major pitfalls when trying to develop another. Thus, many master developers choose to enter partnerships with other developers who have particular specialties. A master developer with expertise in retail development, for example, might bring in office developers, apartment developers, or hotel developers to develop, own, and/or operate portions of the project. Federal Realty Investment Trust and Post Properties, for example, have worked together on a number of projects that combine retail and apartments, an arrangement that allows each to draw on the expertise of the other to create a successful development.

In some cases it is advisable to develop partnerships simply to spread the risk. For example, the Peterson Companies is developing Downtown Silver Spring in a partnership with Folger Pratt, an office developer, even though the Peterson Companies is proficient in office development. The partnership allows each developer to focus on specific aspects of a very large and complex town center project while also spreading the risk financially.

Evaluating Sites and Conducting Market Analyses

The identification of a site suitable for a town center is as much an art as a science: it is based on the observations of an experienced person who has a thorough understanding of both the market and of town center development.

The constraints that determine whether a site will be appropriate for town center development differ from those that affect single-purpose projects. And, although the sites for mixed-use development vary widely, they generally have several features in common. First, they must either be substantial in size or have enough holding capacity to accommodate multiple uses within an urban, street-oriented environment. Most town centers are built on sites that range in size from ten to 50 acres (four to 20 hectares).

Second, because such facilities are likely to generate considerable auto and pedestrian traffic, sites for town center projects should provide visual exposure,

be within easy reach of existing thoroughfares, and offer numerous access points. Although some town center sites have succeeded without these qualities—including Haile Village Center and Market Street at Celebration, both of which are profiled in this book—town centers that lack good access and exposure will generally perform less well financially.

Third, town centers are usually located on infill sites, which offer proximity to multiple markets; for example, sites are often located near the heart of a mature residential or business community, or within a transitional area between different uses and activities. To succeed, a town center must become a focal point for the immediate area.

Fourth, sites for town centers must be located within a jurisdiction that is favorably disposed toward flexible or mixed-use zoning. If the parcel does not already carry mixed-use zoning, approvals for mixed-use development must be achievable within a reasonable period of time and with a reasonable amount of effort.

Once a site has been identified as a suitable candidate for a town center, more in-depth analyses are required to confirm or counter the initial evaluation. In the case of town center developments, determining market potential is really a matter of assessing multiple market potentials: first, each element of the project should be evaluated for its ability to stand alone, as a marketable and financially feasible development;

■ Quantitative identification of potential market absorption, by time period and product line, for the specific site;

■ Determination of the overall development potential for the specific town center project under analysis.

The development potential for public, non-revenue-generating, or ancillary uses should also be considered at this time, to determine both the level of potential support for such uses from the public and nonprofit sectors, as well as their potential contribution to other uses within the project. To assess a proposed cultural facility, for example, the developer would need to determine whether the facility would attract patrons; whether it would benefit other uses; how it would affect parking demands; and whether sufficient public, institutional, or other support would be available to make such a use financially feasible.

While the market analysis should keep in mind that each element of the project should be able to stand on its own as a marketable and financially feasible development, the assessment must also consider the market synergy resulting from a combination of complementary uses in a single complex, and the market potential that can be tapped by the creation of a new kind of real estate product and place. Analysis of other town center projects in the region can be helpful in this regard.

There are essentially three kinds of market synergy that can be achieved in a mixed-use project. The first is derived from direct, on-site market support. For example, office workers, hotel guests, or residents will support a certain volume of nearby retail and restaurant business, and office tenants will generate a certain level of business for a nearby hotel and a certain number of occupants for nearby residences. Market analysis techniques similar to those described in this chapter can usually be used to calculate this first kind of synergy. Estimates of the on-site market for retail space are particularly critical, because on-site uses often provide a significant market for retail.

Phillips Place enjoys good access and visibility from busy arterials in Charlotte, North Carolina.

second, market studies should consider the synergy that results when complementary uses are combined in a single complex. Overall market synergy should be seriously evaluated only after the developer has determined that a sufficient market exists for each major use in and of itself.

Market analysis for town center projects involves

■ Data gathering, field research, and statistical analysis to determine the current and projected levels of supply and demand for each potential use within specified market areas;

A Hampton Inn & Suites, a cinema, and Post Properties apartments add synergy to the retail and dining establishments of Phillips Place.

country that combine luxury condominiums with luxury hotels; the residents of the condos have the direct benefit of access to the luxury services of the hotel, as well as the indirect benefit that comes from the "image" of being associated with the hotel. To take advantage of the marketing power of the hotel brand, the names of many of these projects feature the hotel name—for example, the Ritz-Carlton Hotel and Residences Georgetown, in Washington, D.C.

Hotels can contribute to synergy by enhancing the marketability of office and residential components. Similarly, retail and restaurant uses can provide an attractive and convenient shopping environment for hotel guests, improving the marketability of the hotel component. Other uses and amenities—such as civic, recreational, cultural, or entertainment facilities—contribute to this kind of synergy by enhancing the project's image and environment and making the project as a whole, as well as its individual components, more visible and marketable. While in the first type of synergy the main beneficiaries are retail and hotel components, in the second type the main beneficiaries are office and residential components, which gain marketability from the amenity value of the other uses.

The third kind of synergy is derived from the fact that mixed-use developments, by virtue of their larger scale, variety of uses, multiple buildings, attractive public spaces, and large construction budgets, offer the

The second kind of synergy derives from the indirect benefits of amenities and other uses. For example, retail and hotel uses do not directly generate revenues for office or residential space, but they can serve as important amenities for those uses, which can lead to faster lease-up at higher rents. Millennium Partners, a New York–based firm, has undertaken numerous downtown mixed-use projects around the

Good design can reveal hidden markets for main street office and residential products that are uncommon in suburban markets. The popularity of the main street design of Winter Park Village, in Winter Park, Florida, encouraged the developer to add this office space to the project. *Lee S. Sobel.*

space on the property. Thus, good urban design and place making can sometimes unearth market potential not previously identified—although it is unwise to bank on this eventuality.

In the first two types of synergy, some uses generate markets or value and others benefit from them; in the third type, the creation of a sense of place, all uses tend to benefit evenly. This synergy is indicative of a principal goal of town center and mixed-use development: to create a project of sufficient size, diversity, impact, and design quality that it becomes greater than the sum of its parts—a place or a district, rather than simply a building or project. Some projects, for example, have been developed in areas where market analyses did not show strong support for any of the proposed uses as freestanding entities because none could establish a sufficient sense of place to overcome the site's shortcomings; however, once the uses were developed together, in sufficient scale and with the right design, they succeeded.

At the same time, overly optimistic assumptions about synergy have been the weak points in many mixed-use projects, particularly where uses were oversized or questionable for the location. Experts emphasize the need to ensure that each major component has viable market support from the surrounding market—a strategy that implies, essentially, that the project should be financially feasible even if little or no synergy occurs; if the synergy turns out to be significant, then that should be viewed as an attractive bonus. This conservative approach becomes even more important when retail, office, entertainment, hotel, and other uses are phased in over time, or when phasing is uncertain, as in the case of performing arts centers, museums, and similar facilities over which the master

opportunity to create a whole new sense of place for an area or district. In fact, well-designed public spaces can be the defining element of a project, and its single most important amenity. At Winter Park Village, in Winter Park, Florida, for example, an area that lacked an established office market, the developer found the design of the town center and retail main street was so compelling that it created an opportunity to develop office

developer has little, if any, control. In general, developers attempting to assess synergy in a project must temper analysis with seasoned judgment and experience.

Feasibility Analysis

Once the market has been analyzed, a specific program must be developed and tested to determine financial feasibility. Although the process is iterative, it is described here as essentially a three-step procedure.

- Defining alternative development programs that specify the mix and scale of uses, critical mass, initial configuration, timing and phasing, and land assembly.
- Determining the financial feasibility of each program by estimating development costs, operating costs and revenues, and long-term cash flow. The purpose of this step is to identify the financially optimal program.
- Structuring financing: this includes making decisions about the mix, by project component, of debt and equity and construction and permanent financing—and determining the number and type of public and private financing sources to be involved.

These steps, perhaps the most critical in the development process, require input from the entire development team—market analysts, planners, architects, engineers, contractors, financial analysts, financial institutions, and property managers—all working closely with the developer. The process usually requires several iterations until the best fit is found. Fundamentally, the program must be marketable, feasible, and financeable, and must be able to clear the public approval process.

The following discussion is presented primarily from the point of view of a private developer seeking the optimal program and most profitable development strategy for a given site. If the development is approached from another point of view, the process may differ.

The development program—essentially the grand plan, laid out in some detail—must ultimately specify the mix and scale of uses; the configuration and massing of the project; the timing and phasing of elements; and the plan for land assembly, if the land is not already assembled.

Mix and Scale of Uses

As the first step, the principal components of the development program must be specified (for example, housing units by type, office or retail square footage, number of hotel rooms), taking into consideration timing, phasing, allocated acreage, and alternatives. The mix and scale of uses are derived from several sources—including the creative ideas of the developer and his or her team—and are influenced by a number of factors: the market analysis; the characteristics of the site; the physical constraints and opportunities; the financing environment; any applicable zoning regulations; and the developer's specific objectives and capabilities, including those that are determined by financing.

To determine the mix and scale of uses, the developer first identifies the cornerstone use and complementary uses, then develops several alternatives for configuring and phasing the project. The market analysis will have yielded information on the relative market support for each use; on the basis of that analysis, the developer can make a preliminary determination of the project's cornerstone use. When market support is relatively balanced among uses, the cornerstone use cannot be identified until a full financial analysis—including a sensitivity analysis, to determine how the addition or exclusion of alternative uses will affect the project's overall financial performance—has been completed.

In most privately sponsored projects, the cornerstone uses will become obvious at an early stage; in fact, one use might already have surfaced as the assumed cornerstone even before the formal market analysis begins. Either retail or residential uses, for example, are often assumed to be the cornerstones in many town center and urban village projects, and the market analysis is undertaken primarily to determine the size and timing of these uses and the market for other, complementary uses.

Whatever scale and mix of uses are chosen, the uses must be compatible and appeal to similar markets. Some of this compatibility occurs naturally; for example, a first-class hotel operator is not likely to

be attracted to a mixed-use project unless its office, residential, and retail portions are planned to be equally upscale. Because the retail portion of a project usually cannot succeed unless it appeals to multiple markets—and because much of the retail market will be off site—compatibility issues are most likely to arise between the retail portion and the rest of the project. If, for example, the retail market is more downscale than the market for the other uses,

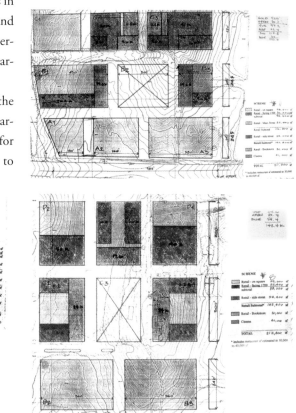

The developers and designers of Southlake Town Square, in Southlake, Texas, went through numerous iterations before settling on the final mix and urban design for the project. These three scenarios show alternative locations for the cinema (in red), a large bookstore, and four different categories of retail. *David M. Schwarz/ Architectural Services, Inc.*

resolving the "image conflict" is critical, as the retail portion usually plays a major role in creating the project's image and identity. In most cases, if the retail component cannot be brought in line with the rest of the project, then it should not be undertaken unless it is deemed to be the primary use. An alternative is to develop very modest retail shops and cafés, and ground-floor residential units that can be converted to office and retail uses in the future. Examples include projects such as Riverside and downtown Celebration, where ground-floor residential is, in fact, being converted into office space. This approach can help establish the types of diverse activities and street life that potential residents and tenants anticipate in town center projects, until adequate demand exists for more substantial retail and office uses.

While retail is perhaps the most important use in most town centers, and thus requires considerable attention, housing is an essential ingredient that distinguishes town centers from simple shopping centers. Todd Zimmerman, of Zimmerman Volk Associates, a residential real estate consultant with extensive experience in projects involving urban housing products, believes strongly that multifamily housing should be included early in town center projects to establish a human presence and a minimum level of everyday activity on the street.

When people actually live within a town center—whether it is above shops and offices, or in rowhouses and apartment buildings—they quickly assume ownership of the public realm: watching over streets, parking areas, and public spaces; noting any shortcomings in the appearance and maintenance of shops and infrastructure; and taking part in the life of

Residential is the cornerstone use in Post Properties's mixed-use projects. Pictured is Riverside near Atlanta. *Steve Hinds.*

the town center simply by carrying out their daily routines. The comings and goings of residents, office workers, moviegoers, diners, shoppers, concertgoers, people watchers, walkers, and delivery people all contribute to the round-the-clock rhythm of place that occurs in a well-rounded town center. Housing provides "eyes on the street." Notes Thomas Brink, of RTKL Associates, "Lighted residential windows above the shops at night impart a sense of reassurance."

The most common mistake among developers of early town centers was to underestimate the market for housing. In many cases, underestimates continue to occur simply because the normal residential market analysis, which looks for sales and leasing of "comparable" housing—cannot find lofts, live/work units, apartments over retail, and urban townhouses

Although the developer of Mizner Park, in Boca Raton, Florida, did not initially want to build residential units above retail, these units have been extremely popular and represent the most consistently successful element of the project.

itation on the number of floors and the intensity of the entertainment uses, it made little financial or place-making sense to sacrifice the second-floor retail space for residential units, which would have weakened the critical mass of the commercial core. Instead, the developers chose to create urban housing adjacent to the two-story commercial core. In Valencia Town Center Drive, in Valencia, California, it made sense to avoid locating housing near the regional shopping mall, which connects to one end of the main street.

to use as a basis for comparison, especially in suburban settings. While caution may have been warranted in the past, projects like Addison Circle, CityPlace, Haile Village Center, Kentlands, Lakelands, Mashpee Commons, Miami Lakes, Mizner Park, Orenco Station, and Riverside have provided robust evidence of untapped markets for town center housing all over the country. While some town center projects, particularly those developed on the scale of a regional mall, may be too oriented toward entertainment and commercial uses to place residential above commercial facilities, in many cases the decision to exclude residential development results in a missed opportunity to add vitality to new places while tapping an underserved market.

Easton Town Center, in Columbus, Ohio, was approved for a maximum of two stories, and both stories were permitted as commercial use. Given the lim-

Lofts (pictured here), live/work units, and other urban residential products new to suburban Portland, Oregon, have proven highly successful in Orenco Station Town Center.

While these two markets might well have supported housing over retail, the logistics for the particular projects dictated placing housing adjacent to, rather than above, ground-floor retail. Other projects, such as CityPlace, in West Palm Beach, Florida; Pentagon Row, in Arlington, Virginia; and Paseo Colorado, in Pasadena, California; place housing directly on top of large-format destination retail.

Project Configuration and Critical Mass

Once the mix and scale of uses have been determined, an initial configuration must be developed that indicates how the uses will be massed, both individually and collectively, on the site. Critical to this effort is the configuration and framing of streets, open space, and public areas, as these are usually critical elements in establishing a sense of place for any successful town center or mixed-use project. The configuration should also take into account maintenance and management issues, because these will affect operating costs once the project is open. Precise designs or sizes need not be indicated, but each use, including mixed-use buildings, should be placed in a suitable location on the site. The purpose of this exercise is essentially to test the program for a physical fit.

A key goal in the development of an initial configuration is to ensure that the necessary critical mass is achieved. Critical mass depends, in turn, on scale and density, and on physical and functional integration; it must also be linked to the phasing plan for the project. The scale and density required to achieve critical mass will vary with the market, the location, and the regulatory framework. In some small projects, achieving critical mass may simply be a matter of attaining sufficient density and creating an appropriate mix of uses and tenants. In more ambitious projects, which seek to create a stronger sense of place and identity, scale may be very important as well, particularly when the project must overcome the ill effects of surrounding uses or is designed to compete on a regional scale. Thoughtful planning and design are crucial at this early stage to ensure physical and functional integration.

Physical integration means that buildings and activities are interconnected via a network of pedestrian-oriented streets, walkways, and public spaces, rather than developed as isolated pods or pads that are primarily automobile oriented. Functional integration refers to the synergy between various uses; it is the fine-grained, carefully orchestrated arrangement that determines, for example, where different types of retail shops are located in relation to one another and in relation to the restaurants, cafés, cinemas, and other uses that make up the core of a town center. (Pet shops, for instance, are best not located adjacent to restaurants; loud, late-night entertainment is best kept separate from residential units.)

Numerous alternative concept plans, reflecting several options for the mix and scale of uses, are generally drawn up for the initial massing and configuration. Although the initial conceptual plans are only preliminary and need not include much in the way of detail, the final conceptual design provides the foundation for the completed project—and as such, is a fundamental step in the development process.

Timing and Phasing

Most town center or mixed-use projects are not constructed *en masse* but are phased over time. In addition to being a practical necessity, phasing is one of the means by which many developers minimize their risks and hedge their bets. While phasing may be the only logical approach in very large mixed-use projects, smaller projects may benefit as well. There will always be tradeoffs, however, between developing the project in increments and all at once. Each situation dictates a different phasing strategy, and no one approach is best; nonetheless, developers considering phasing decisions for town centers should keep a number of issues in mind.

Inherent uncertainties in the development process should be recognized upfront, and flexibility must be built into the phasing plan from the start. In mixed-used development, the list of risks (both seen and unforeseen) is long. Because predevelopment planning and construction for town center projects frequently require long periods of time, the likelihood that the overall development climate will change during the planning process is greatly increased. In addition, mixed-use projects—by definition—involve separate land use markets, which have their own cycles. If the market for one of the uses should sour during the planning process, this could wreak havoc on carefully laid plans, especially when a painstakingly crafted balance of uses is important to a project's success. For example, when internal changes within the industry caused the cinema market to sour in the late 1990s, many cinema operators pulled out of town center projects, creating significant problems for the developers. Because of the potential for such difficulties, it is important for developers to seek flexibility during the approval process so that they can respond to fluctuations in single-family, multifamily, office, and retail markets.

In addition, because the first phases of the project will set the tone for everything that follows, these phases must succeed on their own in order to ensure that the project starts off on the right foot. In fact, some town center and mixed-use projects that were developed in stages suffered from "image problems" after the first component was constructed and was not an initial success. If the first phase does not succeed, the developer may well not get the opportunity to build a second phase.

Several strategies can help to ensure the success of the initial phases of town center projects. The first is to establish a central gathering place or to create a demonstration section of a main street. National commercial tenants, in particular, are becoming more and more savvy about town center projects and are actively looking for locations along double-loaded main streets. To create such locations early in the project, the developers of Southlake Town Square, in Southlake, Texas, carefully constructed the front portions of facing blocks, while leaving the rear portions for a later phase. (This strategy also allowed the developers to avoid triggering parking requirements that call for parking decks to be constructed as each major block within the town center is completed.) Because more than one developer is often involved as mixed-use, entertainment, hotel, and various residential elements are moved forward, it is all the more important—and all the more challenging—to begin establishing the town center by developing entire blocks and streets.

The second strategy is to build several uses at once to create an initial critical mass without overbuilding any single product category. In the initial phases of his projects, George de Guardiola, the developer of Abacoa Town Center, in Jupiter, Florida, prefers to avoid a speculative approach, and advises developers to only "design what you can lease." Todd Zimmerman recommends building a multifamily component early on, to inject the town center with vitality and round-the-clock activity.

Third, while the current phase is important, the developer must always be thinking ahead. One of the biggest oversights in town center and mixed-use projects is to focus exclusively on the first phase, preempting options for effectively integrating subsequent elements into the development program. The more intricate and complementary the integration of various uses, the more crucial it becomes to plan each building phase carefully, both to accommodate further development and to ensure that each phase is functionally and financially viable.

Fourth, it is crucial, while juggling the demands of various phases of development, to avoid overtaxing the staff; the development team's capacity to undertake the various elements of the project simultaneously should be carefully monitored and managed to ensure that the project can proceed in a timely fashion without overwhelming the staff.

Fifth, one particularly important piece of advice: "Don't sell your front door": selling off developed and undeveloped parcels too early in a town center project can mean missing out on the accrued value of the property as the town center is built out and achieves critical mass. Developers need to have "patient money" during the development of mixed-use or town center projects in order to realize their long-term value. In practical terms, this means working to create the financial wherewithal and structure that allow for such patience in terms of equity and debt financing and the phasing of infrastructure.

Finally, successful development may sometimes require that portions or phases of the property be strategically sold off to other developers or owners. Ownership of Reston Town Center, for example, has evolved over time: the original developer, the Reston Land Corporation and Himmel & Co./MKDG, sold the entire project after completion of the first

Phase II of Reston Town Center, in Reston, Virginia, will add residential units and more residential-oriented public spaces to Phase I of the town center, which featured high-rise office, ground-floor retail, an urban plaza, and an ice skating rink. *Sasaki Associates.*

phase; the first completed phase was sold to Equity Office Properties, and the land for the second phase (now being developed) was sold to Terrabrook.

Reston Town Center's well-known Phase I focused predominantly on office buildings and on the shops and restaurants of Market Street. Phase II will expand office, retail, and restaurant space and add residential uses to the mix. "Bringing a broad range of homes to Reston Town Center will make it a *real* place," explained Street-Works development manager Jon Eisen, a consultant on the project. "Adding this element to the already thriving town center guarantees additional success."

The plan for Cornelius Town Center, a small-scale, mixed-use development in North Carolina initiated by the town of Cornelius, calls for three initial phases. The first involved the demolition of old warehouse and mill structures that were on the site, the construction of new public roads and utilities, and the development of a new, 40,000-square-foot (3,720-square-meter) grocery store and seven small retail shops. The second phase provided for additional new infrastructure, such as site lighting, and the construction of a new, 25,000-square-foot (2,320-square-meter) town hall. In the third phase, two- and three-story "main street" buildings, including approximately 40 new townhouse units, will be constructed along the main thoroughfares. The master plan depicts further potential development and a suggested way in which the new infrastructure should continue to evolve beyond the initial phases. Future phases reflected in the master plan include a light-rail station, structured parking for commuters and visitors, a police station or other civic use, the renovation of a mill building, and the addition of multifamily residential units. The master developer in this case is the town of Cornelius, which is in charge of planning and phasing; the town is providing infrastructure and delineating land uses, then selling parcels to developers for development.

Land Assembly and Purchase

Land for town center projects must be assembled on a scale—and at a price and associated lease or purchase terms—that realistically reflects opportunities for development. Acquiring too much land can create heavy carrying costs that can undermine financial feasibility or pressure a developer to build faster than the market will bear. Acquiring too little land, on the other hand, can constrain effective design and programming and leave insufficient room to grow, or to provide parking and amenities.

In general, developers of town centers have a strong interest in controlling adjacent land uses and capturing the values created by the development. This interest may take several forms:

- A desire to discourage directly competitive developments in the immediate environs of the town center;
- A desire to encourage complementary development on adjacent parcels to achieve synergy or critical mass;
- A desire to discourage incompatible or deleterious uses around the fringes of a town center;
- A desire to benefit from rising land values and to take advantage of attendant development opportunities in adjacent areas.

Because town center projects often involve relatively large sites—and numerous landowners—land assembly can be more difficult than in the case of single-use projects. In many instances, land assembly is facilitated by the public sector, which often takes the lead—using condemnation proceedings, if necessary, to acquire the land. If the public sector is not involved, the process is often more difficult, and the developer must first target the owners of key parcels, then diplomatically approach each one individually.

Market factors determine the land price, and a developer negotiating a land purchase price must have a good understanding of the market and how the proposed project will perform financially. Developers can sometimes take advantage of "free look" periods by making an offer and putting down a refundable deposit, but frequently they must put down nonrefundable "earnest money" to obtain an exclusive option to purchase the land; this gives them time to perform due diligence and to evaluate the feasibility of the project. When numerous parcels are involved, the land acquisition process can be very tricky.

When the land is controlled by a single owner, which is often the case in suburban areas (particularly in large greyfield sites, such as aging shopping-center properties), the developer has more flexibility in arranging the purchase or lease of the property and can undertake market analyses and preliminary financial analyses before purchasing the land or even acquiring an option on it. Working with a single landowner also allows the developer to lower carrying costs by arranging for a phased acquisition of the land. This was the case at Phillips Place, in Charlotte, North Carolina.

Whatever the approach or situation, land costs are a critical factor in determining whether a town center project will succeed or fail. In many cases, town center projects can support higher land values than single-use projects, but because land suitable for town center projects is often very expensive, a developer needs to have a clear understanding of the site's true potential before negotiating a land purchase or land lease agreement.

Financial Analysis

Once the program or alternative programs have been selected, they must be tested for feasibility, with the eventual goal of identifying the program that is financially optimal. The purpose of the financial analysis is to define and optimize the development program, to assess the prospects of financial success or failure with reasonable accuracy, and thus to determine whether or not to proceed, and how. The financial analysis for a town center shows capital costs, operating revenues and expenses, and return on investment (ROI); the determination of ROI includes a complex analysis of cash flows and internal rates of return (frequently for five, ten, or 15 years). Any financial analysis must be based on a model that can respond to change.

A key element to consider in the analysis is how the multifaceted nature of town center projects—and of the proposed project in particular—will affect costs and revenues. The financial numbers associated with mixed-use projects are very different from those associated with single-use projects; those differences derive from several factors:

- Because sites for town center projects must appeal to multiple markets, they are usually well located and often very expensive per square foot.
- Because of the complex nature of town center projects, initial planning costs may be greater than for single-use projects. For a large and compli-

cated project, it is not unusual for the developer to have $10 million tied up before making the first draw on the construction loan. In fact, it is easy to invest $1 or $2 million before knowing for sure whether there is a project to develop at all. The complexity of development often results in a higher-than-normal ratio of soft costs to construction costs.

■ Land carrying costs are often quite different from those associated with single-use projects. On the one hand, because of the large size of town center projects, land parcels are often larger, meaning that land carrying costs will be greater than for competing single-use projects on small parcels. On the other hand, because a mixed-use program can be absorbed more quickly than a single-use program, land carrying costs will likely be lower; a 50-acre (20-hectare) parcel planned strictly for office space might take ten years to be built out and absorbed, whereas the same parcel that includes apartments and retail uses, in addition to office uses, may be fully built out and absorbed in only five years.

■ In a mixed-use development, per-square-foot construction costs for each use will likely be higher than the construction costs for the same uses in single-use projects. This is especially true for mixed-use buildings, where the cost of mixing uses will likely result in both higher soft and hard costs, including construction costs, legal costs, and design fees.

■ The amount and cost of common areas and amenities, which must be reflected in the pro forma

analyses for each use, may be larger or smaller than those normally associated with single-use projects.

■ Because of the potential for shared parking, the amount of parking required, and the associated construction costs, will likely be lower than if each use had been developed separately.

■ Depending on the nature of the project, operating costs for mixed-use projects may be higher or lower than for single-use projects.

■ The performance of a town center project may be superior to that of competing single-use projects, including both faster lease-up, higher long-term occupancy rates, and higher rents. For example, according to Gadi Kaufmann, of Robert Charles Lesser & Co., in Chevy Chase, Maryland, the firm's research indicates that town centers can draw from a significantly larger trade area than comparably sized single-use commercial shopping centers.

Because the configurations and success rates of projects differ greatly, it is impossible to say categorically to what degree costs or revenues will vary. The point is that although separate analyses must be performed for each use to ensure that each is viable in its own right, the analyses must also take into consideration the peculiarities of town center projects that will affect costs and revenues.

Perhaps more important, because of the range of factors that are unique to town center development, estimations of costs and revenues are more complicated than for single-use developments—and subject to greater miscalculation. The assumptions about costs and revenues differ significantly—not only between mixed-use and single-use projects but from one mixed-use project to the next; thus, even an experienced mixed-use developer must take care to assess all the appropriate issues before projecting costs and revenues.

Expected returns for town center projects are generally in line with those for other real estate development projects. For example, the publicly traded TrizecHahn Corporation has recently undertaken two major mixed-use projects—Hollywood and Highland,

The success of Phase I of Redmond Town Center, in Redmond, Washington, which opened in 1997, has led to the profitable sale of the project and to a city-approved increase in the total commercial square footage. The next phase will add a 110,000-square-foot (10,220-square-meter) Bon Marché, the town center's first department store, and an upscale, 262-room Hilton hotel. *LMN Architects.*

and Paseo Colorado—for which, on a portfolio basis, the anticipated financial returns were as follows: projected stabilized return on cost, 11 percent; projected stabilized return on TrizecHahn equity, 19 percent; levered internal rate of return to TrizecHahn, approximately 25 percent.

Financial analysis is also a critical part of ongoing asset management. Mixed-use projects often evolve, grow, and improve, and financial performance can frequently change for the better as the project matures. For example, at the Redmond Town Center project, in Redmond, Washington, which was built by Winmar

and first opened in August of 1997, a number of changes in ownership and program have already improved, or are expected to improve, the financial performance of the project. One of four properties in the Pacific Northwest acquired by Macerich and the Ontario Teachers Pension Board (OTPB) in February 1999, the 120-acre (49-hectare), 1,150,000-square-foot (106,840-square-meter) mixed-use complex includes main street retail that offers 100 stores, 15 restaurants and cafés, and entertainment venues. Among the nonretail uses are a 180-room Marriott Residence Inn and 692,000 square feet (64,290 square meters) of office space housing a number of major tenants, including the world headquarters of AT&T Wireless. At buildout, the property is expected to have more than 1.8 million square feet (167,230 square meters) of gross leasable area; among the uses being considered are additional retail space, an upscale residential component, and another hotel.

At the time of the acquisition by Macerich and the OTPB in February 1999, sales at specialty stores (below 20,000 square feet—1,860 square meters) in the core retail area were $285 per square foot ($3,067 per square meter); by July 2001, they had increased 41.4 percent, to $403 per square foot ($4,338 per square meter). The next phase will add a 110,000-square-foot (10,220-square-meter) Bon Marché, the town center's first department store, and an upscale, 262-room Hilton hotel.

Financing

Town center and mixed-use projects are often difficult to finance for a number of reasons.

- Such developments combine several types of products in one project, and are therefore among the largest projects being built today. The correspondingly large mortgage required to finance these projects is often beyond the risk limits of any single financial institution.
- Large town center projects are often phased; each phase may need to be financed separately, with a different lender.
- Lenders and investors may be familiar and comfortable with some uses but not with others; thus, each use in a town center project may have to be financed separately.
- Lenders may view town center configurations—especially main street retailing—as too unconventional and unproven; because it may be difficult to evaluate how the new and unconventional program and design will perform, lenders and investors may exact a premium to compensate for what they perceive as increased risk.
- Because the timetables for town center projects tend to be long (some projects begun a decade ago are still in development), primary returns on equity may not be realized until the later phases of the project. Only a limited number of developers and equity investors are in a position to provide "patient equity."

- For lenders in a production environment, it is often easier and less risky to finance projects that use proven formulas, and to push aside anything that is out of the ordinary. Thus, developers of town center projects often must work harder to obtain the financing they need.
- Because of the complexity and long timeframes associated with town center projects, a developer who hopes to attract equity and debt capital needs a solid reputation for completing sophisticated, long-term projects. Although all lenders and investors will carefully evaluate the feasibility of a proposed project before committing funds to it, they will rarely even bother to assess feasibility unless they are first satisfied that the developer has the expertise to carry the project through to completion.

There has been some speculation regarding the impact of public capital markets on mixed-use and urban real estate. On the REIT side of the equation, Clement Dinsmore notes:

> *Diversification by a REIT into a different property type raises yellow flags with the investment community. Will the REIT become distracted from its main line of business? Will it acquire and be able to integrate the management expertise needed for its investment in a new property type? REIT managers themselves may be wary of the risks of diversification.*

Hence the recent decision by the board of trustees of the Federal Realty Investment Trust to discontinue the development of large, mixed-use projects and to return to the REIT's traditional focus on the acquisition and redevelopment of neighborhood and community shopping-center properties. Dinsmore notes further:

The integration of land uses within a project adds complexity to the evaluation of the property's cash flows and the credit risks that different types of tenants within the project present. The ability of REITs to manage the diversification of their cash flow sources will be essential. The credit analysis required of REIT managers and credit analysts will resemble that which underwriters, rating agencies, and investors currently are undertaking prior to the issuance or purchase of commercial mortgage-backed securities (CMBSs) that are backed by diversified collateral types, including multifamily, retail, and office properties. The learning curve that Wall Street is experiencing in the CMBS market should facilitate the investment community's acceptance of REITs that undertake integrated, multiple-use projects.

Finally, on the debt side of the public markets, Dinsmore observes:

Owners of mixed-use projects may have problems gaining access to the CMBS market, depending upon the complexity of tenant types in the project. Combining different uses within a project presents the creditor with different types of credit risks and different real estate markets to consider. CMBS underwriters and rating agencies have the same credit evaluation tasks as commercial banks and life insurance companies do in considering direct, whole loans to mixed-use projects. Particularly within the last year [mid-1997 to mid-1998], as the volume of loan transactions financed in the CMBS market has mushroomed, underwriters and rating agencies have given first priority to transactions that are more easily and quickly underwritten—the "plain vanilla" loans.[2]

The bottom line is that, given the unconventional design and composition of town centers and other mixed-use projects, financing continues to be a challenge for their developers. According to Lee S. Sobel, a commercial real estate broker with CB Richard Ellis and author of *Greyfields No More,*

The combined talent and experience of the team assembled by CityPlace Partners convinced West Palm Beach to select this group to carry out the ambitious plans for CityPlace. *Elkus/Manfredi Architects Ltd.*

the real estate industry and financial institutions need to work together to put in place the same mechanisms for mixed-use projects that facilitate the financing, development, construction, leasing, sale, and trade of single-use projects. Things have gotten a bit easier in recent years, as the number of mixed-use projects has grown, but we still have a long ways to go before mixed-use achieves equal footing with single-use development.*[3]

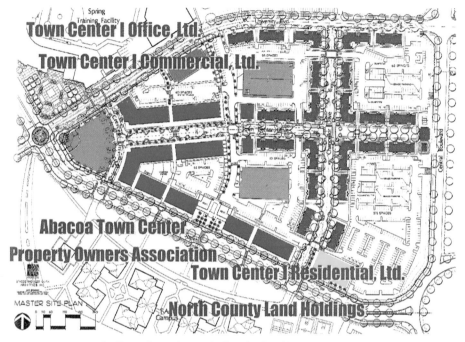

To facilitate financing and allow for flexible exit strategies, Abacoa Town Center, in Jupiter, Florida, is organized into subcomponents: office, commercial/retail, residential, and public space (which is owned by the property owners' association). *George de Guardiola.*

According to Charles Grossman, managing director of Clarion Partners, in New York City, and an International Council of Shopping Centers trustee, banks will often lend only about 60 to 65 percent of the cost for town center projects.[4] Such limitations force developers to seek alternative funding sources and to assume a larger equity stake in town center projects.

De Guardiola maintains that it is crucial to keep project financing as conventional as possible in order to interest banks, equity partners, and future investors in mixed-use or town center projects. De Guardiola

has identified the following basic guidelines for getting such projects financed:

■ Look to industry leaders: identify receptive lenders with experience in mixed-use projects. Abacoa Town Center assembled $65 million from the Bank of America, GMAC Commercial Mortgage, and Lehman Brothers for equity and mezzanine financing.

■ Do not make the financiers think too hard. While it is important to have a good presentation of the town center concept that explains the merits of its planning and design, it is equally important not to overemphasize the uniqueness and unconventional nature of the project. For town center projects to become easier to develop and to succeed, de Guardiola notes that developers "need to elevate economics to the same level as architecture and planning." Conventional financing can work for most mixed-use or town center projects, but it is important to present the facts needed to support the project—including market studies for each component, a description of tenanting strategies, and an analysis of sale prices and rents at competing properties.

■ Divide and conquer. Break up the project into chunks that are understandable to lenders, and that allow for multiple exit strategies. This is especially important in suburban markets, where there is less experience with vertical mixed-use development. Abacoa Town Center is subdivided into residential, office, mixed-use, and common-use areas. This approach yields multiple exit strategies, including long-term refinancing, the potential addition of more financiers, and the option of selling off portions of the project.

■ Minimize conflicts. Delineate property lines for various portions of the project to support more conventional financing and exit strategies. Also, draft clear cross-parking easements that ensure access to parking for all components of the project, regardless of whether they may be sold off in future phases.

- Use good management. Hire people who are fluent in mixed-use development, real estate financing, and exit strategies, and implement their ideas. Let the finance experts make presentations to potential financiers and work out financing arrangements with lenders.

- Pay attention to legal issues. Start all documents with the end in mind. Project elements must be clearly and legally delineated—including easements and common area maintenance and management issues—so that they can be financed, owned, and/or sold separately at some point in the future. Creating the opportunity for a profitable and attractive exit strategy requires effective legal planning and structuring at the outset.[5]

One factor that often works in favor of mixed-use or town center projects is public sector financing. Most local governments view town center or mixed-use projects as being of potential benefit to the jurisdiction—and, as evidenced by projects like CityPlace and by most transit-oriented developments, public/private partnerships or other forms of assistance can play an important role in town center projects. Land write-downs, tax increment financing, municipal bonds, and public improvements at no cost to the project are a few ways that local governments can contribute to a project's financial feasibility and financing.

At Sugar Land Town Square, in Fort Bend County, Texas, a town center that features office, retail, and hotel space, the city of Sugar Land sold bonds for its portion of the hotel project, which consisted of the 60,000-square-foot (5,575-square-meter) Sugar Land Conference Center and 360 spaces of a 525-space parking garage that adjoin the hotel. This

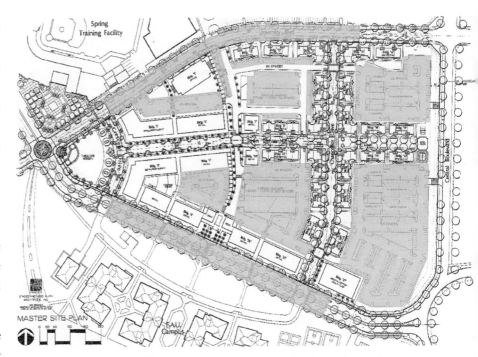

To ensure that shared parking arrangements would be clearly understood—and that parking could be managed and coordinated even if office, residential, and main street portions of the project were eventually sold off—Abacoa Town Center developed a detailed parking plan establishing cross-parking easements. *George de Guardiola.*

required the issuance of $19 million in debt for these two facilities. The city funded $10 million of the $19 million, with the Sugar Land 4B Corporation participating in the project at $9 million. Voters created the 4B Corporation in 1995 to collect a quarter-cent sales tax for development activities within the city. "The conference center/garage will be self-funded," said City Manager Allen Bogard. "Revenues from the hotel occupancy tax will fund $10 million and the remaining $9 million in debt will be funded from sales tax generated from the Town Square project."

perspective, however, developers should fully explore potential public sector support for such initiatives.

The Public Sector and Town Centers

In the give-and-take of getting projects designed, financed, and approved, the famous refrain from the film *Field of Dreams* is heard often: "If you build it, they will come." From the perspective of the public sector, however, it is probably more accurate to say, "If you don't plan for it, they probably won't build it" (hence, no one will come).

Since town centers go against existing regulations and codes in most places in the United States that favor single-use, automobile-oriented development, communities that want town centers to be part of their future need to rethink their planning and zoning codes. For town centers to have any chance of taking root, planning departments and the officials engaged in plan review oversight need to create conditions that are ripe for town centers: specifically, plans and zoning ordinances need to allow mixed uses, narrow streets, higher densities, multistory buildings, and urban open spaces.

While planned unit development (PUD) ordinances may supply some of the necessary flexibility, they often include provisions that are incompatible with town centers. The latent segregation of land uses in portions of some projects—King Farm, in Montgomery County, Maryland, is an example—is an artifact of prior zoning and PUD ordinances. For town centers to be implemented successfully, jurisdictions not only need more flexible zoning regulations but must implement land use and urban design guidelines that specifically support urbanism at the village, town, and urban neighborhood scales.

Much of the innovation that has taken place in land use planning in recent years has recognized the impediments to mixed-use and town center development. Planners have sought to be more proactive by identifying the types of mixed-use centers that are desired, and by indicating their general land use mix,

Abacoa Town Center.

The conference center facility will be leased to the hotel operator.

Tax increment financing (TIF) is often used to help finance parking garages and infrastructure improvements and to pay back public debt on these improvements. Ground leases, like the ones used for Mizner Park and CityPlace, are common as well. A caveat: although public financing or financial assistance can greatly facilitate development, public sector involvement may well complicate and slow the process as well.

Although many developers are hesitant to undertake town center projects without public sector support, many mixed-use or town center projects have gone forward strictly as private ventures. For example, in the case of Abacoa Town Center (Jupiter, Florida) and Santana Row (San Jose, California), and many Post Properties's projects, the sheer strength of the market allowed the projects to proceed without any public subsidies whatsoever. Given the myriad potential benefits that town centers offer from a smart growth

What Municipalities Can Do to Support Place Making

■ Think big. Most cities have a "one-project mentality" and fail to envision the larger picture—how projects fit together to form the city.

■ Emphasize neighborhood scale and context. The allure of places, and how they will look and feel to people, can get lost in regulation. If municipalities emphasize neighborhood scale and the human context, individual projects can become the kinds of places that form neighborhoods and districts and create a human-scale city.

■ Use sound market analysis to inform planning and determine what the desired product is, and put incentives in place that will support the desired outcome.

■ Empower a champion for the project. The developer should be able to work closely with a local government executive who has the power to override or strongly influence department decisions. Leaders need to break the rules—or empower others to do so—when necessary.

■ Take control of planning. Break areas down into districts and connect them with streets and sidewalks. Create—and pursue—a vision of the whole community.

■ Design financial tools upfront. Once you know the location and types of development you want to encourage, create public sector financial tools that can help make the development happen, both by attracting private sector participation and by facilitating the implementation of projects once they are approved.

■ Define edges and entry portals: people should know when they enter and leave a place. Distinctive edges and portals are in keeping with a neighborhood structure, and help create a strong identity for places.

Addison Circle, an urban village project developed by Post Properties, follows many of the principles outlined in the feature box. *Steve Hinds.*

■ Zone for maximum flexibility. To support more organic types of development, cities have to stop micromanaging land uses. The greatest places are made by people who invent something, and this kind of invention happens at a very small scale.

■ Allow creative signage. Every sign in every place within a community should not be the same. Cities can maintain reasonable restrictions on the size and placement of signs without squelching their creative use in place making.

■ Rezone at the worst point. Since rezoning can be one of the most difficult administrative changes to carry out, rezone when the real estate market is at its worst—when there will be fewer objections to trying something new. Much of the zoning imposed in past decades must be completely overturned to allow diverse place making to occur.

■ Consider eliminating or reducing parking requirements. Why would a developer provide insufficient parking for a project? Codes that mandate high parking ratios are outdated, and municipalities should allow greater leeway for the private sector to figure out what works.

■ Focus on funding and creating great streets, sidewalks, and parks. Cities should do this first, upfront, as part of their role in creating and sustaining livable communities.

■ Build pedestrian links between districts. Projects developed as pedestrian-friendly areas still need to be linked to one another by public infrastructure. Cities should plan and build pedestrian links between districts as they are completed. If necessary, they should provide transit links to connect nascent districts.

- Focus on block face dimensions, not setbacks. Cities should regulate the height of buildings and the distance between block fronts. All other setback requirements should be flexible (Post Properties has passed on projects because of disputes involving as little as five feet [1.5 meters] of setback difference).

- Level the playing field for main street retail. Permit parallel parking, don't require parking meters or ticket aggressively, don't close streets to traffic, and do allow trucks to pull up and deliver goods at the fronts of stores.

- Change lighting standards. The size, type, and illumination level for urban lighting tend to be governed by suburban standards that are inappropriate for urban places.

- Improve parks department maintenance programs. These programs are typically understaffed and unable to maintain urban parks and landscaping.

- Alter utility franchise agreements to enable power lines to be buried.

- Change "traffic versus pedestrian" mantras. Pedestrian districts should be accessible and the focus of transit and transportation programs, not isolated enclaves for walking only.

- Condemn holdouts. Use the power of eminent domain to obtain holdout properties that delay progress in land assembly.

- Create regional rather than property-specific affordable-housing programs. The creation of more urban housing and more low-income housing are both worthy goals, but they can't always be interconnected. Pursue them in parallel, without trying to force each individual project to address both needs.

- Take responsibility for historic preservation strategies and funding. Cities do need to care about the preservation of historic structures, but they also need to be proactive about the economics of doing so. It is typically more expensive to adapt and redevelop an old structure than to build new. Developers can play an important role, but they need a lot of help.

- Work with the media—it is an important partner that can help persuade the public to care about places.

Source: Adapted from Art Lomenick, keynote presentation, "Place Making: Developing Town Centers, Transit Villages, and Main Streets," Second Annual ULI Place-Making Conference, San Diego, California, September 18–19, 2000.

location, and transit service options. But few plans have gone so far as to articulate and specifically support the types of buildings, streets, open spaces, and mix of uses required for town centers. Overlay districts and parallel codes (those permitting both conventional subdivisions and traditional neighborhood development) are increasing in popularity, but unless such codes are adopted and implemented as part of a specific plan, there is little incentive for developers to experiment. In taking the next step, places like Chapel Hill, North Carolina, and Santa Monica, California,

have not only created districts where village centers and town centers were supported, but have chosen to concentrate commercial uses in these districts by restricting the amount and type of commercial development permitted in adjacent areas. As mentioned previously, other tools and techniques the public sector can use to move town center projects forward include land assembly; density bonuses; tax increment financing; and provisions for parking, transit stations, and other infrastructure.

In addition, the public sector can take an active role by placing civic uses within the town center. Town centers have always been settings for town

Civic uses, such as post offices, add a level of authenticity and permanence to town centers that commercial uses cannot. Note that this is the U.S. Post Office for Mashpee, Massachusetts, not the "Mashpee Commons Post Office."

halls, courts, libraries, schools, post offices, museums, police stations, and other institutional and cultural facilities. Civic and cultural institutions provide a town center with the kind of credibility and authenticity that cannot be manufactured through architectural styling or through themes or "back sto-

ries" that purport to invent a "history" for a place. Civic institutions also draw a wide range of people undertaking a wide range of activities, introducing a level of diversity that further distinguishes authentic town centers from projects that are limited to commercial uses. Thus, the public sector can use civic and cultural institutions as building blocks in the creation of places that are more than just urban-style shopping centers—places that are the heart and soul of an entire community, rather than simply a convenience for those who happen to live nearby.

Since town centers are a new concept for many suburban communities and involve significant departures from the large, greenfield sites and surface parking lots that governments, religious institutions, and cultural and community institutions are often accustomed to, it may take time to persuade decision makers to consider town centers as sites for civic and institutional buildings. As the town center is constructed and the landscaping of the public spaces matures, however, these sites become increasingly attractive. Thus, if a library, town hall, or other civic or cultural institution cannot be secured in the first phases of a town center project, it is crucial to reserve sites for the future addition of such uses.

Historically, churches, guildhalls, town halls, and courthouses were some of the most distinctive buildings in town centers, and were located on the most prominent sites. Similarly, civic institutions in the town centers of today often adopt an architectural style that is distinct from that of the residential, commercial, and other uses in the town center. However, to protect the overall integrity of the town center, the design of civic institutions needs to be consistent with the urban character of town centers and main streets. Since civic institutions may be added many years after the project is originally constructed, and there may not be a "town architect" to mediate the design process, it is prudent to have the town center's original designer create plan and design guidelines that specifically address the design parameters for civic institutions.

Recognizing their community orientation and potential, public officials often come out in support of town center projects. A word of caution, however: it is important, for developers and public officials alike, to avoid contributing to unrealistic expectations. Even when there is strong preleasing and public support, it takes time for the commercial elements of a projects to be realized; funding and construction of civic uses can take even longer. Unrealistic expectations as to how quickly a town center will come together can lead only to disappointment.

While elected officials and planners receive a lot of attention in the effort to get town centers approved and built, another group of often-neglected specialists play pivotal roles in the implementation of projects: building inspectors, public works officials, fire chiefs, traffic engineers, and parks officials. Unfortunately, the land use, transportation engineering, and urban design of town centers often go against every rule that these specialists have relied on for decades, and against the very standards and codes that it is their job to enforce.

As developers and project managers of town centers soon discover, their projects often require changes or variances in building codes, transportation and civil engineering requirements, parks and recreation standards, design standards for schools and other civic buildings, and fire and safety standards. These standards often dictate wide rights-of-way and curb radii; detached, single-story buildings; deep setbacks; and a host of other requirements embedded in plans, policies, laws, regulations, and practices that are, taken collectively, antithetical to town centers and main streets. It isn't that building inspectors, public works officials, fire chiefs, traffic engineers, and parks officials are unsympathetic to town center projects, but that they are not typically empowered to change policies, only to enforce them. Thus, developers and project managers should engage these specialists early in a project, identify where and how conflicts with regulations may arise, and develop solutions that will satisfy the intent of the regulations without damaging the integrity of the project.

The problem is that local government employees often lack the authority to change policy or allow for flexibility. Thus, strong leadership within the public sector may be required to overcome the inflexible standards and rules that can impede the development of town centers. Political leaders can also empower specialists within the public sector to make the changes necessary for great places to be created. Many local governments that are actively pursuing town center developments, such as Montgomery County, Maryland, are taking a proactive approach by assigning a high-level planner or redevelopment official to champion and/or run interference for the project, reduce the red tape and obstacles, and facilitate the process of acquiring the necessary approvals.

The next chapter revisits five pathbreaking town center projects that were developed beginning in the 1980s and that represent important precursors to the burgeoning number of today's town centers, main

streets, and urban villages. Most of these projects continue to be used as models, and have important lessons for the developers of today's town centers.

Notes

1. See the diagrams and discussion at the beginning of Chapter 4 on the relationships between shopping centers and town centers.

2. Clement Dinsmore, *The Impact of Public Capital Markets on Urban Real Estate* (Washington, D.C.: Center on Urban and Metropolitan Policy, Brookings Institution, July 1998), 15–17, 21.

3. Lee S. Sobel, *Greyfields No More* (San Francisco: Congress for the New Urbanism, 2002).

4. Dave Bodamer, "Urban Retail Panel Term 'New Urbanism'," *Shopping Center Today* (http://www.icsc.org/srch/sct/current/page22.html [August 3, 2001]).

5. Adapted from George de Guardiola, "Place Making and Mixed Uses: Regulatory, Financing, and Management" (presented at the Second Annual ULI Place-Making Conference, San Diego, California, September 2000).

Breakthrough
Projects Revisited

The new generation of town center developments that is emerging today had its beginnings in the years between 1983 and 1990, with the opening of five major town center projects: Miami Lakes Town Center, in Florida; Princeton Forrestal Village, in New Jersey; Mashpee Commons, in Massachusetts; Reston Town Center, in Virginia; and Mizner Park, in Florida. These five pioneering examples of town center development continue to inspire and to educate designers, developers, and public officials throughout the United States. Reston Town Center and Mizner Park, in particular, remain benchmarks against which more recent projects are measured.

All five projects have continued to evolve since they were initially established, and their histories provide insights not only into the maturation process that all town center projects can be expected to experience, but also into some of the pitfalls that such projects can encounter. This chapter describes the more recent evolution of these town centers, examines the problems they have faced, and details some of the keys to their continued resilience and success.

Miami Lakes Town Center

Miami Lakes Town Center was the earliest of these town center projects; its first and second phases were completed in 1983 and 1985, respectively. Like several of today's town centers, Miami Lakes Town Center was a mixed-use development created within a maturing suburban community—in this case, the 3,000-acre (1,210-hectare) Miami Lakes master-planned community (MPC), for which planning had begun in 1957. The center incorporated many of the elements typical of contemporary town centers: specialty retail and entertainment uses (including a movie theater and a health club); residential and office uses above street-level retail space; an integrated hotel with a streetfront entrance; and a "main street" design theme.

The success of the town center since its inception—in particular, the success of the apartments

Miami Lakes Town Center lies at the heart of Miami Lakes, a 1960s-era master-planned community with an unusual spiral road network. Phase I (top half of the drawing) was completed by the mid-1980s. Phase II (bottom half) is currently being developed.
University of Miami/Jean-François Lejeune.

Top: Entering from a major arterial, Main Street wraps around the fountain plaza in Miami Lakes Town Center. The architecture is colorful but utilitarian, and the scale provides a strong sense of enclosure.

Bottom: Miami Lakes's narrow, gently curving Main Street, angled parking, and tight spaces give it a village center atmosphere and vivid sense of place.

and construction of multifamily housing on a large parcel of land directly adjacent to the town center is underway. The cinema has been updated and expanded, and pedestrian traffic has been rerouted so that moviegoers pass along the shops on Main Street after they leave the theater. During the 1990s, the retail tenant mix shifted from predominantly local and regional establishments to one in which national chains had a much stronger presence. Several national chains have recently chosen not to renew their leases, however, and the composition of the main street retail is entering yet another transition. The developer is now considering new strategies that will bolster the attractiveness of the town center as a retail location and help build a critical mass of retail.

The town center can be expected to continue to play a prominent role in the life of the community, particularly from a civic perspective: the residents of the MPC voted to incorporate as a municipality in the fall of 2000, and the town center is a potential location for new municipal government offices and a city hall. The continued accumulation of higher-density multifamily housing around the town center is also expected to bolster the local market for town center businesses.

Town centers, like all retail formats, are not immune from competition, or from market fluctuations that can affect their retail and office tenants. Over time, these fluctuations will test the contention that because of their mixed uses, civic character, and community orientation, main streets and town centers will be more resilient than single-use retail strips and centers. In support of this perspective, it should be noted that Miami Lakes Town Center, Mashpee Commons, Mizner Park, and Reston Town Center have already weathered major recessions and downturns and continued to expand.

What keeps developers, architects, planners, and public officials coming back to Miami Lakes is its urban design: the narrow, gently curving, tree-lined Main Street; the vertical mix of uses; the tight sense of

Apartments above Johnny Rockets, on Main Street at Miami Lakes Town Center.

over the ground-floor retail on Main Street, which have maintained very high occupancy rates for nearly 20 years—has surprised many observers. The dining and entertainment facilities, the health club, and the hotel have also remained relatively stable and profitable throughout these two decades, and Main Street and the fountain plaza have become popular settings for community celebrations, street fairs, and holiday events.

Miami Lakes Town Center has continued to grow and evolve: a block of urban townhouses was added as an extension of the original two-block Main Street,

enclosure experienced on Main Street and in the fountain plaza; the incorporation of the hotel into the streetscape; and the way in which new blocks have been successfully woven into the fabric of the town center. As the town center approaches its 20th anniversary, it maintains a strong sense of place that is likely to continue to attract residents, visitors, and new commercial tenants for many years to come.

Princeton Forrestal Village

Princeton Forrestal Village was developed as a mixed-use commercial center within Princeton Forrestal Center—a large office campus, encompassing several million square feet of office space, developed by Princeton University. Forrestal Village featured 225,000 square feet (20,900 square meters) of office space, 208,000 square feet (19,320 square meters) of retail space, a full-service Marriott hotel, and a 12,900-square-foot (1,200-square-meter) child care center. The urban design of Forrestal Village incorporated many of the

features now common in town center projects, including a pedestrian-oriented main street, traditional-style architecture, and gathering places (Village Square and Market Plaza). It did not, however, include residential uses.

The center of the project is Village Square—a small, landscaped park with a central fountain and park benches. The six-story, 300-room Marriott Hotel overlooks the square. Main Street is a two-block collection of shops, with two floors of commercial office space above. Cars are allowed on Main Street, but the emphasis is on the pedestrian. The streetscape includes copper streetlamps, deciduous trees, ample sidewalks for shoppers, and plenty of wooden benches for sitting and resting.

Village Square at Princeton Forrestal Village. *Sasaki Associates, Inc.*

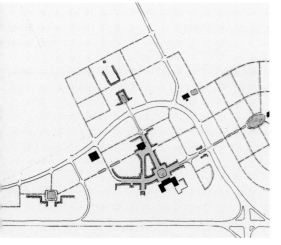

Princeton Forrestal Village introduced pedestrian-oriented streets, bike paths, walkways, and public gathering places within the Princeton Forrestal Center office campus. *Sasaki Associates, Inc.*

The square lines of the rectangular brick buildings are broken up by archways, balconies, and bay windows. The building facades contain various patterns of light brick on dark, and vice versa. To avoid the enormous parking lagoons that dominate most suburban malls, the designers provided several heavily landscaped smaller lots and a covered two-level parking deck.

Forrestal Village has experienced mixed success, in part because of a very competitive environment, unfortunate timing, and a retail strategy that did not work as originally planned. When the project opened, in 1987, the office market in the area was overbuilt, as it was in many parts of the country at that time. As a result, office leasing was sluggish from the outset: nine months after opening, only 25 percent of the office space had been leased. Retail leasing fared better at first, with 85 percent of the space leased within nine months after opening, but retail traffic did not materialize as promised, partly because a similar retail center that opened at the same time diluted what was already a very competitive market. The Marriott hotel, the best performer, exceeded occupancy projections during its first six months of operation.

The real estate recession that soon followed, in the late 1980s and early 1990s, however, led to poor performance for the project overall and forced it into the hands of its lender, the Bank of New York. New managers subsequently transformed the retail portion into a factory outlet center. Originally built for $119 million, the project was reportedly bought

Archways, brick facades, and well-lit storefronts characterize the architecture of Princeton Forrestal Village. *Sasaki Associates, Inc.*

by Gale & Wentworth for $29 million, in 1993, and was subsequently sold off in separate pieces during the 1990s for a total of $45 million.

Among the problems that the project faced was its location within an office-dominated environment, which made it difficult for the development to be perceived as a town center. Moreover, the mix of uses and the development strategy relied heavily on office space—already overabundant in the area at the time—and the retail was positioned and sized in a way that made it difficult, during a recession, for the retail to find a niche and hold its own in a competitive market (the retail tenanting strategy was upscale, and included such tenants as Rodier and Ralph Lauren). Finally, there was no attempt to diversify the town center by introducing civic uses or residential units. Although live/work rowhouses that might appeal to a white-collar, high-technology workforce would not appear in town center projects for many years, apartments might have provided attractive housing options convenient for Forrestal

Center's workforce. Forrestal Village was essentially a shopping center that had adopted the theme of a traditional main street. While most town centers suffer from one or more of these shortcomings, Forrestal Village's flaws may have been more fatal in Princeton, where sophisticated residents and workers can choose to experience Princeton itself as well as other traditional towns and cities in the region, including New York and Philadelphia.

One of the most important lessons to be learned from Forrestal Village is that while an underperforming retail component will certainly hurt a project overall, it is not necessarily a fatal flaw. New owners were able to reposition the retail component to keep it leased and attractive to customers, and the office and hotel components have performed well despite the retail problems. More recently, the performance of all the components has improved—especially that of the office and hotel components, which have achieved high occupancy rates and competitive rents. (In 1999, the office component was named one of the New Jersey office buildings of the year.) The retail portion also seems to be doing well as an outlet center, though it continues to suffer from lingering image problems.

In spite of its initial failure, Forrestal Village was a pioneering, visionary effort: in a location dominated by freestanding office buildings and retail facilities that were surrounded by parking, the developers dared to arrange office, retail, and hotel uses in a traditional main street format. The project was a risky venture that, unfortunately, was completed just before a major real estate recession, which hurt its performance. Nonetheless, the developer, Toombs Development Company; the architect, Bower Lewis Thrower; and the planner, Sasaki Associates, must be credited with taking a bold and creative step that established a new precedent for office, retail, hotel, and mixed-use development in the suburbs.

The pedestrian-oriented streetscape of Princeton Forrestal Village.
Sasaki Associates, Inc.

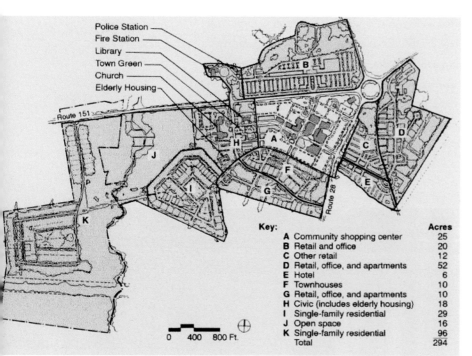

Key:		Acres
A	Community shopping center	25
B	Retail and office	20
C	Other retail	12
D	Retail, office, and apartments	52
E	Hotel	6
F	Townhouses	10
G	Retail, office, and apartments	10
H	Civic (includes elderly housing)	18
I	Single-family residential	29
J	Open space	16
K	Single-family residential	96
	Total	294

The original plan for Mashpee Commons, which transformed the New Seabury Shopping Center into the kernel of a town center; Phase I is high-lighted in white. *Imai/Keller, Inc.*

Mashpee Commons

Planning and design for Mashpee Commons began way back in 1985, when the developers—Douglas S. Storrs and Arnold B. Chase—created a plan to transform the existing, 75,000-square-foot (6,970-square-meter) New Seabury Shopping Center, originally built in 1968, into a three-block, mixed-use downtown based on the design principles of historic New England town centers. Instead of expanding the shopping center or clearing the site to start from scratch, the developers hired architect Randall Imai, of Imai/Keller, Inc., to help create a town center by dividing larger buildings into a series of smaller shops, and adding new facades,

tree-lined sidewalks, and new buildings to create double-loaded streets (that is, streets lined with buildings on both sides). New entrances and display windows broke up the facades of larger buildings, and a liner building was added to the back of the original grocery store, creating storefronts where there had been blank walls.

Large parking lots were redesigned and located at the rear of the new and renovated buildings. A street network was developed to create the three-block core of the downtown, and a town common was planned for the western terminus of the main street. A church and municipal library were built on two sides of the town common site. The original downtown plan for

The original six-screen cinema, fronting a plaza along Steeple Street, continues to draw audiences to Mashpee Commons.

Mashpee Commons called for the addition of 150,000 square feet (13,940 square meters) of commercial space and 100 residential units, located on the second floors of the new buildings.

The original phase of the project encompassed about 25 acres (ten hectares).[1] At the time, Mashpee Commons consisted of 150,630 square feet (13,990 square meters) of space, about 60 percent of which was retail, with the remainder divided between office, dining, and entertainment (a six-screen Hoyts cinema). The site was originally zoned highway commercial, with no residential permitted, and the existing planning regulations called for wide streets and 40-foot (12-meter) setbacks, which were at odds with the mixed uses, shallow setbacks, and narrow streets in the Mashpee Commons plan. Although the town granted the variances, it did not change existing zoning and subdivision regulations or create an overlay district.

Because state and local street standards would have required wider, suburban-style roads, all the streets in Mashpee Commons were designated as driveways and service roads instead of being adopted as public streets by the town. The developers actively recruited civic uses, incorporating a site for a new town post office directly within the project, and donating land for a library and a nearby church. Other portions of the property include fire and police stations, medical offices, and a 24-unit housing facility for seniors. The town has also constructed a new high school and middle school on adjacent parcels.

Ironically, the original neighborhood shopping center had been named for a nearby MPC that had sought to avoid being associated with the town of Mashpee; the developer felt that the association would hamper efforts to market the project to upscale Cape Cod homebuyers. A major reversal occurred in the mid-1980s, however, when the project was redeveloped in a town center format and the Mashpee post office was relocated there: it was suggested that the project be renamed to reflect its growing importance to the town, and "Mashpee Commons" was born.

In 1988, the developers hired Duany Plater-Zyberk & Company to create a plan for the 294 acres (119 hectares) of land that had been assembled.[2] The goal was to create a series of villages with small-lot, single-family homes and townhouses in a

mix of retail, office, restaurant, and municipal uses. This plan called for an additional 450,000 square feet (41,810 square meters) of commercial space and 380 single- and multifamily dwelling units.

Mashpee Commons has been widely hailed as a ground-breaking example of the transformation of an older, conventional shopping center into a town

Since the regulations of the Massachusetts Department of Transportation require much wider streets, all streets within Mashpee Commons are private.

center. The narrow streets, generous sidewalks, and on-street parking created pedestrian-friendly shopping streets, and the two-story, wood-and-brick buildings enclosed the outdoor spaces, creating a sense of place that evoked traditional New England towns and villages. The project was not without shortcomings: there were no residential units; the plazas were very modest; and the project lacked a true center of gravity, such as a village green or town square. In addition, the project was encircled by surface parking lots and did not connect with any of the town's existing neighborhoods. The developers knew, however, that the remaining 250 acres (101 hectares) would provide the opportunity to transform Mashpee Commons into something larger and more diverse if the initial phase succeeded.

After a slow start during the recession of the early 1990s, Mashpee Commons took off: since 1992, store revenues have risen between 10 and 35 percent annually. According to a 1999 report in *New Urban News,* Mashpee Commons, with average annual rents of $30 per square foot ($322 per square meter) for retail, "falls in the top 10 percent of community shopping centers in rent and sales per square foot."[3] Office rents are $10 to $12 per square foot ($107 to $129 per square meter).

The project has continued to evolve over the past decade and now offers more than 280,000 square feet (26,010 square meters) of commercial space. Recent additions include 13 apartments over retail, completed in June of 1998—two studios, nine one-bedroom, and two two-bedroom units. The apartments are located above Talbots, Banana Republic, and Gap Kids stores, in a 26,000-square-foot (2,420-square-meter) mixed-use building at the corner of Market and Steeple Streets, the main intersection of Mashpee Commons.

As with most early town center projects, financing was difficult, and local realtors, developers, and public officials were particularly skeptical about the construction of apartments over retail. A number of citizens also expressed concern—despite monthly rents that ranged from $500 to $1,300—about the types of people who might be attracted to urban-style apartments. The response to the apartments was impressive: a waiting list of more than 80 people engaged in a bidding process that resulted in rental rates 20 percent above expectations. The apartments also attracted a wide spectrum of tenants, including young singles, professionals, and retirees. The developers took this as a strong endorsement of town center housing in Mashpee, and proof that the market would support the continued development of the

This block, with apartments over mainstream retailers, was completed in 1998. Although initially opposed by some neighbors (who were concerned about the types of people who might be attracted to urban-style apartments), the residences proved highly popular: a waiting list of 80 people engaged in a bidding contest that yielded rental rates 20 percent higher than the developer had anticipated.

In 1999, a new clock tower was added to Mashpee Commons's signature building.

100 apartment units originally approved. Two new buildings, constructed in 2002, will provide an additional 36 units.

The developers continued to tweak the original development—reworking the tenant mix, updating and renovating the buildings and streetscape, and expanding the programmed events. One of the most visible changes was the replacement of the original clock tower. After having spent years looking out on the clock tower from their offices across the street, the developers decided that the original clock tower was out of scale with the building on which it was mounted. The addition of the new clock tower, in 1999, demonstrated the developers' commitment to the traditional design of the town center—as well as their determination to "get it right."

The major area of new development has been the North Market Street shopping area, located just to the north and across Route 151 from the core area. While the original Mashpee Commons core was predominantly specialty retail and dining, the North Market section, permitted in 1993, focuses more on neighborhood retail, and includes a large grocery store, a video store, a liquor store, a beauty parlor, a dry cleaner, a commercial mail service, and two banks.

With mostly one-story buildings, a drive-through bank, and more conventional architecture, North Market Street also relaxes the traditional urbanism of Mashpee's original core somewhat; however, it also features a one-story-high, one-block-long liner building, about 24 feet (7.3 meters) deep, that creates a pedestrian streetscape and conceals a large parking lot.

These liner buildings conceal a large parking lot that serves Mashpee Commons's North Market shops.

The successful tenanting of the small storefronts in this building persuaded the developers, in 2000, to build four additional liner buildings in the original core of Mashpee Commons. These modest, one-story buildings transformed what was once a single-loaded street facing a large parking lot into a more urban, double-loaded street. Two larger buildings—a new, two-story, 25,000-square-foot (2,320-square-meter) Gap building, and an unconvention-

of the Boch Center for Performing Arts, which will occupy nine acres (3.6 hectares) in the easternmost neighborhood.

Beginning in 1997, the developers met with a selectmen's subcommittee—made up of members of the board of selectmen, members of the planning board, the town planner, and local citizens—for more than 18 months in preparation for a vote at a town meeting. After reviewing the aesthetics and the traffic, wastewater, and fiscal impacts of the proposal, the subcommittee determined that the neotraditional format would require four amendments to the town's zoning code. This set the stage for a dramatic, New England–style town meeting in October of 1998: each amendment to the town zoning code would require approval by a two-thirds majority, which is typically very difficult to achieve. After substantial debate, the first amendment passed by a slight margin; the next three amendments passed unanimously. While these votes represented a crucial victory, local, regional, and state permitting have continued to impose delays: nearly three years later, none of the neighborhoods had yet broken ground.

Mashpee Commons is an example of the sort of uphill battle typically encountered when developers attempt to build town centers and other smart growth urban forms in what is essentially a no-growth environment. It is ironic that the Cape Cod project has been waylaid by zoning laws that mandate highway-oriented sprawl and prohibit traditional New England town planning and design. The developers have succeeding in creating an attachable fragment of urbanism, but public sector commitment and support will be necessary if the urban pattern is to be continued. Specifically, planning for the development of adjacent parcels must ensure that streets and walkways will be interconnected, and must provide for smooth transitions from predominantly residential neighborhoods to more commercial, mixed-use areas. The five existing roadways that project outward from the nearby rotary and cut through Mashpee Commons continue to represent

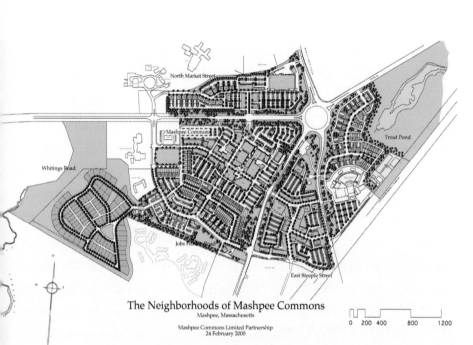

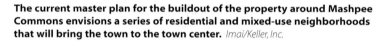

The current master plan for the buildout of the property around Mashpee Commons envisions a series of residential and mixed-use neighborhoods that will bring the town to the town center. *Imai/Keller, Inc.*

ally designed CVS pharmacy—terminate the views looking down the street to the east and west. The small shops (350 to 425 square feet—33 to 39 square meters) have provided opportunities for smaller, startup operations and locally owned businesses to gain a foothold in Mashpee Commons, and have also allowed the developers to expand the commercial core while reducing the visibility of surface parking lots.

The final act for Mashpee Commons, however, is the campaign the developers have been waging to transform the commercial center into a full-fledged town center: plans call for the addition of four new neighborhoods that would include additional residential, office, and retail space; and for the construction

major barriers to the creation of a pedestrian-friendly environment. Traffic-calming measures are needed so that pedestrians can walk comfortably from the core of Mashpee Commons to the North Market Street section, and to the performing arts center and neighborhoods planned to the east, west, and south of the commercial core.

Such changes can be brought about only through progressive reforms supported by local, regional, and state agencies. Just as Mashpee Commons's developers had to relearn how to build a traditional main street, state and local officials now need to rediscover the types of streets, buildings, and public spaces that characterize the historic towns and villages found throughout New England—and make it legal to build them once again.

In a story that is reminiscent of the histories of other town center projects, developer Doug Storrs notes that in the early years, residents would remark on the fact that the project was "owned" by the developers, revealing an uneasiness about the role that Mashpee Commons played within the community. In recent years, however, the development is increasingly referred to simply as "Mashpee," a shift that reveals the growing affinity that many local residents feel for the place, and the gradual merging of the town center's identity with that of the town itself.

Mashpee Commons is fundamentally important in the evolution of town centers for several reasons. First, it demonstrated that retail space could be successfully developed in a main street format. Second, it demonstrated that a conventional shopping center could be converted into a main street and town center format. Third, it illustrated the fact that private developers can add value and a sense of place to a retail development project, making it something more than simply a shopping center. By focusing on the creation of a community-oriented town center with a mix of uses, including residential and civic uses, the developers of Mashpee Commons created a diverse urban place that adds value to all of the various components, creating both a profitable development and momentum for further growth and expansion over time.

Reston Town Center

In the four decades since it was initiated, the large MPC of Reston, Virginia, has grown into a full-fledged suburban city with about 63,000 residents, 2,200 businesses, and a diverse mix of land uses spread over 11.5 square miles (29.8 square kilomters) of northern Virginia. While Reston is predominantly residential and suburban in character, its core—with an abundance of high-rise office space and urban streets and plazas—is one of the most urban examples of a town center project.

The master plan for the community designated a 460-acre (186-hectare) area as a "town center district"; the district included an 85-acre (34-hectare) "urban core" that was intended to function as Reston's downtown. Planning for the town center began in 1982, but was entirely overhauled after a ULI Advisory Services panel determined that the original plan failed to provide the density and diversity that would be needed to create the type of downtown that was envisioned. A new plan was crafted, and Reston Town Center Phase I Associates and Himmel/MKDG began development of Phase I of the town center, a 20.6-acre (8.3-hectare) portion of the urban core.

When Phase I opened, in October of 1990, it incorporated 530,000 square feet (49,230 square meters) of office space; 240,000 square feet (22,300 square meters) of retail, dining, and entertainment space; an 11-screen cinema; and a 430,000-square-foot (39,950-square-meter), 514-room Hyatt Regency. The $185 million project was intensely focused around a

Reston Town Center is now a major regional destination, drawing over 5 million visitors each year. *Sasaki Associates, Inc.*

two-block main street (Market Street) that featured a generous, brick-paved plaza with outdoor seating and a large fountain across the street from a temporary ice-skating rink.

Although the town center won numerous architectural and urban design awards, it struggled during its early years, which happened to fall during a national recession. The project steadily gained momentum, however, and gradually expanded over the next decade. In 1993, the popular temporary skating rink was replaced with a permanent, glass-roofed pavilion that doubles, during warmer months, as a venue for concerts, holiday celebrations, and special events. Since there are no civic institutions in the core, the plaza and pavilion provide much of Reston Town Center's community character.

As evidence of just how much the town center has been adopted by the community, Thomas D'Alesandro, vice president of Terrabrook (the new owners of the undeveloped land in Reston Town Center) and a longtime veteran of Reston's development, notes that people would simply take over Fountain Square for private outdoor parties and wedding receptions, rearranging the outdoor furniture and never imagining that they might need the permission of a property manager.

Reston Town Center was soon holding several dozen events per year, and by 1996 it was estimated that there were more than 5 million annual visitors.

A permanent pavilion, added in 1993, has become a key attraction for winter ice skating, summer concerts, and community events at Reston Town Center.

The town center has become the "downtown" not only for Reston, but for western Fairfax County and eastern Loudoun County as well, with visitors regularly traveling from within a 60-mile (48-kilometer) radius.

Reston Town Center changed ownership and management twice during the 1990s, and although the Market Street area changed little, the properties immediately adjacent to Phase I have changed dramatically. The Spectrum—a large, suburban-style shopping center—was constructed to the immediate north of Phase I. The center generated considerable controversy within Reston—including public opposition from Robert E. Simon, the town founder, who had returned after 30 years and become a community activist. While opponents viewed the Spectrum as a retreat from the traditional urbanism that was already well established along Market Street, the developers defended the addition of large-scale retailers, in a more conventional format, as a means of creating a critical mass of retail space that would ultimately benefit the entire urban core.

More recently, a new office tower with ground-floor retail (One Freedom Square) began the westward expansion of the original core onto a third block. Because of the construction of the Spectrum and this additional office space, all but one of the surface parking lots in the urban core have been redeveloped as structured parking decks.

Residential development was initiated, in May of 1997, with West Market, a high-density neighborhood of townhouses and condominiums just west of Town Center Parkway. West Market has added 440 upscale residential units to the town center district, with prices ranging from $460,000 to $500,000 for the townhouses, and from $160,000 to the low $200,000s for condominiums. West Market's streetscapes are more urban than those of Reston's other residential areas: buildings are pulled close to the sidewalks, and parallel parking spaces line the streets. Although the neighborhood itself is pedestrian-friendly and is theoretically within walking distance of Market Street's shops and restaurants, West

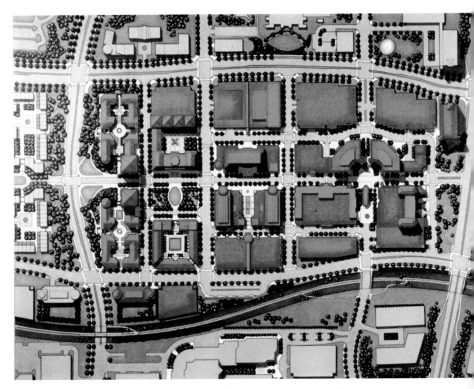

The full buildout of Reston Town Center's urban core, currently under construction, is shown here. The original Phase I, focused on Fountain Square, is located in the center of the eastern half of the core. Phase II will continue the street grid to the west, adding two additional public spaces and several private courtyards, and a mix of moderate- and high-density residential, office, and retail; a swath of high-density residential will also be added to the east. *Sasaki Associates, Inc.*

Market residents are unlikely to cross Town Center Parkway—which was engineered for high-speed traffic—on foot. Once Market Street is extended to the edge of West Market, however, residents' desire to walk to the core will grow much stronger; the introduction of crossing signals and traffic-calming techniques could facilitate the creation of a pedestrian connection between West Market and the core.

The West Market section added the first housing to the town center district, in the form of urban townhouses and condominiums.

Residential development has also occurred just east of the core, where Stratford Tower, a 14-story condominium building, now terminates the view down Market Street. In addition to the tower, the nine-acre (3.6-hectare) project includes Stratford Court, a group of four four-story condominium buildings. Unfortunately, Stratford's location (across Reston Parkway, a divided highway), luxury-priced units (ranging from $150,000 to almost $500,000), and controlled access cause it to function more like a gated community than an integral part of the town center.

With these developments nearing completion, Terrabrook was ready to move forward with Phase II of the urban core. Currently under construction, Phase II lengthens Market Street from two blocks to five blocks. The Market Street spine, which was essentially a short main street in Phase I, is also being expanded along the new north-south roadways, Explorer Street and St. Francis Street. Democracy Drive, which runs parallel to Market Street, is also being extended one block west, and will feature development on both sides of the street. Phase II of the project will incorporate a gradual transition from the intense specialty retail, entertainment, and dining mix and high-rise office towers of Phase I (and the adjacent Freedom Square and Explorer Square blocks) to the somewhat more neighborhood-oriented retail, employment, and high-density residential mix of Phase II. The transition will revolve around Explorer Square, a town green located at the center of Phase II that will provide a counterpoint to the more urban Fountain Square plaza of Phase I. Mixed-use office towers will be to the east and south of the green, a new hotel with ground-floor retail will be on the north side, and two high-density apartment blocks—with retail on the corners facing the green—will lie to the west. Explorer Square will also include an open-air amphitheater for concerts and other events, relieving some of the pressure on the pavilion and Fountain Square plaza.

The 600 urban apartments to be built in the two new residential blocks that will run along Town Center Parkway are arguably the most important addition to the urban core. While residents of the West Market and Stratford developments will have to contend with crossing the wide, high-speed parkways around the urban core, residents of the Phase II apartment blocks will live within easy walking distance of shops and services throughout the urban core.

The design of parking structures has evolved as Reston Town Center has been developed. One of the project's weaknesses was that it lacked liner buildings and ground-floor storefronts to conceal some of the parking garages, which currently create not just "B" streets (streets that are primarily utilitarian rather than pedestrian-oriented) but significant dead zones just off Market Street. More recent parking structures have incorporated liner buildings, which make the structures more attractive while also expanding the amount of street frontage lined with retail. With the addition of retail tenants along both sides of Democracy Drive, the town center now enjoys a retail shopping loop that connects with and extends the original two blocks of retail along Market Street.

The following characteristics are the principal sources of Reston Town Center's strength:

■ A high-density assembly of office, retail, hotel, entertainment, and—with Phase II—residential uses;

■ A solid main street, and a very strong center of gravity (the Fountain Square plaza, which will soon be joined by a second center, the town green of Phase II);

■ The incorporation of a major hotel and cinema into the streetscape (both have entrances directly from Market Street);

■ A permanent, civic-oriented skating rink and performance pavilion;

■ The successful evolution from surface parking lots to structured parking decks as the project has grown.

Depending on the long-term performance of the Spectrum shopping center, there may be the potential to narrow the New Dominion Parkway and fill in the Spectrum site over time, extending the urban fabric of the core even further.

Top: In Phase II, the tallest mixed-use buildings will be located along Market Street, with urban-style apartment blocks on either side. *Sasaki Associates, Inc.*

Bottom: Two walls of the cinema are lined with shops, forming a continuous, high-quality pedestrian network. Garages—added later, along Democracy Drive—are now concealed by liner shops, creating a retail loop with Market Street.

space. As one of the few town centers that includes substantial office space, Reston Town Center provides an important model for the integration of office space into a town center format.

One of the most urban town centers to date, Reston features numerous high-rise buildings in a variety of architectural styles, more completed space than virtually any other town center, and a high-density "downtown" atmosphere. Future plans include a metro station within 1,000 feet (304 meters) of the town center that would provide a transit connection to the Dulles Corridor and the Washington metropolitan region. Finally, Reston offers an excellent example of how a town center can be phased, over time, to become a larger, more diversified, mixed-use district.

Mizner Park

Just two months after Phase I of Reston Town Center opened, another pathbreaking project was reaching completion over 1,000 miles (1,610 kilometers) to the south, in Boca Raton, Florida. Mizner Park, which opened in December 1990, is unique for many reasons, among them its distinction as the first enclosed shopping mall to be replaced by a town center. The leading role played by the Boca Raton Community Redevelopment Agency (CRA), in partnership with Crocker & Company, also presaged the many public/private partnerships that would come to play a strong role in town center development (particularly in City-Place, in West Palm Beach, which would come about a decade later). In contrast to its contemporaries, Mashpee Commons and Reston Town Center, Mizner Park incorporated residences as a cornerstone use right from the start, arranging both apartments and offices above ground-floor retail space.

In 1987, the Boca Raton CRA recommended that the 15-year-old Boca Raton Mall be redeveloped as a mixed-use complex. When Crocker & Company purchased the 28.7-acre (11.6-hectare) site a few months later, the stage was set for an extended round of negotiations between the CRA and the developer to

On Market Street in mid-July, shoppers stroll and window shop beneath a mature canopy of trees.

Reston Town Center is especially noteworthy among town centers because it incorporated office space as the cornerstone use. The project's location within the rapidly growing Dulles corridor—a booming office corridor during the 1990s—afforded ample opportunity to attract office tenants; even in this highly competitive suburban office market, the center succeeded in commanding a premium for its office

Top: The Boca Raton Mall opened in 1974 and was moribund by the late 1980s, when the Boca Raton Community Redevelopment Agency targeted the site for redevelopment. The mall closed in 1989 and was demolished to make way for Mizner Park. *Boca Raton Community Redevelopment Agency.*

Bottom: Mizner Park completely transformed the site of the former shopping mall, creating a premier public space where a mix of residential, retail, and office space—including dining, entertainment and, now, civic uses—supports a variety of activities. *Crocker & Company.*

decide the fate of the property. The CRA proposed that the city purchase the property (through a $58 million bond issue that would be repaid through tax increment financing), take ownership of all 28.7 acres (11.6 hectares) of the site, and lease back 12 acres (4.8 hectares) of land, on which Crocker & Company would construct new buildings. This ground-lease arrangement assumed that the project would be successful, and that the higher property values would lead to increased tax revenues, which would be used to retire the debt. When some citizens expressed concern over the bond issue, Crocker & Company requested a voter referendum that revealed overwhelming support for the redevelopment initiative.

The site was then cleared to make way for Mizner Park, which would come to represent the antithesis of the enclosed mall it replaced. In the center of the site, where the mall stood, is a long rectangular public space that forms the heart and soul of the project. Some have likened the space to a fragment of a boulevard, and others simply call it a linear park, but the space also has some of the qualities of a grand European plaza. In contrast to most projects, where the public space takes the form of a small square or green, the public space at Mizner is wide, runs the entire length of the project, and is heavily landscaped with tropical foliage, benches, fountains, colorful gazebos, and a network of brick-paved walkways. In the decade since they were

on both sides of the plaza, provide continuous shelter from the sun and rain. To break up the monotony of the large buildings, portions of each structure are recessed, and the heights of individual structures vary between three and six stories, creating an ensemble effect. Parallel on-street parking spaces line both sides of the streets, and parking decks are tucked in the rear of each of the four blocks; multiple passageways at midblock bring visitors directly from the garages to the walkways in front of the shops.

When the ULI Project Reference File on Mizner Park was published, in 1992, the project offered 156,000 square feet (14,490 square meters) of retail, dining, and entertainment (including an eight-screen cinema); 136,000 square feet (12,630 square meters)

Mizner Park's tropical climate helped to create a lush landscape where, just a few years earlier, there had been nothing but parking lots and a shopping mall.

first planted, Mizner Park's palm, banyan, and other tropical trees have matured into a dense, shady canopy that provides quiet places for strolling and sitting, and that greatly enhances the open plazas and the central fountain area.

Wrapped around this grand public space are brick-paved streets lined with pink buildings, of varying heights, that create a strong sense of enclosure. The deep and arcaded walkways in front of the shops,

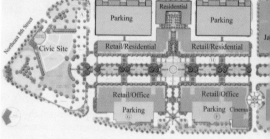

Top: Mizner Park's long street walls are broken up by variations in the heights of buildings and through the use of balconies, windows, and railings, which create an ensemble effect.

Bottom: The site plan for Mizner Park. *Boca Raton Community Redevelopment Agency.*

The popular outdoor dining area at Mizner Park, where seating spills out of the numerous restaurants that are at the base of a large apartment building added in a later phase.

of residential space (for 136 apartments); 106,000 square feet (9,850 square meters) of office space; and an outdoor amphitheater. The project was completed at a total cost of $59.5 million. Subsequent phases have added a nine-story, 112-unit apartment building; 24 three-story streetfront townhouses; the 40,000-square-foot (3,720-square-meter) International Museum of Cartoon Art (now defunct); an 80,000-square-foot (7,430-square-meter) Jacobson's Department Store; and an eight-story, 180,000-square-foot (16,720-square-meter) office building. The most recent addition is the Boca Raton Center for the Arts, at the northern end of the project.

Mizner Park's strength lies in its ability to create a sophisticated, European-style urban atmosphere with a unique sense of place. Mizner Park's ambience derives from very basic architecture that is enriched by a grand public space and by elements of civic art that include the arcaded entrance, fountain area, and entranceway tower. In Tony Nelessen's visual preference surveys, which are administered to people throughout the United States, the outdoor dining plaza below the apartment tower consistently ranks as one of the most popular images.

The bold ground-lease arrangement also provided a model for other cities to consider, particularly with respect to revitalization efforts involving greyfield shopping mall properties. The courage to include housing over retail and line the back of a parking garage with townhouses has also had rewarding results, in the form of extraordinary demand for all units. The residential, in fact, has been the most successful aspect of the project. Rents for the residences whose wrought-iron balconies overlook the plaza have appreciated dramatically, proving that even within a mile (1.6 kilometers) of apartments and condominiums overlooking the beachfront, there is an extraordinary demand for "rooms with a view" of an urban streetscape. The one drawback of Mizner Park's ground lease is that it complicates (but does not preclude) the sale of the townhouses, many of which are occupied as rental units.

That the project has aged well is due less to the modest architecture of the buildings than to the graceful maturation of the public space. Richard Heapes, who worked on the design of Mizner Park while on staff at Cooper Carry Architects, notes that Mizner's buildings were designed and built within a very condensed time frame. Since no one knew how successful the project would be, the structures were not built for the ages and will require updating in the years ahead. Shortcomings—such as the plainness and uniformity of the buildings, and the fact that the large columns are hollow—are often noted by architects but seldom

The addition of urban townhouses on the western border of the site provides an excellent transition between the commercial core of Mizner Park and the neighborhood of single-family homes directly across the street. The townhouses line (and conceal) one of Mizner Park's large parking garages.

ficult for them to remember which of the four parking decks they parked in.

The project has also faced its share of criticism over the years for the substantial amount of public investment that was required to make it feasible, and for the slow progress in the construction of the community and cultural facilities. One of the lessons that both the developer and the city learned is not to oversell a project's civic elements to the public in the early stages of the project, before fundraising is complete and financing has been secured. The recent construction of the Boca Raton Center for the Arts shows how much local commitment and perseverance are required to ensure that civic elements fall into place on sites that have been reserved at the outset of the project.

Given the ground-lease arrangement with the city, Mizner Park's leasing decisions have been subjected to additional scrutiny. Some members of the community, for example, are concerned about the increasing dominance of high-end, upscale retail and dining tenants, and have pressured the developer and city officials to add more moderately priced venues. The addition of the American Café and Ruby Tuesday—moderately priced, family-oriented restaurants—was considered a concession to these pressures.

The downtown redevelopment plan envisioned a corridor of pedestrian-friendly, mixed-use urbanism running from Mizner Park south through the downtown. Transforming the adjacent hodgepodge of strip malls, office buildings, and older shopping centers—all under separate property ownership—has proven to

by the public, which is more immersed in the urban space, the atmosphere, and the visual variety that the storefronts present. Charlie Siemon, a land use attorney who was also instrumental in the early planning and development phases of Mizner Park—and who has lived and worked there for many years—points out a more relevant problem associated with the excessive harmony of the building materials and colors: it can be disorienting to visitors and make it dif-

Mizner Park's grand public space, with its combination of hardscape and green areas, has become an attractive public gathering place for both residents and visitors.

Mizner Park's center of gravity: a centrally located fountain facing the large outdoor dining area.

be a more daunting challenge than the acquisition of the ready-made greyfield mall site for Mizner Park. Mizner Park, however, has succeeded in creating an attachable fragment of urbanism—a new downtown for Boca Raton that planners and city officials have been working to connect with other parts of the city. The owners of adjacent properties, including a strip center that terminates the southern end of the plaza, also see the benefit of trying to make connections to Mizner Park and to build on its success.

Mizner Park remains a preeminent case study of a town center created on a redevelopment site through an innovative public/private partnership. The project continues to thrive and has served as an inspiration for many other town center initiatives, including CityPlace, in West Palm Beach. It also possesses perhaps the most attractive urban public space of any town center project (CityPlace being the one possible exception). At a time when few would have believed that it was financially feasible, Mizner Park bucked local and national trends and proved that

main streets focused on an open-air plaza, with apartments and offices over retail, could be successful—both financially, and as a format for urban-oriented revitalization.

Notes
1. The first phase of the project was written up in 1991, in the ULI Project Reference File.
2. The original architect, Randall Imai, has continued to be the primary architect for ongoing site and building design in Mashpee Commons and is now a principal in the firm Imai/Keller, Inc.
3. Rob Steuteville, "New Downtown Thrives; Awaits Neighborhoods," *New Urban News* 4, no. 2 (1999): 10–13.

CHAPTER 7

CityPlace

West Palm Beach, Florida

One of the largest and most ambitious town center projects built to date in the United States—and one of the most urban—CityPlace successfully transformed a failed private sector venture in a blighted area into the opportunity of a lifetime for downtown West Palm Beach. The result of a highly creative public/private partnership forged by the vision and tenacity of a strong mayor, CityPlace offers a sophisticated urbanism that evokes some of the ambience of a European city.

The development includes a mix of national retailers, local and regional specialty shops, ten destination restaurants, nearly 600 residential units (including private townhouses, live/work lofts, and rental apartments), a restored 1920s church adapted to serve as a multipurpose cultural center, a Muvico 20-screen cinema complex fashioned after the Paris Opera House, and a $3.5 million "show" fountain in the center of a grand, Italian-style plaza. Additional office, hotel, and convention space is planned for later phases.

Background and Site Characteristics

Part of a ten-block, 72.9-acre (30-hectare) tract located in the heart of West Palm Beach, CityPlace is ten minutes from the Palm Beach International Airport and near the intersection of I-95 and Okeechobee Boulevard, a major thoroughfare that leads to Palm Beach and popular beach destinations along the Atlantic Coast. Affluent communities such as Palm Beach, Hobe Sound, Delray Beach, and Boca Raton are all nearby, as are attractive shopping districts like Worth Avenue (which is across the intercoastal waterway), and West Palm Beach's earlier success story, the Clematis Street district. Much of the CityPlace site had been assembled and cleared by a failed private sector redevelopment effort in the late 1980s. In the 1990s, the city completed the land assembly by demolishing structures on key sites and making some additional acquisitions.

The CityPlace development team was led by Kenneth Himmel, managing partner of CityPlace Partners and head of the Palladium Company, a development firm. Himmel's experience with previous projects—including Copley Place (Boston), Pacific Place (Seattle), Reston Town Center (Reston, Virginia), and Water Tower Place (Chicago)—brought tremendous strength to the project. To design CityPlace, Himmel brought on Howard Elkus, of Elkus/Manfredi Architects Ltd., in Boston, who had also served as the lead designer for Himmel's Copley Place, Pacific Place, and Water Tower Place projects.

The site is bordered to the west, along Sapodilla Avenue, by the Kravis Center, a performing arts center, and the School for the Performing Arts; the Florida Ballet is woven into the northeastern corner of the site. The southern portion of the site is separated from the northern portion by Okeechobee Boulevard; there are plans to build office space in the center of the boulevard's landscaped median and on the southeastern corner of the site, on each side of the boulevard. A large convention center is planned for the southwestern corner of the site, and a cluster of uses—including a hotel, offices, and a parking garage—are planned for the western portion of the site, to support the convention center.

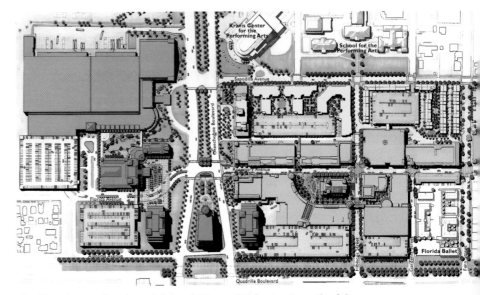

CityPlace is transforming a blighted 73-acre (30-hectare) swath of downtown West Palm Beach into a town center that acts as a regional destination. *Elkus/Manfredi Architects Ltd.*

Development

While West Palm Beach enjoyed proximity to beaches and to the many affluent communities in the region, it enjoyed none of their advantages; by the 1980s, the downtown had become even less active than the typical nine-to-five setting, and held little appeal either to city residents or to outside visitors. It also included a number of poorly maintained, underutilized buildings and large pockets of vacant land.

One such pocket was the area where CityPlace is now located: nearly 73 acres (30 hectares) of land that Henry Rolfs had quietly assembled—using 20 different real estate agents—in the short span of nine months. Unfortunately for Rolfs, his grand plan for the Downtown/Uptown project, which he hoped would be a gateway to Palm Beach, was started in 1986, and the enterprise collapsed with the real estate depression of the late 1980s and early 1990s. Although the project failed, Rolfs's success in assembling the land would later relieve the city of the burden of doing so—a significant advantage, as land assembly often impedes downtown redevelopment projects.

At about this time a new mayor, Nancy Graham, came into office, and was faced with the challenge of

Mixed-use buildings with retail on the ground floor and residential above overlook the plaza on Rosemary Street. The Pottery Barn shown is a one-story store with a two-story facade. The church plaza attracts large groups of visitors during the day...

...and by night. *Elkus/Manfredi Architects Ltd.*

improving a downtown that no one much cared about. With very few resources at her disposal, Graham began trying to figure out where to start. In 1993, while attending the Mayors' Institute on City Design, a program sponsored by the National Endowment for the Arts, Graham heard Charleston mayor Joe Riley speak about his city's successful revitalization. Riley's speech

opened her eyes to the importance of good urban design in revitalizing cities. Upon returning to West Palm Beach, however, Graham discovered that all the attractive, exciting urban places she had learned about were illegal to build in her city. Clearing the path for redevelopment would mean overhauling the city's planning and regulatory codes, creating a new master plan for the downtown that would incorporate new urbanist principles, appointing new staff and commissioners who were receptive to change, and undertaking some catalytic moves involving land acquisition, demolition, and street improvements.[1]

Eventually, Graham succeeded in nurturing the Clematis Street district until it was transformed into an attractive, pedestrian-friendly retail street. She also found creative ways to use the city's limited resources to push redevelopment forward. When a decrepit Holiday Inn stood in the way of redevelopment, Graham had the city purchase the building for $1,000 at a foreclosure sale and proceeded to throw a New Year's Eve party featuring the implosion of the structure. The site is now home to the Meyer's Amphitheater at Sunset Park.

Graham was also instrumental in getting a new fountain built near city hall, in Centennial Plaza, as a focal point for people to meet and mingle, and she supported and helped to connect a growing hub of arts and cultural institutions, including Ballet Florida, Dreyfoos School of the Arts, the Fine Arts District, the Kravis Center for the Performing Arts, the Montgomery Art Center, the Norton Museum of Art, the Palm Beach Opera, and the Palm Street Artists Studios.

The CityPlace site was adjacent to the revitalized areas, but much of it had previously been razed, creating a vast no-man's-land in what Graham described as "the gateway to downtown West Palm Beach." The city lacked both the funds needed to acquire the site and the development expertise needed to carry out the type of urban, mixed-use development the mayor envisioned. Graham convinced the city to accept some financial risk (by borrowing $20 million from Florida's Sunshine Fund to acquire the site), then to launch a national search for a development team capable of carrying out a major redevelopment project. The city issued a request for proposals (RFP) and fielded a number of strong development proposals, eventually selecting the team that would become CityPlace Partners.

Using the $20 million it had borrowed, the city acquired the site, with the understanding that the developer would repay the amount through lease payments, and would have the option to buy the property once the project was built. The city also supported $55 million in bonds, to be repaid through tax increment financing (TIF); the money would be used to create a high-quality public space and to pay 30 percent of the construction costs for the parking structures. The agreement with the developer stipulated that if the amount of TIF money collected in any given year was too low to meet the assessments on the bonds, the developer would make up the difference for that year. As credit enhancement—to help get the project financed—the city's maximum exposure on the bond was $4 million of debt reserve for five years. Of the $142 million financed by the developers, 77 percent came from commercial banks (led by Key Bank, which provided first mortgage construction and mini-perm financing); the remaining 23 percent represented equity investment by the Palladium Company and an equity partner, a pension fund based in the Midwest.

With the city's money on the table, the developer's mantra "time is money" took on added significance—"time" now meant both the developer's money and the city's money. Graham had the site and a skilled development team, but she knew that "in order to get them to do something great that meets your vision you have to make it easy for them to do it." The city responded by taking on all of the permitting work for the project—a decision that

A grand staircase brings visitors up past the balconies of Legal Seafood to a small plaza with a fountain, which serves as a meeting place for the establishments—several restaurants and the Muvico 20-screen cinema— that surround the plaza. *Elkus/Manfredi Architects Ltd.*

provided an enormous boost to the development. Elkus, with 20 years of experience working on similar projects, commented that "the stage had been set by the city and the path had been cleared, in terms of approval, like no project I have ever been involved with; to have 18 months between the winning of the project and the ground breaking is unprecedented."[2]

Mix of Uses

Because the developers of CityPlace knew from the start that the unique place they envisioned would require an equally unique mix of shops, restaurants, and entertainment, they avoided relying solely on the large chains that are typical of shopping malls and eschewed discount retailers. Instead, they assembled a core of experienced main street retailers, including Ann Taylor; Pottery Barn; Restoration Hardware; Williams-Sonoma; a 30,000-square-foot (2,790-square-meter) Barnes & Noble; and a 16,000-square-foot (1,490-square-meter) FAO Schwarz. They also assembled a variety of anchors, including Macy's; the 92,000-square-foot (8,550-square-meter) Muvico Parisian 20-screen cinema; and a 23,000-square-foot (2,140-square-meter) Publix grocery store. Finally, they recruited ten high-profile "destination" restaurants, including Angelo and Maxie's, Legal Seafood (which originated in Boston), the Cheesecake Factory, and Mark's. The several dozen smaller shops sprinkled around the project—mostly higher-end fashion, home, and lifestyle retailers—range in size from 200 to 3,000 square feet (19 to 280 square meters).

To gain entry into the project, Macy's agreed to create a new store concept—a two-story, 110,000-square-foot (10,220-square-meter) building that is smaller than its traditional department stores and specifically designed for an urban environment. Muvico, a Ft. Lauderdale–based cinema operator, blended into the urban atmosphere by housing its 20-screen theater in a building that was designed to evoke the grandeur and elegance of the Paris Opera House, then including upscale concessions, a supervised chil-

Residential properties sold very quickly in CityPlace, though some were purchased as investment property and are not occupied year-round.

dren's playroom, and valet parking. FAO Schwarz created a two-story, custom-designed building as well. Even retailers that did not drastically alter their internal layouts were willing to experiment with their external appearance: Pottery Barn, for example, negotiated a two-story facade on a one-story store; the second floor is actually occupied residential space.

The retail, dining, and entertainment mix is only part of the CityPlace story, however, as the project includes plans for three office towers, totaling 750,000 square feet (69,680 square meters), and a diverse assortment of 586 housing units. While some developers view housing as an unproven use and an unnecessary risk for town center projects, the CityPlace team viewed the provision of diverse housing types as a means of generating the 24-hour street life the project was aiming for—and as central to the project's long-term success.

CityPlace's extraordinary mix of housing options is concentrated close to the major cultural institutions, and includes 51 private townhouses, 33 garden apartments, 128 luxury rental apartments in high-rise buildings, 264 mid-rise rental apartments in three buildings, and 38 rental flats and 56 live/work lofts above the storefronts on Rosemary Avenue. Much of the higher-density housing is located in apartment buildings that run the entire length of Sapodilla Avenue and envelop the large parking garages located within the interiors of two blocks. Townhouses and live/work units sold at a rapid pace. One note of caution, however, concerns the fact that many of the units appear to have been purchased as second homes and investment property, meaning that they remain unoccupied for long periods of time. Developers of town center projects might want to consider residency requirements, such as those used in Celebration and other projects, to discourage speculation, to ensure that units are occupied, and to create the sort of 24-hour street life that residential uses can bring to town centers.

Streets, Layout, and Parking

The mixed-use core of the site centers on the large church plaza, and consists of four large blocks that are further broken up by alleyways (service roads) and side streets. Rosemary Avenue, the central spine of the site, runs from Okeechobee Boulevard through the key internal crossroad at Hibiscus Street, and continues straight through to Fern Street, which forms the northern boundary of the site. The pattern of streets and blocks in CityPlace provides multiple connections to adjacent downtown neighborhoods and cultural sites.

The streets of CityPlace are lined with parallel parking spaces and a mix of street trees, climbing trellises covered with flowering vines, and a variety of

Cars, buses, trolleys, delivery vehicles, and pedestrians all share the streets at CityPlace.

large potted plants. Sidewalks range from six to ten feet (two to three meters) in width and are even wider at key intersections, where they are protected from traffic by bollards and lampposts that expand the pedestrian space and help narrow the distance that people must traverse to get from one side of the street to the other. The sidewalks themselves are composed of tile mosaics that add to the Mediterranean theme. At each of the five intersections within the site, the streets are paved with brick, to heighten drivers' awareness that they are in a pedestrian zone.

Parking is provided in four large decks located in back of the multistory buildings on either side of Rosemary Avenue. In the northern half of the site, the parking decks are concealed in the interiors of blocks and are accessible by means of a service alley. Parking decks in the southern half of the site back up to a rail line that runs between the site and Quadrille Boulevard. Although utilitarian in design, the decks are connected with CityPlace's buildings, streets, and plazas via attractive pedestrian passageways.

The facades of long buildings at CityPlace are broken up into shorter sections, creating the appearance of an ensemble of smaller buildings. A variety of colors and architectural elements yield much greater visual diversity than is found in many town center projects and represent a departure from the "all-pink" styling of many South Florida projects. The streets are lined with parallel parking spaces, palm trees, and trellises with flowering vines. *Elkus/Manfredi Architects Ltd.*

Buildings

Following in the footsteps of Addison Mizner,[3] Elkus, Himmel, and Mayor Graham undertook an intense, seven-day tour of southern Mediterranean architecture and urbanism, seeking inspirational buildings, plazas, fountains, and urban landscapes. While traveling, Elkus and his design team "measured the height and width of arcades from Venice to Rome." The designers were interested in two things. "We were seeking the right scale of those spaces, to make it feel good for the pedestrian walking in those arcades, and to make it work well to showcase the tenants that have to do business in those arcades."[4]

To develop an area encompassing five city blocks without creating the sameness of a "project," the designers worked hard to incorporate unique design features into buildings, walkways, and landscaping throughout CityPlace. The buildings offer columns of various styles; the walkways, crosswalks, and plazas are composed of various combinations of stone, brick, and tile; and plantings complement the architecture, instead of being in a uniform pattern composed of identical trees and plants. In a 1998 interview with the *South Florida Business Journal*, Elkus described the intent of CityPlace's architecture:

I think it's an architecture of freedom. You can be as informal or formal as you want within that context. You can be your most relaxed self or you can be eloquent. This is not a great, formal, columned statement . . . but there is a greater unity in the overall approach than, say, on Clematis Street, which can be southern Mediterranean and South Beach. You

CityPlace provides an extensive urban landscape of plazas, courtyards, grand staircases, fountains, balconies, and arcaded walkways for cafés, restaurants, and outdoor events. Calm, pedestrian-friendly street design and on-street parking allow pedestrians and cars to happily coexist. *Elkus/Manfredi Architects Ltd.*

Top: Two-story commercial buildings curve gently around the central plaza, focusing attention on the historic church building.

Bottom: The careful restoration and adaptive use of the 1920s-era Spanish Colonial Revival church has created a community resource and lends authenticity and a sense of place to the project. *Elkus/Manfredi Architects Ltd.*

will not find the use of pink within CityPlace. We don't think it belongs within the palette that we've chosen. It has been so exaggerated in all-pink developments that by the elimination of pink we're making sure CityPlace doesn't run that way.[5]

Because of variations in style, color, elevation, and material, the facades of the large buildings along Rosemary Avenue appear to be composed of many smaller buildings. The architectural details play off the southern Mediterranean theme, and feature exposed rafters; canvas awnings; tile and metal rooftops; and wrought-iron and wooden balconies on the upper floors, where residential units overlook the street life below. "It's an architecture of the out-of-doors," explains Elkus, "of a very different climate. It embraces landscaping. It does not have hard edges between the inside and the outside. It uses patios, arches, and trellises between the buildings and surrounding them."[6]

The former First United Methodist Church and the central plaza that surrounds it represent the heart and soul of CityPlace. Built in 1926, the church was one of the largest Spanish Colonial Revival structures of its day—large enough to provide shelter for victims of a 1928 hurricane for nearly 11 months while their homes were being rebuilt. Carefully restored and adapted at a cost of $5 million, the building features an 11,000-square-foot (1,020-square-meter) hall that is used for cultural performances, community events, and art exhibits. More important, the church building is a visual anchor that lends the project a sense of history and authenticity, of the sort that cannot be fabricated. To preserve dramatic views of the building, the project's designers created a large, Italian-style plaza in front of the church and curved the commercial street wall to form a crescent that encloses the plaza.

Public Gathering Spaces

The church plaza itself is the project's center of gravity, providing a grand public room that draws visitors from West Palm Beach and Florida's entire Gold Coast region. The plaza's strong sense of enclosure; the presence of the freestanding church building; the high concentration of outdoor dining areas that spill out into the plaza (including a café on the back side of the church building); and the urban landscaping (including benches, fountains, and plants and trees in large terra-cotta pots)—all contribute to the strongly European atmosphere.

Victor Dover, a Miami-based urban designer, has observed that the large plaza area might have benefited from the addition of a street that would have curved around the church and run parallel to Rosemary Avenue. The addition of this street would have increased the connectivity throughout the site and further activated the plaza and storefronts by adding slow-moving traffic and on-street parking. Nonetheless, Dover agrees that the space is a marvelous gathering place as it is and a major new landmark in southeastern Florida.

The project also includes a dramatic fountain: a solid piece of civic art by day, at night the fountain

The fountains are a favorite place for families to gather and for children to play, even on a rainy day like this one.

provides shows of water, light, and fog choreographed to music. Smaller plazas, courtyards, and fountains are located on both the first and second levels of the project, and the streets can be closed for festivals and events.

Marketing, Management, and Performance

CityPlace gained momentum quickly: the retail space was 60 percent leased at ground breaking, and 80 percent leased one year prior to opening, which was in October of 2000. Residential space was snatched up even faster: 51 townhouses, ranging in price from $252,000 to $418,000, sold out in just ten days. The 33 condominiums, some as small as 766 square feet (70 square meters) and at prices ranging from $139,000 to $349,000, sold in just three weeks. Even more impressive was the fact that all these units were sold the summer before any residential construction had even begun. Apartment leasing initially moved more slowly, which some observers attributed to the absence of neighborhood retail uses in and around CityPlace. The addition of a Publix grocery store is expected to accelerate leasing since residents will no longer have to drive to obtain basic grocery items and sundries.

On the basis of the project's performance during its first eight months, CityPlace management expects retail sales to average between $450 and $500 per square foot ($4,843 and $5,381 per square meter) in the first year. The ten restaurants have also performed exceptionally well—so well that on weekends, there are long waits for seating, during which patrons visit the shops and stroll through the plaza. Total retail revenues for the first year of operation were around $60 million.

CityPlace enjoys the coordinated marketing and management of a regional shopping mall, and municipal support in the programming of community festivals and events. The project is also having a positive impact on adjacent properties—and cultural institutions, such as the Kravis Center, are initiating projects to improve the connections between their sites and CityPlace. To protect the city's prior redevelopment effort in the Clematis Street district, the downtown development authority and the developer have funded a free waterfront trolley system that connects the district with CityPlace in a continuous loop, seven days a week, 12 hours a day. In its first six months of operation the trolley trans-

ported over 300,000 people between the two sites.

The impact of CityPlace goes beyond the development site, however: there has been a dramatic increase in development activity in downtown West Palm Beach that observers attribute to CityPlace. While there was initial concern that CityPlace might hurt the revitalized section of Clematis Street, Bill Fountain, director of the downtown development authority, credited CityPlace with helping to attract national retail stores, such as the Gap and Banana Republic, to Clematis Street. There has been an unprecedented upsurge in residential development downtown, and renewed interest in office and commercial development, which did not exist before CityPlace was built. "I think we have already seen the benefit of CityPlace." Fountain said. "By creating their economic climate they are spinning off lots of other opportunities. It is churning the marketplace."[7]

Experience Gained

- Keep it real. The preservation and adaptive use of the Spanish Colonial Revival church represented an investment in the unique identity of the project, establishing a connection to local history and to the community that gave greater authenticity to the entire project.
- Create a center of gravity. The grand, Italian-style plaza provides the project with a powerful focal point that attracts people to CityPlace not just as a place to shop, but also as a place to live, to work, to dine, to attend cultural and entertainment events, and simply to gather with friends and family.

- Adopt a local or regional vernacular. The project's southern Mediterranean theme—evoked not only through stylistic elements but through the indoor/outdoor character of the buildings and spaces—provides a strong sense of place that is connected to the vernacular traditions of Florida's early Gold Coast communities.
- Create rooms with a view. Don't underestimate the power of high-quality urban public spaces to generate strong demand for town center residences of all types.
- Consider taking steps to ensure that town center housing is purchased by people who intend to live there and contribute to the life of the downtown, not merely as investment property that may sit empty for long periods of time.

CityPlace is an example of how quickly large-scale redevelopment projects can proceed when municipalities and the private sector work closely together to realize a shared vision. A number of actions on the part of local government are key to this kind of success:

- Enact compatible local regulations. In West Palm Beach, regulatory reforms had already removed major impediments to compact, mixed-use development in the downtown; at CityPlace, these were used to encourage the town center format.

- Assemble (or help to assemble) the land. Although CityPlace had an advantage, in that land assembly had been largely completed by an earlier owner of the property, the city continued to assemble key parcels that made possible a project of this scale. Land assembly is particularly crucial on infill sites, where property ownership is often fragmented into many small parcels. While municipalities may not have the resources to take the lead in assembling land, they can use their power of eminent domain to acquire isolated holdouts that would otherwise obstruct the project.
- Provide strong local leadership and support. Public sector support can make or break a town center project and, in this case, CityPlace moved forward with the backing of a strong mayor who had a clear vision of how the property should be redeveloped and the willingness to take bold steps to support the project.
- Provide necessary public financing. When a city is willing to take on risk by putting up public funds to obtain property and to make infrastructure improvements, it can jump-start redevelopment projects and gain much more control over them. (A caveat: this added level of control can help or hinder a project, depending on how good the marriage is between the municipality and the developer.) For publicly initiated projects, it is important to control the property and the process to guarantee that the outcome is compatible with public objectives. Because it controlled the property, West Palm Beach was able to conduct a competitive RFP process that allowed the city to select a development team whose experience in town center development was based on traditional urban design principles, making the best possible partnership between public and private sector partners.
- Divide and conquer. By taking on all the permitting to push the project through the approval process, the city allowed the development team to focus on what it did best—financing, building, and leasing the project.

Project Data: CityPlace

General Information

Project type	New town center for an existing city
Web page	http://www.cityplaceweb.com/
Location	West Palm Beach, Florida, on Okeechobee Boulevard, just east of I-95
Acres/hectares	72.9/30
Parking	3,300 spaces in four parking garages—approximately 5.5 spaces per 1,000 square feet (93 square meters) of leasable retail space
Investment to date	$550 million ($220 million retail component)

Owners

CityPlace Partners, New York; the Related Companies, L.P., New York; the Palladium Company, New York; the O'Connor Group, New York; the Related Group of Florida, Miami; the Ohio State Teachers Retirement System; the City of West Palm Beach

Developer

The Palladium Company, New York

Master Planners and Architects

Elkus/Manfredi Architects Ltd., Boston (cultural arts center: Rick Gonzalez, REG Architects)

Landscape Architect

Bradshaw Gill & Associates, Ft. Lauderdale

Commercial Uses

Building Area by Type of Use

Use	Square Feet/Square Meters
Retail	600,000/55,740
Office (three buildings)	750,000/69,680

Retail Uses

Number of establishments	78
Lease rates (per square foot/square meter)	Low $30s/low $300s
Tenant mix	Balanced mix of national chains (including Barnes & Noble, FAO Schwarz, Macy's, Pottery Barn, and Restoration Hardware) and unique local and regional establishments; a Publix supermarket; ten restaurants
Range of shop sizes	Most smaller shops range from 200 to 3,000 square feet (19 to 280 square meters), with a half-dozen larger stores and restaurants

Hotel Uses

440 rooms (planned)

Residential Uses

Unit Type	Number of Units
Private townhouses	51
Garden apartments	33
Luxury rental apartments	128
Mid-rise rental apartments	264
Rental flats	38
Live/work lofts	56
Total	570

Civic Uses

Harriet Himmel Gilman Theater for Cultural and Performing Arts, a central plaza, and assorted small urban open spaces

Development Schedule

City contract awarded	1996
Ground breaking	December 1998
Opened	October 2000
Buildout date	2003

Notes

1. The master plan was eventually developed by Duany Plater-Zyberk & Company and by the Gibbs Planning Group.
2. Carole Clancy, "CityPlace Architect Draws Inspiration from Italy," *South Florida Business Journal*, May 15, 1998, 3A.
3. Addison Mizner (1872–1933) was a Florida architect and developer who popularized Mediterranean architecture in Boca Raton and South Florida—particularly the Spanish Colonial style, which he employed in projects such as the Cloister Inn of Boca Raton.
4. Clancy, "CityPlace Architect."
5. Ibid.
6. Ibid.
7. Darcie Lunsford, "CityPlace Sparks Downtown Homes," *South Florida Business Journal* (Miami-Dade edition), May 1, 1998, 1A, 2.

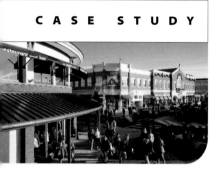

Easton Town Center

Columbus, Ohio

Unlike all the town center developments that preceded it, Easton Town Center is essentially a super regional shopping center in an open-air, main street format. As such, it not only presents a prime example of main street retailing and town center development, but a new model for how to program and design a regional shopping center.

With over 1.5 million square feet (139,350 square meters) of retail space (including both Phase I and Phase II), Easton Town Center is the commercial hub of a 1,200-acre (490-hectare) master-planned community taking shape about eight miles (13 kilometers) northeast of downtown Columbus, Ohio. A mixed-use town center with a mid-America theme that reflects its location near the city of Columbus, Easton Town Center was envisioned by its creators as a leisure-time destination center that would be based on traditional main street and town center design principles.

Development and Mix of Uses

The story of Easton Town Center parallels the story of the Limited, Inc., a multiline retail chain headquartered in Columbus.[1] Both Easton and the Limited originated with the vision of Leslie Wexner, the founder, chairman, and chief executive officer of the Limited, Inc. In the early 1980s, building on its 18 years of constant growth, the Limited, Inc., started to operate as a venture capitalist, creating new businesses and purchasing existing specialty retailers. As part of this expansion, Wexner formed a real estate development unit within the Limited. An early project was the 1,200-acre (490-hectare) country club community of New Albany, just a few miles east of Easton.

In 1986, Wexner started purchasing farmland in the northeast quadrant of Columbus; the property, which centered around Morse Road, was within the city limits and just within the I-270 beltway. He envisioned a multiuse development of retail, office, residential, hotel, and entertainment venues, but his principal goal was to establish a business park for the Limited's national headquarters and operations center. The land was a large infill parcel surrounded by low-density development, and the city was encouraging further development by offering a ten-year, 100 percent abatement of property taxes for all new development in the area. With each purchase of a parcel, Wexner's development team had to win zoning approval for conversion from agricultural to commercial use. By the time Wexner announced the start of construction, in early 1996, the fully assembled parcels formed a contiguous 1,200 acres (490 hectares), an area twice the size of the local Ohio State University campus.

Meanwhile, the recession of the early 1990s led to drastic corporate restructuring at the Limited, Inc. As a publicly traded company focused on maximizing shareholder value, the Limited responded by spinning off its various store brands as freestanding businesses and by shedding all but its core activities.

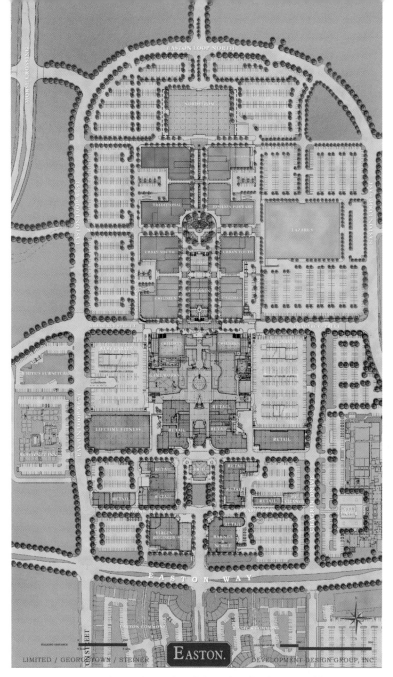

Easton town center is a major regional shopping destination, with over 1.5 million square feet (139,350 square meters) of retail space. Phase I of the development is located on the lower half of the site plan, and Phase II is on the upper half. *Development Design Group.*

One of the noncore businesses was Easton, 50 percent of which the Limited sold to the Georgetown Company, of New York.

Easton and its environs continued to develop during Easton Town Center's startup phase. The 4 million square feet (371,610 square meters) of office space that had been constructed by the end of 1995 provided a local and regional presence for Chase Manhattan Mortgage Corporation, Price Waterhouse, and M/I Schottenstein Homes, and housed the world headquarters for the Limited, Inc., and for the catalog distribution center for Victoria's Secret. The widening of nearby I-270 from six to 12 lanes also had begun in anticipation of increased traffic.

A preexisting flexible zoning district in the middle of the Easton property provided the developer with some latitude for mixing uses, and the municipality was very cooperative in moving Easton Town Center and the other elements of Easton forward. Additional time was needed to negotiate parking requirements, particularly the cross-parking formulas that showed how office and retail would share portions of the same lots and structures. The one way in which the city provided financial assistance was by establishing a TIF arrangement to help cover the costs of necessary public infrastructure, including the parking structures and some road work. The remainder of the project was privately financed. Although lenders were hesitant at first about the concept of the town center, financing proceeded smoothly once the preleasing accelerated and the high caliber of tenants became clear.

The project is being jointly developed by Steiner + Associates and the Georgetown Company, the developer of Easton, and is being managed by Steiner for a partnership of owners consisting of Steiner; the Georgetown Company; the Limited, Inc.; and Arnold Schwarzenegger. Steiner + Associates, which

led the project development team, is the trendsetting development and management firm best known for its work on urban entertainment centers (UECs). Yaromir Steiner, the founder of the firm, was previously president of Constructa, the developer of CocoWalk, in Miami. Steiner views Easton Town Center as a step forward in the evolution of UECs, and as a step "backward"—toward the streets, buildings, and public spaces of traditional cities and towns.

Phase I, which opened in July 1999, incorporates 750,000 square feet (69,680 square meters) of retail, entertainment, and dining in an open-air environment that features a large town square and urban-style streets and public spaces. Phase I was so successful that the schedule for Phase II was accelerated (it opened in the fall of 2001), and the original plans were expanded to provide an additional 800,000 square feet (74,320 square meters) of commercial space—in essence, creating a super regional mall. Phase II features over 400,000 square feet (37,160 square meters) of department stores, including Nordstrom and Lazarus as anchors; additional restaurants; a mix of "best of class" retailers; and office space. The project also includes an apartment/townhouse section and two hotels—a Hilton and a Residence Inn by Marriott. Although the apartment/townhouse complex is located across the street from the commercial core, the architecture of the complex is stylistically connected with that of the town center. The final phases will add multifamily housing and a vertical mixing of uses.

Easton Town Center is the first phase of a larger district plan that calls for additional office and commercial space, residential neighborhoods, parks, and other features radiating out from the town center.

The Easton property is located near the I-270 beltway and is surrounded by development on all sides, making it the last "large infill" parcel within the city limits of Columbus. According to Tim Rollins, chief operating officer of Steiner + Associates, the 34-acre (14-hectare) town center was an early part of the overall development plan, intended to "provide a definite center to help identify the project overall." When fully built out, Easton is projected to incorporate some 5 million square feet (464,520 square meters) of retail, office, entertainment, and residential space and to employ 40,000 workers.

The design of Easton Town Center involved a collaborative planning process that took place over a period of two years, with Cooper, Robertson & Partners focusing more on site planning and the Development Design Group on architecture. The two firms considered the best of past town center designs—including Country Club Plaza, in Kansas City, Missouri, and Reston Town Center, in Reston, Virginia—to see what had worked, and adapted what they had learned to the needs of the Columbus marketplace.

Streets, Layout, and Parking

The rectangular site consists of two large districts, the original Phase I town center district to the south, and the new Phase II—also known as the Fashion District—to the north. Both the surface and structured parking are located at the periphery of the site, including two major parking decks located near the center of the site, at its eastern and western edges.

On the southern portion of the site, two narrow east-west streets about 1,000 feet (300 meters) long cut through the site and border the northern and southern edges of a formal square; both streets have on-street parking, to slow down cars traveling through the town and to keep the wide sidewalks safe for pedestrians. Two one-block streets run north-south on the edges of the square, connecting the cross streets and creating a classic town square pattern. The Fashion District features a

Easton Town Center has a mix of commercial uses in one- and two-story buildings. Some buildings feature small stores on the ground floor and office space on upper floors. *Development Design Group.*

central north-south street—the Strand—which terminates at the Nordstrom building and two cross-streets.

Streets within the project were kept private to make the traditional main street design possible and to allow the streets to be closed for weekly farmers' markets and special events. At the edge of the project, however, the intimate private streets within the grid give way to public streets with wider configurations, including Easton Way, a wide, four-lane street with a large median, which separates the town center from the new townhouses, apartments, and hotels being built by separate developers.

Phase I included 3,800 parking spaces: over 6.3 spaces per 1,000 square feet (93 square meters). The internal streets offer parallel parking spaces, but most parking is provided in the two multilevel parking garages and surface lots. The surface parking lots are located behind all four blocks in the southern half of the site. The northern half of the site is completely surrounded by surface parking lots.

All town center projects face the challenge of providing adequate and accessible parking while avoiding the creation of a sea of parking; creative solutions to isolating and concealing vast amounts of parking are often hard to find. Easton Town Center's strategy was to place the parking on the outer periphery—roughly in a grid pattern—in rectangular lots or in parking structures that are separated by streets or buildings. These rear lots feed into retail side streets that run perpendicular from the central, north-south retail spine that runs through the site. The use of the two large parking structures lined with retail buildings and smaller surface lots that are flanked by buildings on two or three sides allows parking in the southern half of the site to be more effectively concealed than in the northern half.

Buildings

The majority of the buildings in Easton Town Center are one to two stories tall, although many of the facades appear to be taller. Buildings are pulled close to the sidewalks, providing a strong sense of enclosure on the project's narrow interior streets and in the town square. Smaller stores and cafés at street level fill out Easton's rigid street grid. Office space is located on the second level, above the stores.

Easton Town Center's version of the Crystal Palace provides a climate-controlled retail and dining area protected from the region's winter weather. *Development Design Group.*

Borrowing a method used by filmmakers and animators, the designers used storyboards to plan Easton Town Center's buildings, adapting the vernacular themes common to midwestern American towns in the first half of the 20th century to contemporary uses. The Barnes & Noble Bookstore is designed to resemble an old "Carnegie" town library, and a 95,000-square-foot (8,830-square-meter) fitness center is housed in a two-story building that is reminiscent of a 1920s high school with 1950s additions. There are other suggestions of adaptive use, including an "old" fire station that now houses a bakery, and an "old" Bijou theater—complete with art deco references—that appears to have been reincarnated as a Pottery Barn.

Easton's centerpiece, Easton Station, is an enclosed pavilion designed to resemble a traditional midwestern train station. The ensemble—which houses a 30-screen cinema, a high-tech video arcade, and other entertainment-oriented tenants—is one that Disney's Imagineers might have dreamed up: the plaza in front of the "old" train depot appears to have been retrofitted with a glass roof in the style of the Crystal Palace. Although the enclosed pavilion departs from the open-air format of town centers and main streets, the building provides an example of how enclosed retail spaces can be integrated into the streetscapes of town center and main street projects.

The illusion of adaptive use is an effort to introduce a greater sense of authenticity—to evoke an actual town composed of individual buildings that have been constructed during different eras and modified over the course of decades. While most people would not be fooled into thinking that Easton was, in fact, a much older place than it is, the architecture nevertheless stirs feelings of familiarity and comfort in visitors, and has been well-received.

Public Gathering Spaces

Easton offers many types of public spaces, including the town square, the main streets, a "pop fountain," and generous outdoor seating areas for restaurants. Phase II has added an interactive children's garden and a reflection pool where children can sail model boats. The town square, the project's center of gravity, is heavily landscaped and includes both "hard" and "soft" features—paved walkways, fountains, benches, four large panels of lawn, and foliage. The designers have succeeded admirably in creating a square that is capable of accommodating large public events but that does not look empty and lifeless at other times.

The pop fountain, which is extremely popular with children, sends water shooting high in the air to

A traditional town square represents the center of gravity for Easton Town Center. *Development Design Group.*

Most buildings along the square are pulled up close to the sidewalk. The buildings have metal awnings, make generous use of brick, and offer ornamental architectural elements drawn from local and regional influences. *Development Design Group.*

the accompaniment of music and lights. An attraction in and of itself, the fountain operates from early spring through October. The main streets and outdoor dining areas round out Easton Town Center by providing the kinds of public open spaces that are essential to the urban fabric of traditional town centers.

Mix of Uses

Easton Town Center features an impressive array of tenants: about 30 percent of the Phase I retail and entertainment establishments are completely new to the Columbus market. Although timing and market factors were favorable, the developers credit the unique town center concept with enabling the project to succeed in attracting so many prominent chains to the region for the first time. The developers also took care not to overload on national chains, which would

have watered down the local flavor of the project, and spent considerable time and effort actively recruiting over 20 local and regional businesses.

Phase I of Easton Town Center is designed to offer patrons a variety of ways to spend their leisure time. As a lifestyle center, it has no true anchors. Shops are laid out around a town square and along urban streets. The development team wanted not just any main street, but a Columbus main street. They sought out local restaurateurs to develop new dining concepts based on local preferences; two that have succeeded are the Brio Tuscan Grille and the Ocean Club, which serve Italian fare and seafood, respectively. Local fast-food providers include C. V. Wrappers and Panera Bread. Large-format, sit-down restaurants include the Cheesecake Factory, Fadó Irish Pub, Hama Sushi, and P. F. Chang's China Bistro.

Easton Town Center is distinguished by an enviable mix of leisure and entertainment tenants as well, including Life Time Fitness, a Minneapolis-based health club that, in addition to aerobic studios, a sauna, and fitness equipment, also offers two swimming pools, two basketball courts, squash courts, climbing walls, and a child care facility. Entertainment and media venues include Barnes & Noble; Virgin Records Megastore; Jeepers, an indoor amusement park for children; a 35,000-square-foot (3,250-square-meter) Game Works; the Shark Club, a billiards and bowling venue; Round Midnight, Columbus's first-ever all-night jazz club; the Funny Bone Comedy Club; and a 30-screen multiplex cinema and restaurant that was originally a partnership between Planet Hollywood (now gone) and AMC Theatres. Lifestyle retailers include Pottery Barn,

Easton Town Center has provided an urban-style gathering place for thousands of Columbus residents born and raised in the suburbs. *Development Design Group.*

Restoration Hardware, Smith & Hawken, and Williams-Sonoma; fashion venues include Abercrombie & Fitch, Ann Taylor, Baby Gap, Gap, Gap Kids, Banana Republic, Bath and Body Works, Eddie Bauer, J. Crew, Talbots, Victoria's Secret, and World Foot Locker.

Easton Town Center's nighttime ambience. *Development Design Group.*

The 40-acre (16-hectare) Phase II expansion extends the two-story, open-air design of Phase I along a boulevard that leads to the Fashion District, an 800,000-square-foot (74,320-square-meter) regional mall anchored by a freestanding, 170,000-square-foot (15,790-square-meter) Nordstrom store and a Lazarus department store. The Fashion District features such tenants as Anthropologie, Benetton, Brookstone, the Container Store, Jos. A. Bank, Harry and David, the Limited, the Limited Too, Pottery Barn Kids, the Sharper Image, and Wilsons Leather.

Although Easton Town Center is limited to retail, entertainment, and office uses, adjacent development is creating a more well-rounded mix of uses, including 50,000 square feet (4,650 square meters) of office above retail, and a high-density, 700-unit townhouse district—Easton Commons—which is being developed just south of the town center. Two hotels have been built, one on either side of the town center: the 310-room Columbus Hilton and Towers and a 120-room Residence Inn by Marriott. A third hotel, a 150-room Courtyard Marriott, is also being constructed. An apartment and townhouse project has been built directly adjacent to the project, and the 5 million square feet (464,520 square meters) of office space approved for Easton's 1,200 acres (485 hectares) will add major workplaces.

Marketing, Management, and Performance

Steiner + Associates manages Easton Town Center as a shopping center property, handling all management and marketing, including programming for a large number of festivals and events. Despite skepticism

Groups of people enjoying a daytime event in the town square. Easton Town Center attracted an incredible 11 million visitors in its first year—5 million more than the developer had projected. *Development Design Group.*

about the developer's projections for 7 million visitors within the first year, Phase I actually drew an astonishing 11 million visitors in its first 12 months of operation. As a result, the project's financial performance has far exceeded everyone's expectations, generating over $150 million in sales in its first year. National retailers are achieving average annual sales of approximately $480 per square foot ($5,165 per square meter), and restaurants are achieving sales of over $700 per square foot ($7,535 per square meter). The outstanding performance of Phase I fueled the expansion and rapid acceleration in the preleasing and development of Phase II.

Experience Gained

■ Like Mashpee Commons more than a decade earlier, Easton Town Center proved that open-air town center and main street projects need not be limited to southern climates or to urban areas that already draw large numbers of tourists.

■ Regional and super regional shopping centers can be successfully configured as main street developments. Given the abundance of highly similar enclosed shopping malls across the country, new developments are increasingly likely to adopt main street and town center formats as a way of differentiating themselves—and, at the same time, tapping into underserved demand for shopping in a town center environment.

■ Shopping malls and main streets can be successfully integrated through careful urban design, but retailers accustomed to the highway visibility and parking in front found in conventional shopping centers must be willing to relax their individual orientation and embrace a formula where the town center as a whole becomes the destination.

■ The UEC concept can be successfully expanded, diversified, and opened up through an urban design approach that employs a more traditional urban fabric of urban streets and squares.

■ Easton Town Center's success in attracting tenants that were new to the Columbus market suggests that town center and main street formats may help to lure national tenants to markets that they did not previously find attractive.

■ The successful recruitment of national chains should not distract developers from the more difficult and important job of adding a meaningful assortment of local and regional players, which adds variety and helps distinguish the project from competitors.

■ The time and energy invested in the detailed planning and design of public spaces are well spent. In Easton Town Center's case, such efforts produced a central square that is large enough to handle crowds but not so large that it seems empty when there is no event. The town square provides a center of gravity for the project and is an important defining element for the town center as a whole.

■ Good urban design should not only focus on creating places that feel good but that work from a business viewpoint—for example, by supporting cross-shopping (when the same customers shop in stores on opposite sides of a street), by facilitating pedestrian movement, and by providing added attractions for customers.

■ Layering architectural and urban design elements from a range of eras helps to create visual variety and to convey the sense that a place has evolved slowly over time.

Notes
1. This section is adapted from David Takesuye et al., "Easton Town Center," *ULI Project Reference File* 30, no. 18 (October-December 2000).

Project Data: Easton Town Center

General Information

Project type	Town center for master-planned community
Web page	http://www.eastontowncenter.com
Location	Columbus, Ohio, metropolitan area
Acres/hectares	33.8/13.7, plus 40-acre (16-hectare) expansion area
Parking, Phase I	6.35 spaces per 1,000 square feet (93 square meters) of leasable space; total of 6,495 spaces projected at buildout

Owners and Developers

Steiner + Associates; the Georgetown Company; the Limited, Inc.

Master Planners and Architects

Development Design Group; Cooper, Robertson & Partners; Meacham & Apel Architects

Commercial Uses

Total Leasable Space

Phase	Square Feet/Square Meters
Phase I	599,865/55,730
Phase II	8,230/770

Building Area by Type of Use

Use	Square Feet/Square Meters	
	Phase I	Phase II
Retail, dining, and entertainment	672,230/62,450	349,145/32,440
Office	52,500/4,880	83,178/7,730
Other (department stores)	N.A.[a]	407,000/37,810
Total	724,730/67,330	839,323/77,980

Number and Size of Establishments

Type of Establishment	Number	Average Size, Phase 1 (Square Feet/Square Meters)
Retail	72	8,330/773
Office	15	3,500/325
Total	87	

Retail Uses

Tenant mix	About two-thirds national chains and one-third local and regional establishments
Lease rates (per square foot/square meter)	$24–$32/$259–$344, with tenant allowances of up to $150/$1,615
Lease terms	Triple net; average length five to ten years

Hotel Uses

Two hotels (with a total of 510 rooms) adjacent to the town center

Residential Uses

None within the town center; adjacent development of 800 luxury apartments and townhouses (monthly rents for the apartments are $635–$2,000)

Civic Uses

Main street and town square

Financial Information, Phase I

Site acquisition costs	$16,000,000
Site improvement costs	9,000,000
Construction costs	78,000,000
Soft costs	32,000,000
Total development costs	$135,000,000

Project Schedule

Planning began	October 1996
Ground breaking	June 1998
Phase I completed	June 1999
Phase II completed	Fall 2001

a. Not applicable.

CASE STUDY

Haile Village Center

Gainesville, Florida

One of those rare developments that lives up to its name, Haile Village Center is a carefully composed mix of single-family building types, gently curving streets and lanes, mature landscaping, and village-scale public gathering places. All these elements combine to give the project the ambience of a true village center.

The view down Main Street to the Meeting Hall on a quiet morning.

While traditional villages were surrounded by the natural landscape and agricultural lands, Haile Village Center is located in the heart of Haile Plantation, a 1,700-acre (690-hectare) suburban master-planned community (MPC) located about three miles (five kilometers) outside of Gainesville, Florida. Development of Haile Plantation, which began in 1978, was based on cutting-edge suburban planned unit development (PUD) and environmental conservation practices of the time: the neighborhoods were clustered around a golf course, and a system of trails was used to connect generous amounts of open space.

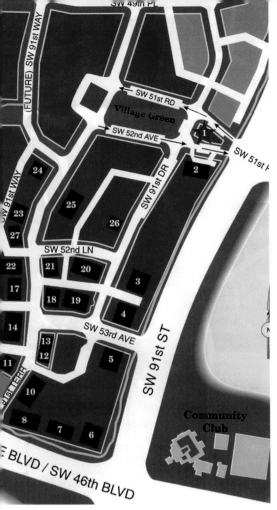

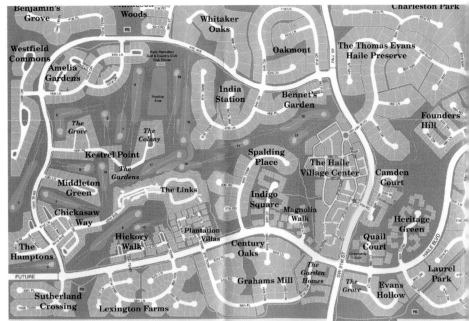

Above: Haile Village Center is located within the Haile Plantation master-planned community, just outside of Gainesville, Florida. *Haile Plantation Corporation.*

Left: Haile Village Center site plan. *Haile Plantation Corporation.*

Single-family homes (which now range from the low $100,000s to $600,000) are grouped by market segment along suburban streets and culs-de-sac.

Despite this conventional suburban format, the 1978 master plan included plans for a town center and three village centers, all of which were envisioned as mixed-use, pedestrian-oriented urban settings that would incorporate squares and plazas.

Background and Site Characteristics

Since Haile Plantation has very little property along the nearest major roadways, and regulations prevented commercial development in these locations, the original plan for multiple centers was abandoned in favor of a single village center to be located near the geographic heart of the MPC—an arrangement that maximized access for Haile Plantation's 8,000 residents but placed Haile Village Center off the beaten path for outsiders.[1] The center is about five miles

(eight kilometers) from I-75, and lies within a few miles of several major arterials, including Tower Road and S.W. Archer Road. The village center is not visible from either of these arterials, however, and only modest signage announces the center's location to passersby.

The village center's 50-acre (20-hectare) site is ringed by Haile's suburban neighborhoods and is adjacent to a portion of the golf course. The village center is accessed from Haile Boulevard to the south and from S.W. 91st Street to the east. There are no direct street connections to adjacent neighborhoods, although the trail system does provide pedestrian connections. The long side of the rectangular site runs along S.W. 91st Street—which, until recently, terminated within Haile Plantation. The roadway was recently extended to connect with a major east-west arterial leading to Gainesville, a change that is expected to provide much higher traffic counts and bring more people from outside Haile Plantation to the village center.

The topography of the site consists of gently rolling slopes that gradually rise upward to the east of the main street, and slope down toward a pedestrian trail and open space to the west of the main street, where a wetland forms the edge of the village center. A small pond at the southern entrance of the village center is surrounded by large live oaks, from which Spanish moss hangs in long locks. The mix of mature live oaks, laurel oaks, sweet gums, hickories, and loblolly pines that has been preserved throughout the site is one of the key ingredients of the village center, contributing a sense of time and place to this relatively new project. Newly planted street trees include live oaks, shumard oaks, overcup oaks, sable palms, washingtonia palms, and a few northern white oaks.

The incorporation of mature landscaping contributes to Haile Village Center's charm and strong sense of place.

In the years leading up to the final planning and design of Haile Village Center, developers Bob Kramer and Matthew Kaskel visited dozens of traditional towns—including Annapolis, Maryland, and Fredericksburg, Virginia—as well as a wide assortment of Florida towns such as Key West, St. Augustine, and others with historic main streets and village centers. Kramer and Kaskel noted the desirable qualities of each place and developed a mental pattern language of streets, buildings, and spaces that they adapted for their village center. The result was that Haile Village Center was conceived as a traditional neighborhood, and planned and designed according to the principles of the new urbanism. But while many projects adopt generic new urbanist principles for the design of traditional neighborhood developments (TNDs), Kramer and Kaskel were careful to design Haile Village Center's streets, buildings, landscaping, and gathering places to evoke the particular village character they desired. For example, carriage lanes, a type of rear access road appropriate to a village setting, were substituted for alleyways, which are commonly used in TNDs.

Development

As described by the developers, the development strategy for Haile Village Center was to design a center that would meet some of the everyday needs of Haile Plantation residents living within one mile (1.6 kilometers) of the center. Growth has been incremental, market-driven, and consistent with the character of a community-oriented village center. As the center has grown and evolved, it has attracted more visitors from outside the MPC, but the tenant mix at the center defies the conventional categories of shopping centers. Apart from the corner store and restaurants, the developers have not recruited business owners or tenants; from the developers' perspective, shopping center–type marketing is inconsistent with the kinds of businesses and customers that are drawn to the village center.

While it can be difficult to gain approvals for TNDs, the entire MPC had been approved back in the late 1970s, when state and regional agencies assessed the impacts of the Haile Plantation (because it was categorized as a development of regional impact—a DRI), and the county approved platting under an existing PUD provision. The prior impact assessments and approvals paved the way for the development of the village center; the only additional requirements were some further studies and amendments that focused primarily on traffic and environmental impacts.

According to Kramer, because the project had a number of unconventional aspects—including the unusual location, low traffic counts, and a vertical mix of uses—and because the plans called for the incremental development of small buildings, the developers had difficulty finding major lenders that were willing to finance the project. (For example, a national builder of multifamily housing that wanted to build a component of the village center found that its regular institutional investors were not interested in projects of less than $20 to $40 million.) As a result, the Haile Plantation Corporation financed about 75 percent of the development of the village center through local sources of capital.

The only design review is conducted by Kramer, who acts as the town architect, providing would-be builders with copies of the *TND Series* of home plans. Scott Tonnelier, developer and builder of three houses in Haile Village Center (including the Clean Air Florida Home, which was developed in association with the American Lung Association of Florida), describes this informal mechanism as a "very strict design review process with regular follow-up visits during construction."[2] Kramer also hands out copies

The developers' promotion of "great good places" finds a home.

of Ray Oldenburg's *The Great Good Place* to would-be café and restaurant operators.[3] His efforts are having a visible impact, with the opening of the Third Place Café in the spring of 2000.

Mix of Uses

Haile Village Center provides a balanced mix of single- and multifamily residences, retail shops and services, professional offices, and public space. Among the 55 establishments there is only one chain operation, the full-service SunTrust Bank, which negotiated an exclusive agreement to become the only bank in the village center. Although there are a few tenants of the sort that might be found in community shopping centers, neither the demographics of the local market nor the location of the center currently fits the standards used by national retail chains. Most of the commercial establishments are what Larry Loesch, proprietor of the Write Impression printing and gift shop and head of the merchants' association, describes as "destination businesses." While the retail and service shops do not rely primarily on drive-by customers, most of them depend on business from both Haile Plantation residents and outside customers.

Retail businesses and restaurants include a corner store (that sells prepared foods and basic grocery items), a florist, a jewelry shop, a stationery and gift shop, two clothing stores, a café and pub, a family restaurant, and an ice cream parlor. Professional and service-oriented businesses include two law firms, a bank, a cabinetmaker, a builder, real estate offices, a dance studio, a dentist, an optician, a preschool, a dry cleaner, a day spa, a veterinarian, a counseling center, insurance offices, and an interior design business. The village center has also attracted a half-dozen small corporate offices, including the headquarters for Gumby's Pizza. The majority of these businesses occupy ground-floor space in buildings that have apartments on the second floor.

Streets and Parking

The streets in the village center are much narrower than those found in Haile Plantation's other neighborhoods, and form a tight, irregular grid pattern lined with brick sidewalks, regularly spaced shade trees, and rustic lampposts. The main street is about 2,000 feet (609 meters) long and 40 feet (12 meters) wide, but the roadway narrows to 21 feet (6.4 meters) at some points. The gentle curve of the main street provides a series of changing views that unfold gradually as visitors walk along the street. As visitors approach the center of the village, the street straightens to reveal a view of the Meeting Hall. The Meeting Hall and village green sit at the halfway point of the main street, and side streets extend out from this spine to form a village center district, as opposed to a thin commercial strip or isolated main street.

Some single-family homes are also served by rear lanes, between 11 and 12 feet (3.4 and 3.7 meters) in width, that were consciously designed as carriage lanes

Top: On-street parking is encouraged along the main street, both for the convenience of shoppers and for its traffic calming effects.

Bottom: One of Haile Village Center's carriage lanes—narrow, rustic roads without curbs that lead to the backs of homes. Carriage lanes were common in historic villages.

Pergolas (above) and thin storage buildings (below) are strategically placed to screen parking areas.

rather than as the more urban alleyways found in many TNDs. As is the case with many TNDs and town center projects, the streets are owned and maintained by the community management association because their dimensions would have been prohibited by local street standards. Parking is provided in unmarked on-street parallel spaces, in parking courts at the interiors of blocks, and in small lots that are located behind buildings and screened by landscaping, storage sheds, and a pergola that doubles as a performance stage for farmers' markets and community celebrations.

Buildings

Throughout the village center, building lots are organized into modules 18 feet (5.5 meters) wide, which can be combined to create larger lots where the developers deem it appropriate. A variety of traditionally styled brick and stick-frame buildings—containing a mix of retail shops, service businesses, and restaurants, with residences on the upper floors—line the sidewalks. Porches, arcades, awnings, stoops, and balconies extend the buildings over and onto the sidewalks and toward the streets, creating transitions between public and private space and giving the streets a stronger sense of enclosure.

Kramer has personally designed many of the 40 buildings in the village center, including an impressive

The streetscape includes brick sidewalks, a variety of street trees, and appropriately scaled lampposts.

range of commercial, mixed-use, civic, and residential structures. With the pattern and character of the village center now established, Kramer is more comfortable working with outside architects to design additional single-family homes and the multifamily section currently under construction. Because the buildings in the village center were designed and constructed over a period of seven years and feature variations in materials, massing, frontages, and styles, they succeed in evoking the ambience of historic towns and main streets that have evolved more slowly over time. The seasoned quality of the village center is further reinforced by the organic nature of its design, including its gently curving streets, its carriage lanes, and the fact that the buildings and sidewalks were designed around mature trees.

All residences within the village center are within a five-minute walk of the village green and the main street businesses, and all are permitted to have garage apartments and home occupations, including bed-and-breakfast inns. In addition to the apartments above the shops and offices, there are currently about three dozen single-family homes adjacent to the village core. These houses are also designed in traditional styles and are situated on deep, narrow lots, with the buildings pulled up close to the sidewalk. Homes typically include wood railings and fences, small courtyards, patios and side yards, and porches and balconies with beaded-board ceilings. Most houses have detached or semi-detached garages in back, and over half of the homes

Top: Buildings within the village center are detached, individually designed structures, most of which have retail and office on the ground floor and residential above.

Bottom: Any of the narrow-lot single-family homes in the northern portion of the village center could be converted to a bed-and-breakfast; above their garages, many homes offer residential flats that can be rented out.

Top: An ornamental pavilion transforms the small traffic circle at the northern edge of the village center into an attractive public space.

Bottom: The village green and the Meeting Hall are the center of gravity for the village center.

have some living space over their garages (of these spaces, six are designed as rental apartments).

Public Gathering Spaces

The primary public spaces within the village center are the village green and the main street itself, which can be closed off to traffic for special events like the weekly farmers' market. There are also small pocket parks, a tot-lot, and pedestrian paths that lead to the nearby pond and golf course. Civic elements include the Meeting Hall, the offices of the Haile Plantation community association, a preschool, a sheriff's substation, and a commercial postal center with mailboxes and vending machines for purchasing stamps. In terms of their scale, understated style, and composition, the Meeting Hall and the village green are perfectly suited to each other and to the village character. The fenced tot-lot located between the Meeting Hall and the main street sees plenty of use but is the one space that seems to be somewhat less evocative of the village atmosphere.

The Meeting Hall, which terminates the view down the main street at the village green, provides a key gathering place for both public and private events, including concerts, community celebrations, weddings, receptions, and private parties. A local minister who performed a wedding ceremony in the hall shortly after it first opened now holds Sunday-morning services there.

Holiday festivals and special events—such as this Founder's Day celebration—draw as much as 70 percent of Haile Plantation's population, as well as residents from the surrounding area. *Haile Plantation Corporation.*

Marketing, Management, and Performance

Currently about half of the commercial buildings in the village center are owned and managed by the Haile Plantation Corporation, and the other half are owned and maintained by the people who operate shops and businesses there. Most of these business owners live within Haile Plantation, making it unique

among town center and main street projects, which are typically geared toward preleasing space to regional and national chains. The Haile Plantation Corporation and the Village Center Homeowners' Association are responsible for the maintenance of the streets and public spaces, and the corporation collaborates with the merchants' association in organizing events and undertaking local marketing.

Since there is little drive-by business and the merchants cannot afford an expensive advertising program, they rely on local advertising magazines, the community newsletter, and word of mouth. They also benefit from the wide variety of events held at Haile Village Center, including holiday celebrations, arts and crafts festivals, sporting events, and a weekly farmers' market. Kramer reports that the most popular events have drawn as much as 70 percent of the population of Haile Plantation.

The large number of service businesses and professional offices has provided Haile Village Center with a stable tenant mix that holds down the center's turnover rate. The center is also home to a core of service-oriented retailers who are adept at developing and maintaining a loyal customer base. Businesses that have had a more difficult time becoming established include the Village Market (a corner store) and some of the early restaurants and cafés.

Throughout changes in the management of the corner store, Kramer remained committed to the idea of maintaining such an establishment, noting that "You don't have much of a place without one." While the Haile Corporation subsidized the store for some time, its performance improved dramatically after Kramer moved it to a central location on the main street; sales have since risen by 50 percent. Now self-sustaining, the Village Market is owned by a resident of the village center, and the developers are no longer involved.

Haile Village Center stands as an exception to the rule against burying commercial centers inside MPCs. While the project's design is worthy of emulation, the center's success is more a testament to the developers' vision and perseverance than the result of a shrewd development strategy or a strong site location. Generally speaking, a town center project will perform much better when at least a portion of the center is easily accessed and visible from major arterials. The developers' unsuccessful attempts to attract a small-scale, high-quality grocer and a pharmacy to the village center early in the project bear this out—although, under the appropriate circumstances, such establishments can serve as important anchors and be successfully incorporated into a traditional center. Now that a Publix grocery store has opened in a nearby community shopping center (with better traffic counts and roadway visibility), it is highly unlikely that such a facility will be added to Haile Village Center.

Haile Village Center has provided the community with the type of special gathering place that is missing in many American suburbs. The center has also enhanced property values in the MPC and greatly contributed to the community's status as a desirable place to live. As such, the village is an attractive model for community developers, especially because of its charming, small-scale design. However, it is a less attractive model for town center developers looking for development opportunities outside of an MPC or TND environment. The lack of visibility and exposure detracts from both the center's competitiveness and its attractiveness to national chains, which are critical to the success of most town centers. The strategy of selling retail parcels to individual tenants, moreover, will make it difficult to control tenant mix and manage the center over time.

Nevertheless, the developers are clearly profiting from the development of the village center, and their holdings have continuously increased in value as the project is built out and continues to mature. Haile Village Center's shortcomings are also its strengths. Because of its unconventional approach—its reliance on small, independent tenants; its charming village design; and its incremental phasing—Haile Village Center has created a sense of place that is hard to find in new retail and town center environments, and residents seem to like it just the way it is.

Experience Gained

- Developing a community-oriented village center or main street without large amounts of capital requires patience—and "patient money." It takes time to establish the concept; to assemble a well-rounded mix of businesses; to finance a series of small, mixed-use buildings; and to work with builders and small-business owners to design buildings that contribute to the village ambience. Development of this type requires developers who have a long-term investment outlook, and who can wait for return on investment to increase as the center is built out.

- The best way to create a place that looks as if it had been built in small increments, over time, is to do just that. When buildings are designed one lot at a time, developers can make adjustments in response to what they have learned from previous phases of the project.

- Mature landscaping and traditional building materials greatly enhance the authenticity of new projects.

- Town centers that are located within MPCs, remote from major thoroughfares, are challenging propositions. Vision, talent, and leadership are critical to the success of such ventures. Because of Robert Kramer's combined talents as developer, architect, and urbanist, Haile Village Center has had the advantage of a "town founder" throughout its development. Kramer's attention to detail, business acumen, and low-key leadership have allowed the project to stay the course.

Notes

1. The developer did reserve land for a second village center north of Haile Village Center and is beginning to look at development options for that property now that a major roadway adjacent to the property has been completed.
2. Scott Tonnelier, interviewed by the author, January 21, 2000. For more on the Clean Air Florida Home, see http://www.tonnelier.com/10haile.htm.
3. Ray Oldenburg, *The Great Good Place* (New York: Paragon House, 1989).

Project Data: Haile Village Center

General Information

Project type	Village center in a 1980s master-planned community
Web page	http://www.haileplantation.com/indexhvc.html
Location	Alachua County, Florida
Acres/hectares	50/20
Parking ratios	In the mixed-use portion of the project, five spaces per 1,000 square feet (93 square meters), with no additional spaces for the residential space above commercial space; in the multifamily portion, one space per bedroom
Development costs to date	$49.2 million

Owners and Developers
Robert B. Kramer and Matthew Kaskel; the Fleeman family

Master Planners and Architects
Robert B. Kramer and Matthew Kaskel

Building Area by Type of Use

Use	Square Feet/Square Meters	
	Existing	Proposed
Retail	15,000/1,390	80,000/7,430
Office	90,000/8,360	80,000/7,430
Civic	4,700/440	6,200/580
Total	109,700/10,190	166,200/15,440

Commercial Uses
Number of establishments   55

Tenant mix   Neighborhood shops, services, and dining establishments, and a wide range of small professional offices; no major national chains except SunTrust Bank

Size range
(square feet/square meters)   500–3,000/46–280

Civic Uses: Building Area by Use

Use	Square Feet/Square Meters
Meeting Hall	3,200/300
Community association building	1,500/140[a]

Residential Uses
120 units, including apartments over shops; single-family homes on narrow lots; live/work units; and accessory units (apartments over garages); of the accessory units, 30 have been built and another 70 to 80 are permitted. Another 100 multifamily units are under development.

Sales Prices
Townhouses and detached homes start in the low $200,000s and range widely in price: three-bedroom, four-bath, 3,000-square-foot (280-square-meter) townhouses sell for between $275,000 and $295,000.

Development Schedule

Construction began	1994
Projected buildout	2005

a. Including sheriff's office and post office (a total of 3,000 square feet has been proposed).

Market Square

Gaithersburg, Maryland

Market Square is unique among town center and main street projects, in that it is sandwiched between two traditional neighborhood developments (TNDs). On one side is Kentlands—which was begun in 1990 and is one of the oldest and most mature TNDs in the country—and on the other side is Lakelands, a relative newcomer that opened in 1998. These two TNDs have a combined area of 695 acres (280 hectares) and a broad mix of 3,400 residential units, including apartments, townhouses, live/work units, and single-family homes. The neighborhoods include an elementary school, a future middle school, two churches, and a fine-grained mix of neighborhood parks, squares, and plazas. The Market Square site straddles both TNDs in an area sometimes referred to as Midtown, and sits directly across Kentlands Boulevard from Kentlands Square, a 350,000-square-foot (32,520-square-meter) conventional shopping center. Together, Market Square and Kentlands Square shopping center (both developed by the Beatty Companies) offer approximately 600,000 square feet (55,740 square meters) of commercial space.

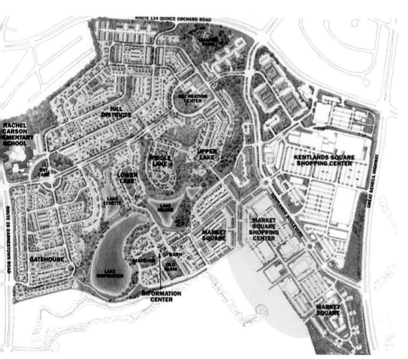

Market Square (highlighted) is located in Gaithersburg, Maryland, between the Kentlands and Lakelands traditional neighborhood developments.

In many ways, Market Square is a tale of two places—one a traditional main street and the other a suburban shopping center. While the Beatty Companies developed Market Square strictly as a commercial area, the project is considered innovative because big-box stores have been successfully incorporated into a main street and urban square, and because the development has been successfully integrated into two TNDs.

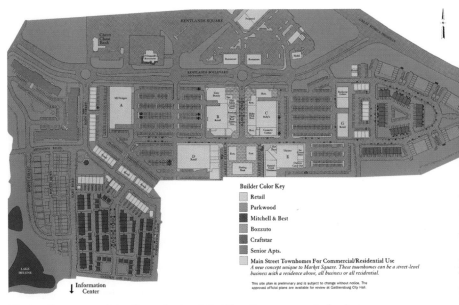

Market Square consists of a main street that functions as a central spine and leads to an urban plaza; parking lots are located behind the buildings and front the big-box retail stores.

Development

The decade-long process that led to the creation of Market Square is a tale of extraordinary efforts on the part of the developer, Gaithersburg's former mayor and planning staff, and the residents of Kentlands, all of whom—despite the odds—remained committed to pursuing a traditional town center format and working out the nitty-gritty details of implementing the unusual concept. With the Lakelands project poised to eventually double the population of Kentlands, Great Seneca Development Corporation, which has managed the development of Kentlands since 1991, was more confident about pursuing additional commercial development. Great Seneca asked the Beatty Companies, the developer of Kentlands Square, to develop Market Square as well.[1] The key to the entire project was the parties' willingness to redraw the boundaries of Kentlands and Lakelands, and to sell off slices of both properties to assemble the land that would be needed for a centrally located town center serving the residents of both projects.

Early proposals that would have brought a large Target store to Market Square and extended the Kentlands Square shopping center format drew a strong negative response from residents, who wanted more input in the planning stages of the project. The town planner, Duany Plater-Zyberk & Company (DPZ), was hired to run a community design workshop and to develop a master plan that would satisfy the residents' desire for a traditional town center; accommodate the requirements of the larger, mainstream retailers that would occupy most of the project's 255,000 square feet (23,690 square meters); and provide a bridge between the two TNDs. The final plan that emerged from the design workshop met with widespread support and was eventually approved by the city.

Approval of the plan, however, did not protect the project from extended battles over building codes, street standards, and other regulations that posed difficulties for the construction of Market Square and the adjacent live/work units. In one instance, after the developer had chosen to adopt for

Market Square the distinctive design of the street signs used throughout Gaithersburg, city staff pointed out that some of the streets in the project were too narrow to become public streets maintained by the city, and that using the same signage for both public and private streets might create confusion for maintenance workers. Clark Wagner, Gaithersburg's urban design director, came up with a simple solution: adding the word "private" inside the logo, to distinguish between the two.

Mix of Uses

Market Square faced numerous challenges in its efforts to assemble a mix of tenants that would meet the needs of the nearby TND residents and tap into the

The Kentlands Stadium 8 theater provides an entertainment dimension for the town center.

affluent and growing regional market. The developer was very successful in recruiting national retailers like Michaels, the Dress Barn, and Zany Brainy. Other large national tenants—such as MJ Designs and Sunny's (an outdoor goods retailer), as well as several smaller establishments—came and went, making it necessary to re-lease 70,000 square feet (6,500 square meters) of space early in the project. Although some turnover is common in the early stages of retail projects, including town centers, in this case the early closures of some Market Square tenants, such as Sunny's and the very successful MJ Designs store, resulted from the closures of the entire national chains.

While the retail portion of Market Square is now almost fully leased, entertainment, leisure, and dining have formed the nucleus of the project. Entertainment became a key component unexpectedly, when the owner of the Kentlands Stadium 8 Theaters identified the project as a desirable setting in a growing, underserved market. Other key elements include the Bally fitness center, Seattle's Best Coffee, Star Diner, and the Wine Harvest, a café and wine and gift shop at the center of Market Street that quickly became the project's "third place." This diverse mix of commercial businesses provides a steady flow of customers throughout the morning, afternoon, and evening hours.

The wine merchant serves as a "third place" for Market Square.

Market Square Retail Mix

Zany Brainy
Bally Total Fitness
Kentlands Stadium 8 Theaters
Potomac Pizza
Taste of Hong Kong
The Cone Zone
Mind and Body Spa
Lifestyles Hair Salon
Seattle's Best Coffee
Rudy's Dawg House
Barbeque Galore
Moby Dick Restaurant
The Wine Harvest

Next Day Blinds
Reeck Floor Care Center
PetSmart
Sun Works Tanning Salon
Coldwell Banker Real Estate
Star Diner
Kensington Dry Cleaners
Arcadia New and Used CDs
Dress Barn
Midtown Skatecenter
Kentlands Flowers & Bows
Simply Wireless
The Sweet Tooth Café

Michaels
Dentist
FreshFields Market
Daviko Gems
Hakuba Grill-Sushi Bar
Colonial Opticians
Buca di Beppo
Tandoori Restaurant
Symbiosis Wireless
Persiano Rugs
Apples to Zebras Gifts
Baja Fresh
My Gym

The Bally fitness center draws a steady flow of visitors to the town center from early morning to late evening.

The entrances of the large retail stores face parking lots.

Two four-story office buildings are also being constructed on the opposite side of the traffic circle, at the entrance to Kentlands Square, and portions of these buildings have been preleased to real estate and law offices. Market Square will also benefit from the addition of an Extended Stay America hotel, to be located directly behind one of the new office buildings. The site just south of the central square has also been discussed as a possible location for a third office building.

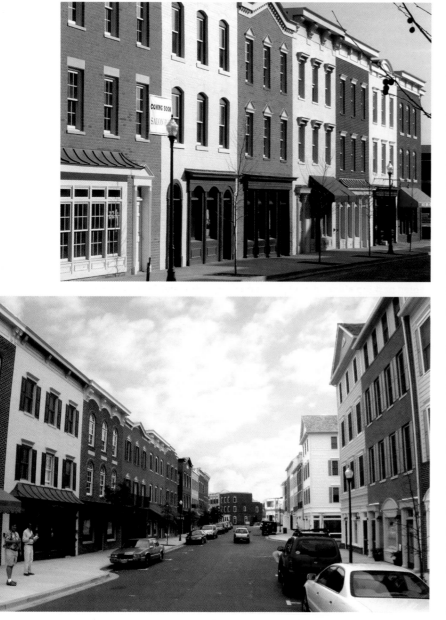

Top: Live/work townhouses along Main Street, directly adjacent to Market Square, offer shops and work spaces on the ground floor, offices on the second floor, and apartments above.

Bottom: Three- and four-story flex housing lines Main Street all the way from Kentlands Square Shopping Center to the central square.

While Market Square itself does not include residential space, it straddles high-density, mixed-use portions of the Kentlands and Lakelands TNDs, which puts hundreds of dwelling units and a growing number of offices and service businesses within easy walking distance of Market Street's shops and restaurants. Directly adjacent to Market Square, Parkwood Homes is building 46 live/work townhouses along one side of Main Street; on the other side, Mitchell & Best has built another 14 live/work townhouses, plus two live/work detached houses. Another 16 live/work "convertibles" fill out the rest of Main Street. The convertible units are currently fully occupied as townhouses; however, the first levels are built to commercial code, which means that the residential facades could be transformed into storefronts with ease.

The Parkwood Homes townhouses are commercially oriented units, with the first two floors designated commercial and the third floor residential. Because of their scale and architectural details—which include ten-foot (three-meter) ceilings (on the ground floor); brick facades; thick wood moldings, cornices, and pediments; and full basements, these buildings create a stronger urban presence than the nearby Market Square buildings. The Mitchell & Best units are more residential in character, with commercial uses permitted only on the ground floor and residential on the second and third floors. These units are currently selling for over $500,000.

The Parkwood Homes units have commanded stiff prices, starting at $369,000 for an unfinished shell and ranging up to $479,000 for a built-out unit. Two of the first purchasers acquired two adjacent townhouses to house their personal care business, Salon Red, and leased out the one-bedroom apartments on the third floor of each unit. The basements provide a tranquil space for the salon's yoga classes, the storefronts are used for the hair-cutting salon, and the second floor provides rooms for massages and facials. A few owners have chosen to live above their stores, but most have opted to rent out the third-floor apartments. In one building, occupied by a mortgage brokerage with 15 employees, all three levels have been converted into offices. Overall, the live/work units have added a lively mix of small shops, professional offices, salons, and service businesses that complement the Market Square stores.

Streets, Layout, and Parking

To reach Market Square, visitors leave the main arterial, Great Seneca Highway; turn onto Kentlands Boulevard, which gently climbs straight toward Market Square; drive past an inconspicuous entrance that leads to the health club and cinema; then turn right, moving through a traffic circle that has an entrance to Kentlands Square on the north side and to Market Street to the south. Visitors who miss the main entrance to Market Square can use a third entrance that delivers them into a large parking lot in the middle of four big-box stores. At this point, a visitor might think that he or she had taken a wrong turn and arrived in the suburban-style Kentlands Square shopping center, rather than in a town center project. As it turns out, this parking lot, and another large lot on the eastern half of the site, are located to the *rear* of Market Street. The entrances to the big-box stores face these lots, but their Market Street sides are lined with small shops and restaurants pulled up close to the street. Market Street itself is a narrow, two-lane road with parallel parking spaces on both sides and brick sidewalks that create a pedestrian-friendly street.

Market Street runs south from Kentlands Boulevard for one block, where it crosses CenterPoint Way, forming the central axis of Market Square. Market Street splits into Market Street East and Market Street West, one-way streets that wrap around either side of the square and provide angled parking in front of half-blocks of shops and offices. CenterPoint Way main-

Angled parking along Market Street West provides additional parking spaces convenient to shops and services.

tains the basic geometry of Market Street—that is, it is built to a similar width and provides two vehicular lanes and parallel parking on both sides—but it serves primarily to circulate traffic and pedestrians from the parking lots to Market Street.

One of the strengths of Market Square is the way in which its streets and blocks interconnect with the adjacent neighborhoods of Kentlands and Lakelands. Efforts to connect town centers, main streets, and TNDs with existing neighborhoods are often vehemently opposed by residents living adjacent to the projects. The residents of Kentlands, in contrast, understood the design principles of TNDs and actively promoted the creation of walkable streets to connect their homes with local shops and restaurants.

Market Square has wrestled with the parking requirements of four big-box retail operations, an eight-screen cinema, and a 23,000-square-foot (2,140-square-meter) health club. Through a combination of five irregularly shaped parking lots, and on-street parallel and angled parking spaces, the plan manages to generate about 5.5 spaces per 1,000 square feet (93 square meters) of commercial space. This comes at a cost, however: the street wall quickly disintegrates as one walks east or west of Market Street along Center-Point Way—a conscious tradeoff on the part of the designers, who wanted to create high-quality pedestrian streets ("A" streets) by concentrating loading docks, utilities, and parking lots on adjacent streets ("B" streets). In Market Square, CenterPoint Way acts primarily as a "B" street, supporting the two "A" streets, Market Street and Main Street.

Buildings

Market Street is anchored by a creative mix of four large, big-box clusters lined with small shops and restaurants. The shops along Market Street range in size from 900 to 3,600 square feet (80 to 330 square meters), and the restaurants range from 3,800 to 6,000 square feet (350 to 560 square meters). The large retailers range from 10,000 square feet (930 square meters) to over 31,000 square feet (2,880 square meters). A 35,800-square-foot (3,330-square-meter) grocery store is located at the western edge of the site. Although the presence of large retailers draws customers to the project, the fact that the only entrances to these stores are located off the parking lots creates a sense that the project is made up of subzones, some suburban and

Smaller shops with storefronts along Market Street.

others urban. Adding entrances, along Market Street, to the larger stores could have increased foot traffic on the main street and helped establish a critical mass of storefronts along the street.

The regulatory code requires each tenant to have a unique facade, a requirement that has generated an eclectic mix of materials, colors, frontages, and signage—all of which were designed by the project's architects, the Development Design Group. The facades of the buildings are primarily of brick and wood, with a mix of canvas and metal awnings lit from above for effect. Although the colorful awnings help distinguish storefronts from one another, they occasionally obscure the signs on adjacent shops and are not deep enough to provide shelter from the rain and sun. The display windows of the many shops along Market Street offer a sufficient amount of glass to create an "A" street, but CenterPoint Way, which has large expanses of blank wall and very few entrances to shops, quickly dissolves into a "B" street. Brick sidewalks reinforce the pedestrian ambience of Market Street and the square, but the sidewalks off Market Street are sometimes too narrow, and end abruptly on the way to the parking lots, as if to remind visitors that they are leaving the urban realm and entering a suburban section of the project.

Mike Watkins, the head of the Washington, D.C., office of DPZ, which is located in Kentlands, a short walk from Market Square, notes that although Market Square's design has shortcomings, it succeeds in creating a distinctive gathering place. Watkins feels that Market Square fulfills many community needs that are not met by projects that are considered more architecturally refined. He also believes that what some architects might view as design flaws—such as the strained mix of colors, materials, and styles in the streetlights, benches, awnings, signage, and garbage cans—are actually new versions of the visual chaos found in real towns. In Watkins's view, this "messy urbanism" helps to create more authentic places in the long run.

Watkins and other members of the Kentlands community lobbied hard to persuade the developer to build two-and three-story structures throughout Market Square, but the developer was skeptical about the economic feasibility of vertical mixed uses. The developer did, however, incorporate three two-story buildings along Market Street, including one that overlooks the central square and is designated for a restaurant and pub. Other buildings create the illusion of a second story through the addition of upper-floor facades and gabled dormers.

Faux second-story facades and dormers create the illusion of taller buildings.

Market Street's sidewalks are lined with an electric mix of materials, colors, and signage.

While multistory buildings are not mandatory for the creation of successful main streets and town centers (cities like Boston and San Francisco have many one-story neighborhood centers and successful

To activate the public space with an indoor/outdoor dining atmosphere, the developer decided to locate two restaurants within the central square, adjacent to the skating rink. This move has provided a steady flow of people through the square at mealtimes and during evening get-togethers and community events, but it has also created financial and design challenges: finishing the facades on three or four sides of a building costs more than finishing the front side only; and when freestanding buildings are positioned within a square, their backs will face storefronts.[2] The second challenge was not entirely resolved, and remains an issue.

Public Gathering Spaces

Taken together, Market Street, the central square, and a fountain plaza in front of the four-story apartment building that overlooks Market Square create a spine of public space in the heart of Market Square. Effectively the civic center for both Kentlands and Lakelands, the square is the setting for sidewalk fairs; an annual art and wine festival; and other events organized by the Kentlands Community Foundation,

The Market Street East block, where single-story commercial buildings meet three- to four-story townhouses.

The decision to locate two restaurants within the central plaza meant that the backs of the restaurants would face the fronts of the shops across the street.

commercial streets), they do help to create a stronger sense of enclosure for the streets and public spaces. Multistory buildings also help to create the vitality that comes from a concentration of workplaces, residences, shops, and restaurants along a single street. In the case of Market Square, the fact that the tallest high-density residential buildings of both Kentlands and Lakelands are clustered around the town center accentuates the project's low-rise profile. Moreover, the transition between three- and four-story townhouses and single-story commercial buildings on the same block is abrupt. The combination of the big-box subzones (which, as noted earlier, have no entrances along Market Street) and the single-story character of the design makes Market Square—with a total of 250,000 square feet (23,230 square meters) of space—appear to be a much smaller project than it is.

the fledgling merchants' association, and the city of Gaithersburg, which is permitted to hold three events annually in the square. Smaller plazas at the northern entrance to Market Street, off Kentlands Boulevard, serve as outdoor dining areas for restaurants on either

Top: The Main Street Pavilion anchors an intimate public gathering space that is lined with the three-story live/work units that are on both sides of Main Street.

Bottom: When it is closed off, Market Street itself becomes a key gathering place for larger events.
Diane Dorney, The Town Paper.

side of the street. On the western edge of the site, across from the live/work units, is the Main Street Pavilion, where a farmers' market is planned.

All of the spaces, and Market Street itself, are still young. It will take time for the street trees and landscaping to mature and for the construction activity on the adjacent Lakelands site to subside. While the sidewalks and the square provide a good foundation for a public gathering space, the addition of a central fountain, shade trees, or other landmarks and urban landscaping would create focal points and add definition to the public space. A portion of the central square is used for an ice skating rink in the winter and, although a popular community amenity, it is not a particularly inviting place: a solid, stark white wall surrounds the ice and obscures the view of the rink at ground level. The rink area is used for a miniature golf course during the warmer months, an unusual amenity for a town center. Community members are already working on a

plan that would borrow a page from Reston Town Center, creating a permanent skating pavilion that could be used for concerts and performances during the summer months.

Marketing, Management, and Performance

Market Square offers a pedestrian-friendly main street with an attractive mix of shops, services, restaurants, and entertainment and leisure activities. The dining and entertainment uses, appealing public gathering places, and strong support from local residents make it possible to promote Market Square as a gathering place for the residents of the dozens of nearby residential subdivisions that lack such amenities. Now that Market Square is more than 90 percent leased, the developer is beginning to craft a more distinctive identity for the project and to take advantage of the opportunity to transform it into a regional destination.

The words "Market Square" have recently been added to the brick walls at the main entrance to Market Street, and decorative strings of lights now outline the rooflines of buildings. The developer has put up locator maps, between the parking lots and the square, to show visitors the locations of shops and restaurants. In addition, the developer has recently recruited a popular Italian restaurant and a 35,000-square-foot (3,250-square-meter) grocery store, and is working hard to identify an appropriate dining and drinking establishment for the last remaining restaurant space, which occupies a prominent two-story building overlooking the square.

Market Square still has some distance to go before it achieves what retail planners refer to as "brand image"—the distinctive level of identity that is represented and reinforced by signs, logos, brochures, banners, locator maps, Web sites, and more decorative—"You have arrived"—points of entry. Watkins would like to see lighting added to the tall spire of the cinema, the tallest structure in Market Square, to act as a beacon and draw more visitors to the square.

Scott Cregger, of the Beatty Companies, reports that despite the unexpected turnover of some major tenants early in the project, most establishments have performed up to expectations. This level of success can be attributed, in large part, to the tenants' proximity to Kentlands Square, the name recognition of the tenants Beatty succeeded in recruiting (e.g., Bally, Michaels, and Zany Brainy), and the commitment of the residents. The first-ever Kentlands/Lakelands Art and Wine Festival—"Tickle Your Palette 2001"—was held in May, and brought hundreds of visitors from both TNDs and the surrounding neighborhoods. As Market Square leases up and matures, the developer may tap into an even greater unrealized potential to bring the project to the next level of development.

Experience Gained

■ Large-format retail stores that require ample parking and roadway visibility present challenges for main street and town center projects; however, they can be accommodated through careful planning and design, and can help draw customers from a larger trade area to the main street.

■ If possible, at least one entrance for each of the large retail stores should be located along a main street, to encourage foot traffic. If the large retail-

ers have no entrances on the main streets, the project appears to be a grouping of two or more subzones rather than a single, coherent place.

■ Town center projects that are part of a TND can expect higher-than-average support from local residents; however, close proximity to a major thoroughfare and strong demographics (beyond the boundaries of the TND) remain key site location criteria. The success of Market Square will depend largely on the same market factors that have made Kentlands Square shopping center successful.

■ Main street and town center projects can deliver high parking ratios even where structured parking is not feasible, if spaces are distributed in smaller lots concealed from the main street, and if plentiful parallel parking is provided on the streets.

■ Since large retailers and cinemas are often unwilling to reinvent their standard prototype buildings with entirely new urban formats, not every street can be a pedestrian-friendly main street. A system of "A" and "B" streets allows developers to create a pedestrian setting with a stronger sense of place on "A" streets, while accommodating large-format buildings, loading docks, waste removal, and parking lots on "B" streets, in alleyways, and to the rear of main street buildings.

■ Town center and main street projects require developers to be shrewd as well as prudent. It is important, for example, to investigate the prospective market for main street office and residential space before writing it off as too risky. The successful development of high-density apartments, condominiums, senior apartments, and $500,000 live/work townhouses within walking distance of Market Square is an indication that upper-floor office and residential space could have been successfully incorporated into the project.

■ Development of all the uses in a mixed-use project is frequently beyond the scope of a single developer. In the case of Market Square, the town center area was divided up into retail and various multifamily components, all bridged by the live/work units, allowing developers to focus on what they knew best.

Project Data: Market Square

General Information

Project type	Main street and town center for a traditional neighborhood development (TND)
Location	Gaithersburg, Maryland, just off Kentlands Boulevard
Acres/hectares	22/9
Parking ratio	5.5 spaces per 1,000 square feet (93 square meters)
Estimated project cost	$13 million[a]

Owners and Developers
Kentlands II, LLC; the Beatty Companies

Master Planner
Duany Plater-Zyberk & Company

Architect
Development Design Group

Commercial Uses

Building area (square feet/square meters)	255,000/23,690
Number of establishments	33

Tenant mix	Four restaurants, an eight-screen cinema, and a mix of smaller local and regional shops and services; about one-third of all retailers are national chains
Range of shop sizes (square feet/square meters)	900–35,800/80–3,330
Lease rates (square feet/square meters)	$30–$40/$322–$430

Residential Uses
No residential uses in Market Square itself; the Kentlands and Lakelands TNDs, which include a mix of apartments, townhouses, condominiums, and single-family homes, are directly adjacent to the project.

Civic Uses
Public square with an outdoor ice skating rink, Main Street Pavilion, and fountain plaza

Project Schedule

Construction began	1999
Buildout date	2001

a. As reported at http://www.reji.com/archive/CREJ/1997/971223/9712235.shtml (May 13, 2001).

Notes

1. Great Seneca Development Corporation, a subsidiary of Chevy Chase Savings and Loan, took over the development of Kentlands when the bank was forced to foreclose on the property. While the TND homes continued to sell at premium prices right through the recession, the financial circumstances of the original developer, Joseph Alfandre, unraveled after the Simon Property Group was unable to consummate a deal to purchase a large parcel of Kentlands for a regional shopping mall on property that eventually became the Kentlands Square shopping center.

2. For examples of how other recent projects have handled freestanding buildings within a town square, see the case studies on CityPlace and Southlake Town Square.

Market Street at Celebration

Celebration, Florida

Celebration is one of the most thoroughly planned and designed master-planned communities (MPCs) ever built, and the town center is certainly no exception. With the Walt Disney Company's financial muscle, a master plan crafted by the team of Robert A. M. Stern Architects, and Cooper, Robertson & Partners, and signature buildings designed by some of today's most prominent architects, Celebration's modest downtown is an urban designer's dream.

Located deep within Celebration's 4,900 acres (1,980 hectares), the town center is located about one mile (1.6 kilometers) from U.S. 192 and I-4, adjacent to the Walt Disney World Resort, and about a 20-minute drive from downtown Orlando. The site sits on the shore of a small lake at the heart of Celebration Village, the central neighborhood of the MPC.

Andrew Ross, a professor of American studies at New York University, spent an entire year living in Celebration's town center, observing the media-soaked Disney town's early days—an experience that he later described in *The Celebration Chronicles.*[1]

Celebration is a 4,900-acre (1,980-hectare) traditional neighborhood development (TND) about a 20-minute drive from downtown Orlando. The town center (highlighted in pink) is located on the lake, in the northern portion of the project known as Celebration Village. *Cooper, Robertson & Partners.*

Surveying the built landscape of his new home from an apartment above Market Street, Ross notes that in contrast to the "concrete and neon thickets of fast-food shacks and discount malls, acres of asphalt parking lots, and subdivisions of dull duplicate housing, the reason for Celebration lay all around."[2]

Unlike the central-Florida sprawl that lies outside Celebration's white vinyl fences, the town center was conceived as a place where people could walk from their homes to local shops and restaurants, parks, schools, the post office, and services. It was designed as a place for residents and visitors to come together—as the sun around which the life of Celebration's neighborhoods would revolve, and as the centerpiece of a new urbanist small town, built for the middle classes, that might serve as a model for broader applications of the new urbanism.

Celebration and its town center have drawn international attention and praise, but they have their critics as well. Some critics note that while the design is admirable, the town center does not seem to make financial sense as a real estate project: few companies except Disney could or would have undertaken such a project in this location, so early in the development of the larger community, and with such an all-star lineup of architects and urban designers. In fact, the Disney brand and financial strength were critical assets that allowed the town center to be located away from major arterials and to be developed in the initial phase of the Celebration traditional neighborhood development (TND). The urban design and mixing of uses in the town center, however, represent an exciting, innovative approach to mixed-use development that can offer many lessons to town center projects being developed under more conventional circumstances.

Development

Planning and approval for downtown Celebration were part of the overall planning and approval process for the Celebration project. The Celebration project itself was part of a larger effort undertaken by the Walt

Celebration's town center represents a dramatic break from the commercial strips and centers that have proliferated in the greater Orlando area.

Disney Company, which wanted to establish a public/private partnership to carry out over $400 million in transportation improvements to benefit the adjacent Walt Disney World Resort. As a result of this larger effort, the Celebration property was de-annexed from the Disney-controlled Reedy Creek District and made part of Osceola County; a Development of Regional Impact study was undertaken—a process that took several years and considerable expense; and a public/private partnership was established to carry out massive roadway improvements in the area.

Many observers were surprised that Disney chose to develop the town center very early in the project. The company gave several reasons for this move: first, to quickly establish the small-town character of the project by focusing, in Phase I, on Celebration Village and the town center; second, to use the town center as a marketing tool to promote residential property sales in the rest of the project. The town center succeeded in the second objective—although, as noted earlier, many observers have called into question the profitability of the town center as a development venture during those early years.

Mix of Uses

The Celebration Company has worked very hard to assemble an attractive mix of stores, restaurants, and services in the town center, including four restaurants, a cinema, a hotel, and an eclectic mix of shops. While some observers claim that the town center has been primarily tourist-oriented right from the start, it has

Gooding's grocery store puts everyday grocery items within walking distance of Celebration's residents.

evolved to include shops and services that cater to local residents, including a small Gooding's grocery store, a dry cleaner, a travel agency, a beauty salon, some home furnishings and interior decorating shops, a coffee shop, a bank, a café and grill, an ice cream and candy shop, a post office (with counter service), and a town hall. Gooding's is, literally, the corner store for the town center, but the Village Mercantile and the coffee shop have acted as "third places" where residents meet.

Most retailers and restaurateurs have relied on the power of the Disney name to attract business. As Tom Zirbe, who relocated his antiques business all the way

The concentration of apartments and townhouses (pictured here) helped to build up the density of Celebration's downtown. All units rented and sold at a brisk pace. *Rick Hall.*

from Honolulu, put it, "Who would have come here without the Disney name? There's not a businessman in his right mind who would move to a community with 1,000 people in the middle of a swamp."[3] But Celebration's core contains an enviable mix of uses in addition to retail—apartments, townhouses, and single-family homes; a hotel; offices; civic uses; and parks—all within easy walking distance of the main street. Brian Shea, of Cooper, Robertson, describes the inclusion of townhouses, in particular, as the key to building up the density of the downtown. He also notes that, as has been the case in so many other town center projects, the local real estate community had very little confidence that townhouses could be sold in the town center—a concern that proved groundless when the units rapidly sold out.

The 115-room Celebration Hotel, located on the lakefront, offers 5,000 square feet (460 square meters) of meeting space and is positioned to attract retreats, weddings, and small corporate events. Marketed as "the closest upscale boutique hotel to Walt Disney World theme parks," it is the latest of the six Florida hotels in Richard C. Kessler's suite of Grand Theme Hotels. In addition to adding vitality to the shops and restaurants of the downtown, the hotel—described in its promotional literature as "a resort destination [with] the simplicity and innocence of turn-of-the-century Florida"—plays off the "traditional town" aspect of Celebration.

The town center mix could have been even more diverse if the 284,000-square-foot (26,380-square-meter) Celebration Health facility, and some of the 1

The Celebration Hotel.

million square feet (92,900 square meters) of office space being built at the Celebration Place office complex and planned business parks along I-4 and U.S. 192, had been concentrated in or near the town center. The hundreds of employees who currently work in these facilities would have provided considerable day and evening foot traffic for the downtown shops and restaurants. The additional commercial space,

however, might have eroded the traditional, small town-atmosphere that is the hallmark of Celebration's downtown and the primary attraction for visitors.

Streets, Layout, and Parking

Most visitors enter the town center via Celebration Avenue, which runs from U.S. 192 (where the Celebration water tower stands as a beacon), then passes a row of village homes and townhouses at the edge of Celebration Village. As the avenue passes the Com-

Market Street at Celebration is the town center of the TND, located adjacent to a manmade lake in the centrally located Celebration Village neighborhood. *Cooper, Robertson & Partners.*

munity Presbyterian Church it curves to the northwest, directing the visitor's view toward the Bank of Celebration (SunTrust), then away from the town center toward the bottom of Water Street and the apartment buildings just north of the downtown.

The view down Water Street, toward the town center. *Cooper, Robertson & Partners.*

side of Market Street were sized to accommodate a variety of buildings along their perimeter, and to allow the interiors of the blocks to be used for parking courts. A smaller block follows the curve around the lake, where shops line Bloom Street's lakeside; apartments wrap around the southern and western sides of the block to enclose a third parking court. A fourth block, just east of the town center, across Sycamore Street, is slated for future development and is currently used as an overflow parking lot.

Market Street itself—a narrow, brick-paved street made narrower by parallel parking on both sides—is only one block long. It is a thoroughly pedestrian space, with a strong sense of enclosure provided by

Water Street, which runs straight into the town center from the north, provides visitors with both a more dramatic view and a more immediate sense of having "arrived" in downtown Celebration. Water Street delivers visitors directly into Market Square, where they are surrounded by some of the town center's most distinctive buildings, and treated to a view down Market Street to the lake. Perhaps the most enticing view of the downtown, however—invisible from both buildings and roadways—is from the edge of the vast nature preserve located across the lake.

The deceptively simple town center plan consists of four blocks clustered around the lake, bisected north to south by Market Street and east to west by Front Street, which runs along the lakefront. The two 450-by-400-foot (137-by-122-meter) blocks on either

Because Market Street is private, management can easily close the street for special events—such as the farmers' market, pictured here. *Cooper, Robertson & Partners.*

three-story buildings that are pulled up to the sidewalks and by rows of palm trees that line both sides of the street. Visitors cross at any point along the street; vehicles move slowly in both directions, and traffic is so calm that drivers occasionally make three-point turns in the middle of the block to change direction or to secure an on-street parking space. The sidewalks are wide, and an arcaded walkway and balconies provide relief from central Florida's midday sun. Like the main streets in most town center projects, Market Street is private, and is owned and maintained by the Celebration Company. Keeping the street private gave the developer more freedom to design and build a traditional main street and allows management to close the street for farmers' markets and other special events. All other streets in the downtown are public.

Parking courts are skillfully concealed within the interiors of blocks.

Front Street is paved (not brick) and zigzags along the waterfront, past the restaurants, the cinema, and the shops. Bloom Street, Sycamore Street, and Campus Street complete the downtown portion of the town's continuous curved grid. Alleyways slipped in behind the buildings, around the parking courts, provide access for deliveries, garbage trucks, and utilities, and help to preserve the high quality of the downtown streetscapes.

Through a combination of small surface lots, parking courts, and on-street parking spaces, the designers of the town center succeeded in assembling 1,000 parking spaces in the downtown area without providing any parking structures. The placement of the buildings and the vehicular entrances skillfully conceals much of the surface parking. Downtown

Charles Moore's tower, which previously housed Celebration's Preview Center, overlooks Gooding's grocery store.

Celebration includes some of the best examples of parking courts in any town center project. The courts provide parking for residents, whose private entrances to their apartments are located at the backs of buildings, as well as for visitors, who have easy access to the shops and restaurants through midblock passageways.

Buildings

The architecture of downtown Celebration was inspired by pre-1940s, small-town, main street America—but unlike the buildings at Main Street, U.S.A., in Disney's nearby Magic Kingdom Park, Celebration's buildings are full-scale, functioning structures where people live, work, and conduct their everyday business.

The architecture throughout the downtown reflects extensive research into vernacular traditions, which were then applied, in various combinations, to emulate the gradual development of town centers historically. The results include a range of styles and influences: Bloom Street's apartment buildings, for example, reflect the influence of "Carolina low-country" architecture; the design of SunTrust's Bank of Celebration building features neoclassical gestures; and the Columbia restaurant offers a mixture of Spanish, Cuban, and Floridian design elements. The composition of the buildings creates an urban fabric of compatible building types.

In Celebration's town center, stylistic flourishes are reserved for the buildings that have been designed by internationally known architects. These include an open-air post office by Michael Graves; a town hall by Philip Johnson; a bank by Venturi, Scott Brown; a cinema by Cesar Pelli; and a preview center by the late Charles Moore. Inspired by the lookout tower built by George Merrick for Coral Gables in the 1920s, from which potential homebuyers could view the town layout, Moore incorporated a similar tower into the Preview Center. Other references to town center precedents include the clock-tower building midway down Market Street, which Stern describes as a "tropical nod" to the clock tower in the town center of Lake Forest, Illinois.[4] The Celebration Company, a wholly owned subsidiary of the Disney Company created to develop and manage Celebration, touts the signature buildings as major downtown attractions and distributes *Architectural Walking Tour* pamphlets to visitors.

While the signature buildings provide visual interest, it is the "background" buildings, with their more subdued traditional architecture, that provide the backbone of the town center. Designed by Cooper,

Robertson & Partners and Robert A. M. Stern Architects, these buildings line Front Street, Bloom Street, and both sides of Market Street. The mix of vernacular influences and the use of detached buildings—a design approach that is maintained even in the larger structures, via midblock passageways to the parking courts behind the buildings—create a consistent *town* scale that falls between the village ambience of Haile Village Center and the more urbane scale and atmosphere of CityPlace, Mizner Park, and Reston Town Center. Two aspects of the design—the fact that all the buildings work together to frame the streets and public spaces, and that all the shops, restaurants, and offices have streetfront entrances—combine to give

An ensemble of three- and four-story "background" buildings along Market Street. The buildings, porches, and balconies, and the rows of palm trees provide a strong sense of enclosure for Celebration's brick-paved Market Street. *Cooper, Robertson & Partners.*

Celebration's downtown a stronger presence than can be found in projects like Kentlands Market Square, which has nearly twice as much square footage.

Although Richard Heapes, currently a retail consultant for Market Street, finds the signature buildings of the town center ill-suited to adapt to alternative uses, the background buildings were designed to be more flexible, and establishments like White Horse Gifts have been reconfigured into larger or smaller spaces to suit their changing needs.

Arcaded walkways provide relief from the central Florida sun for leisurely window-shopping.

The view of the town center from the nature preserve across the lake. Although some have criticized the lakefront orientation of the town center from a retailing perspective, the design draws on Florida precedents in Lake Eola (Orlando) and Lake Mirror Promenade (Lakeland).

The commercial architecture and urban design of downtown Celebration are true to their historic roots, with arcades, street trees, generous sidewalks, large glass display windows, and 12-foot- (3.7-meter-) high ground floors throughout the downtown. Another strength of Celebration's town center design is the flexibility that was built into its structures right from the start. Ground-level apartments on Celebration Avenue are designed so that they can be easily converted to commercial space in the future, and storefronts can be readily divided or consolidated in response to the changing needs of tenants, even where their facades make them appear to be parts of separate buildings.

Criticisms of the design tend to focus on two aspects, both of which concern the town center's commercial elements. The first is that the town center was located two miles from the nearest arterial, which delivers most of the customers that downtown Celebration's shops and restaurants need in order to survive. Ross notes that Peter Rummell, the former chairman of the Celebration Company, acknowledged that "putting these stores in two miles [3.2 kilometers] from route 192 was always the biggest gamble."[5] Unlike Haile Village Center, which had no roadside frontage available, Celebration held a good

deal of roadside frontage, along U.S. 192, that could have been used for the town center. While the town continues to grow at a fast pace, its 4,500 residents (as of June 2001) are nowhere near the number needed to support the amount of retail space in the downtown, which means that the center will continue to rely more heavily on regional and tourist business than on local residents.

The second criticism is that, apart from the Market Street block, the lakefront arrangement precludes the type of cross-street shopping that both mall and main street layouts traditionally encourage. Although the lakefront provides an attractive setting for the restaurants, retail expert Bob Gibbs has observed that "Fish don't shop." Celebration's designers and management have responded to this criticism by noting that the design of the town center is consistent with that of historic inland Florida towns—such as Lake Eola, in Orlando, and the Lake Mirror Promenade, in Lakeland, Florida—which use lakes as focal points for commercial activity. They also note that they wanted to avoid locating the town center adjacent to the placeless sprawl of the Route 192 landscape, which epitomizes the type of development from which Celebration was trying to distinguish itself.

Public Gathering Spaces

The town center enjoys a variety of public gathering spaces, ranging from the formality of Market Square to the liveliness of Market Street to the serenity of the lakefront and the Lakeside Park promenade. The lake-

The Front Street dock.

front, along Front Street, offers movable rocking chairs, a dock with steps for ample seating, and a pavilion; the promenade takes visitors along the edge of the nature preserve across from the town center. There is also a plaza in front of the cinema, and directly across the street is the show fountain, a feature that entices visitors to cross Front Street to explore Lakeside Park and the wetlands area. Located just southeast of the town center, the park includes trails that circle around the lake—providing stunning views of the town center skyline—and lead to the wetlands and wooden walkways on the west side, which link the Lake Evalyn neighborhood to the downtown.

Other nearby gathering places include Founder's Park, which is located between the town center and Celebration School, and the nearby bridge over Water Street, which has become a popular meeting place for Celebration's teenagers. By means of attractively landscaped, brick-paved walkways that lead from the parking courts, between and through buildings, and out onto the commercial streets, downtown Celebration also extends the public space beyond the main squares

Top: Two of Celebration's signature buildings, Philip Johnson's town hall and Michael Graves's post office, glimpsed through the trees and fountain in Market Square.

Bottom: The lakeside promenade.

and thoroughfares. The plaza area that begins in front of the town hall continues past the open-air post office and extends along the back side of Market Street. These types of "interstitial spaces"—among the best to be found in a town center project—are not mere window dressing but are functional, attractive passageways that encourage people to walk from the parking lots and apartments to the shops.

Marketing, Management, and Performance

The property is managed in much the same way as a conventional retail operation: the Celebration Company coordinates marketing and management functions; sets hours of operation; and organizes sidewalk sales, weekly farmers' markets, and special promotions. The promotions include events that take advantage of the town center's open-air setting; during the award-winning holiday-season promotion Now Snowing Nightly, for example, held in the weeks leading up to New Year's Day, snow machines transform Market Street into a winter wonderland for a few minutes on the stroke of every hour from six to nine p.m. A new promotion—the Beach and Seafood Festival—dumped 64 tons (58 metric tons) of sand on Market Street and the lakeside area, creating an impromptu beach. The event drew an estimated 20,000 visitors in its first year. When the festival was over, the sand was swept up and used on a local golf course.

Regular events, in addition to sidewalk sales and the farmers' market, include an annual art show, a Founder's Day weekend, a Fourth of July parade, and various holiday celebrations. According to some reports, the Celebration Company spends considerably more on marketing and promotions than the average shopping mall, but the events serve a dual purpose: they support the town's residential sales, and they help to establish the town center as a regional shopping, dining, and entertainment destination.

After the first years of development, the Disney Company's corporate management decided to nurture Celebration's unique identity, which meant weakening the connection between the town and Disney's corporate identity. At about the same time, the Celebration Company began carefully crafting a new identity and marketing strategy for Celebration's downtown, which they renamed "Market Street at Celebration." As part of a concerted effort to reposition the town center as a local and regional destination—one that would rely less on tourist business—brochures, maps, a Web site, billboards, and promotions were orchestrated to reinforce the Market Street at Celebration brand. By presenting Market Street as the identity of the town center, the marketing effort was intended to change the perception, among nearby residents, that Celebration was simply a high-profile residential project being built by the Walt Disney Company, and to persuade the local and regional market that the center might have something to offer people living outside Celebration's white vinyl fences.

For the Beach and Seafood Festival, Market Street is buried in 64 tons (58 metric tons) of sand. The sand was later used on a golf course. *The Celebration Company.*

In the face of a challenging location and small resident population, the town center's retail shops struggled to make ends meet during the early years, and a bike shop, a candy store, an antique store, some gift and apparel stores, and two restaurants closed and were replaced by other establishments. Zirbe's Antiques,

reportedly the most successful town center business in the first few years of the project, also closed its doors in late 1999, after disagreements with the Celebration Company over the shop's shortened operating hours. Awash in a regional sea of hotels, the 115-room Celebration Hotel also struggled during its first two years, and some observers have suggested that it would have been more successful if it had been built according to the original plan, which envisioned a smaller inn.

The primary attractions have been the two-screen, stadium-seating cinema, the "destination" restaurants, and the Preview Center, which drew thousands of curious visitors who wanted to find out more about Disney's new town. Not surprisingly, the fact that the Celebration realty operation was moved from the Preview Center to a building in the South Village neighborhood raised concerns among downtown business owners, who feared a loss of customers. Although the relocation of the sales operation may deter some visitors from going downtown, it has also made the attractive space in the Preview Center building available for expanding the retail base of the town. Many residents, however, would like to see the space reserved for community purposes.

Market Street's four unique specialty restaurants are the major anchors for the town center. In the effort to market Celebration as a destination, advertising campaigns have focused specifically on the restaurants, and the Celebration Company reports that the restaurants have experienced significant growth in sales every year, ranging from 6 to 20 percent annually. These fine-dining establishments are complemented by the

Market Street Café (providing more affordable breakfasts and lunches oriented toward families and retirees), a coffee shop, a pizza place, and an ice cream shop. Other Celebration businesses, such as Barnie's Coffee and Tea, the Village Mercantile, and AMC Celebration 2, are pleased with their performance to date.

There are now 20 specialty shops and services, and more services are being added through the conversion of downtown apartments. The mix of retailers has changed in response to the marketplace and to the growing number of residents. The addition of a hair salon was met with accolades from residents, who would also like to see a larger grocery, a video rental store, and a hardware store. Because these types of retailers require a large consumer base, the locations being considered are on the perimeter of the community, adjacent to a major commercial artery.

Despite some growing pains, there has been no shortage of shops and restaurants interested in filling vacancies in the town center, and special events held in Market Street at Celebration are very well attended. Perry Reader, president of the Celebration Company, reported in the spring of 2002 that average retail sales had, for the first time, reached the threshold of $300 per square foot ($3,229 per square meter), a respectable figure for most shopping malls and evidence that the town center's promotional efforts and repositioning have paid off. Additional development adjacent to the town center, including a satellite campus of Stetson University, will also bring in business.

With over 20,000 people attending the first day of the annual art show, and the same number attending the recent beach festival, the challenge for event planners has become a matter of avoiding *too much* promotion, and managing parking and traffic flows before, during, and after events. To help with this difficulty, the Celebration Company hired transportation consultants to develop a parking and circulation plan for special events that will ease the peak traffic flows by clearly identifying the streets that are reserved for local resident traffic and turning others into temporary one-way streets. If the town center succeeds in establishing itself as a regional destination and the Celebration population continues to grow toward its potential buildout of 12,000 to 15,000 residents, the Celebration Company is confident that the retail mix will stabilize and prosper.

Experience Gained

- Market Street at Celebration's masterful site plan and architecture represent one of the most extensive applications of new urbanist design principles for a town center project. The connections between the residential neighborhoods of Celebration Village and the town center are seamless; parking and midblock passageways are skillfully handled; and a variety of detached, traditionally styled buildings accommodate a wide variety of uses. Celebration epitomizes, for a small town, the scale and character evoked by the phrase *town center.*

■ Urban design for town centers must follow good commercial design principles that maximize cross-shopping opportunities, allow for the assembly of a critical mass of retail space, and position the center so that it connects with nearby residential neighborhoods while tapping drive-by traffic on adjacent thoroughfares.

■ At the village and town scale, plentiful parking can be sensitively provided, deferring the need for structured parking. In addition, by carefully locating and designing entrances and exits and by lining the perimeter of blocks with buildings, developers can conceal most surface parking in parking courts.

■ Public space should consist of a continuous network of streets and spaces, rather than of isolated pockets of streets and space. Developing such a network means building small, intimate public spaces off the main street, and creating attractively landscaped passageways that connect the spaces between and behind buildings and lead to parking, housing, other parts of the town center, and adjacent destinations.

■ The Disney approach—which was to site the town center in the heart of the new community, away from major roadways, and to create the downtown in the early stages of the MPC's development—was a deliberate strategy that is not likely to be emulated by other developers. Although a town center can establish the character of a larger project and act as a marketing tool, most developers do not have the resources of a corporation like the Walt Disney Company at their disposal; early retail development should be justified by the *existing* market.

■ Promotions and events for town centers and main streets should take full advantage of the unique open-air settings that set these projects apart from enclosed malls and other conventional retail formats.

■ Town centers in MPCs are most often identified with the particular community in which they are located. A comprehensive marketing strategy and "branding" effort should focus on the assets and identity of the town center as an attractive place for visitors as well as residents.

■ Residents and other stakeholders can provide valuable suggestions about retail store hours, product mix, and customer service. Specific promotions involving residents, out-of-town visitors, and area employers can increase traffic during traditionally slow periods.

Notes

1. Andrew Ross, *The Celebration Chronicles: Life, Liberty, and the Pursuit of Property Value in Disney's New Town* (New York: Ballantine Books, 1999).
2. Ibid.
3. Ibid., 82.
4. Beth Dunlop, *Downtown Celebration Architectural Walking Tour* (Celebration, Fla.: Disney Company).
5. Ross, *Celebration Chronicles,* 81.

Project Data: Market Street at Celebration

General Information

Project type	Town center for a new urbanist community
Web page	http://www.celebrationfl.com/market_street/home.html
Location	Osceola County, Florida, one mile (1.6 kilometers) south of U.S. 192 and adjacent to I-4
Acres/hectares	18/7
Parking	1,000 spaces in the downtown
Total development costs	Approximately $40 million[a]

Owner and Developer

The Celebration Company

Master Planners and Architects

Robert A. M. Stern Architects; Cooper, Robertson & Partners

Landscape Architect

EDAW

Building Area by Type of Use

Use	Square Feet/Square Meters
Retail	56,380/5,240
Office	78,067/7,250
Cinema	11,150/1,040
Town hall, post office	3,600/330
Total	149,197/13,860

Commercial Uses

Number of establishments[b]	26
Tenant mix	Specialty retail shops and services; professional offices; two-screen, stadium-seating theater; four destination restaurants; corner grocery store

Size range (square feet/square meters)	715–7,500/70–700, with flexibility to combine and subdivide ground floor space as necessary for tenants

Hotel Uses

115 rooms, with 5,000 square feet (460 square meters) of meeting space

Residential Uses

Approximately 300 units, including townhouses, single-family homes, and 123 rental apartments (45 above retail space)

Monthly rents	From $850 for a one-bedroom, one-bath, 800-square-foot (74-square-meter) apartment to $2,350 for a three-bedroom, 2.5-bath, 2,000-square-foot (186-square-meter) townhouse
Sales prices, townhouses	$275,000–$375,000 and up

Civic Uses

Town hall, post office, lakefront promenade, interactive fountain, and town square

Development Schedule

Ground breaking	Winter 1995
Downtown stores open	November 1996
Buildout date	2004–2009

a. Based on unofficial estimates.

b. Excluding offices.

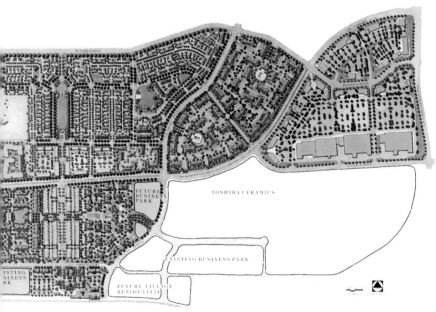

Orenco Station Town Center

Portland, Oregon

Widely praised by local, state, and federal officials as a prime example of transit-oriented development and smart growth, the Orenco Station traditional neighborhood development (TND) received accolades from vice president Al Gore, who visited the project during his 2000 election campaign. A 190-acre (77-hectare) new urbanist community being developed by Pacific Realty Trust, L.P. (PacTrust), and Costa Pacific Homes, Orenco Station Town Center incorporates over 1,800 living units; ten acres (four hectares) of business park uses; and 55 acres (22 hectares) of office and retail commercial uses, including the mixed-use town center and a separate, big-box retail area. Located in a rapidly growing suburb of Portland, Oregon (known as the Silicon Forest, and home to Fujitsu, Intel, and Toshiba), the project takes its name from Orenco (short for Oregon Nursery Company), an early-20th-century company town located just a half-mile (0.80 kilometers) away. The original Orenco, a major West Coast agricultural nursery, was connected to Portland via an electric railway at what was then called Orenco Station.

The master plan for Orenco Station's 190 acres (77 hectares) includes a light-rail station, a town center, single-family and multifamily housing, and a big-box retail area. *Fletcher·Farr·Ayotte, PC.*

Development

A diversified real estate company headquartered in Portland, PacTrust is one of the Pacific Northwest's largest real estate developers and investment property owners concentrating on industrial, office, and commercial income-producing properties. With its in-house site selection, design, construction, leasing, and property management capabilities, PacTrust brought a considerable range of assets to the development, financing, and management of a town center project—with one exception: it lacked expertise in residential development.

When PacTrust acquired the site in the 1980s, the creation of a new urbanist transit village was not even a remote possibility, as the property was zoned for industrial use and located on the outermost fringes of the Portland metro area. In the early 1990s, as market conditions improved and PacTrust began considering the development of the property, Portland's Westside light-rail line was approved, and the zoning for the property was changed to a station-area residential category. Once the light-rail stop was designated to be located on site, the town center zoning called for high-density, mixed-use development on the property.

Since PacTrust is primarily a commercial developer, it formed a joint venture with Costa Pacific Homes, a residential builder headquartered in Beaverton, Oregon, to create a new plan for developing the property. A number of public agencies also played key roles in shaping the project, and a strong public/private partnership (both formal and informal) was forged between the developer and the city of Hillsboro; Washington County; the Tri-Met Transportation Agency; the Metro regional government; the Portland Development Commission; U.S. senator Mark Hatfield; U.S. representative Elizabeth Furse; and many corporate entities and private citizens.

While working with public agencies to satisfy the requirements for transit-oriented development, PacTrust also hedged its bets by selling off parcels just east and south of the town center for the development of

Orenco Station is located in a rapidly growing suburb of Portland, Oregon—known as the Silicon Forest—that is home to Intel, Fujitsu, and Toshiba. The town center is located in the heart of the traditional neighborhood development's residential neighborhoods, adjacent to N.W. Cornell Road (foreground), which carries 25,000 trips per day past the site. *PacTrust.*

more conventional multifamily housing, and by creating a big-box retail section (considered a "slam dunk") on the eastern third of the site. PacTrust itself developed the 50-acre (20-hectare) Crossroads at Orenco Station, a regional retail center that currently includes 150,000 square feet (13,940 square meters) of retail and plans for office, pad retail,[1] and hospitality.

On the multifamily parcels, Fairfield Investments developed a conventional, 600-unit apartment community between the town center and the big-box retail property, and Simpson Housing developed an 800-

Transit Village Design and Development in the Round

The Round project, in Beaverton, Oregon, just west of Portland on the Max light-rail line, has generated considerable debate about the viability of transit villages. At the Round, development is focused around a pedestrian plaza that is bisected by the rail line and enclosed by multistory, mixed-use buildings with retail on the ground floor and residential units above. Some urban designers have criticized the "split-plaza" design, which made it difficult, in the initial phase, to build sufficient space on both sides of the rail line to enclose the plaza and create a strong sense of place.

Planners and designers have also criticized the absence of a main street, which could have attracted customers arriving by automobile. Although the developer and public agencies focused heavily on opportunities to create high-density mixed uses around the new transit line, the site is entirely surrounded by automobile-oriented suburban development. Portland and other cities offer many examples of successful transit-oriented retail; however, when development near a transit station is being incorporated into surrounding suburban areas it is necessary to accommodate the primary mode of local transport—namely, the automobile. Whether or not transit will support retail uses depends heavily on how pedestrian- and transit-oriented the pattern of development surrounding the station is, on the level of ridership, and on standard market factors such as the demographics of the trade area and the relative strength of competing retail.

Other observers believe that the Round's innovative design was not responsible for the failure of the project, which they attribute more to the combination of high land costs and inadequate financing. The major lesson to be drawn from the Round is that developers should not allow a project's transit aspect to distract them from the fundamental principles of real estate development and finance.[1]

1. Steve Coyle, Bill Dennis, Rob Dickson, John Fregonese, and Bill Lennertz, telephone conversations and e-mail correspondence with author.

unit condominium community southeast of the town center near the light-rail station. The key corridor parcel that runs from the rail station to the town center was also sold off to another developer specializing in multifamily housing, but was still undeveloped as of the beginning of 2002. Design guidelines call for this property to be developed in an urban, higher-density configuration.

The rezoning of the site assumed that all commercial uses and higher-density housing would be concentrated in the immediate vicinity of the light-rail station. According to Mike Mehaffy, project manager for PacTrust, this idea superimposed a "radial density formula that had no organizing features," and ignored the major arterial just north of the station. The 25,000 cars that drive through the site each day via N.W. Cornell Road convinced the developer that

the town center needed to be located along the arterial, rather than one-third of a mile (0.5 kilometers) away, at the rail station. Citing the failure of other transit-oriented projects—such as the Round, in Beaverton, just a few rail stops to the east—the developer persuaded planners and public officials that the success of the town center's retail would depend on customers' arriving not only by rail, but also by foot—and, especially, by automobile.

"We made the point that we needed flexibility to be able to create a strong neighborhood design with a sense of place, and to respond to market conditions," said Mehaffy. "We managed to persuade the jurisdictions that blindly following a density formula was a very bad idea. We therefore committed to deliver an equal number of units overall, with flexibility in the configuration." He described the final location of the town center, north of N.W. Cornell Road, as creating an "amenity axis": the north-south roadway (N.E.

Orenco Station Parkway) extends from the light-rail station along the main street to Central Park, and the town center commercial area runs east-west along the arterial (N.W. Cornell Road). In the end, according to Ken Grimes, the lead architect of Orenco Station, "All the traditional rules of zoning and planning were thrown out the window."

Although the town center was considered more experimental than the big-box and multifamily areas of Orenco Station, predevelopment focus groups and surveys of early homebuyers identified the town center as the most desired amenity—a finding that led PacTrust and Costa Pacific to rethink their phasing strategy and develop the main street core sooner than they had originally planned. The construction of the town center has since been credited with accelerating the appreciation of land values throughout the project, leading many on the development team to second-guess the early decision to sell off large parcels to other developers.

In programming the retail, Richard Loffelmacher, PacTrust's retail specialist, has worked hard to create "good chemistry" in Orenco Station Town Center, carefully selecting strong local restaurants, neighborhood services, and retailers. "We could have had two dozen beauty salons in here if we hadn't been selective," notes Loffelmacher. The main street is currently anchored by a Starbucks coffee shop and three neighborhood restaurants (Italian, Indian, and a combination steakhouse and bar). Other shops and services located in the town center include an optician, a dentist, a cleaning and alterations shop, a wine and cigar shop, a psychologist, a floral and gift shop, a clothing store, a title company, a real estate company, and a stockbroker. A 30,000-square-foot (2,790-square-meter) organic grocery store and 14,000 square feet (1,300 square meters) of retail space (with affordable loft housing above) opened in September 2001, and negotiations are under way with additional tenants.

Orenco Station's development team was also careful to distinguish between competitive and complementary retail. PacTrust developed the town center and the big-box portions of Orenco Station simultaneously, and took care to ensure that their commercial components do not overlap.

The Site, Streets, Layout, and Parking

Located about ten miles (16 kilometers) west of downtown Portland, the Orenco Station Town Center site had little in terms of distinctive natural features or

The project draws its identity from the nearby town of Orenco and from the light-rail station that connects the project with downtown Portland.

amenities. "There isn't a river, there isn't a lake, there aren't any great views," explained John Kohlmoos, sales manager for Costa Pacific.[2] What sets the project apart are its new urbanist design elements; its location adjacent to Portland's Westside light-rail line, in Hillsboro; and a seven-acre (three-hectare) town center with ground-floor retail, loft residences, and live/work townhouses.

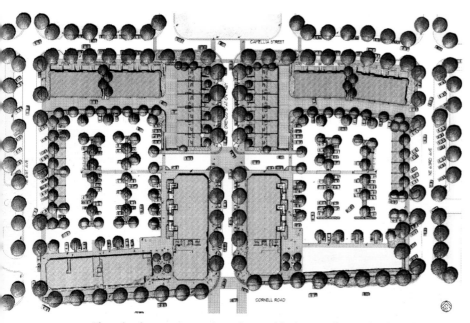

The mixed-use core consists of a two-block area where mixed-use buildings line a short main street; midblock access is provided to the parking courts that are located behind the buildings. *Fletcher•Farr•Ayotte, PC.*

The 190-acre (77-hectare) TND site is crisscrossed by two major roadways—N.W. Cornell Road and N.W. 229th Street Avenue. The town center is located in the western portion of the site, in the cen-

ter of the residential sections of Orenco Station that border N.W. Cornell Road. One block deep and four blocks long, the town center focuses on a one-block main street that runs between the busy main arterial, N.W. Cornell Road, and the rectangular Central Park. A row of short, square blocks along the arterial give way to the long rectangular blocks that parallel Central Park, and lead toward the irregular blocks at the northern edge of the site.

Just east of the town center, the interconnected streets, alleys, and sidewalks of the town center yield to the more conventional suburban streets and parking lots of the multifamily housing and big-box retail parcels. Orenco Station Parkway, the backbone of the plan, provides a main street promenade that leads from the light-rail station to the town center and beyond, to Central Park, which is surrounded by cottages and bungalows. The long, straight parkway is designed so that it terminates with a view of the distant hills.

Only one subsidy was used for the project— a federal Congestion Mitigation Air Quality grant of $500,000, which was used to add pedestrian amenities—including special pavers, bollards, benches, street trees, and lighting—along Orenco Station Parkway. Design guidelines call for buildings to line both sides of this section of the parkway, and for front doors and porches to face the street, creating a comfortable pedestrian environment. Construction of these buildings, however, has not yet begun, and the absence of a street wall makes the relatively short distance between the rail station and the town center appear much longer than it is.

Parking in the town center is provided on the street, in parallel parking spaces, and in lots and recessed spaces tucked beneath the rear of the live/work buildings. Some lofts have 11-foot- (3.4-meter-) high rear garages that are equipped with lifts, permitting two cars to be stored (the overhead space can also be

The lifts inside these garages enable loft residents to enjoy the same amount of storage area that they would have in a standard two-car garage—but at a lower cost, and using half the land area.

used for general storage). Providing the $4,000 lifts was less costly than building two-car garages, and allowed the designers to reduce the amount of land area used for parking within the town center.

Buildings

According to Bob Boileau, of Fletcher•Farr•Ayotte, PC, the architecture of the town center was inspired by historic photos of the area and by older buildings from the pre–World War II era that have survived to the present day. The designers drew on these sources to develop an architecture and urban design intended to provide both a strong "sense of place" and a "feeling of permanence." The mixed-use buildings along the main street of Orenco Station Town Center feature brick and wood facades, bay windows, balconies, wrought-iron railings, and metal awnings. Two identical, 16,725-square-foot (1,550-square-meter) mixed-use buildings, with retail on the ground floor and two-story lofts above, frame the entrance to the town center's main street. The corners of the buildings have commercial office space on the upper floors; the residences above the retail, which are designed to look like the lofts found in older industrial buildings, have polished concrete floors, two-story ceilings with exposed

Two identical three-story, mixed-use buildings frame the entrance to Orenco Station Town Center's main street. The buildings along the main street feature brick and wood facades, bay windows, balconies, wrought-iron railings, and metal awnings.

Shops and work spaces for the live/work units are located off lower-level terraces; raising the residential space above street level maintains privacy.

beams, and fixtures with an industrial look and feel. By providing a strong sense of enclosure for the two-lane main street, these three-story buildings create an "outdoor room"; on-street parking, wide sidewalks, street trees, and lampposts add to the pedestrian-friendly ambience.

Top: Shops and restaurants are concentrated on the first block off the main arterial.

Bottom: A short block of live/work townhouses provides a transition between the retail block and the single-family homes around Central Park.

As one moves north from N.W. Cornell Road, one of the two major roadways that run through the community, the half-block of main street retail transitions to a shorter block of three-story, live/work townhouses that mimic the style and materials of the retail block but are less deep and massive. Each townhouse has a split entry: one flight of stairs leads up to the main living area, which sits above the street, affording added privacy; another, shorter, set of stairs leads down to a work space that is ADA-accessible and can be converted to retail.

Designed as walkups with a "brownstone" character, the live/work townhouses provide a gradual transition from a commercial to a more residential ambience; in the townhouse portion of the block, planting strips and narrower sidewalks replace the tree wells and wider sidewalks of the retail section, and lower-level terraces lead to the work spaces and the planting strips.[3] The large bay windows of the townhouses and lofts provide views of the urban streetscape to one side, and of the quiet green of Central Park to the north.

The transition to the detached, single-family cottages and bungalows clustered around the spacious Central Park is more abrupt—and, in retrospect, if the strength of the market for the lofts and townhouses had been better established, the designers and the developer would have considered extending the three-story walkups all the way around Central Park.

Public Gathering Spaces

Orenco Station Town Center provides a fine-grained mix of public gathering spaces—including, in addition to Central Park and the main street—pocket parks,

The lofts and live/work townhouses provide a "room with a view"—something that is hard to come by in most multifamily projects.

small plazas, and greens. Although residents appreciate the spaciousness of Central Park, some feel that its size, in relation to that of the surrounding cottages and bungalows, undermines the sense of intimacy and enclosure of the main street. The designers expect a stronger sense of intimacy and enclosure to evolve, however, as the young trees planted around the green

Top: The spacious green of Central Park, with a view of the distant hills.

Middle: Distinctive pavilions give character to the park.

Bottom: At the southern end of Central Park, adjacent to the commercial main street and live/work units, benches, lampposts, and gravel surfaces create a more urban ambience.

mature. Because the parks and plazas called for in local parks and recreation standards are generally much larger than those that would be considered appropriate for traditionally styled towns and main streets, conflict often arises over the design of parks and other urban open spaces for TNDs and town center projects. In the case of Orenco Station Town Center, the size of the park was the result of a compromise: local standards would have required an even larger park.

Marketing, Management, and Performance

The commercial and office space in Orenco Station Town Center has enjoyed broad market acceptance: over 90 percent of the commercial space and over 80 percent of the office space was occupied by mid-2001, and rents are up to 15 percent higher than those for comparable space in the area. Careful and selective leasing continues as the town center and live/work space fills up, and a number of prospective clients have been turned away.

The lofts and townhouses, for which there were no local comparables on which to base sales expectations, have sold at prices that shattered records for attached housing products in the area. In 1996, there were two attached-home sales in the Hillsboro market, both in the $100,000 range. Orenco Station has already recorded 25 sales in the town center alone, and another 92 just north of the town center. One live/work townhouse sold for over $500,000, and another two units that had been combined sold for almost $800,000. Sales prices on lofts have ranged from $124,000 to $388,000, at a price of about $190 per square foot ($2,045 per square meter), versus a typical price of $130 per square foot ($1,400 per square meter) for attached residential properties.

Experience Gained

Project success depends on a strong foundation:[4]

- Create a vision for the project and remain committed to it. The power of the vision will depend on the capacity of the architecture and urbanism to evoke a strong sense of emotional connection in potential residents and visitors.
- Create excitement in the marketplace.
- Differentiate the project from other developments.
- Generate support from lenders, government jurisdictions, and the public.

Viable retail is critical to the performance of a town center:

- Provide maximum exposure for retail. In the case of Orenco Station, ensuring maximum exposure meant locating the town center so that it would front a busy arterial, rather than locating it adjacent to the light-rail station itself.
- Understand the difference between competitive and complementary retail. The developer, Pac-Trust, was able to distinguish the commercial mix of the town center from the big-box portion of Orenco, which was developed simultaneously. The developer also learned from the mistakes of potential competitors—such as the Round, a transit village in nearby Beaverton—which PacTrust believed relied too heavily on transit riders to support retail establishments.

- Provide access for all modes of transportation: cars, pedestrians, bicycles, and public transportation.
- Provide an anchor—although not necessarily a big-box or traditional shopping-center anchor. At Orenco Station Town Center, Starbucks serves as an anchor because of its prominent street visibility and high name recognition. The restaurants also act as destinations for the town center.

All elements of the town center must be market-driven:

- The town center creates value for the rest of the project; surveyed residents named the town center as the number one amenity, and the town center was credited with increasing land values throughout the project.
- The market for higher-density, mixed-use projects in the suburbs is evolving rapidly. Although real estate investors base their strategies, in part, on the success of comparable projects in the past, a well-worn financial disclaimer can apply as well: "Past performance is no guarantee of future profits." Conduct market surveys that reveal the *potential* market among today's homebuyers, rather than the needs of past homebuyers.
- Getting the right mix of tenants requires patience, a well-crafted leasing plan, and the recruitment of hard-to-find elements like good local and regional restaurateurs.

Create inviting urban open space:

- Provide a system of parks (a "string of pearls") running through the project.
- To create a sense of enclosure and foster a strong pedestrian environment, provide wide sidewalks and narrow streets lined with buildings.
- Add balconies, stoops, windows, and doorways facing the sidewalks to provide "eyes on the street"; increase the sense of safety and security; and provide town center residences with "a room with a view"—a feature rarely found in suburban settings.

Don't sell your front door (or the areas leading to your front door):

- At Orenco Station Town Center, the sale of the property linking the town center to the light-rail station has delayed development of that key parcel and suspended the full buildout of the transit village.
- The construction of the town center has accelerated the appreciation of property values throughout the project. The sale of the property adjacent to the light-rail station came too early in the project and sacrificed much of this created value.

- The parts of Orenco Station that are considered the weakest are those that were sold to multifamily developers who delivered density without creating a strong neighborhood character. It is crucial to retain design control over all parcels to ensure consistency with the project's vision. When parcels are sold off, carefully worded agreements providing for design review are essential.

Place making is a cooperative venture. In the case of Orenco Station Town Center, the public/private process worked because

- The public sector and the community stepped in and determined what the regional goals would be;
- The developer was willing to craft a development strategy that responded to these goals;
- The jurisdictions were willing to sit down with the developer and cooperate in the evolution of a project that was economically viable and that also had a strong sense of place.

Notes
1. Development isolated on satellite sites, loosely connected to shopping centers.
2. Rosemary Leonetti, "New Urbanism Success Story: Planned Community Wins National Awards and Sells Lots of Homes"(http://www.office.com/global/content/article/printme/ 0,3232,16740,00 [November 1, 2000]).
3. Strips of ground between the street and sidewalk, planted with trees and plants.
4. This section is adapted from a presentation on Orenco Station by Bob Boileau at ULI's Second Annual Place Making Conference, September 18, 2000, San Diego, California. Also based on discussions with Mike Mehaffy, project manager, PacTrust.

Project Data: Orenco Station Town Center

General Information

Project type	Transit village in a new urbanist community
Web page	http://www.orencostation.com
Location	Hillsboro, Oregon, ten miles (16 kilometers) west of Portland
Acres/hectares (town center only)	7/3
Estimated investment to date	$20 million

Owner and Developer

Master developer and owner, PacTrust (Pacific Realty Associates, L.P.); residential developer, Costa Pacific Homes

Master Planners

Fletcher•Farr•Ayotte PC; Iverson Associates

Landscape Architecture and Engineering

Walker ◆ Macy; Alpha Engineering, Inc.

Commercial Uses

Building Area by Type of Use

Use	Square Feet/Square Meters	
	Actual	Proposed
Retail and dining	70,000/6,500	92,000/8,550
Office	31,000/2,880	41,000/3,810
Total	101,000/9,380	133,000/12,360

Commercial Lease Rates and Terms

Rates (per square foot/square meter)	$20–$24/$215–$258
Terms	Triple net, no subleasing

Retail Uses

Number of establishments	15
Tenant mix	Primarily neighborhood specialty shops, services, and dining, with two national chains (Starbucks and Orvis)
Range of shop sizes[a] (square feet/square meters)	550–3,000/50–280

Residential Uses

Unit Type	Unit Size (Square Feet/ Square Meters)	Number of Units
Loft residences above shops	650–1,900/60–180	22
Live/work townhouses	2,300–2,500[b]/210–230	28

Sales and Rental Prices

Sales prices, lofts and townhouses	$124,000–$500,000+
Rental prices, apartments in adjacent multifamilysection	$700–$1,200 for luxury units; "granny flats" adjacent to the town center rent for $500–$700 per month

Project Schedule

Site planning	1995
Ground breaking	1998
Buildout date, town center	2002

a. Excluding the grocery store.
b. Including 450 square feet (42 square meters) of work space.

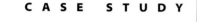

Southlake Town Square

Southlake, Texas

Developed on land that was formerly occupied by an egg farm and horse farm, and surrounded by $500,000 homes on large suburban lots, Southlake Town Square has resurrected the classic Texas courthouse square after a hiatus of nearly 100 years. The initial phases of Southlake Town Square represent the heart of what is projected to grow into a 2.5-million-square-foot (232,260-square-meter) development. Located in Tarrant County, on 130 acres (50 hectares) centered between Dallas and Fort Worth, just northwest of the Dallas–Fort Worth International Airport, the project already includes nearly 400,000 square feet (37,160 square meters) of commercial space, a town hall, a post office, a library, and both a town square and a larger city park; future plans call for a hotel, townhouses, and residential lofts.

Southlake Town Square is also intended to create an actual town center for the City of Southlake, a booming suburb of over 21,000 people (up from 7,082 in 1990), many of whom have come from cities and towns across the nation to take high-paying jobs in the corporate corridor between Dallas and Fort Worth. Southlake Town Square thus confronts many of the place-making challenges faced by suburban communities throughout the United States—including rapid growth, a transient population, an automobile-dependent transportation system, the suburban mindset of local residents, and large-scale retail and civic uses that are difficult to incorporate into town centers and main streets. The project has come to terms with both the civic and commercial aspects of these challenges through a traditional town center grid focused on a courthouse square.

Background and Site Characteristics

In the firm's first venture into the world of "open-air, mixed-use lifestyle centers," Brian Stebbins, of Cooper & Stebbins, L.P., acted as the managing partner for Southlake Town Square and was heavily involved in all phases of the project. For the planning and design of the project, Stebbins hired David M. Schwarz, whose previous experience included well-known Texas projects such as the Ballpark in Arlington, a traditionally styled urban baseball stadium for the Texas Rangers; Sundance Square, a 14-block revitalization effort in downtown Fort Worth; and Bass Performance Hall, also in Fort Worth. Schwarz inherited an earlier conceptual plan for the site that was laid out in conventional suburban fashion—with separate, single-use pods of regional retail, neighborhood retail, office, entertainment, restaurant, and civic uses.

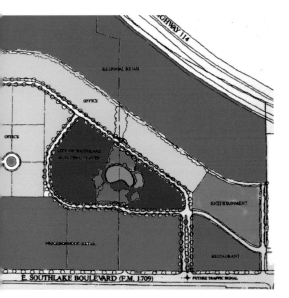

The original plan for the Southlake Town Square property was a conventional single-use arrangement (color added). David M. Schwarz/Architectural Services, Inc.

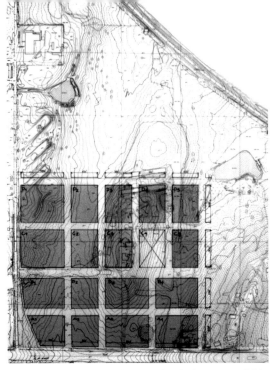

To experiment with site layouts, the designers overlaid historic block patterns—like downtown Fort Worth's—on the property. After generating multiple plans for short, traditional blocks, they eventually settled on a 12-block layout. David M. Schwarz/Architectural Services, Inc.

As part of the site-planning process, Schwarz superimposed the historic grid of downtown Fort Worth on the Southlake Town Square property to reveal the scale and potential of the site. Working from this starting point, Schwarz transformed the seven single-use islands of the original plan into 12 mixed-use blocks, all interconnected by a bent-grid street network focusing on a large town square. The developer questioned the approach and asked Schwarz for evidence that the 24-plex cinema and big-box retail uses originally envisioned for the project could be incorporated into the proposed block and street pattern. Schwarz responded with drawings and plans illustrating the adaptability of the proposed urban fabric, and began presenting slide shows to the developer (and, later, to the public) that showed historic town centers and traditional types of urban public gathering spaces.

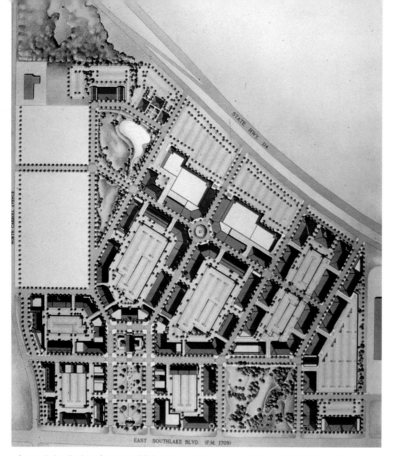

The original plan for Southlake Town Square positioned buildings along East Southlake Boulevard to enclose the square and screen it from the heavy traffic on the arterial. The final plan, pictured here, shows the addition of the town hall on the square and the open view from the arterial that the city required. *David M. Schwarz/Architectural Services, Inc.*

On the basis of Schwarz's recommendations and its own vision for the property, the developer decided to pursue the concept of an open-air town center, reserving the northern portion of the site for the potential inclusion of a large cinema and-big box retailers.[1] The design team then worked through the final plan, first delineating the public space and then the blocks (which were made large enough to contain parking lots or garages at the interior, surrounded by buildings), and finally mapping the uses. At 350 feet (106 meters), the longest block is somewhat longer than the designers would have preferred for pedestrian comfort, but the length was necessary to accommodate the parking garages.

To create shorter walking distances between the parking areas and the commercial streets, the designers incorporated midblock breaks along each block face. This technique works particularly well around the town square, which is broken up into three segments, creating a fine-grained mix of short block segments, streets, passageways, and a variety of public spaces. It becomes less effective on the side streets (essentially "B" streets) away from the square, where the street wall gives way to parking areas on at least one side of the street, creating a less attractive pedestrian environment. Future plans call for the construction of liner buildings, up to 80 feet (24 meters) deep, to help mask these parking areas and to create building fronts on both sides of the street.

Development

Peter Cooper and Brian Stebbins met while both were involved in the development of retail, hotel, and office projects in Australia and New Zealand in the 1980s. When they returned to the United States (they formed their partnership in 1989), they initially focused on power centers in Texas, where they felt the real estate cycle had bottomed out. In 1995, they shifted the focus of their business to master-planned developments—specifically, "open-air, mixed-use lifestyle centers"—which, they believed, had the potential for greater appreciation than conventional shopping centers, through long-term ownership.

The team identified the future site for Southlake Town Square after a nationwide search for an area that would support the type of mixed-use center they wanted to develop. The site was attractive for its strong demographics, its location in a rapidly growing corridor between Dallas and Fort Worth, its proximity to the regional airport, and the opportunity it afforded to assemble a large, undeveloped property from two existing parcels. After the Rouse Company decided not to pursue the construction of a shopping mall on the property, Cooper & Stebbins put together a three-way partnership with the two families that owned the property.

Although the City of Southlake had designated the site as a village center in a 1995 corridor study that envisioned mixed uses in a master-planned format, the study produced very little regulatory guidance, outside of a sign ordinance that addressed some landscape issues. The zoning for the property was a mix of commercial and planned unit development districts that allowed some flexibility but prohibited residential uses. As Stebbins noted, "The city had these romantic dreams of a downtown but no rules."[2] Working with Schwarz, Stebbins transformed the earlier plan—first from the single-use, big-box format to a hybrid mix of big boxes and a town square area, and finally to the current plan, in which big boxes were completely supplanted by the Grand Avenue promenade, and the 24-plex cinema was replaced by a 200-room inn.

The development environment was initially highly charged, with considerable disagreement over the zoning of the site. The surrounding area was suburban in character, and many nearby homeowners wanted to see the site remain essentially undeveloped, or wanted it to be developed as a golf course. The preconstruction planning and negotiation took three years before the $75 million first phase broke ground in the fall of 1998. The developer and designer used examples of great public spaces, main streets, and town centers to convey to public officials and Southlake's citizens the concept behind the project. As Schwarz noted, "Making great places is a matter of unquantifiable values, not objective principles. It's much easier to sell values using images of great places rather than abstract principles"—like mixed use and compact development.

In support of the project, the city created a 408-acre (165-hectare) tax increment reinvestment financing zone that included all of the Southlake Town Square property. The tax increment financing (TIF) zone collects property taxes on development within the zone and uses this money to pay off bonds for public improvements. These funds have been used to pay some costs for the construction of the town hall and the public streets and parking decks, and 100 percent of the costs for the public park. A school district also benefits from the TIF and is using a portion of the funds generated to finance school facilities.

Mix of Uses

Southlake Town Square combines a nearly equal amount of retail and office space, evenly divided between ground-floor retail and second-floor office space. The retail currently includes 62 shops and services, including ten restaurants and cafés; the office space houses a wide variety of businesses and professional services. The developer is also assembling an enviable assortment of civic uses: the town hall build-

The town hall adds a dramatic civic presence to the town square and enhances the authenticity of the town center. The decision to locate the town hall in the square required the city to spend additional money to create brick facades on all four sides of the building. *Steve Hall/Hedrich-Blessing.*

ing houses the city council chambers, an office for the justice of the peace, the office of the Tarrant County commissioner, the county tax office, the city's first public library, and a subcounty courthouse.

The eight-acre (three-hectare) post office block includes neighborhood retail uses to serve the adjacent residential neighborhoods, as well as visitors and workers in Southlake Town Square.[3] While modern post offices are increasingly designed as drive-through facilities that require extensive parking areas for delivery vehicles, the 22,000-square-foot (2,040-square-meter) full-service mail distribution center in Southlake Town Square was brought up to the street and designed to look like a small-town post office. The post office is attached to four one-story buildings that were designed to look as if they had evolved over time, and these buildings screen the parking areas located in the rear.

Residential uses are the one crucial component that is so far absent. The ultimate plan for the project calls for the Grand Avenue promenade to be lined with ground-floor retail, with two-story residential lofts above, and to terminate at a hotel at the northern end of the street. A large residential neighborhood is to be located on the eastern third of the property, just north of the park. While Southlake Town Square is far ahead of the pace set by most town center projects for incorporating civic uses, it will not evolve into a full-fledged town center until it gains full-time residents in and around the commercial core. The developer plans to begin construction of the first residential neighborhood in 2002.

Streets, Layout, and Parking

The design team established a hierarchy of streets in a bent-grid pattern that emphasizes the intersections between streets. In creating the hierarchy, Schwarz notes, "We identified which [streets] were important and why, not just in terms of how they look but what they do." The streets surrounding the town square were designed as traditional downtown shopping streets, with on-street parking and pedestrian amenities. Two of these streets provide the main entrances to the project, then run north from Southlake Boulevard along either side of the square. From the northern end of the square, the views down both these streets are terminated by buildings at the corners of the blocks, providing a strong sense of enclosure to the space. The extension of Grand Avenue, yet to be developed, will act as a long promenade and as the primary streetscape connecting the square to the northern section of the project. All other streets act as short connectors that provide alternative travel paths for movement within the site, or as throughways that pass completely through the site and connect to major arterials.

In part because of their newness, the sidewalks, curbs, walkways, and even the brick crosswalks appear rather spartan, and while great streets do not require expensive materials, the introduction of more variety in surface materials could enhance the pedestrian character of the project and reinforce the impression that this is a place that has evolved over time.

One large difference between Southlake Town Square and other town center projects is that *all* of the project's streets are public. This means that city approval is required before streets can be closed off for festivals and events. It has also created challenges for the design team, which had to incorporate the 70-foot (21-meter) right-of-way required on public streets. Schwarz addressed the challenge by adding generous sidewalks, rows of street trees, and angled parking on both sides of the primary pedestrian streets, as well as by "necking down" intersections to decrease the walking distance for pedestrians crossing streets. While these design features do slow traffic and improve the pedestrian quality of the streets, the 70-foot (21-meter) rights-of-way, the 14-foot- (4.3-meter-) wide sidewalks on the blocks surrounding the town square, and the 11-foot- (3.4-meter-) wide sidewalks on all others, create a space that some consider too open to establish a strong sense of enclosure, given that Southlake's buildings are only two stories high. The relative size of the open space will decrease, however, as the street trees mature and create a canopy around the square.

Schwarz describes the urban fabric as a pattern of street–building–alley–garage–alley–building–street, an arrangement that made it possible to maintain the street wall and the enclosed spaces by locating most parking, deliveries, and services behind buildings. Schwarz notes that while an individual developer cannot control what might occur on adjacent properties, the interconnected blocks and street grid make Southlake Town Square a "very attachable fragment of urbanism."

Schwarz considers the most important element of the design, however, to be the parking. "Parking controls everything," he commented. "It's the driving force." In addition to the angled and parallel spaces

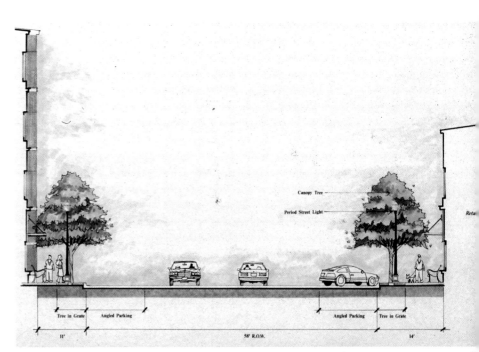

Top: A typical street section at the town square. *David M. Schwarz/Architectural Services, Inc.*

Bottom: Unlike the streets in many town centers, those in Southlake Town Square are all public—and, as such, are subject to the engineering and design standards set by the state department of transportation. *David M. Schwarz/Architectural Services, Inc.*

on streets, the plan incorporates parking decks and surface lots. Decks are freestanding, except where the topography made it possible to add liner buildings and to conceal the garage.

Although the construction of parking decks was required to support the amount of commercial space permitted, the developer was allowed to calculate parking needs on a block-by-block basis. By phasing the development so that partial blocks were completed on opposite sides of the street and square, the developer was able to delay the requirement to build the garages until after substantial amounts of commercial space were operational, rather than being forced to construct the garages upfront. Thus, development could be completed on two sides of each block without triggering the requirement to construct a parking deck. This phased development approach also made sense from a place-making perspective, which calls for two-sided streets and enclosed spaces to be created early in the project to establish a sense of place.

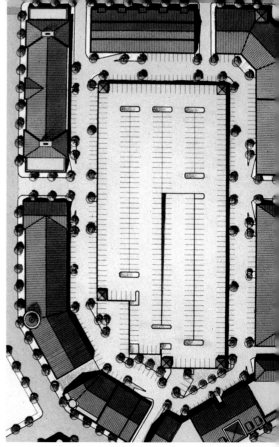

The buildings line the perimeter of the blocks, creating a pedestrian-friendly street wall and screening the parking garages in the interiors of the blocks. *David M. Schwarz/Architectural Services, Inc.*

Buildings

Unlike many town center projects, which consist of a combination of larger and smaller buildings, deep big boxes, and shallow liner buildings, Southlake Town Square is composed of large, two-story buildings on the perimeters of blocks. The blocks surround the square and run along Grand Avenue, and the buildings offer floor plates of between 15,000 and 35,000 square feet (between 1,390 and 3,250 square meters)—ample enough to accommodate large retailers and to achieve the large amount of square footage approved for the project. Most of the buildings are a half-block long, and many wrap around the corners of blocks and follow the curve of the street. To break up this mass, the designers used multiple facades on the fronts of buildings, creating the impression that four to five smaller buildings had been built side by side over a period of time. This approach allowed the developer to accommodate a great deal of commercial space (275,000 square feet—25,550 square meters) in

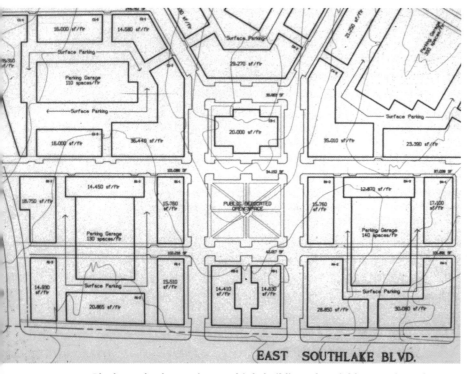

Blocks are broken up into multiple buildings that yield approximately 100,000 square feet (9,290 square meters) per block. *David M. Schwarz/Architectural Services, Inc.*

Multiple facades break up large structures and create the impression of an ensemble of buildings. *Steve Hall/Hedrich-Blessing.*

the first seven buildings constructed around the town square, with two to three sides of each block still remaining to be built.

Another difference between Southlake Town Square and other town center projects is that the design team did not formally define building typologies, urban design guidelines, or vernacular architectural styles. "We shied away from any type of geographic identity," Stebbins said.[4] The developer wanted an appealing town center that would feel vaguely familiar to a city of newcomers drawn from throughout the United States. Schwarz did, however, exert some control by handpicking the architects to design the facades of individual buildings—an approach that

also helped to ensure variety in the streetscape, which is more difficult to achieve when a single architect designs all the buildings.

As a result, the architecture of Southlake Town Square is consciously eclectic, consistent with pre–World War II American main street architecture but with influences drawn from multiple regions and styles. Downtown Fort Worth's Western Union Building was one local source of inspiration, but other buildings employ art deco, Victorian, Romanesque, and midwestern themes. The numerous stylistic influences that were used to break up large buildings into distinct facades designed by different architects was a way of "compressing time," creating in just a few years an environment that would have taken a century to evolve.

What distinguishes the architecture of Southlake Town Square, however, is not its stylistic flair but the collective effect of well-mannered "background buildings." Outside of varied cornices, an occasional dormer, a second-floor railing or awning, and modest towers on some of the street corners, the overall effect is that of an ensemble cast with one star: the town hall.

The town hall supplies that extra measure of civic reality that often escapes town center and main street projects. In the case of Southlake Town Square, the imposing four-story building assumes the most prominent site in the town, within the square and in front of some of the major retail and office tenants that had been visible from East Southlake Boulevard before the town hall was constructed. Although the original plan called for the square to be completely enclosed and blocked off from the busy four-lane arterial, the developer lobbied hard to have the new town hall located in Southlake Town Square—and, to secure this civic anchor for the project, agreed to maintain a clear view from East Southlake Boulevard, at the southern border of the site, across the square to the town hall. In addi-

One building, many facades facing the town square. *Steve Hall/Hedrich-Blessing.*

tion, all the parking for the 80,000-square-foot (7,430-square-meter) town hall was assigned to surface lots located off the square and behind the commercial buildings, eliminating the moat of parking that might otherwise have been required.

Pleased with the early results of Southlake Town Square, the city hired Schwarz to design the new town hall building. Since the backs of the commercial buildings faced onto parking lots (and future garages), the developer was able to leave these relatively plain and undecorated. Because the town hall, in contrast, would be located within the town square, all four sides of the building would be in full public view. This greatly added to the cost of the building, which amounted to $15 million, but the design garnered strong public support.

At an urban design conference in Charleston, South Carolina, in March 2001, a panel of observers commended Southlake Town Square for achieving some of the best architecture to be found in a town center project. This is not to say that there is no room for improvement; the shop awnings are mostly decorative, and there are no arcaded walks that might provide relief from the Texas sun and rain; moreover, the rather staid, straightforward character of the project, albeit one of its strengths, also begs for some relief—some flights of fancy in architecture, landscape design, or public art that could humanize the setting, much the way that the fountains and civic art of Country Club Plaza do. Such elements can be added over time, however, and the developer's and designers' obvious care and attention to detail have already led the public to embrace this very young project for what it is—the town square for the city of Southlake, Texas.

Public Gathering Spaces

The town square is obviously the centerpiece of the project—the center of gravity around which the buildings and activities revolve. The square is actually a series of three half-block panels: the first is occupied

With no arcades and small decorative awnings, the fronts of buildings offer little relief from the Texas sun and rain. *David M. Schwarz/Architectural Services, Inc.*

Southlake residents and visitors enjoy an art festival in the town square.
David M. Schwarz/Architectural Services, Inc.

by a pond and pavilion; the middle panel is made up of the central square, which is crisscrossed by walkways that meet at a central fountain; and the northernmost panel is occupied by the town hall. Each panel offers a variety of public gathering spaces that take on an increasingly urban character as visitors move from the arterial toward the town hall.

Including the town square, the project features a total of 13 acres (five hectares) of public parks and open space. One of the largest park areas, located just one block away from the square along the busy East Southlake Boulevard, was inspired in part by the designs of Frederick Law Olmsted; it encompasses meandering trails and preserves the largest cluster of mature trees on the property. The streets also provide a network of pedestrian space that extends the

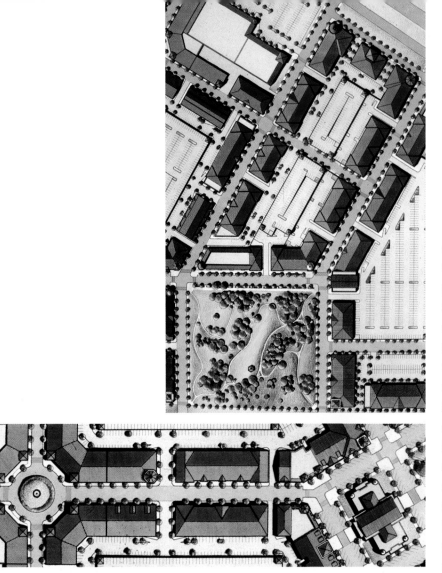

Top: A large, Olmstedian park just east of the town square provides a peaceful setting. *David M. Schwarz/Architectural Services, Inc.*

Bottom: Grand Avenue provides a central spine of pedestrian-oriented public space that extends from the town square into the heart of the site. *David M. Schwarz/Architectural Services, Inc.*

public realm from the square, to the new post office block, up the Grand Avenue promenade, and across the site to the residential neighborhood planned just north of the park.

The square is oversized in relation to the two-story buildings that surround it, but the addition of the four-story town hall has scaled down the space, and the trees planted along the streets and around the

square will continue to enhance the human scale of the space as they mature. A combination of tall lamp-posts and short, lighted bollards also provides a more intimate scale within the square at night. Landscaping elements and outdoor furniture were carefully chosen to avoid a contrived, "project" atmosphere—an effort that is generally successful in the central square, but that falters around the manmade pond and the pavilion of Ruskin Park, which have a somewhat more artificial quality that seems out of place at the East Southlake Boulevard entrance to the project. The awkward landscaping along the boulevard, which is more rural and suburban than urban, derives, in part, from a shift in the plan, which originally called for buildings at this location to close the square. As mentioned earlier, in return for agreeing that the new town hall would be located within the town square, the city required the developer to leave the square open, providing a view of the building from the busy, four-lane arterial on the south side of the square. In the resulting trade-off, the town square and the town center gained a very visible, signature civic building, but the objective of enclosing all four sides of the public square had to be abandoned.

Indeed, it's difficult to argue with success; the town square has clearly been triumphant as a gathering place, drawing thousands of people to concerts, holiday celebrations, and special events. The opening events for Southlake Town Square were attended by thousands of city residents and Mayor Rick Stacy, who proclaimed, "This is a new beginning for our city—a foundation for our future."[5]

The pavilion in the square is used for musical performances and other events that draw crowds to Southlake Town Square. *Steve Hall/Hedrich-Blessing.*

Marketing, Management, and Performance

Cooper & Stebbins set about recruiting retailers from a target list of 200 prospects, beginning with children's retailers, then women's and men's stores, then home furnishings, then restaurants. Stebbins acted as an ambassador for the town square concept, and personally wooed a variety of national, small regional, and local retailers. The developer also hired Dallas-based United Commercial Realty to market and lease the project, although Stebbins continued to personally promote the project to prospective retail and office tenants. Preleasing for the retail component was very strong; the recently completed post office block, for example, was over 50 percent preleased before construction began.

The project was an immediate success from both a commercial and a community perspective. In March 2000, just one year after the project opened, retail space was 100 percent occupied, as was more

than 80 percent of the office space. Six of the 17 national retailers reported that their Southlake stores had the best opening-day sales of their entire national chains, and none of the retail tenants turned over during the first year. Over 6,000 residents turned out for the first Fourth of July celebration and over 20,000 for the second; an estimated 25,000 people attended a weekend Art in the Square festival the first year, and 40,000 the following year. Management has been amazed at the small amount of litter that remains after the public events, which Stebbins takes as a sign that community members view the town square as their own and take pride in its appearance.

Angled parking spaces line the traditional downtown shopping streets. The festive lighting is reminiscent of Country Club Plaza, in Kansas City. *Steve Hall/Hedrich-Blessing.*

Experience Gained

- When presenting town center and main street projects for public review, provide images of similar types of historic places and focus on their traditional, underlying values rather than on abstract principles like smart growth, mixed use, and compact development. "Making great places is a matter of unquantifiable values, not objective principles."

- It is important to establish a strong sense of place in the initial phase of the project. For Cooper & Stebbins, this meant building the town square first. For other projects, establishing a sense of place may be as simple as completing both sides of a single block before beginning the next phase. In Southlake Town Square, the parking deck formula allowed the developer to build two sides of each block without triggering construction of the parking decks.

- Incorporating civic institutions on prominent sites reinforces the traditional community orientation of town centers, which is part of what citizens respond to. Civic uses can bring public sector commitment to the project and instill a long-term sense of public ownership and pride in a place.

- Contemporary institutional uses, such as town halls, courthouses, libraries, and post offices, can be woven into a traditional urban fabric without sacrificing the character of the project—or the space needs, parking needs, and accessibility requirements of the institutions.

- Traditional town squares, plazas, greens, promenades, and courthouse squares come in a great many shapes and sizes, and visits to a variety of these will provide insight into what is most appropriate for the town center being planned. In the case of Southlake Town Square, while the square may seem oversized to some, it has turned out to be a very functional and popular public gathering place for the community.

- TIF, TIF, TIF. The opportunity to finance significant portions of the expensive infrastructure that is often required for high-density town center projects makes tax increment financing an invaluable tool where it can be negotiated. This means that developers must be able to make a strong case for the public benefits of the town center project—a case that is easier to make when significant civic uses and public gathering spaces are incorporated.

Notes

1. See graphics and additional discussion in chapter 5.
2. Kelli Rodda, "Southlake Leads National Trend by Creating Downtown Lifestyle," *Real Estate Quarterly*, June 19, 1998, 3A, 7A.
3. The "Post Office Square" area, located just northwest of the town square, does not appear on the original master plan that accompanies this case study.
4. Rodda, "Southlake."
5. Dave Lieber, "Foundation for the Future," *Star-Telegram* (Fort Worth, Texas), March 21, 1999.

Project Data: Southlake Town Square

General Information

Project type	Town center
Web page	http://www.southlaketownsquare.com/
Location	Southlake, Texas, between Southlake Boulevard and State Highway 114
Acres/hectares	130/53 (42/17 in Phase I; 8/3 in Phase II)
Parking	Approximately 1,800 parking spaces: 3.47 spaces per 1,000 square feet (93 square meters)
Investment, Phase I	$75 million

Owner and Developer
Cooper & Stebbins, L.P.

Master Planner and Architects
David M. Schwarz/Architectural Services, Inc.

Building Area by Type of Use

Use	Square Feet/Square Meters		
	Phase I	Phase II	Buildout
Retail	220,000/20,440	37,000/3,440	700,000/65,030
Office	160,000/14,860		1,800,000/167,230
Civic	80,000/7,430a	22,000/2,040b	
Total	460,000/42,740	59,000/5,480	2,500,000/232,260

Commercial Uses: Lease Rates

Use	Base Rent (Per Square Foot/ Square Meter)	Tenant Improvement Allowance (Per Square Foot/ Square Meter)
Office	$16+/$172+	$15/$161
Retail	$22+/$236+	$20/$215

Retail, Service, and Restaurant Uses

Number of establishments	89
Tenant mix	National retail chains, including Eddie Bauer, the Container Store, the Gap, Pottery Barn, and Williams-Sonoma
Range of shop sizes	100–10,000 square feet (9–930 square meters), with some larger stores, including a 24,000-square-foot (2,230-square-meter) Container Store and plans for a two-story Barnes & Noble

Hotel Uses
Two planned

Residential Uses
None currently; lofts and townhouses planned for future phases

Civic Uses
A town hall, a post office, a library, and a city park

Development Schedule

Land acquisition	1995
Project planning, design, and approvals	1995–1997
Ground breaking	Fall 1998
Opening, Phase I	March 1999
Opening, Phase II	2001
Estimated buildout date	2010

a. Town hall.
b. Post office.

CASE STUDY

Valencia's Town Center Drive: A Developer's Perspective

Gary M. Cusumano

Gary M. Cusumano is chief executive officer and president of Newhall Land, a California real estate company founded in 1883 that is developing the new towns of Valencia and Newhall Ranch.

To meet the needs of our growing new town, Valencia, California, which has been under development 30 miles (48 kilometers) north of downtown Los Angeles since the late 1960s, we began building Town Center Drive—Valencia's half-mile- (0.8-kilometer-) long new main street—in the early 1990s. Unfortunately, those years coincided with the depths of the worst recession in Southern California since the Great Depression.

But the Newhall Land and Farming Company, the developers of Valencia, decided to go ahead and start constructing the $200 million Town Center Drive anyway. Valencia's 1965 master plan, prepared by Victor Gruen, had set aside the location for a town center, and all subsequent development had been planned in such a way as to integrate that site into Valencia and make it the heart of the community. Thus, by the early 1990s, the site was surrounded by Valencia's three main arterials and was the focal point for Valencia's 25-mile (38-kilometer) paseo (walkway) system.

The overall plan for the buildout of Valencia Town Center Drive (colors indicate an early phasing plan for the project; orange areas represent the final phases). *EDAW.*

We began master planning and infrastructure work in 1991 and broke ground on our first building in 1995; additional buildings were constructed as the market dictated. In November 1998, we celebrated the grand opening of Town Center Drive with the first annual Bella Via street-painting festival. When the street was completed, in 2002, it had 16 low- and mid-rise buildings, including five office buildings with approximately 400,000 square feet (37,160 square meters) of office space as well as ground-floor retail space; two upscale apartment complexes with a total of 560 units, which anchor the western end of the street and overlook the Town Green; 114,234 square feet (10,610 square meters) of retail space for national and local retailers; several restaurants and coffeehouses; the six-story, 244-room Hyatt Valencia Hotel and an adjacent 26,000-square-foot (2,420-square-meter) con-

ference center; the 52,000-square-foot (4,830-square-meter) Spectrum Health Club; and the 108,000-square-foot (10,030-square-meter) Valencia Entertainment Plaza, which has a 12-screen multiplex and additional restaurants and retailers. The two-story, 790,000-square-foot (73,390-square-meter) Valencia Town Center regional mall, designed by RTKL Associates, Inc., anchors the eastern end of the street.

Conceived in the late 1980s and planned in 1991, Town Center Drive was one of the pioneers in the development of new suburban main streets and town centers, and was the first true new main street or town center to be completed in California. As a result, Newhall Land had no familiar models to follow when planning, designing, programming, constructing, and leasing our new main street. How did we do it, and what lessons did we learn along the way that can benefit other place-making developers?

Planning Our Main Street

We wanted to create a public realm that would strengthen Valencia's heart and identity—and, most important, provide a place where all kinds of people could come together for a wide variety of everyday activities. We wanted to create a community hub for Valencia's 42,000 residents and a regional hub for the 200,000 residents of the surrounding Santa Clarita Valley.

We began our planning process by touring and studying main streets from Santa Barbara, California, to Annapolis, Maryland, and we learned from all of them. We talked to developers, municipal officials, store owners, and planners to learn what worked on a main street—and what didn't. We also received considerable guidance from skilled real estate professionals, architects, and planners, each of whom had their own (usually differing) ideas about the necessary ingredients for a successful new main street. Many were participants in a one-day design charrette that we conducted in 1993.

Newhall Land envisioned Town Center Drive as a contemporary version of the small-town main streets of the pre–World War II era: these were streets that had a broad mix of uses—office, retail, restaurants, entertainment, housing—and that attracted residents, workers, and visitors from early morning until late at night, seven days a week. Newhall Land particularly wanted to bring office uses to Town Center Drive,

Streets in the town center are 53 feet (16 meters) wide from curb to curb, with 14-foot- (4.3-meter-) wide sidewalks, and angled parking. *EDAW.*

both to generate additional jobs in the community and to enable more residents to work closer to home.

To create a pedestrian-friendly environment, another key component of a main street, we decided that the ground floors of the low- and mid-rise office buildings would contain retail uses and restaurants. The street itself would be relatively narrow, to strengthen the pedestrian-friendly atmosphere and to slow traffic. We would plant mature trees up and down the street. Abundant open space—a Valencia tradition—would include landscaped plazas, landscaped courtyards at the entrances to buildings, and plazas or water gardens at strategic locations. We would install public art, such as murals and bronze statues, along the street.

Designing Our Main Street

We decided that Town Center Drive buildings would follow a Southern California architectural theme—like State Street, in Santa Barbara—but we did not want a homogeneous, heavily urbanized design. We wanted Town Center Drive to have the look of a main street that had developed over time, where the styles and sizes of buildings were different from each other yet complementary. We took special care to integrate the Valencia Town Center regional mall into the street, both physically and architecturally. The tallest office buildings, for example, were placed in the middle of the street to create a focal point along Town Center Drive. Adjacent buildings gradually step down in height to complement the two-story mall.

To avoid turning Town Center Drive into a busy traffic artery, we made the roadway just 53 feet (16 meters) wide from curb to curb, and lined it with

Sketches indicate the variety of uses that the town center buildings and public spaces were designed to support. *EDAW.*

sidewalks that were ten to 14 feet (three to 4.3 meters) wide. We added angled curbside parking to further calm through-traffic, then tucked the vast majority of the parking behind the buildings, in multistory parking structures and a few surface lots. To create a true main street ambience and provide pedestrian-friendly opportunities for window-shopping, we held the building line to the sidewalks.

Programming Our Main Street: The Right Tenant Mix and Uses

If Town Center Drive was going to succeed, programming the right balance of national and local uses and tenants was critical. We had two principal goals: first, to level out the ups and downs of the various market segments; second, to achieve a mix of uses that would complement and support each other. Office, for example, feeds retail by supplying customers for the stores and restaurants, and retail supports office by providing those amenities that create a more attractive location for employers.

We programmed Town Center Drive's retail to complement, not compete with, the middle-market orientation of the regional mall, which serves as the street's eastern anchor. We focused on higher-end men's and women's apparel, home furnishings, and gift shops, as well as restaurants and cafés. Above all, we

Town Center Drive includes a mix of retail, service businesses, restaurants, entertainment, hotel, residential, and office uses. Office uses include the corporate headquarters of the Princess Cruise Line. *EDAW.*

Top: Main street retail leading to one of the shopping mall entrances. *EDAW.*

Bottom: Entertainment Plaza, in front of the cinema. *EDAW.*

wanted to avoid a "chain row." We looked for distinctive shops and restaurants, large and small, that really serve local needs and demographics. We carefully mixed national tenants, like Ann Taylor and Talbots, with local businesses and retailers, like Valencia Florists and Paper Mulberry. Town Center Plaza—a 26,000-square-foot (2,410-square-meter) retail and office building—was planned to provide space for local professionals and stores.

Office and retail were just the start. Although it is one use that is often lacking from the new main streets and town centers that are springing up in suburbs across the country, we knew that a hotel would be a key component for the success of Town Center Drive. In addition to being a destination unto itself, a hotel creates an important spillover effect: it puts people (particularly business travelers) onto a street, especially in the evening.

Before entertainment retail had become a real estate development fad, we recognized that an entertainment center (movie theaters, in particular) would be a regional draw that could really strengthen our street. So we planned the 108,000-square-foot (10,030-square-meter) Valencia Entertainment Plaza. We also worked to bring the Spectrum Health Club onto Town Center Drive—which, in fitness-conscious Southern California, would provide an early-morning to late-evening draw, seven days a week.

Finally, to anchor the western end of the street, we planned upscale apartments that would supply customers—and even workers—for the retail and commercial uses up and down Town Center Drive. They would also provide that all-important pedestrian traffic that creates a feeling of movement and excitement on a street.

Building Town Center Drive

In the early 1990s, Town Center Drive was still a paper street. We needed a "lone soldier" to prove to prospective tenants and users that Town Center Drive really would get built. Thus, in Valencia's relatively new office market, in the midst of the lingering recession, we had to construct a three-story office building with ground-floor retail.

On September 15, 1995, we broke ground on 24300 Town Center Drive: it was the first speculative office building that had been constructed in greater Los Angeles since 1990. The three-story, 57,000-square-foot (5,300-square-meter) building, which was designed by Johnson Fain Partners, was completed in September 1996. With this lone soldier leading the way, we completed the Spectrum Health Club in June 1997. That same month, Princess Cruises (one of the nation's three largest cruise companies) signed a 15-year lease for the top five stories (132,000 square feet—12,260 square meters) of a six-story Town Center Drive building that was completed in fall 1998. Peter Ratcliffe, president of Princess Cruises, said that one reason his company moved 750 of its employees from West Los Angeles's high-profile Century City to Valencia was "the city-center environment being developed along Town Center Drive."

As Southern California's economy continued to improve and market demand rose in the mid- to late 1990s, we added more buildings to Town Center

Drive, including the hotel, the conference center, and retail buildings. But some key parcels on and near Town Center Drive remained empty. Then, in 1999, Princess Cruises announced plans to move its entire corporate headquarters to two new buildings at Town Center Drive: a four-story, 84,000-square-foot (7,800-square-meter) building on Town Center Drive itself and a five-story, 127,000-square-foot (11,800-square-meter) building one block away. The original 750 Princess Cruises employees moved into these new buildings in early 2001.

Why did Princess Cruises make this remarkable commitment to Valencia? New suburban main streets like Town Center Drive offer corporations (and their employees) the desirable combination of a close-to-home suburban location and a pedestrian-friendly environment with a mix of everyday uses. During lunch hours, employees can walk—not drive—to a restaurant, bookstore, dry cleaner, or doctor's office.

Valencia Town Center Drive has become a popular venue for art fairs, sidewalk sales, and community performances and events. *EDAW.*

Living with Our New Main Street

Unlike some developers who construct their new main street or town center all at once, we developed Town Center Drive piece by piece, over the course of a decade, to meet market demand and our budget requirements. By early 2001, approximately 80 percent of the street was complete. With the full lease-up of Town Center Drive's first apartment building, market demand for housing on the street was so strong that we abandoned plans for a new office building opposite the

Town Green, and instead sold the land for the construction of an upscale apartment complex, with ground-floor retail in some areas.

Unlike many new so-called main streets, which are little more than open-air shopping centers, Town Center Drive is a true public realm, with a full mix of traditional main street uses—including office, residential, retail, entertainment, hotel, and open space—and is physically integrated into the Valencia community. Town Center Drive brings jobs and services to Valencia, and has created a long-missing hub for Valencia and the surrounding Santa Clarita Valley.

Experience Gained

We did a lot of things right on Town Center Drive that have made this new main street a true place, a public realm for Valencia's 40,000 residents, and a regional hub for the Santa Clarita Valley's 200,000 residents. But we should have done some things differently. For example, although we designed the ten- to 14-foot- (three- to 4.3-meter-) wide sidewalks on Town Center Drive to accommodate several uses—from window-shopping to restaurant patios—they are not wide enough, in areas that have street furniture, to allow two couples to pass each other easily. If we had it to do over again, we would have made the sidewalks wider. Now all we can do is remove some of the planters along the buildings to facilitate pedestrian traffic.

We also neglected to put an adequate Town Center Drive "window," or presence, on McBean Parkway, a major arterial that bisects our new main street. Many Town Center Drive buildings present a blank wall to McBean Parkway, which is a problem because a blank wall encourages people to bypass Town Center Drive. The architectural design should have extended from the facade and around the corner of each building.

Finally, we have not yet attracted a civic use—like a library, a post office, or an educational institution—to Town Center Drive. Civic uses are essential building blocks for creating a genuine place, because they bring legitimacy to a main street or town center, they bring strong pedestrian traffic, and they do not pack up and leave in a few years, creating holes in the overall development.

Perhaps the greatest lesson in planning and building Town Center Drive has been the importance of sticking to our convictions and taking the time to get what we wanted. In the late 1980s, for example, when we were planning the two-story Valencia Town Center regional mall, we wanted the future Town Center

The McBean Parkway presented major challenges to connecting two portions of the town center and led to a development strategy that created a more independent mixed-use area south of the Parkway.

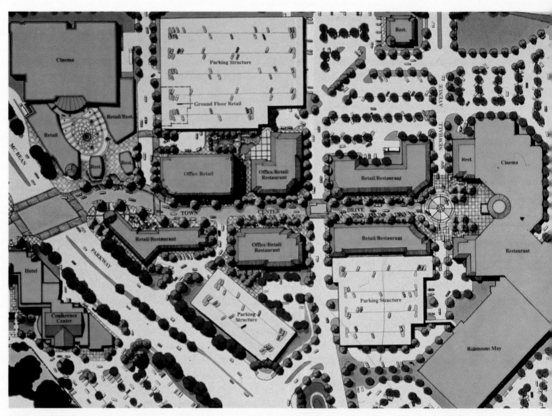

Town Center Drive was perhaps the first main street designed to connect directly to a regional shopping mall, terminates the street to the east. *EDAW.*

Drive to connect with the mall's main pedestrian entrance. So, the mall's master plan broke the "ring of parking" that traditionally surrounds most shopping centers and set aside an area that would become the first block of Town Center Drive. Although prospective department store anchors were opposed to any change in the standard regional mall formula, we insisted on constructing the mall to our specifications, and signed the anchors after a year of negotiations.

We also had to stick to our guns to sign the right uses for the most critical location on Town Center Drive: the two buildings that form the easternmost end of the street and provide the transition into the

main pedestrian entrance to the regional mall. We had expected to sign restaurants for those two retail spaces, but many restaurants that wanted to be on Town Center Drive preferred to locate in available space two blocks away, near the Entertainment Plaza. We didn't panic, and we didn't rush out to sign any tenants we could get to plug that key gap on the street. Instead, we waited two years until we could attract an appropriate restaurant and a Talbots retail store to complete the programming mix that best serves Town Center Drive and the mall.[1]

Note

1. In 2001, Town Center Drive won ULI's Award for Excellence in the mixed-use, large-scale category.

Project Data: Town Center Drive

General Information

Project type	Mixed-use new suburban main street connected to a two-story regional mall in a master-planned new town
Web page	http://www.valenciatowncenter.com/info/towncenter.cfm
Location	Valencia, California, 30 miles (48 kilometers) north of downtown Los Angeles on the I-5 corridor
Acres/hectares	80/32
Total development costs	$200 million

Owner and Developer

Newhall Land and Farming Company

Master Planners

RTKL Associates, Inc.; Skidmore, Owings & Merrill LLP

Architects

Johnson Fain Partners; Altoon + Porter Architects

Building Area by Type of Use

Use	Square Feet/Square Meters
Retail	114,234/10,610[a]
Office	400,000/37,160
Entertainment	108,000/10,030
Health club	52,000/4,830
Conference center	26,000/2,420
Total	700,234/65,050

Commercial Uses: Rents

Use	Average Monthly Rent (Per Square Foot/Square Meter)
Retail	$2.25/$24.00
Office	$2.35/$25.00

Retail Uses

Major national and regional retailers and restaurants, a 12-screen multiplex, and a health club. The adjacent Valencia Town Center mall has 110 specialty retail tenants.

Hotel Uses

244-room Hyatt with a 26,000-square-foot (2,420-square-meter) conference center

Residential Uses

560 rental apartments

Public Space

Plaza, main street, and town green

Development Schedule

Planning began	1991
Project opened	November 1998
Buildout date	Summer 2002

a. In addition to the 790,000-square-foot (73,390-square-meter) mall.

CHAPTER 8

A Compendium of

Planning and Design Ideas for Town Centers

"To create a great place takes passion, and it happens at the point of execution, one person at a time, across specialties. That's where great places are created—somebody has to care."

—ART LOMENICK

The town centers, main streets, and urban villages that are being planned and built today are being driven by broad social, economic, cultural, and demographic trends. These exciting, multifaceted projects also represent some of the best prospects for delivering on the promise of smart growth. When compared with low-density, single-use development, mixed-use, pedestrian-oriented town centers can achieve many of the benefits touted by smart growth advocates, including increased transit usage, reduced dependence on automobiles, and lower environmental impacts. Through the creation of interesting, diverse, and community-oriented gathering places, these projects also represent the potential restoration of a viable public realm in American towns, cities, and suburbs.

The wide range of projects featured in this book do not represent blueprints that can be copied: no one project can be held up as offering solutions to every single challenge involved in planning and designing town centers, main streets, and urban villages. Collectively, however, these projects offer a range of insights and lessons—summarized in this chapter—that can inform the efforts of developers, planners, designers, and policy makers working to bring town centers into being.

Defining the Character of the Town Center

In planning and designing a town center, urban village, or main street development, it is critical to identify at the outset the essential character desired for the place to be created—the total fabric—so that the whole can, in fact, become greater than the sum of its parts. All the projects discussed in this book are essentially attempts to create urban settings; the basic question comes down to what degree of urbanism is to be built. Is this going to be a village center in a low-density suburban area; a town center for a traditional neighborhood development, master-planned community, suburban town, or edge city; or a neighborhood center, urban district, or downtown core for a city? The answer to this question should completely drive the design of the project. Once you know which type of urban place you want to create you can begin to match the buildings, streets, public spaces, landscaping, and architectural details to the type of place being created.[1]

The village-scale qualities that make Haile Village Center succeed, and the buildings and public spaces that create an ideal town-scale setting in Celebration's town center, differ radically from the more urban scale and composition of places like CityPlace, Mizner Park, and Reston Town Center. The buildings, streets, open spaces, and tenants of these projects are not interchangeable.

In addition to defining the essential character of the development, it is important to think in terms of "the experience of place." The experience of place goes beyond the functional roles of buildings and infra-

Top: A village atmosphere has been defined at Haile Village Center, where detached, stick-frame and brick buildings and rustic walkways line a gently curving main street that terminates in a view of the Meeting Hall.

Middle: Celebration is a sophisticated town center with a small-town atmosphere. Although Celebration's buildings are detached, they are larger and more stately than those of Haile Village Center, and Market Square is more formal than Haile's fountain park.

Bottom: Mizner Park—featuring taller, attached buildings; arcaded walkways; and a grand public space—creates an urban district with a European character.

The public art, decorative elements, and lighting added to Kansas City's Country Club Plaza over several decades have added a human touch to the 1920s shopping village. *Kevin Klinkenberg.*

structure and the flow of pedestrians past shops and restaurants. The experience of place encompasses elements such as symbolism, playfulness, clarity, legibility, and serendipity. There should be a sense of exploration, mystery, and discovery about what might be waiting just around the next corner. There should be signs of a human touch in the design of buildings and outdoor settings, and a sense of art, history, culture, community, and humanity in the shaping of buildings, landscapes, streetscapes, and even basic infrastructure, which should appeal to young and old, male and female, and people from all walks of life.

Shape a Place from the Start

While the intent in town center development is to create a unique and interesting place, that goal will rarely be achieved overnight. Because of their size and complexity, most town center projects are phased, with different developers building different portions of the project. In developing a phasing plan, it is extremely important to establish a strong sense of place in the early stages of the project. For example, instead of building an isolated block of stores or buildings on one side of a street, it is preferable to build two half-blocks on two sides of a street, with buildings facing one another and parking in the rear. This arrangement will create a sense of enclosure—a *sense of place*—that is lacking on single-loaded streets.

Establishing a significant urban plaza or green in the initial phase can strengthen the sense of place. Especially when adjacent areas include busy roadways, suburban subdivisions, retail strips, and office parks—

One side is not enough. (Mount Pleasant Town Center, Mt. Pleasant, South Carolina.)

Two-sided streets and enclosed public spaces should be completed in the first phase of a town center to establish a sense of place. (CityPlace.)

all of which detract from the sense of place in a town center—deflected or terminated vistas can reinforce the sense of being immersed in a distinctive setting. A new store, a restaurant, or a movie theater may draw people at first, but they will return again and again because of the overall sense of place achieved through the quality and attractiveness of the streets, buildings, walkways, and public gathering spaces.

Create a Center of Gravity

Nothing is more powerful for a town center than a strong center of gravity, a focal point that provides a gathering place for people and an identity for the project. The center of gravity may be the main street itself, but more often it is an urban park, a plaza, an outdoor dining area, a fountain, a transit station, a clock tower, or some other place to which people are naturally drawn. A center of gravity helps visitors remain oriented to the larger setting, provides dramatic views of the town center, and offers an outdoor setting for meeting, mingling, lounging, and conversing. The central public space should also be adaptable—providing performance space and seating for special events, as well as flexible space for kiosks and exhibits at art fairs and farmers' markets. Notes Thomas Brink, of RTKL Associates, in Baltimore: "It's critical to activate the edges of a public space, or it will be underutilized."

The center of gravity may or may not overlap with the highest concentration of commercial activity. While attractive gathering places and commerce can reinforce one another, there needs to be a balance between the community orientation of the public realm and the commercial activity around, and often within, the outdoor areas of town centers. The role of public space is not simply to act as an accoutrement to commercial activity, but neither should it be a pristine enclave, divorced from the excitement of the shops, restaurants, and other commercial facilities of town centers. While it makes sense to cluster dining and entertainment uses around a plaza or green to create a hub of activity, people should also be able to rest, stroll, or gather for quiet conversations without feeling that they are trespassing on private property or obliged to purchase something.

Public space is the great equalizer for town center projects. Whereas town center housing is often aimed at high-end homebuyers and renters, and

At CityPlace, the grand plaza, fountain, and historic church building create a powerful center of gravity. *Elkus/Manfredi Architects Ltd.*

many shops may cater to upscale households, the public spaces provide gathering places for people from all walks of life: this community-oriented role is central to what makes town centers much more than "inside-out shopping malls," and helps justify the public sector's support of such projects. A center of gravity that is also a resplendent public space can transform an attractive commercial setting into a genuine town center that serves as a focal point for the surrounding neighborhoods; attracts visitors from throughout the community and the region; and provides an amenity that will bolster the long-term viability of the property.

Attention to detail—materials, color, texture, lighting, planters, and foliage—adds authenticity to new projects. (Post Riverside, Atlanta, Georgia.) *Steve Hinds.*

The Closer They Get,
the Better You Should Look

The litmus test for town center urban design, however, remains the eye of the beholder. As the European architect and urbanist Léon Krier has observed, good architecture is something that should become increasingly interesting and engaging the closer you are to it. A town center skyline, punctuated by a clock tower or steeple, provides visual interest from the highway; the approach to the town center should unfold into an interesting drive along a main street filled with people, storefront displays, outdoor cafés, public spaces, street trees, awnings, signage, and display lighting. On the street, the architecture should provide an immersive setting that is more than simply a container for com-mercial activities. The design should recognize the changing visual experience that visitors encounter as they walk along streets and through public spaces; should provide comfort and shade for pedestrians; and should incorporate expressions of time, place, history, and culture.

Materials and encroachments (balconies, arcades, awnings, and porches) should not only respond to the overall local climate but to the seasonal and day-to-night changes that create patterns of shadows and light; affect visitors' comfort and the visibility of window displays; and contribute to the overall aesthetic qualities of the center. Something as simple as the ornamentation above a doorway, the scrollwork on a park bench, or a tile mosaic along a public walkway or windowsill can become an object of fascination and delight.

Urbandizing: A Primer on How Town Centers Can Compete with Retail Malls and Strip Centers

There has never been a better time for downtown shopping districts to regain the customers lost to strip centers and regional malls. The same is true of the new main streets and town centers being built today. And yet so many of the recent, expensive efforts to revitalize downtowns or build new town centers have struggled.

What's missing?

Quite often, a solid foundation of everyday retail trade is missing. Main street retailers must follow the same merchandising and retail principles used by the best major mall developers to satisfy consumer wants and needs. *Urbandizing* applies the science of merchandising to the real-life needs of main streets and town centers. These include

- The need for great storefront design with exciting visual appeal;
- Traffic patterns that guide people to stores;
- Strategic tenant mix;
- An inviting, clean, and secure shopping environment;
- Ample, close-by parking;
- Regular, generous shopping hours;
- The best in marketing, advertising, and management.

It is important, however, that town centers not lose their distinctive physical and lifestyle qualities. The architectural details that can help blend the best of the old with the best of the new. The traditions and rhythms, the local heritage, the sense of place that attract us back to town centers and main streets.

Still, many new town centers and downtown redevelopments have struggled because of the lack of everyday commerce. Town centers need not look like malls or try to replace malls. Instead, they must adopt the best of mall merchandising principles to win back the retail dollar.

These are the steps to urban retailing.

Step One: Storefronts

Winning stores attract and hold attention and indicate immediately the type and quality of merchandise. Proper window display, entry design, signage, lighting, and fixtures are all part of the strategy to draw shoppers inside.

This must happen quickly. Retailers, indoor or out, have only about eight seconds to capture the attention of a shopper walking by a storefront. For those driving by town center storefronts in their cars, this "window" of opportunity may only be two or three seconds.

Storefronts must always be up to date. Primary architectural treatments should be updated at least every five years. This is a generous schedule; in leading shopping centers, storefronts are redone as often as every two years. In addition, a common storefront team must work with all retailers on a town center block.

Overall, keep storefronts simple and clean; let the merchandise take center stage. These merchandise displays should be rotated every one to five days; many leading national chains rotate merchandise daily. In the town center setting, this will encourage people to drive by and see what's new. Unfortunately, conventional planning wisdom has often restricted vehicles from main street, eliminating the constant exposure to storefronts and merchandise displays that leads to sales.

Window displays don't have to be over-elaborate or expensive, just fresh and inventive. Main streets must be always changing, always new, always interesting.

Retail follows fashion, and fashion changes frequently. Shoppers will not believe a store has fashionable new clothing on the inside if it is outdated or worn on the outside.

Step Two: Circulation

A typical regional mall has two to four large anchor stores to lure shoppers from its geographical territory. These are usually major national department stores. Through carefully developed sight lines and pedestrian traffic patterns, these anchors are then used to pull shoppers through the mall so they walk past the smaller shops and their merchandise.

The town center setting does not necessarily need large retail department stores to serve as anchors. Many other attractions can function in the same way as department stores, as a regional draw for shoppers. These include live theaters, movie theaters, art and convention centers, and farmers' markets. Town center developers and management should look carefully at what they have to attract shoppers. Putting the unique features and qualities of a town center at the service of business will help maintain these cultural resources for everyone.

Remember, the location of anchors or attractions is more important than their type. They should be at the periphery of the town center retail district or the ends of downtown blocks. This is contrary to the historic downtown setup that placed the anchor in the middle of a block of shops. Instead, corner anchors force shoppers to parade by all the smaller, more specialized stores in between.

Signage, storefront displays, and windows must then work together to help lure shoppers along the retail path. The best shopping path leads people to walk down one side of a street, cross over at the end of a block, and then walk down the opposite side. Thus, the traditional downtown street, running between stores, is not necessarily bad; it keeps shoppers from zigzagging back and forth and skipping stores.

Most important, every retail district must have one main shopping path.

Parallel main streets or alleyways developed for shops distract from a productive pedestrian traffic pattern. The best malls direct shoppers in a path that brings the greatest number of stores into the clearest view; they make it difficult to get off the retail "trail." The trail is often a straight, 1,000-foot [305-meter] section of a main street, but in larger urban districts and town centers this can also be a "loop" that takes shoppers around several blocks, via interconnected streets and sidewalks with shops on both sides of the street, where the layout is much like that of large regional shopping malls.

Every shopping district should also have a main intersection, approximately halfway along its length, to allow people to orient themselves. This intersection should have an interesting focal point that draws people toward the middle of the downtown. Often a strong vertical element aids in this task. Most historic downtowns have such dramatic landmarks that can, with imagination, be integrated into a total retail strategy—and new town centers can achieve the same effect.

This area is equivalent to the main court of a shopping mall. Here, we should find an information booth, a play area for children, stroller rental, and signage leading to other shops. Views from three or four directions must possess strong visual interest to pull shoppers past stores in each direction.

Fortunately, most town centers do have a main cross-street intersection that can act like a magnet to pull people, creating such a focal point. Traffic patterns must be organized, however, so people can park or be dropped off for easy access to this area. Once shoppers reach this focal point, pedestrian pathways, tenant mix, signage, and storefront design will all be used to move shoppers through the retail district.

A major impediment to the smooth circulation of shoppers through a retail district is "dead" space—empty storefronts or nonretail storefronts like offices or branches of a bank. A frontage of 30 feet without retail is often enough to cause shoppers to stop in their tracks and turn around.

Empty storefronts should be filled immediately with merchandise from other stores, or with local displays. When nonretail spaces do occur on a block, shoppers must be pulled past these points by strong merchandising and design in the stores on either side. Retail flow must not be interrupted.

Step Three: Strategic Tenant Mix

Leading shopping centers carefully arrange their tenant types and positions.

The main shopping strip is where all shoppers begin their retail journey. It should feature stores that thrive on impulse buying, like shoe stores, fashion stores, and toy stores. In contrast, destination shops should be at the ends of shopping avenues.

Stores will have higher sales if grouped by type of merchandise as well as by price point. Examples include men's clothing, housewares, or restaurants. This encourages the comparison shopping needed to ensure value and stimulate spending.

Not every type of shop, however, needs to be on the main shopping streets. Many businesses, like used-record shops or coin dealers, do well on second-level or side streets. These are usually destination shops owned by one or two individuals. They have less staff available to monitor for shoplifting or other potential problems, and they likely cannot afford the rent on Main Street.

If possible, restaurants should be carefully located to encourage movement past storefronts. New town centers often cluster restaurants around a plaza or outdoor dining area, sometimes connected to an entertainment section of a project. Since restaurants are often primary destinations in town centers, they should only be grouped where they will reinforce the movement of pedestrians past shops—as they walk between parking areas, entertainment areas, and the restaurants.

Sidewalk seating and benches can often distract or impede shoppers as much as restaurant or food-court seating. Avoid locating benches or seating too close to the pedestrian walkway. Also, avoid excessive grouping of seats. It is very uncomfortable and intimidating for pedestrians to have to pass a gauntlet of inspectors. An uncomfortable shopping experience leads to a permanently lost customer.

Service stops should be at the outer edges of town center shopping districts. Examples include barber shops, shoe repair shops, bakeries, and dry cleaners. These businesses will generally prefer the lower rents found in these edge areas. Moreover, service shops in these locations can be easily reached by people coming from their cars or by nearby residents on foot. Items can be left off on the way into the heart of the retail district or picked up on the way out.

Step Four: Streetscape and Landscaping

Sidewalk and pedestrian-mall paving, benches, and trees are all important elements of the main street shopping experience. But they can have an extremely negative impact on shoppers if not done properly. Contrary to many current projects and ideas, these treatments need not and should not be ornate or overly expensive. Otherwise, they will compete with and distract from storefronts. The business of town center retail districts should be business, not to awe or overwhelm.

Paving, for instance, should be of a quality material but kept fairly simple. Busy, trendy, and colorful or intricate designs disorient shoppers. Well-done brushed concrete will succeed over expensive granite.

Benches should be oriented to afford clear views of storefronts. They must also be placed far enough from regular shopping circulation routes so that transients or rowdy teenagers don't intimidate or frighten shoppers.

Not too rich, not too gaudy applies to street trees as well as paving and benches. Trees make a downtown inviting and provide shade and human scale. But again, we have often overused them in town center schemes. What looks good on a site plan often contradicts good retail practice. Trees must be landscaped to fit the stores, not the other way around. Generally, fewer will do, in smaller clusters, to avoid obstructing storefronts or signage.

Mall developers have tended to two paths in recent years. One group follows the principles outlined here. The other, at great expense, builds the ornate and trendy. Typically, these "showcase" malls have much lower sales per square foot than the more practical, focused ones.

Step Five: Parking

The epitaph of our day may eventually be "My kingdom for a parking spot."

The most successful shopping centers have learned this lesson well. Parking must be plentiful, secure, close to shopping, and free or inexpensive. Employees must be encouraged to park in the more distant spots, by means of employee parking stickers or a shuttle system during peak shopping times. Nearby overflow parking must be available on peak shopping days.

Unfortunately, many downtown redevelopments of the sixties and seventies ended up reducing the total parking count by converting head-in diagonal parking to parallel parking. This was a serious mistake because it reduced the number of parking stalls on Main Street and the likelihood that shoppers would find a place to park.

When possible, install diagonal parking so shoppers know they have a good chance of finding a parking space. While driving down Main Street, shoppers will view storefronts and window displays and begin their retail decisions. With modern merchandising, many purchasing decisions are actually made before the customer ever crosses the threshold of a store. Head-in, angled parking is better than parallel parking in the main street setting as it permits a greater parking density. Overflow parking must be available behind the stores but it should not be the primary parking area. We want people viewing and walking past storefronts. Overly aggressive town center parking enforcement only thwarts retail plans. We are creatures of habit. People turn to the same parking spot again and again, usually the first one they used at a particular mall, strip center, or shopping district. These patterns are almost impossible to change.

This has been borne out at many shopping malls. At one grand opening, only a temporary lot was available. Afterward, shoppers persisted in using this lot, instead of the intended main lots, even though it was difficult to reach and use.

Similarly, town centers cannot simply tear up old lots and expect users to find somewhere else to park. They won't. Many of these shoppers will never come back. High-profile, intensive efforts must accompany any change in parking locations.

Clean and safe can never be overdone in retail, especially with parking, which tends to be the most intimidating part of the shopping experience. Sidewalks should be steam cleaned daily. Parking lots should be cleaned daily, resurfaced or repaved regularly, and feature good lighting and attractive landscaping. Security in parking areas must be visible at all times.

Retail parking garages must be more user-friendly, less intimidating than garages for office workers. Pedestrian stairwells and elevators should be centrally located, with clear signage and graphics.

The rush to "mall over" downtowns was a terrible mistake. The exclusion of all automobile traffic in favor of pedestrian traffic was counterproductive. Successful town centers need people driving by Main Street storefronts to stimulate impulse and latent buying.

Too often, pedestrian malls broke all the retail rules. Elaborate "state park" landscaping, for instance, blocked the views to stores and intimidated shoppers by creating spaces where people could hide. In one retail survey after another, consumers continue to cite security and safety as the number one potential negative in the shopping experience.

Step Six: Lighting

Lighting is extremely important in retail but is often misused in town center shopping districts. Streetlights should be simple rather than ornate, and their placement must not obstruct storefronts.

A down light or cut-off lens should be used whenever possible to avoid excessive glare, which can be especially common with globe-type and "cobra head" lighting. Glare from building lights and signage must not be allowed to compete with storefront design or the presentation of merchandise.

The main street setting presents special lighting problems. The inside of a store must be brighter than the outside environment to draw attention, but daylight or streetlights and their reflections foil this principle in many town centers. This problem can be solved by generous use of indoor lighting, even during the day. Similarly, the use of energy-saving bronzed or darkened glass should be avoided in favor of a clear view to merchandise.

Step Seven: Management

Most malls benefit from single ownership or management. They are leased, maintained, and marketed as a unit. This is undoubtedly one of the greatest challenges facing downtown development districts, but is less of a problem for new town centers. To prosper, town center shopping districts must be managed like the best shopping centers, where stores help each other.

All stores in a town center retail district should have the same hours and days of operation. Never let one tenant close while the others remain open. Sunday hours should also be strongly encouraged, and all stores should have their hours of operation clearly posted.

Today's time-stressed, two-income families can't afford and won't tolerate hit-or-miss shopping. They shop at malls or strip centers as multiple errand destinations because they know that all stores will be open.

The establishment of a central leasing agent to negotiate rents, coordinate tenant mix, and promote town center shopping districts is crucial. A top-notch leasing agent can draw in a significant number of new stores, including major national tenants. Often, one national chain will only come into a retail venue if certain other stores are present. An experienced leasing agent can put together these deals.

Don't be overly intimidated when national chains join the Main Street picture. Many of these retailers are the best in the business. Other town center retailers can learn from their sophisticated merchandise presentation and marketing techniques. Do insist, however, that these national retailers design storefronts and interiors that are suited to regional architecture, materials, and culture.

Main street stores must share in the maintenance of sidewalks, trash cans, windows, and storefronts, as well as security. Police officers or security guards must always be visible to shop-pers. Even when there are no apparent threats, they will be available to help shoppers who are locked out of their cars or who have flat tires.

Like mall tenants, town center stores must be willing to share expenses for these efforts. An empty main street storefront hurts every other store. Cooperation on promotional efforts, common store hours, and signage can go a long way toward increasing retail activity.

City zoning and planning boards must also be more flexible in order for town centers to grow and change with new retail trends. Examples include outlet centers or the so-called category killers for items like office supplies, home furnishings, or health and beauty aids.

These stores often open in strip centers or malls, where the needed space is available. Unless town centers find ways to accommodate such new retailing formats, they will continue to lose out to malls. A way must also be found to introduce flexibility into rent structures, making it easier for stores to expand or contract as business dictates.

Today, shoppers are expecting good service and value for their retail dollar. Town centers cannot survive solely on boutique shopping or festival and holiday celebrations. All downtowns, new or old, malled or open to traffic, must embrace the best in modern retailing. This will lead to the everyday retail traffic that builds sales and sustains town center development. This is the route back to Main Street U.S.A.

Source: Adapted from Robert J. Gibbs, Gibbs Planning Group, "Urbandizing: A Primer on How Downtowns Can Compete with Retail Malls and Strip Centers," *Planning & Zoning News* 11, no. 1 (November 1992). Reprinted by permission of the Planning and Zoning Center, Lansing, Wisconsin 48917; © 1992; all rights reserved.

Mind the Store

As Georgia Chapman noted nearly four centuries ago, "Keep thy shop and thy shop will keep thee." While it is important to establish a sense of place and a special character for a town center, certain rules of commerce must be obeyed as well. Each of the uses, especially the retail, must compete in a marketplace where tried-and-true formulas still work; to ensure that the project remains competitive with more conventional formats, developers of town centers should adopt many of these formulas as well. The accompanying feature box on "urbandizing" outlines how main streets and town centers can create unique downtown environments while avoiding potential pitfalls, and can incorporate the established merchandising strategies used in more conventional retailing operations.

The well-mannered shop: Green's Market, in the Lakelands traditional neighborhood development, Gaithersburg, Maryland.

Planning the Streets and Circulation System

Planning a successful street, circulation, and parking system is a fundamental challenge of town center development. The creation of active, pedestrian-friendly streets is what sets town center and main street developments apart from other commercial and residential projects.

Be Streetwise

The circulation system within a town center should be made up of an interconnected network of streets and walkways that form a grid, which provides multiple routes for cars, bikes, and pedestrians to move from one block to the next. The grid itself can be as varied as the streets: it may be a rigid grid, of straight streets and square blocks, or it may be a modified grid, in which streets radiate outward from important landmarks and focal points, curve gently to reveal an ever-changing panorama, or flow around plazas and squares in a complex pattern.

Unfortunately, the geometry necessary for the design of pedestrian-friendly streets remains outlawed in much of the United States. Faced with standards that require wide, high-speed streets and that prohibit on-street parking, developers may need to retain ownership of, and maintain, the internal street network of town centers—or, at the very least, of the principal main street. Ownership allows developers to build narrow streets with shallow setbacks and tight corners, and permits uses and activities that are normally prohibited, such as sidewalk cafés and street closings for special events.

The downside of private streets, notes Brink, is that they "can reinforce the idea of your development as a private enclave—which is not positive for building neighborhoods and cities." Brink also notes that private streets involve a significant initial cost, as well as ongoing maintenance costs. "If possible," he advises, "the developer should work with the city to amend streetscape standards to allow new streetscapes, and to have the city fund and maintain the streets as well."

Town centers require a hierarchy of street types. "A" streets are the pedestrian-oriented main streets where the business activity and the public life of the town center are concentrated. "B" streets are less pedestrian-focused and accommodate utilities; parking garages and lots; dumpsters; and heavier, faster traffic. Alleys, a specific type of through-block street commonly found behind the backs of buildings in town centers, provide rear access to the buildings and allow utilitarian functions—service deliveries, garbage collection, small amounts of employee parking, and utility work, for example—to occur off the main street. Too often, town centers are envisioned as consisting *entirely* of high-quality main streets, with no provision for the utilitarian needs of shops, restaurants, cinemas, and residential buildings. In fact, the absence of "B" streets can wreak havoc on the pedestrian quality of a town center's main streets by pushing utilitarian activities out in front of the stores.

The curb radius—the radius of the circle formed by the curve at the corner of the curb (essentially a measurement of the sharpness of the curb corner)—is also an important element of street design for town centers. The longer the radius, the faster the speed at which cars can make a turn, which is why curves are very long and gradual at expressway entrances and exits. In town centers it is important to use shorter curb radii to create sharper turns, and thereby slow down automobiles (which are required to stop for stop signs, crosswalks, or traffic lights anyway, and should not be speeding around corners without slowing down). The 25-foot (7.6-meter) curb radius commonly required for suburban streets needs to be reduced to a more urban standard for town centers, preferably in the five- to ten-foot (1.5- to three-meter) range, depending on the width of the sidewalk.

There is less agreement regarding the use of bulb-outs at intersections. Some urban designers believe that bulb-outs should always be included at intersections because they can reduce the width of streets and make it easier for pedestrians to cross, while also defining parallel parking lanes. However, if the town center already has narrow, urban streets with on-street parking, bulb-outs are probably unnecessary. Some maintain that bulb-outs are fine for suburban settings, where streets are wider and more challenging to cross, but that they clutter the streetscape in town centers and more urban settings. More importantly for developers, bulb-outs are more difficult to engineer and construct, especially for drainage, and will add to the cost of infrastructure.

Depending on how formal the urban character of the place is, street trees may or may not be regularly spaced, and may or may not be all the same species. Care must be taken to prevent street trees and plantings

A wide curb radius encourages faster vehicular movement and creates bloated intersections that make it more difficult for pedestrians to reach shops on the opposite side of the street. (Mount Pleasant Town Center, Mt. Pleasant, South Carolina.)

Top and bottom: Because they are seldom needed for managing traffic within town centers, and because they tend to enlarge intersections and to push building frontages too far apart, traffic circles and decorative land-scaping for intersections should be used sparingly in town centers.

Top: Parking lots, blank walls, service entrances, and utilities should be located to the rear of buildings, along alleyways, or clustered along "B" streets like this one. (Kentlands Market Square.)

Bottom: "B" streets make it possible to maintain high-quality pedestrian-oriented "A" streets—like Main Street, in Miami Lakes Town Center.

from obscuring too much of the storefronts, signage, and store entrances from motorists and pedestrians. The planting strip between the sidewalk and the street may be continuous or, as the streetscape becomes more urban, contain a mix of planters, tree wells, bike racks, and street furniture.

Sidewalks and walkways are the most basic element of pedestrian-friendly environments. Walkways need to be wide enough to accommodate the amount of pedestrian activity anticipated, and should be free of obstructions (like lampposts and trees); they also need to lead somewhere, and not come to an abrupt dead end.

Attention to the quality of walkways should not end with the sidewalks along main streets. Visitors must feel comfortable using parking decks and the parking areas located behind buildings, which means that these areas must be well lit and maintained, and that the passageways leading to and from parking areas to the main street must be perceived as safe, clean, and attractive. Clear wayfinding graphics and signage are also critical. Passageways that cut through blocks and connect with small courtyards and other fragments of urban space (the "interstitial space" between the primary streets and public spaces) represent opportunities to extend the fabric of the public realm and should not be treated as throwaway spaces. Unfortunately, these in-between, off-the-beaten-track spaces are regularly ignored in town centers, where the passageways leading to and from parking areas are often weedy, neglected areas, and any space other than the main street, formal squares, and parks is unkempt, leftover space where nothing is done. Some of this space should be left as simply utilitarian, but more of it can and should be used to create a more fine-grained variety of public and semipublic space. While some areas will be purely functional, others afford enough enclosure for the creation of intimate public spaces that are quieter than the streetfront areas. Shop windows and entrances can also open up onto the passageways themselves, extending the street fabric and making the passages safer, well lit, and more attractive, and enabling the shops along the passageways to benefit from the steady flow of foot traffic past window displays.

Finally, it is important in the early stages of development to identify adjacent roadways that represent barriers to pedestrians so that the developer, transportation planners, and the municipality can work together on traffic-calming solutions. If a project is completely surrounded by wide, high-speed

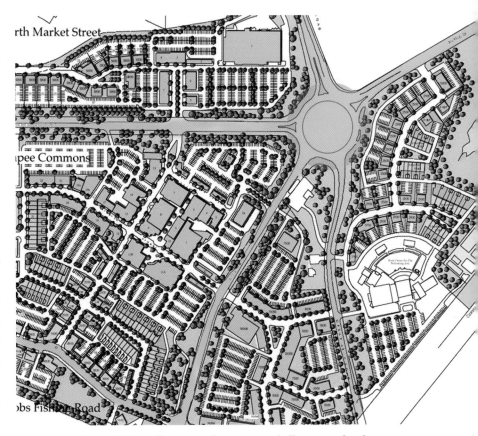

The design of preexisting, adjacent roadways poses challenges to developers' efforts to build and connect walkable districts on both sides of such roadways. Pictured: detail of Mashpee Commons plan. *Imai/Keller, Inc.*

Main Streets versus Through-Streets: Ask the Traffic Engineer

Question: What is the magic number for traffic on downtown streets: the number that works well for business vitality; the number that ensures that streets aren't choked with traffic; the number above which you should consider other options, like a well-designed bypass or ring road?

Response: Ideally, for great walkability on your main street, you want two-lane, two-way streets with a 25-mile-per-hour design and posted speed. You need short blocks, on the order of 350 to 600 feet (107 to 183 meters), which increases walkability. Add parallel parking, or perhaps angled parking if the building density is greater. Buildings should be pulled near the street, and sidewalks should be a safe and generous ten to 12 feet (three to 3.7 meters) wide. Especially in warm climates, shade should be provided liberally, by means of street trees and awnings. In other words, traffic volume is generally not an input but the result of careful design. Determine the types of streets and pedestrian character of the town center you want, then do the transportation.

Now, if you must deal with through-traffic, some diversion may be necessary. Try very hard to divert traffic no more than one block away. The history of bypass highways is one of lost urban retail vitality. A decent downtown grid will diffuse most congestion by enabling vehicles to take many alternative routes, whereas the collector-arterial system of the suburbs is designed to concentrate all traffic onto a small number of wide thoroughfares.

A two-lane street, with peak-hour directional flow rates of 800 to 1,000 vehicles per hour for each lane, works well. If necessary, convert that to a daily figure by using a rough multiplier of ten and doubling for the other direction; that yields 16,000 to 20,000 average daily trips. Arterials designed according to the criteria in the American Green Book, the standard reference for traffic engineers, are harder to cross at four lanes, and very hard at six, because of high speeds. Vehicle speed is the key to everything.

Retailers have rules of thumb for needed volumes, but in reality the customer mix, market area, price, competition, and a dozen other factors are just as important. Except for the highest-volume places, bypasses are generally bad for building or rebuilding downtowns. They generally lead to congestion—and, more importantly, to unwalkable places "out there."

Source: Adapted from Richard Hall, "Main Streets versus Through-Streets: Ask the Traffic Engineer," *Town Paper* 3, no. 5. Reprinted with permission.

roadways, it is likely to evolve into a pedestrian-friendly island to which all visitors drive—much like a conventional shopping center—regardless of how close high-density housing and offices might be.

Be a Blockhead

Short blocks (600 feet maximum, but preferably shorter) are the rule for town centers and main streets. Where blocks become too long, midblock passageways can be introduced to create links between blocks, and through buildings to parking areas. To maintain an urban streetscape and avoid "dead zones" (where, for example, parking lots front the street), blocks within town centers should be lined with buildings on as many sides as possible.

Whether blocks are squares or rectangles will be largely determined by the street pattern. Irregularly shaped blocks can add to the variety of an urban setting and create interesting opportunities for small plazas, parks, and distinctive buildings (e.g., Manhattan's famous Flatiron Building) that can enhance the unique character of a place.

When planning streets and blocks, developers must also keep in mind what types of establishments might need to be accommodated. Multiplex cinemas, large civic buildings, hotels, and big-box retailers present special challenges within a town center context; if not handled sensitively, such structures can appear to consume an entire block and create long dead zones in the streetscape.

Parking Is Power

According to Robert Davis, the developer of Seaside and partner in a major downtown redevelopment project in Albuquerque, New Mexico, the major difference between historic town centers and contemporary town center projects is that "We're going to have to figure out how to stockpile a whole lot more cars." In the words of Disney's chairman, Michael Eisner, "Form follows parking."[2] David Sucher, the author of *City Comforts,* has gone so far as to say that good urban design "begins with the location of the parking lot."

Regardless of where a town center project is located, developers, planners, and designers all focus on parking as a key variable in making town center equations work. Given the mix of uses assembled in town center projects, shared parking represents a real opportunity—particularly where office, retail, dining, and entertainment uses are combined. Residential units introduce more complexity, since residents demand that parking be both safe and reserved for

The drop-off area of Don Shula's Hotel, in Miami Lakes, is located just off Main Street. *Chris Podstawski.*

their exclusive use. But whatever the particular mix of uses, the project needs to provide parking ratios that can satisfy prospective retail and office tenants and local governments. The challenge is to accommodate as much parking as possible without sacrificing the urban qualities of town centers and main streets, and to do so without allowing parking infrastructure costs to bankrupt the project. It is because of the complexity and cost of addressing parking needs that parking is one of the most common areas for public/private partnership arrangements in support of town centers.

In town centers, parking is typically located to the rear of and at the edges of projects (e.g., Mashpee Commons's surface lots and Mizner Park's garages); in parking courts within the interiors of blocks (e.g.,

The Lake Forest Parking Plan: Recommended Principles for Town Centers

Parking facilities should accommodate six distinct types of daily uses: long-term, all-day employee parking; shopper, business, and patron parking; errand parking of 15- to 20-minute maximum duration; all-day commuter parking; service vehicle parking; and bicycle storage.

Long-term parking space should be concentrated in large facilities at the periphery of the downtown. These facilities should be located in direct contact with major vehicular approach routes.

Short-term patron parking space should be located in the most convenient areas of downtown and related to vehicular access capacity. Patron facilities should be regulated to discourage their use for long-term parking.

Errand parking space should be widely distributed throughout the area. Strict enforcement of time regulation should ensure short duration of stay and high turnover of this type of space.

Service parking should either be provided in communal areas, such as special service courts for loading and unloading, or in individual on- or off-street loading areas.

Source: Michael Davidson, "Centripetal Forces: Town Centers Are Back," *Zoning News* (October 1998): 1–4.

Celebration); in structured parking, preferably behind occupied buildings (e.g., Southlake Town Square and CityPlace); and on the street (in virtually all town centers). Parking courts, decks, and on-street parking can weave a great many parking spaces into the traditional street and block patterns of compact town centers. Because a main street surrounded by large expanses of asphalt can seem like little more than a dressed-up shopping center, surface lots must be designed and located more carefully. Since parking structures generate significant vehicular and pedestrian traffic, urban designers typically treat them as anchors and work to integrate garages within the retail core of town centers.

Surface lots remain unavoidable for most projects, however, especially in suburban areas where the economics of projects do not support the construction of parking garages. Developers can avoid the negative effects created by a "sea of parking" by dividing large parking areas into many smaller lots—which can be more easily concealed by the placement of buildings, site topography, and landscaping—and distributing them throughout a site. The largest lots can be concentrated along the least desirable borders of a site (often near a busy high-

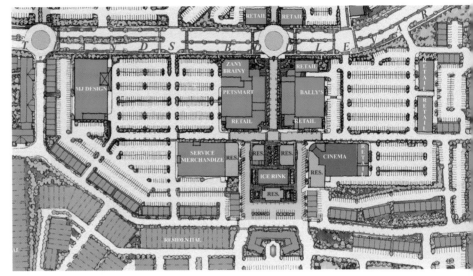

Top: At Washingtonian Center, in Gaithersburg, Maryland, shops have structured parking above and on-street parking in front.

Bottom: Parking is power at Reston Town Center, where large parking structures fuel the high-rise office buildings and the hotel, entertainment, and retail uses. Here, however, the lack of liner buildings and shops at the street level creates a less-than-attractive "B" street.

Top: In Kentlands Market Square, parking is concentrated in the large surface lots where the entrances to the big-box stores are located—an arrangement that preserves the central north-south spine of Market Street and allows Main Street to maintain an unbroken chain of high-quality pedestrian frontages composed of live/work buildings (in purple). *Development Design Group.*

Bottom: Parking lots in Kansas City's County Club Plaza have gradually been replaced by parking garages that have been skillfully concealed in the fabric of the blocks. *Kevin Klinkenberg.*

way), but at least one side of the town center should always be bordered by something other than a parking lot, preferably something that connects it with a neighborhood. Lastly, parking lots can be configured so that the streets and blocks of the town center can be extended in the future, as parking decks and transit become feasible.

Valet parking can be employed to make certain uses, such as restaurants, more viable, while reducing parking space requirements. Valet attendants can park cars in less accessible, less desirable areas, freeing up spots for self-parkers who are visiting other uses.

Designing and Configuring Buildings

Double-loaded streets are a good starting point, but creating a main street means much more than putting two strip centers face-to-face. And while beautiful urban public spaces can act as powerful attractors, what will leave a lasting impression is what people see around them as they walk down the street; sit in outdoor dining areas or on street benches; or linger in the public spaces on their way to and from shops, restaurants, and entertainment venues. Unlike the exteriors of shopping malls and strip shopping centers, the architecture of town centers and main streets must maintain a high level of visual interest.

The height of buildings, and the extent to which they are attached to adjacent structures, are key factors in determining whether an area is perceived as a village, a small town, or a more urban setting. Traditional commercial centers in hamlets and villages are characterized by low-rise, detached buildings that are reminiscent of single-family houses, whereas centers in larger towns and cities are characterized by attached buildings of increasing height (as property values warrant).

The placement of buildings will also determine the character of the streets and open spaces. Buildings that are pulled close to the street will accommodate pedestrians by providing easy access, window displays, and shelter (by means of awnings, arcades, and colonnades). Buildings that terminate vistas, line two sides of a street, and surround open spaces provide the sense of enclosure that is part of what distinguishes town centers from shopping centers.

Make Sure the Architecture Is Urban

Beyond the simple but crucial issues of the scale and positioning of buildings, the language of the architecture represents the primary means of communicating the overall character of the town center. Some projects strive to incorporate authentic local and regional architectural styles, while others—through liberal architectural interpretations—attempt to distill the essence of a New England village, a midwestern main street, or the buildings of a western courthouse square.

While there is a considerable consensus about essential urban design principles for town centers, there is much less agreement about architectural styles. Some have advanced a loose traditionalism, based on the Arts and Crafts style, as an adaptable middle ground that is both appropriate to the scale and composition of American town centers and that falls between the extremes of classicism and modernism. Others prefer a stricter interpretation of historical styles. Still others advocate reaching for innovative, original styles, considered more in tune with today's *zeitgeist,* as long as they conform to traditional urban layouts. Many town center and main street projects have come under fire for their reliance on thin, inaccurate, or overly nostalgic treatments of traditional styles. As urban designer Victor Dover has commented, "We certainly don't want to replace bad modern architecture with bad traditional architecture."

The dangers of excess appear at both ends of the architectural spectrum: heavy use of eclectic historical styles is sometimes viewed as inauthentic, and the absence of such styles is sometimes viewed as shallow and commercial. As is the case with good urbanism generally, the past is the best source for models of good urban architecture: historic buildings may or may not be used as literal models with

respect to architectural style, but they clearly demonstrate how to achieve compatibility with the street and the square, and how to accommodate a mix of uses and adapt over time. The look backward, however, has to be informed by sidelong looks at the current demands of retail, dining, office, residential, and institutional tenants.

Brink notes that the designer must also address whether the buildings can and should be contextual—that is, maintain a visual connection to adjacent neighborhoods. A town center is the center of a neighborhood and a community, which means that the project's relation to its surroundings is a beginning point for establishing its authenticity. The quality of design in surrounding neighborhoods will be an important factor in determining how "contextual" the project becomes.

In many cases, however, where town centers are being built in suburban areas, the surrounding neighborhoods possess very little in the way of local and regional architectural traditions, and little of the character of the urban neighborhoods that are traditionally connected to town centers. It then becomes necessary to rediscover earlier architectural traditions, creating new blocks and neighborhoods that can provide a transition from the commercial core of the town center to the existing low-density suburban neighborhoods on the edge. Live/work buildings, urban rowhouses, and townhouses have been used very effectively in this way in a number of projects, including Kentlands Market Square, Mizner Park, and Orenco Station Town Center.

Town centers need to be planned and developed as the centers of larger communities—with smooth transitions from suburban neighborhoods . . .

. . . to more compact neighborhoods with a more urban character, where buildings are closer together and multifamily, live/work units and mixed uses are permitted, and finally . . .

. . . to town centers, where the commercial core is located and where attached, multistory, mixed-use buildings frame the urban streetscape and the public spaces. *Michael Morrissey.*

Top: A low-rise urban atmosphere is created at Phillips Place, in Charlotte, North Carolina, where two-story buildings are pulled up to the sidewalk, and angled parking and planting strips between the street and the sidewalk provide pedestrian comfort.

Bottom: Shaping urban space in CityPlace in West Palm Beach: taller buildings, more urban buildings, and a narrower street provide a stronger sense of enclosure.

Buildings need to be good urban citizens—helping to shape the urban realm outside their walls, while simultaneously serving the functional needs of their tenants. The mixed-use buildings that line the main street in Miami Lakes Town Center, an early predecessor of today's town centers, have sufficient height and massing to create a strong sense of enclosure along the street and around the central fountain, despite the fact that they have a bare minimum of architectural embellishment, which relies more on color than on architectural detail to set the atmosphere.

Allow for Flexibility

Buildings must also allow for flexibility as tenants change. Initially, the buildings at Miami Lakes Town Center had the small internal dimensions of historic main street structures that were intended for small, "mom-and-pop" operations. By the 1990s, when the center began to attract national retailers, the square footage on the ground floor proved too small to comfortably accommodate contemporary retailers like Victoria's Secret (which, because of the shallowness of the building, takes up an entire half-block of frontage).

Today's town centers have learned from Miami Lakes and other examples, and now incorporate generous internal spaces that can more easily be reconfigured to accommodate tenants of various sizes. In Celebration, White's Books and Gifts started out as a large store on the Bloom Street waterfront. As Celebration leased up and White's decided that it required less space, it went from 4,000 square feet (370 square meters) to less than 2,400 square feet (220 square meters), and the vacated square footage was reconfigured to accommodate multiple shopfronts. At the other end of the spectrum, projects that Federal Realty Investment Trust is working on, such as Pentagon Row (Arlington, Virginia), Santana Row (San Jose, California), and Bethesda Row (Bethesda, Maryland), incorporate large blocks of buildings, with footprints of 100,000 square feet or more, that are designed to adapt to the needs of commercial uses on the ground floor and residential

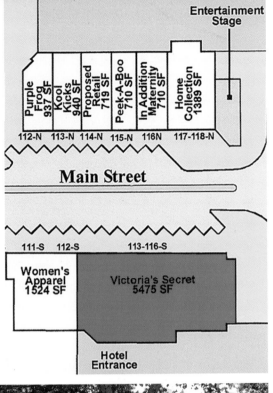

Top: Smaller, mom-and-pop–scale stores with shallow depths (north side of Main Street) were combined over the years to meet the needs of the larger national and regional retailers that were attracted to Miami Lakes Town Center (south side of Main Street). *The Graham Companies.*

Bottom: Victoria's Secret, in Miami Lakes Town Center, takes up a long stretch of storefronts originally designed for multiple shops that were smaller and shallower.

or office uses on the upper floors. The added complexity at this scale has led Federal Realty to partner with apartment developers, such as Post Properties and AvalonBay, to configure the residential portions of the shared structures.

Focus on Facades

One of the most common practices in today's town centers is to construct large, multipurpose buildings, which often run the length of an entire block, then add a series of distinctive facades that mimic the appearance of many smaller buildings connected side by side. Examples can be found in many town center projects—including Southlake Town Square and Federal Realty's main street projects, where different architects were hired to design a variety of facades to make one building look like an ensemble of three or four buildings. This strategy is an important part of what architects describe as the need to "compress

Top: The excessive use of similar materials throughout a town center reinforces a "project" atmosphere that is reminiscent of shopping malls.

Bottom: Varied storefronts and colors are used to create the appearance of separate buildings at Santana Row, in San Jose, California. *Street-Works.*

time"—that is, to make it appear, through the architecture and urban design of places, as if a series of buildings had been constructed over a long period of time rather than within a matter of months.

The effective design of streetfront buildings involves many details, and it is a challenge to ensure that buildings simultaneously achieve the visual variety of compressed time and perform properly as good urban buildings, which should address the street and shape the public spaces. Even multistory, mixed-use

Arcades can provide sheltered pedestrian walkways but should not be so deep that they cast heavy shadows or so low that they obscure storefronts. To ensure that pedestrians remain engaged with the storefronts, sidewalks should not extend beyond the edges of arcades.

buildings with varied facades that are brought up to the sidewalk can fall short if the character of the entrances, shop windows, awnings, lighting, balconies, and sidewalks is inconsistent with a human-scale, pedestrian environment. It's not simply that the commercial buildings of strip centers and shopping malls are inconsistent with town centers—it's that so much of what main street architecture is all about concerns the facades and encroachments of buildings—awnings, stoops, balconies, and porches. Facades and encroachments are not simply ornamental architectural features; they establish the relationship between the buildings and the public realm, and are essential to the creation of environments where the indoors and the outdoors flow together. This interrelationship between indoor and outdoor space is a crucial factor in the design of town centers and main streets; and, although it may be difficult for casual visitors to explain, it is almost impossible for them to ignore.

Dine Alfresco

Town centers and main streets are not shopping malls. The focus of activity is on outdoor streets, walkways, parks, plazas, squares, and courtyards. Dining alfresco—watching people walk by while you feast under the trees and the stars, surrounded by interesting architecture, trickling fountains, and dramatic lighting—can be a major attraction for a town center. In fact, one of the main things that town centers can do to distinguish themselves from conventional shopping centers and highway-oriented restaurants and entertainment venues is to blur the line between outdoor and indoor environments.

Dining alfresco in Reston Town Center.

Too often, town centers miss opportunities to increase their indoor/outdoor appeal. These balconies and rooftops at Mashpee Commons (top) and Market Square at Kentlands (bottom) represent missed opportunities for enhancing visitors' level of engagement in the visual spectacle that the town centers offer.

Sidewalk cafés, pubs, and restaurants with balcony seating, and storefronts that can spill out into the street to create open-air markets, are all elements that contribute to the indoor/outdoor appeal of town centers. As cities like Toronto have proven, a project need not be located south of the Mason-Dixon Line to embrace the outdoors. The key is to incorporate architecture and building technology that will allow the town center to adapt to the local climate and seasonal changes. In four-season climates, for example, space heaters and removable glass walls and windows can make year-round use of sidewalk space possible. Winter also presents opportunities for snow festivals, ice skating, and other outdoor activities that are impossible in warmer climates. And not every balcony or terrace needs to be occupied by restaurants and shops—some can simply provide places for people to linger and take in the panorama of the town center.

Usable balconies and roof decks are a major missed opportunity for most town centers. Where drinking and dining establishments include balconies and roof decks, patrons are often willing to wait longer for seating in these areas, so that they can enjoy the views of the street life and public spaces below. In town centers where multistory buildings would make them possible, balconies are too often absent. In single-story town centers, the addition of roof decks to buildings that surround key public spaces and that occupy the corners of key intersections could add vitality above street level.

Know Your Fronts from Your Backs

Unlike shopping malls, where almost all storefronts are internally oriented, and strip shopping centers, which have a single clear "front" and utilitarian sides and backs, buildings in town centers can have many public sides, which can create both cost issues and design issues. Striking a balance between the demands of cost and good design is not always easy. While not every side of a building needs to be finished (finishing and detailing every side of a building is very costly), it is important to reduce the number of dead zones in a project—areas where sidewalks face parking areas, blank walls, or long stretches of display windows that are unbroken by entrances.

In historic downtowns, the backs of buildings typically faced each other across alleyways. Because these were service areas that were not intended to be viewed by the public, the owners of the buildings did not expend resources decorating them. The same is true today. As David Schwarz, the designer of Southlake Town Square, has commented, because people do not expect the rear of buildings, where parking and utilities are concentrated, to be refined—and because it is important to economize in town center design—"We let backs be backs."

In today's town centers, major problems can occur when the backs of buildings face major streets, the shopfronts of other buildings, or adjacent neighborhoods. As Brink notes, "A main street project that turns its back on its surroundings creates a disconnect and begins to read as an inauthentic, privatized place." Thus, while it may be necessary to let "backs be backs," the design should minimize visitors' exposure to unrefined buildings at the major points of access to the project. Building backs that are near high-traffic pedestrian pathways should be more refined, and alleyways and service courts should be used where possible, so that backs face each other and not adjacent neighborhoods or roadways.

The biggest challenge occurs when freestanding buildings are set within a public space and surrounded by blocks of storefronts. Prominent examples include the courthouse in Southlake Town Square (Southlake, Texas) and the restaurants in Market Square (Kentlands, Maryland).[3] Orenco Station Town Center and Valencia Town Center Drive also offer examples of facades that have been extended around the corners

Top: When parking and service areas are concentrated behind buildings, developers can economize—using no-frills architecture and letting "backs be backs." Pictured: Southlake Town Square. *David M. Schwarz/Architectural Services, Inc.*

Bottom: Concentrating parking and service areas behind buildings allows more attention to be paid to the details of facades and the pedestrian quality of the streetscape. Pictured: Southlake Town Square. *David M. Schwarz/Architectural Services, Inc.*

of buildings that face busy arterials so that passing motorists are greeted by a "window" into the town center instead of by a blank wall.

It is important to remember that people do not experience the main street side of a project in isolation from the rest of its streets, passageways, and buildings. The atmosphere of a main street should not immediately disintegrate when a visitor turns a corner to walk down a side street. Rather than think in terms of short, isolated main streets with exposed backs and sides, developers and designers should plan main street and town center projects so that they can grow into districts, spreading gradually out onto side streets. The key is to begin with a block structure, which puts buildings around the perimeter and accommodates parking behind the buildings.

Cinemas and hotels create special issues when it comes to the treatment of backs and fronts. These two uses can add vitality to town centers—but, given the size of the buildings and the parking requirements, they must be carefully adapted to support a town center format. The buildings that house cinemas and hotels, and their entrances, should take up only a small portion of a main street. Many cities offer examples of good urban hotels—with restaurants and shops lining the ground floor—that are appropriate for town centers. Parking can be located behind buildings and in structured parking, and drive-up, valet entrances for check-in can be located on secondary streets.

The freestanding multiplex cinema, surrounded by parking, represents the antithesis of the type of urban cinema that town centers need. Large multiplex buildings can be attractively accommodated through the use of liner stores, which can help conceal the large blank walls that would otherwise deaden the street.

Cinemas can also be located on a second level, which eliminates the blank facade at street level. Cinema entrances and exits should be strategically placed to ensure that visitors entering and exiting the cinema pass the retail stores on the main street, rather than simply passing into and out of nearby parking lots. Another strategy adopted by town centers is to eschew multiplex cinemas in favor of smaller "art house" cinemas that incorporate fewer screens and cater to a narrower, upscale audience.

Miami Lakes's cinema has undergone two expansions since it first opened in the mid-1980s. The latest expansion rerouted pedestrian traffic to bring moviegoers exiting the cinema onto Main Street.

Storefront Design and Merchandising

One of the toughest habits for conventional retail developers to break, in the creation of town centers, is the use of extrusions typical of strip center retail storefronts. Long accustomed to spending significant sums of money for the various faux towers, ersatz cornices, and other details that festoon the upper facades of buildings to present an attractive profile from surrounding roadways, developers and their architects are now faced with shifting their priorities and the expenditure of capital from the tops of buildings to the street and pedestrian level, where a rich public realm is desired and where shoppers reside. Fortunately, the urban-savvy tenants of today are pushing developers to respond.

Retail storefronts, after all, are about seduction, or the conversion of browsers on the sidewalk (or in the car) into consumers. It has been this way since the formation of medieval market towns. The diagram in figure 1 illustrates the millennium-old roles of a storefront: showcase the product, identify the merchant, and therefore distinguish the shop/merchant from others on the street. In today's world of urban retailing, the storefront presentation is also the first brand statement that a retailer makes to a potential consumer. It tells the consumer that the store and the products/services that reside within are hip/cool, conservative, value-priced, or any other of a range of messages that can cue and trigger the consumer into action. These messages can reside solely within the merchandising displays and signage, or can be presented in tandem with the actual design of the storefront.

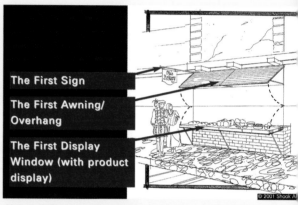

Figure 1: The storefront should showcase the product, identify the merchant, and distinguish the store from others.

Regardless of the approach, the design of the storefronts should create a pattern of transition and visual relief for the pedestrian. Despite its style-neutral design, the storefront in figure 2 represents all the elements of a well-designed storefront. The bulkhead serves to separate the storefront from the shaft of the building, and to provide a place for signage. The base, with its contrasting, and usually rich and highly detailed material, underlines the merchandising presentation within the display window.

Both the base and the transom serve to bracket and feature the display windows. The entry area is set back just enough to allow the creation of smaller display windows perpendicular to the viewing angle of the pedestrian, and to create a small area for the shopper to gather things or kids before heading into the store. The height and width of the display window approximate the field of vision of human sight, and the window is lit adequately during the day to focus the viewer's eye upon the merchandise. At night, the lighting spills out into the street, reducing the level of lighting that is required by streetlights.

Figure 2: The elements of a well-designed storefront.

And to top it off, a small "watermark" sign is placed on the glass to overtly feature a particular store brand, and to subliminally communicate the uniqueness and quality of the establishment. Awnings and arcades can be incorporated as conditions dictate. Obviously, the degree of detail and distinctiveness one can achieve within this construct is virtually limitless. These rules are not bound by history or style except where a particular style might eliminate basic storefront elements such as the bulkhead, transom, and display windows.

Old habits do indeed die hard. The more conventional developers will counter that such approaches cost more, are exhausting to implement, and are more difficult to manage than standard approaches. All true, by the way, if taken to the extreme. Fortunately, a number of technologies and management practices are being developed and used that deliver the detail within financial expectations.

Source: Terry Shook, AIA, president and cofounder of Shook in Charlotte, North Carolina. Portions of the feature box were excerpted from material used in a summer course on urban retailing taught by Terry Shook and Bob Gibbs at Harvard University's Graduate School of Design.

Create a Room with a View

Town centers and main streets offer something that cannot be found in most suburban communities: *a room with a view.* Apartments, townhomes, and condominiums overlooking public plazas, fountains, parks, squares, and main streets are something very new for many Americans, and something very hard to come by outside of major cities.

To make town center housing appealing to renters and homebuyers, developers need to locate the units carefully in relation to performance spaces, restaurants, shops, and parking areas. Town center residents are typically provided with parking that is reserved for their exclusive use. Units located above stores and offices normally include private entrances that are away from the main public areas.

Most important, it is essential to rediscover the ways in which traditional urban housing types achieved a delicate balance between public and private space. A number of basic building practices can be used to create dwellings that allow residents to view and listen to the street life when they want to, and to retreat into the privacy of their homes at other times. Examples of such strategies include raising the first floors of rowhouses a few feet above the street; insulating units sufficiently from the sounds of adjacent buildings, garages, and the street; carefully positioning windows and doors (so that, for example, windows of adjacent residences do not peer directly into one another); providing landscaping to screen private yard spaces; and including side yards, courtyards, and terraces in the building design.

Understanding Urbanism

Ultimately, developing a successful town center or urban village requires an understanding and love of urban places and urban design, and a desire to create a great place that can outlive short-term retail fads, adapt to change, and evolve into a true community center. Town center and urban village development is about profitably configuring land uses, buildings, and open space within a pedestrian-friendly street system, in order to create a whole that is greater than the sum of

Top: Rooms with a view of Riverside's parks and public spaces, in Atlanta. *Steve Hinds.*

Middle: Rooms with a view of CityPlace's fountains, grand public space, and Spanish Colonial Revival church building.

Bottom: Rooms with a view in Portland, Oregon's, Orenco Station Town Center.

its parts. It is about place making and city building, and requires a broad understanding of these endeavors.

Such understanding of urban place making has become scarce during the past 50 years. Richard Heapes, of Street-Works, in Alexandria, Virginia, an urban designer who has been involved in the creation of many town center and main street projects—including one of the earliest, Mizner Park, and one of the most recent, Santana Row—bemoans the fact that the architecture, urban planning, and landscape architecture professions have lost a basic understanding of how to design urban places. The emphasis on uniqueness, experimentation, and self-expression in academic circles—schools of architecture and landscape architecture—prevents students from understanding how urban buildings can work together to form a viable public realm—and from understanding that to create such a realm, the buildings must conform to some basic parameters in setbacks, heights, and frontages. Planning schools have become heavily focused on policy making and social science, and the study and teaching of physical planning has become a lost art. "I can't get a landscape architect who will simply do a shade tree over a park bench," Heapes laments, "or an architect who can do a good, basic main street retail facade." Heapes now hires people with more general skills, whom he can train—people who do not bring preconceptions to the work. For the storefronts at Santana Row, Heapes has dispensed with architects completely and is working directly with the commercial tenants on the facades.

J.C. Nichols, developer of Country Club Plaza, in Kansas City, and cofounder of ULI. Nichols personified the type of well-rounded generalist who understood the art, science, and business of place making. *J.C. Nichols Company.*

The key for many is found in the title of Jan Gehl's book *Life Between Buildings.*[4] By emphasizing the building as a work of art—an object to be admired and surrounded by open space—modernists reversed the traditional relationship between buildings and open space. The modernist legacy made it virtually impossible to create the types of main streets and enclosed public gathering places that had defined traditional town centers and created an inviting public realm—a realm where the "life between buildings" can occur.

In similar fashion, new urbanist Andrés Duany believes that the excessive specialization of the professionals involved in planning and development has created barriers to good urban design. Duany identifies J. C. Nichols, the cofounder of ULI and the developer of Country Club Plaza, as the type of development professional needed today: someone who has a general knowledge of many different fields and is guided by a larger vision of place making.

As Art Lomenick has observed, great places are created at the point of implementation, one small act at a time, by a multitude of individuals. But for main streets and town centers to be successful, there must be people who assume a larger responsibility, engage issues large and small as they emerge, and ensure that problems are resolved in a way that does not compromise the look, feel, and function of the project. Place making is much like making a motion picture: it requires the careful orchestration of the specialized talents and skills of many people, and of many economic and design elements, all of which must work together to create a successful production.

The final thought here for those who would pursue town center and main street development is to assemble a team that is resourceful, managerial, and multitalented, and that truly understands real estate and urbanism—a team that can both make good business decisions and stay focused on the ultimate goal of creating attractive, exciting, memorable places that will be successful for many years to come.

Notes
1. See the discussion of the "rural-urban transect" in chapter 4.
2. Russ Rymer, "Back to the Future: Disney Reinvents the Company Town," *Harper's,* October 1996, 65–76.
3. See discussions of both situations in the chapter 7 case studies.
4. Jan Gehl, *Life Between Buildings: Using Public Space,* trans. Jo Koch (New York: Van Nostrand Reinhold, 1987).

An enduring precedent for town centers that continues to adapt and mature gracefully: Country Club Plaza, in Kansas City. *Kevin Klinkenberg.*